THE RIVER WAR

VOL. I.

The River War Volume 1

An Historical Account of the Reconquest of the Soudan

By Winston Spencer Churchill

First published 1899

This edition 2022

Scrawny Goat Books

Scrawny Goat Books
124 City Road
London, EC1V 2NX

scrawnygoatbooks.com

ISBN 978-1-915645-08-1

THE RIVER WAR

AN HISTORICAL ACCOUNT OF THE RECONQUEST OF THE SOUDAN

BY

WINSTON SPENCER CHURCHILL

AUTHOR OF 'THE STORY OF THE MALAKAND FIELD FORCE, 1897'

EDITED BY COL. F. RHODES, D.S.O.

Illustrated by Angus McNeill, Seaforth Highlanders

IN TWO VOLUMES

VOLUME I

EVELYN BARING, 1ST EARL OF CROMER,

THIS BOOK IS INSCRIBED

TO

THE MARQUESS OF SALISBURY, KG

UNDER WHOSE WISE DIRECTION

THE CONSERVATIVE PARTY HAVE LONG ENJOYED POWER

AND THE NATION PROSPERITY

DURING WHOSE ADMINISTRATIONS THE

REORGANISATION OF EGYPT HAS BEEN MAINLY ACCOMPLISHED

AND UPON WHOSE ADVICE HER MAJESTY DETERMINED

TO ORDER THE RECONQUEST OF THE SOUDAN

PREFACE

The first object of this book is to relate in exact military detail the operations directed by Lord Kitchener of Khartoum on the Upper Nile from April 1896 to February 1899, which I have called 'The River War,' and which resulted in the reconquest of the Egyptian Soudan. But in order that the reader may understand, and even sympathise with the emotions which these events excited, I have prefixed a general survey of the geography, aspect, and history of the country, and have tried to show its connection with Egypt and Great Britain. This summary was originally intended to occupy about thirty pages, but it has distended itself to five lengthy chapters, which must make their own excuses.

At Chapter VI. the military chronicle begins, and thereafter I have described every incident which exercised an appreciable influence on the course of the campaigns. I anticipate that the accounts of the various actions will provoke some disagreement. Each sees a tumult from a different point of view, and the narratives I have examined are frequently contradictory.

Uncertainty is inevitable; but I must observe that all statements of fact in this book are based upon he written evidence of independent, disinterested eyewitnesses, and that in nearly every action I have had the advantage of comparing the personal account of the officer who commanded, both with the official reports and with the private letters of his subordinates. I shall therefore hope that the story is at least as accurate as any other that is likely to be written.

I am under great obligations to Colonel Rhodes, who has not only assisted me with his store of knowledge and experience, gained during many years of war in the Soudan, but has also procured me much valuable information which I could not have otherwise obtained. His name on the title-page may win the tale a popularity with the officers of the Egyptian service which is not courted in the text.

I desire to acknowledge the help and kindness I have received from most of the principal actors in the River War, from the Cairene authorities, and from the Intelligence Departments. Many of those who have supplied me with narratives, or who have undertaken the no less tedious task of reading the proofs, have done so on the understanding that their names should not be mentioned. I therefore offer them mv thanks in a general form.

At Chapter XV. I am able to supplement the evidence of others by my own observation. I was attached to the 21st Lancers on condition that I paid my own expenses to and from Egypt; and as I hold, with Napoleon, that war should support war, I wrote a series of letters to the 'MORNING POST' newspaper to cover the outlay. By the courtesy of the proprietors of that journal I have been permitted to reproduce whatever passages from them I desired. They are not in quite the same style as the rest of the narrative, but they have the merit of being the actual impressions of exciting days.

The maps and plans are the most expensive — perhaps the most valuable— part of these volumes. For their topographical features I am indebted to the Director of Military Intelligence. The positions and movements of the troops are taken from the statements and diagrams of mv various informants. I have every reason to believe them correct. It is of course absolutely impossible for anyone to understand a campaign or an action without continually referring to the map, and I trust that the reader will not be irritated by my repeated exhortations to him to do so.

The footnotes marked with asterisks show where each map may be found as soon as it is likely to be useful in explaining the text. Those signed 'Editor' are by Colonel Rhodes. The others are mine. For the most part they explain themselves; and it is only necessary for me to state that the first time a military officer's name is mentioned, his full designation with whatever rank he then held is printed as a note.

I will not venture to pronounce upon the artistic value of the sketches with which Mr. McNeill has adorned the account: but I think that they are in every detail scrupulously accurate.

The military criticisms of all kinds are my own; yet while I accept the fullest responsibility for them, I am entitled to state that they have been carefully discussed with several distinguished soldiers in the British, Indian, and Egyptian services, and, although admittedly matters of controversy, have not been found unreasonable.

A long book does not justify a long preface, and I hasten to conclude. It is not for me to say whether these pages contain anything of the slightest merit, but I assert with some pride that I have written, without fear or favour, only what I believe to be fair and true; and I venture to think that, if the reader take the trouble to follow the account on the maps which explain it, he will know as much about the River War as I have been able to learn in twelve months of diligent study.

WINSTON SPENCER CHURCHILL.
35a Great Cumberland Place,
London: September 25, 1899.

LIST OF PRINCIPAL WORKS CONSULTED

Fire and Sword in the Soudan (SLATIN), 1895.
Ten Years' Captivity in the Mahdi's Camp (OHRWALDER), 1892.
Mahdism and the Egyptian Soudan (WINGATE), 1891.
England in Egypt (MILNER), 1893.
Ten Years in Equatoria (CASATI), 1880–1889. 2 vols.
Life in the Soudan (WILLIAMS), 1882.
The Ruin of the Soudan (RUSSELL), 1892.
'83 to '87 in the Soudan (WYLDE), 1888. 2 vols.
Life of Emin Pasha (SCHWEITZER), 1898.
Lord Cromer (TRAILL), 1897.
Journals at Khartoum (GORDON), 1885.
Life of Gordon (BOULGER), 1887.
Colonel Gordon in Central Africa (HILL), 1884.
With the Camel Corps up the Nile (GLEICHEN), 1886.
From Korti to Khartoum (WILSON), 1885.
The Campaign of the Cataracts (BUTLER), 1885.
The Egyptian Soudan: its Loss and Recovery (ALFORD & SWORD), 1898.
Letters from the Soudan (KNIGHT), 1896.
Towards Khartoum (ATTERIDGE), 1896.
Sirdar and Khalifa (BURLEIGH), 1898.
With Kitchener to Khartoum (STEEVENS), 1898.
The Downfall of the Dervishes (BENNETT), 1898.

GOVERNMENT PUBLICATIONS

Report on the Soudan, 1883 (LIEUT-COL. STEWART), Egypt, No. 11, 1883.
Report on the Administration of Egypt (LORD CROMER). Egypt, No. 1, 1895.

*Report on the Progress of Reorganisation in Egypt (*MR. VILLIERS STUART), Egypt, No. 2, 1895.

Report on the Administration of Egypt (LORD CROMER), Egypt, No. 1, 1896.

Correspondence respecting the Lawsuit brought against the Egyptian Government in regard to the Appropriation of Money from the General Reserve Fund to the Expenses of the Dongola Expedition. Egypt, No. 1, 1897.

Report on the Administration of Egypt (LORD CROMER), Egypt, No. 2, 1897.

Reports on the Province of Dongola (SIR WILLIAM GARSTIN, MR. C. E. DAWKINS), Egypt, No. 3, 1897.

Report on the Administration of Egypt (LORD CROMER), Egypt. No. 1, 1898.

Correspondence with the French Government respecting the Valley of the Upper Nile, Egypt, No. 2, 1898.

Further Correspondence with the French Government, Egypt, No. 3, 1898.

Agreement between H.R.M.'s Government and the Government of H.H. the Khedive, relative to the Future Administration of the Soudan, Egypt, No. 1, 1899.

Declaration relative to the British and French Spheres of Influence in Central Africa, Egypt, No. 2, 1899.

Report on the Soudan, 1899 (SIR WILLIAM GARSTIN), Egypt, No. 5, 1899.

Handbook of the Soudan, 1898 (compiled in the Intelligence Division of the War Office by Captain Count GLEICHEN).

Report on the Nile and Country between Dongola, Suakin, Kassala, and Omdurman, 1898 (compiled in the Intelligence Division of the War Office by Captain Count GLEICHEN).

And various other Blue Books and Official Reports.

Table of Contents

LIST OF ILLUSTRATIONS

Contents

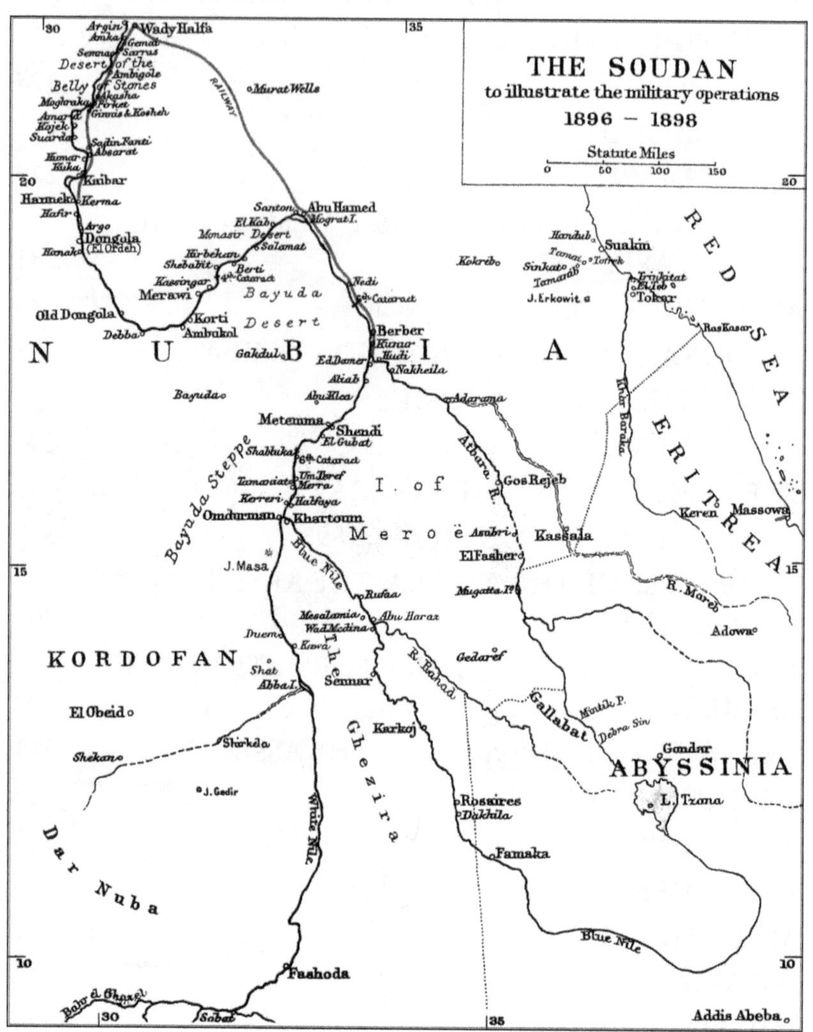
THE SOUDAN
to illustrate the military operations
1896 – 1898
Statute Miles
0 50 100 150
Wady Halfa
Desert of the Belly of Stones
RAILWAY
Murat Wells
Kerma
Dongula (El Ordeh)
Old Dongola
Merawi
Korti
Ambukol
Abu Hamed
Bayuda Desert
Berber
N U B I A
Metemma
Shendi
Bayuda Steppe
Omdurman
Khartoum
I. of Meroë
Atbara R.
Suakin
RED SEA
ERITREA
Kassala
Massowa
Keren
Blue Nile
White Nile
KORDOFAN
El Obeid
Sennar
The Ghezira
Gedaref
Gallabat
ABYSSINIA
Gondar
L. Tzana
Adowa
Rosaires
Famaka
Dar Nuba
Fashoda
Bahr el Ghazal
Sobat
Addis Abeba

CHAPTER I
THE MILITARY SOUDAN[1]

Aut Nilus, aut nihil

The scope of the work—The Soudan and the Nile—The real Soudan—The Military Soudan—The desert—The river—The banks—The vegetation—At sunset—Desolation—Extent—Lost in the desert—The eternal river—Its source—The annual miracle—The scale of the account.

He who may be attracted by interest or driven by idleness to examine this book will find therein a tale of blood and war. The extremes of fortune are displayed, and he may read of battles that were massacres — of others that were mere parades, of joyful victory or forlorn defeat, of exultation or of disappointment. In the story of the long and fierce contention he may remark occasions of shameful cowardice and reckless heroism: of plans conceived in haste and emergency: of schemes laid with slow deliberation: of wild extravagance and cruel waste; of economies more barbarous still; of wisdom and incompetence. He may observe men under many conditions, but mostly unfortunate, and applaud or condemn their behaviour.

He may study a peculiar warfare fought under varied circumstances, the like of which have not been seen before. And if he should be persuaded or compelled to follow the long road from initial tragedy to final triumph, he may admire the perseverance of a vigorous race who pursue their policies in spite of delay and disaster to victorious ends.

* * * * * *

The north-eastern quarter of the continent of Africa is drained and watered by the Nile. Among and about the headstreams and

1 Map, 'The Soudan,' page xiv.

tributaries of this mighty river lie the wide and fertile provinces of the Egyptian Soudan.

Situate in the very centre of the land, these remote regions are on every side divided from the seas by five hundred miles of mountain, swamp, or desert. The great river which has already called them into being is their only means of growth, their only channel of progress. It is by the Nile alone that their commerce can reach the outer markets, or European civilisation can penetrate the inner darkness. The Soudan is joined to Egypt by the Nile, as a diver is connected with the surface by his air-pipe. Without it there is only suffocation.

The town of Khartoum, by the confluence of the Blue and White Niles, is the point on which the trade of the south must inevitably converge. It is the port whence goods are shipped across the desert ocean. It is the great spout through which the merchandise collected from a wide area streams northwards to the Mediterranean shore. It marks the extreme northern limit of the fertile Soudan. Between Khartoum and Assuan the river flows for twelve hundred miles through deserts of surpassing desolation. At last the wilderness recedes and the living world broadens out again into Egypt and the Delta. It is with the events that have occurred in the intervening waste that these pages are concerned.

The real Soudan, known to the statesman and the explorer, lies far to the south — moist, undulating, and exuberant. But there is another Soudan, which some mistake for the true, whose solitudes oppress the Nile from the Egyptian frontier to Omdurman. This is the Soudan of the soldier. Destitute of wealth or future, it is rich in history. The names of its squalid villages are familiar to distant and enlightened peoples. The barrenness of its scenes has been drawn by skilful pen and pencil. Its ample deserts have tasted the blood of brave men. Its hot, black rocks have witnessed famous tragedies. It is the scene of the war.

This great tract, which may conveniently be called 'The Military Soudan,' stretches with apparent indefiniteness over the face of the continent. Level plains of smooth sand — a little rosier than buff, a little paler than salmon — are interrupted only by occasional peaks of rock — black, stark, and shapeless. Rainless storms dance tirelessly over the hot, crisp surface of the ground. The fine sand, driven by the wind, gathers into deep drifts, and silts among the dark rocks of the hills, exactly as snow hangs about an Alpine summit; only it is a fiery snow, such as might fall in hell. The earth burns with the quenchless thirst of ages, and in the steel-blue sky scarcely a cloud obstructs the unrelenting triumph of the sun.

Through the desert flows the river — a thread of blue silk drawn across an enormous brown drugget; and even the blue thread is brown for half the year. Where the water laps the sand and soaks into the banks there grows an avenue of vegetation which seems very beautiful and luxuriant by contrast with what lies beyond. The Nile, through all the three thousand miles of its course vital to everything that lives beside it, is never so precious as here. The traveller clings to the strong river as to an old friend, staunch in the hour of need. All the world blazes, but here is shade. The deserts are hot, but the Nile is cool. The land is parched, but here is abundant water. The picture painted in burnt sienna is relieved by a grateful flash of green.

Yet he who had not seen the desert, nor felt the sun heavy on his shoulders, would hardly admire the fertility of the riparian scrub. Unnourishing reeds and grasses grow rank and coarse from the water's edge. The dark, rotten soil between the tussocks is cracked and granulated by the drying up of the annual flood. The character of the vegetation is inhospitable. Thornbushes, bristling like hedgehogs and thriving arrogantly, everywhere predominate and with their prickly tangles obstruct or forbid the path. Near to the river they often form an impenetrable jungle, and, though more scattered as the bank is left, they stretch out hardily into the desert sand, following the reëntrants and thrusting their roots deep in search of percolating moisture.

The soldier thinking of *zeribas* may applaud their usefulness. The artist may find beauty in the delicate buds and long white spines. But the traveller, pricked all over and his clothes torn, will judge these insufficient apology for their existence.

Smaller than the thorn-bushes, but quite as numerous, the caustic plant abounds. Its long stalks are garnished with pale green leaves, and from the jointed branches large, luscious-looking fruits depend.

But when the unwitting hand grasps these pretentious apples, they burst at once and expose their contents. They are only bladders puffed with air and filled with a poisonous white milk, which produces blindness if by chance it is squirted in the eye. These are malignant growths. Only the palms by the brink are kindly, and men journeying along the Nile must look often towards their bushy tops, where among the spreading foliage the red and yellow glint of date clusters proclaims the ripening of a generous crop, and protests that Nature is not always mischievous and cruel.

The banks of the Nile, except by contrast with the desert, display an abundance of barrenness. Their characteristic is monotony. Their attraction is their sadness. Yet there is one hour when all is changed. Just before the sun sets towards the western cliffs a delicious flush brightens and enlivens the landscape. It is as though some Titanic artist in the hour of inspiration is retouching the picture, painting in dark purple shadows among the rocks, strengthening the lights on the sand, gilding and beautifying everything, and making the whole scene live.

The river, whose windings give the impression of a lake, turns from muddy brown to silver-grey. The sky from a dull blue deepens into violet in the west. Everything under that magic touch becomes vivid and alive. And then the sun sinks altogether behind the rocks, the colours fade out of the sky, the flush off the sands, and gradually everything darkens and grows grey, like a man's cheek when he is bleeding to death. We are left sad and sorrowful in the dark, until the stars light up and remind us that there is always something beyond.

In a land whose beauty is the beauty of a moment, whose face is desolate, and whose character is strangely stern, the curse of war was hardly needed to produce a melancholy effect. Where everything is hot and burning, the caustic plants appear superfluous. In deserts where thirst is enthroned, and where the rocks and sand appeal to a pitiless sky for moisture, it was a savage trick to add the mockery of the mirage. Yet a philosopher might draw comfort from the reflection that strife is rightly relegated to unprofitable regions, and may acidly observe that those who seek to destroy each other have no right to rail at Nature.

The desolation of the theatre of the River War, though appalling, will be realised more easily than its vast area. Distances that the eye cannot measure are appreciated with difficulty and vagueness by the mind. Africa in the atlas looks neither enormous nor obstructed. Those, indeed, who have travelled by march or caravan may understand the size by observing the distance between two places on the map and reflecting on the weary days that were consumed in journeying from one to the other. Memory, by modelling on the smooth, page mountain, valley, and ravine, by painting in forest marsh and scrub, by recalling successive camping grounds and reflecting on the tedious hours of hot sun and constant movement, may create a true impression of the oppressive distance. But those who have only travelled by railway in the developed countries of Europe will find grave difficulty in estimating the extent of the enormous territories over which science has not yet established her authority.

The area multiplies the desolation. There is life only by the Nile. If a man were to leave the river, he might journey westward and find no human habitation, nor the smoke of a cooking fire, except the lonely tent of a Kabbabish Arab or the encampment of a trader's caravan till he reached the coast-line of America. Or he might go east and find nothing but sand and sea and sun until Bombay rose above the horizon. The thread of fresh water is itself solitary in regions where all living things lack company. The terrors of these wastes are made known to the traveller who by stupidity or misfortune should lose his way. The camp may be within a few miles. Yet in the darkness, if once the true direction has been lost, he must be content to wait for morning. In the dragging hours of the night the desolation will oppress his mind and assail his nerve. Daylight may restore his courage and reveal the road; but while he lives he will remember the desert. With such a one we may return to drink at sunrise from the river.

The thirst of the night is quenched and its anxieties dispelled by the sweet and cool water; nor will he who is thus refreshed ungratefully forget to thank the God he worships, that when He made the world, He also made the Nile.

In the account of the River War, the Nile is naturally supreme. It is the great *motif* that recurs throughout the whole opera. The general purposing military operations, the statesman who would decide upon grave policies, and the reader desirous of studying the course and results of either, must think of the Nile. It is the life of the lands through which it flows. It is the cause of the war. It is the means by which we fight; the end at which we aim. Imagination should paint the river through every page in the story. It glitters between the palm-trees during the actions. It is the explanation of nearly every military movement. By its banks the armies camp by night. Backed or flanked on its unfordable stream they offer or accept battle by day.[2] To its brink, morning and evening, long lines of camels, horses, transport mules, and slaughter cattle hurry eagerly.

Emir and Dervish, officer and soldier, friend and foe, kneel alike to this god of ancient Egypt and draw each day their daily water in goatskin, bottle, or canteen. Without the river none would have started. Without it none might have continued. Without it none could ever have returned.

All who journey on the Nile, whether in commerce or war, will pay their tribute of respect and gratitude; for the great river has befriended all races and every age. It has borne with an impartial smile the stately barges of the Pharaohs and the unpretentious sternwheel steamers of Cook. It has seen war with the *balista* and the short Roman sword, and has witnessed the military employment of quick-firing guns and Lyddite shells. Kingdoms and dominations have risen and fallen by its banks. Religious sects have sprung into life, gained strength in adversity, triumphed over opposition, and relapsed into the obscurity of non-existence. The knowledge of men has grown, withered, and revived. The very shape and structure of the human form may have altered, but the Nile remains unchanged.

A cynic might observe that this is true of all other rivers, and that every natural feature proclaims the insignificance of man. But the thought seems less unwelcome of the Nile, and we remember that its mission has always been to relieve and vivify. Through all the centuries it has performed the annual miracle of its flood. That surprising phenomenon has been uninterrupted. Every year when the rains fall and the mountain snows of Central Africa begin to melt, the headstreams become torrents and the great lakes are filled to the

---

2 The author is here thinking only of the actions of the River War.—EDITOR.

brim. A vast expanse of low, swampy lands, crossed by secondary channels and flooded for many miles, regulates the flow, and by a sponge-like action prevents the excess of one year from causing the deficiency of the next. Far away in Egypt, prince, priest, and peasant look southwards with anxious attention for the fluctuating yet certain rise. Gradually the flood begins. The Bahr-el-Ghazal from a channel of stagnant pools and marshes becomes a broad and navigable stream. The Sobat and the Atbara from dry watercourses with occasional pools, in which the fish and alligators are crowded, turn to rushing rivers. But all this is remote from Egypt. After its confluence with the Atbara no drop of water reaches the Nile, and it flows for seven hundred miles through the sands or rushes in cataracts among the rocks of the Nubian desert.

Nevertheless, in spite of the tremendous diminution in volume caused by the dryness of the earth and air, and the heat of the sun — all of which drink greedily — the river below Assuan is sufficiently great to supply nine millions of people with as much water as their utmost science and energies can draw, and yet pour into the Mediterranean a low-water surplus current of 61,500 cubic feet per second. Nor is its water its only gift. As the Nile rises, its complexion is changed. The clear blue river becomes thick and red, laden with the magic mud that can raise cities from the desert sand and make the wilderness a garden. The geographer may still in the arrogance of science describe the Nile as 'a great, steady-flowing river, fed by the rains of the tropics, controlled by the existence of a vast head reservoir and several areas of repose, and annually flooded by the accession of a great body of water with which its eastern tributaries are flushed';[3] but all who have drunk deeply of its soft yet fateful waters—fateful, since they give both life and death—will understand why the old Egyptians worshipped the river, nor will they even in modern days easily dissociate from their minds a feeling of mystic reverence.

Amid these regions and along the river was fought the war with which these pages are concerned. I do not exaggerate its importance. Even in the present day it is only one among the various great enterprises of the State. In the near future it will seem almost insig-

3 *Encyclopaedia Britannica.*

nificant. The past in relation to the present is but a fleeting moment; nor is it to be expected that when others occupy the world, the events I have chronicled will attract their attention. Each generation exults in the immediate possession of life, and regards with indifference, scarcely tinged by pride or pity, the records and monuments of those that are no more. The greatest events of history are insignificant beside the bill of fare. The greatest men that ever lived serve to pass an idle hour. The tremendous crash of the Roman Empire is scarcely heard outside the schools and colleges. The past is insulted as much by what is remembered as by what is altogether forgotten. Yet — since the desire to live extends beyond the span of life, and men long for a refuge in memory, when the world shall have slipped from beneath their feet like a trapdoor; since we may credit ourselves with the sympathy posterity will continue to owe; and since some chroniclers, desiring in a distant age to write for his present a history of our past, may, rummaging among old books, find this — I have set forth in the expression of the times a true and impartial account of events which, though they will be forgotten in a century, nevertheless extended over thirteen years of strife and involved the untimely destruction of three hundred thousand human lives.

CHAPTER II[1]

THE REBELLION OF THE MAHDI

'Thrice is he armed who hath his quarrel just"

The Soudan—Its beasts—Its inhabitants—Their history—The spirit of Empire—The rule of Egypt—Its magnificence—Its shame—The army of occupation—Two personalities—General Gordon in the Soudan—His administration—The force of fanaticism—Its influence on the revolt—A just quarrel—A leader—Early days of the Mahdi—Sharif Abba Island—Mohammed's protest—His disgrace—The implacable Sheikh—A taunt—Fame of the Mahdi—Abdullahi—His fortunes—The great conspiracy—Rebellion—The first success—The *Hegira*—The Mudir of Fashoda—Destruction of Yusef Pasha—Spread of the revolt—Egyptian politics—British intervention—Hicks Pasha—Destruction of his army—Triumph of the Mahdi—His work.

That part of the earth's surface geographically known as the Egyptian Soudan extends from Assuan to the Equator, and from Suakin to Darfur. The previous chapter has described the scenery and character of the northern portion of this wide region, in which the operations of the British troops have taken place: a great river flowing through greater deserts. South of Khartoum the land becomes more fruitful. The numerous tributaries of the Nile multiply the areas of riparian fertility. A considerable rainfall, increasing as the Equator is approached, enables the intervening spaces to support vegetation and consequently human life. The greater part of the country is feverish and unhealthy, nor can Europeans long sustain the attacks of its climate. Nevertheless it is by no means valueless. On the east the province of Sennar used to produce abundant grain, and might easily produce no less abundant cotton. Westward the

1 Map, 'The Soudan,' page 14.

vast territories of Kordofan and Darfur afford grazing-grounds to a multitude of cattle, and give means of livelihood to great numbers of Baggara or cow-herd Arabs, who may also pursue with activity and stratagem the fleet giraffe and the still fleeter ostrich. To the south-east lies Bahr-el-Ghazal, a great tract of country occupied by dense woods and plentifully watered. Further south and nearer the Equator the forests and marshes become exuberant with tropical growths, and the whole face of the land is moist and green. Amid groves of gigantic trees and through plains of high waving grass the stately elephant roams in herds, which occasionally number four hundred, hardly ever disturbed by a well-armed hunter. The ivory of their tusks constitutes the wealth of the Equatorial Province. So greatly they abound that Emin Pasha is provoked to complain of a pest of these valuable pachyderms:[2] and although they are only assailed by the natives with spear and gun, no less than twelve thousand hundredweight of ivory has been exported in a single year.[3]

All other kinds of large beasts known to man inhabit these obscure retreats. The fierce rhinoceros crashes through the undergrowth. Among the reeds of melancholy swamps huge hippopotami, crocodiles, and buffaloes prosper and increase. Antelope of every known and many unclassified species; serpents of peculiar venom; countless millions of birds, butterflies, and beetles are among the offsprings of prolific Nature. Nor would the daring sportsman who should survive his expedition fail to add to the achievements of science and the extent of natural history as well as to his own reputation.

The human inhabitants of the Soudan would not, but for their vices and misfortunes, be disproportioned in numbers to the *fauna* or less happy. War, slavery, and oppression have however afflicted them until the total population of the whole country does not exceed at the most liberal estimate three million souls. The huge area contains many differences of climate and situation, and these have produced peculiar and diverse breeds of men. The Soudanese are of many tribes, but two main races can be clearly distinguished: the aboriginal natives, and the Arab settlers. The indigenous inhabit-

---

2 *Life of Emin Pasha,* vol. i. chapter ix.
3 *Ibid.*

ants of the country were negroes as black as coal. Strong, virile, and simple-minded savages, they lived as we may imagine prehistoric men—hunting, fighting, marrying, and dying, with no ideas beyond the gratification of their physical desires, and no fears save those engendered by ghosts, witchcraft, the worship of ancestors, and other forms of superstition common among peoples of low development. They displayed the virtues of barbarism. They were brave and honest. The smallness of their intelligence excused the degradation of their habits. Their ignorance secured their innocence. Yet their eulogy must be short, for though their customs, language, and appearance vary with the districts they inhabit and the subdivisions to which they belong, the history of all is a confused legend of strife and misery, their natures are uniformly cruel and thriftless, and their condition is one of equal squalor and want.

Although the negroes are the more numerous, the Arabs exceed in power. The bravery of the aboriginals is outweighed by the intelligence of the invaders and their superior force of character. During the second century of the Mohammedan era, when the inhabitants of Arabia went forth to conquer the world, one adventurous army struck south. The first pioneers were followed at intervals by continual immigrations of Arabs not only from Arabia but also across the deserts from Egypt and Morocco. The element thus introduced has spread and is spreading throughout the Soudan, as water soaks into a dry sponge. The aboriginals absorbed the invaders they could not repel. The stronger race imposed its customs and language on the negroes. The vigour of their blood sensibly altered the facial appearance of the Soudanese. The faith of Islam appears to possess a strange fascination for negroid races. For more than a thousand years the influence of Mohammedanism has been permeating the Soudan, and, although ignorance and natural obstacles obstruct the progress of new ideas, the whole of the black race is gradually adopting the new religion and developing Arab characteristics. In the districts of the north, where the original invaders settled, the evolution is complete, and the Arabs of the Soudan are a race formed by the interbreeding of negro and Arab, and yet distinct from either. In the more remote and inaccessible regions which lie to the south and west the negro race remains as yet unchanged by the Arab influence. And between these extremes every decree of mixture is to be found.

In some tribes pure Arabic is spoken, and prior to the rise of the Mahdi the orthodox Moslem faith was practised. In others Arabic has merely modified the ancient dialects, and the Mohammedan religion has been adapted to the older superstitions; but although the gap between the Arab-negro and the negro-pure was thus filled by every intermediate blend, the two races were at an early date quite distinct.

The qualities of mongrels are rarely admirable, and the mixture of the Arab and negro types has produced a debased and cruel breed, more shocking because they are more intelligent than the primitive savages. The stronger race soon began to prey upon the simple aboriginals; some of the Arab tribes were camel breeders; some were goat-herds; some were Baggaras or cow-herds. But all, without exception, were hunters of men. To the great slave-market at Jeddah a continual stream of negro captives has flowed for hundreds of years. The invention of gunpowder and the adoption by the Arabs of firearms facilitated the traffic by placing the ignorant negroes at a further disadvantage. Thus the situation in the Soudan for several centuries may be summed up as follows:—The dominant race of Arab invaders was unceasingly spreading its blood, religion, customs, and language among the black aboriginal population, and at the same time it harried and enslaved them.

The state of society that arose out of this may be easily imagined. The warlike Arab tribes fought and brawled among themselves in ceaseless fend and strife. The negroes trembled in apprehension of capture, or rose locally against their oppressors. Occasionally an important Sheikh would effect the combination of many tribes, and a kingdom came into existence—a community consisting of a military class armed with guns and of multitudes of slaves, at once their servants and their merchandise, and sometimes trained as soldiers. The domination might prosper viciously till it was overthrown by some more powerful league. Although the Arab race impressed itself on the negro so strongly, yet the power of numbers was asserted, and in the fifteenth century the old negro tribal names of Fung, Hameg, &c, reappear, while the Arab classifications are forgotten. During the sixteenth century the Fung tribe became all-powerful, and with rare fortune maintained its supremacy until about 1750, when the Hameg arose and destroyed it. The Hameg broke up after a brief spell of rapine and oppression, and the Soudan relapsed into the anarchy from which it had never been very far removed.

All this was unheeded by the outer world, from which the Soudan is separated by the deserts, and it seemed that the slow, painful course of development would be unaided and uninterrupted. But at last the populations of Europe changed. Another civilisation reared itself above the ruins of Roman triumph and Mohammedan aspiration—a civilisation more powerful, more glorious, but no less aggressive. The impulse of conquest which hurried the French and English to Canada and the Indies, which sent the Dutch to the Cape and the Spaniards to Peru, spread to Africa and led the Egyptians to the Soudan. In the year 1819 Mahomet Ali, availing himself of the disorders alike as an excuse and an opportunity, marched up the Nile with a great army. The Arab tribes, torn by dissension, exhausted by thirty years of general war, and no longer inspired by their neglected religion, offered a weak resistance. Their slaves, having known the worst of life, were apathetic. The black aboriginals were silent and afraid. The whole vast territory was conquered with very little fighting, and the victorious army, leaving garrisons, returned in triumph to the Delta.

What enterprise that an enlightened community may attempt is more noble and more profitable than the reclamation from barbarism of fertile regions and large populations? To give peace to warring tribes, to administer justice where all was violence, to strike the chains off the slave, to draw the richness from the soil, to plant the earliest seeds of commerce and learning, to increase in whole peoples their capacities for pleasure and diminish their chances of pain—what more beautiful ideal or more valuable reward can inspire human effort? The act is virtuous, the exercise invigorating, and the result often extremely profitable. Yet as the mind turns from the wonderful cloudland of aspiration to the ugly scaffolding of attempt and achievement, a succession of opposite ideas arise. Industrious races are displayed stinted and starved for the sake of an expensive Imperialism which they can only enjoy, if they are well fed. Wild peoples, ignorant of their barbarism, callous of suffering, careless of life but tenacious of liberty, are seen to resist with fury the philanthropic invaders, and to perish in thousands before they are convinced of their mistake. The inevitable gap between conquest and dominion becomes filled with the figures of the greedy trader, the inopportune missionary, the ambitious soldier, and the lying speculator, who disquiet the minds of the conquered and excite the sordid appetites of the conquerors. And as the eye of thought rests on these sinister features, it hardly seems possible for us to believe that any fair prospect is approached by so foul a path.

The desire to prevail is not, however, a matter of reason but of constitution. It is only one form of the spirit of competition, the condition of our continued existence. All the vigorous nations of the earth have sought and are seeking to conquer. Even the feeblest cling to their possessions with desperation. The Spaniards fought for the last remains of their empire with the last remains of their strength. Few features strike the reader of modern Egyptian history so strongly as the desire of the educated classes to hold or regain the Soudan. In a nation where public spirit is almost unknown, Cherif Pasha resigned rather than consent to the abandonment of the southern provinces. Even cataleptic China protests against dismemberment. The instinct may not be wise, but it is apparently healthy; for, as in the Roman State, when there are no more worlds to conquer and no rivals to destroy, nations exchange the desire for power for the love of art, and so a gradual, yet continual, enervation and decline turn from the vigorous beauties of the nude to the more subtle allurements of the draped, and then sink to actual eroticism and ultimate decay. The writer of a tale of war may not follow such an argument even to the depths which average men can plumb; nor can he examine the question whether a conspiracy for the arrest of development is justified by the unexpected powers which the science of man has snatched from Nature. It is only possible to recognise the desire to prevail—the spirit of empire—as a great fact, which practical men must reckon with; and then perforce return to the Egyptians with the reflection that, if even noble races soil themselves by pursuing the path of conquest, it would be well if mean breeds avoided it altogether.[4]

---

4 'One thing is certain, that the Egyptian should never be allowed out of his own country.'—*Colonel Gordon in Central Africa*, April 11, 1879.

From 1819 to 1883 Egypt ruled the Soudan. Her rule was not kindly, wise, nor profitable. Its aim was to exploit, not to improve the local population. The miseries of the people were aggravated rather than lessened; but they were concealed. For the rough justice of the sword there were substituted the intricate laws of corruption and bribery. Violence and plunder were more hideous, since they were cloaked with legality and armed with authority.

The land was undeveloped and poor. It barely sustained its inhabitants. The additional burden of a considerable foreign garrison and a crowd of rapacious officials increased the severity of the economic conditions. Scarcity was frequent. Famines were periodical. The Egyptians had only pressed upon the tortured face of the Soudan the bland mask of an organised Government.

Corrupt and incapable Governors-General succeeded each other at Khartoum with bewildering rapidity. The constant changes, while they prevented the continuity of any wise policy, did not interrupt the misrule. With hardly any exceptions the Pashas were consistent in oppression. The success of their administration was measured by the Ministries in Egypt by the amount of money they could extort from the natives; among the officials in the Soudan, by the number of useless offices they could create. There were a few bright examples of honest men, but these, by providing a contrast only increased the discontents. The rule of Egypt was iniquitous. Yet it preserved the magnificent appearance of Imperial dominion. The Egyptian Proconsul lived in state at the confluence of the Niles. The representatives of foreign Powers established themselves in the city. The trade of the south converged upon Khartoum. Thither the subordinate governors, *Beys* and *Mudirs*, repaired at intervals to report the state of their provinces and to receive instructions. Thither was sent the ivory of Equatoria, the ostrich feathers of Kordofan, gum from Darfur, grain from Sennar, and taxes collected from all the regions. Strange beasts, entrapped in the swamps and forests, passed through the capital on their journey to Cairo and Europe.

Complex and imposing reports of revenue and expenditure were annually compiled. An elaborate and dignified correspondence was maintained between Egypt and its great dependency. The casual observer, astonished at the unusual capacity for government displayed by an Oriental people, was tempted to accept the famous assertion which Nubar Pasha put into the mouth of the Khedive Ismail; 'We are no longer in Africa, but in Europe.' Yet all was a hateful sham.[5]

The arbitrary and excessive taxes were collected only at the point of the bayonet. If a petty chief fell into arrears, his neighbours were raised against him. If an Arab tribe were recalcitrant, a military expedition was despatched. The ability of the Arabs to pay depended on their success as slave-hunters. When there had been a good catch, the revenue profited. The Egyptian Government had joined the International League against the slave trade. They continued however, indirectly but deliberately, to make money out of it.[6]

In the miserable, harassing warfare that accompanied the collection of taxes the Viceregal commanders gained more from fraud than force. No subterfuge, no treachery, was too mean for them to adopt. No oath or treaty was too sacred for them to break. Their methods were cruel, and if honour did not impede the achievement, mercy did not restrict the effects of their inglorious successes; and the effete administrators delighted to order their timid soldiery to carry out the most savage executions. The political methods and social style of the Governors-General were imitated more or less exactly by the subordinate officials according to their degree in the

---

5 'The government of the Egyptians in these far-off countries is nothing else but one of brigandage of the very worst description.'—*Colonel Gordon in Central Africa*, April 11, 1879.

6 A very concise description of the methods of the Egyptian Government in the collection of their revenue throughout the Soudan, and a clear testimony to the source from which it was derived, is found in Lieut.-Colonel Stewart's report (1883). He wrote:—'Say the annual tribute of the tribe was 5,000*l*. Having no money, and no wealth but their cattle, it was evident that they were quite unable to pay the sum. In such cases the Kordofan merchant (Djellab) would offer to pay it, if the tribe would supply him with an equivalent in slaves, say 1,000. Should the required number of slaves not be forthcoming, then the tribe would agree to pay the balance by selling him cows at a certain rate. Should the tribe fail in the bargain, the merchant would refuse to pay the Government, and the latter would have to send troops to harry the tribe. These troops would probably plunder and destroy far more than was necessary, with the result of still further impoverishing the tribe, making the Government detested, and the people only too willing to seize any opportunity of escaping from it.'—*Egypt*, No. 11, 1883.

provinces. Since they were completely hidden from the eye of civilisation, they enjoyed a greater licence in their administration.

As their education was inferior, so their habits became more gross. Meanwhile the volcano on which they disported themselves was ominously silent. The Arab tribes obeyed, and the black population cowered.

The authority of a tyrannical Government was supported by the presence of a worthless army. Nearly forty thousand men were distributed among eight main and numerous minor garrisons. Isolated in a roadless country by enormous distances and natural obstacles, and living in the midst of large savage populations of fanatical character and warlike habits, whose exasperation was yearly growing with their miseries, the Viceregal forces might depend for their safety only on the skill of their officers, the excellence of their discipline, and the superiority of their weapons. But the Egyptian officers were at that time distinguished for nothing but their public incapacity and private misbehaviour. The evil reputation of the Soudan and its climate deterred the more educated or more wealthy from serving in such distant regions, and none went south who could avoid it. The army which the Khedives maintained in the Delta was, judged by European standards, only a rabble. It was badly trained, rarely paid, and very cowardly; and the scum of the army of the Delta was the cream of the army of the Soudan. The officers remained for long periods, many all their lives, in the obscurity of the remote provinces. Some had been sent there in disgrace, others in disfavour. Some had been forced to serve out of Egypt by extreme poverty, others were drawn to the Soudan by the hopes of gratifying peculiar tastes. The majority had harems of the women of the country,[7] which were limited only by the amount of money they could lay hands upon by any method. Many were hopeless and habitual drunkards. Nearly all were dishonest. All were indolent and incapable.

Under such leadership the finest soldiery would have soon degenerated. The Egyptians in the Soudan were not fine soldiers. Like their officers, they were the worst part of the Khedivial army. Like

7 'In one district the commander of the troops was carrying off not only the flocks and herds of the natives, but their young girls.'—*Colonel Gordon in Central Africa* (Campaign of Gessi Pasha).

them, they had been driven to the south. Like them, they were slothful and effete. Their training was imperfect. Their discipline was lax. Their courage was low. Nor was even this all the weakness and peril of their position; for while the regular troops were thus demoralised, there existed a powerful local irregular force of Bazingers,[8] as well armed as the soldiers, more numerous, more courageous, and who regarded the alien garrisons with fear that continually diminished, and hate that continually grew. And behind regulars and irregulars alike the wild Arab tribes of the desert and the hardy blacks of the forests, goaded by suffering and injustice, thought the foreigners the cause of all their woes, and were delayed only by their inability to combine from sweeping them off the face of the earth. Never was there such a house of cards as the Egyptian dominion in the Soudan. The marvel is that it stood so long, not that it fell so soon.

The names of two men of extraordinary character and great fame are for ever connected with the actual outburst. One was an English general, the other an Arab priest; yet, in spite of the great gulf and vivid contrast between their conditions, they resembled each other in many respects. Both were earnest and enthusiastic men of keen sympathies and passionate emotions. Both were powerfully swayed by religious fervour. Both exerted great personal influence on all who came in contact with them. Both were reformers. The Arab was an African reproduction of the Englishman; the Englishman a superior and civilised development of the Arab. In the end they fought to the death, but for an important part of their lives their influence on the fortunes of the Soudan was exerted in the same direction. Mohammed Ahmed, 'The Mahdi,' will be discussed in his own place. Charles Gordon needs no introduction. Long "before this tale begins his reputation was European. The fame of the 'Ever-victorious Army' had spread far beyond the Great Wall of China.

The misgovernment of the Egyptians and the misery of the Soudanese reached their greatest extreme in the seventh decade of the present century.[9] From such a situation there seemed to be no issue other than by force of arms. The Arab tribes lacked no provocation. Yet they were destitute of two moral forces essential to all rebellions.

8 Soudanese riflemen.—EDITOR.

9 The nineteenth century. [Footnote to the new edition].

The first was the knowledge that better things existed. The second was a spirit of combination. General Gordon showed them the first. The Mahdi provided the second.

It is impossible to study any part of Charles Gordon's career without being drawn to all the rest. As his wild and varied fortunes lead him from Sebastopol to Pekin, from Gravesend to South Africa, from Mauritius to the Soudan, the reader follows fascinated. Every scene is strange, terrible, or dramatic. Yet, remarkable as are the scenes, the actor is the more extraordinary; a type without comparison in modern times and with few likenesses in history. Rare and precious is the truly disinterested man. Potentates of many lands and different degree—the Emperor of China, the King of the Belgians, the Premier of Cape Colony, the Khedive of Egypt—competed to secure his services. The importance of his offices varied no less than their nature. One day he was a subaltern of sappers; on another he commanded the Chinese army; the next he directed an orphanage; or was Governor-General of the Soudan, with supreme powers of life and death and peace and war; or served as private secretary to Lord Ripon. But in whatever capacity he laboured he was true to his reputation. Whether he is portrayed bitterly criticising to Graham the tactics of the assault on the Redan; or pulling the head of Lar Wang from under his bedstead and waving it in paroxysms of indignation before the astonished eyes of Sir Halliday Macartney; or riding alone into the camp of the rebel Suliman and receiving the respectful salutes of those who had meant to kill him; or telling the Khedive Ismail that he 'must have the whole Soudan to govern'; or reducing his salary to half the regulation amount because 'he thought it was too much'; or ruling a country as large as Europe; or collecting facts for Lord Ripon's rhetorical efforts, we perceive a man careless alike of the frowns of men or the smiles of women, of life or comfort, wealth or fame.

It was a pity that a man, thus gloriously free from the ordinary restraining influences of human society, should have found in his own character so little mental ballast. Mercury uncontrolled by the force of gravity was not on several occasions more unstable than Charles Gordon. His moods were capricious and uncertain, his passions violent, his impulses sudden and inconsistent. The mortal enemy of the morning had become a trusted ally before the night. The friend he loved to-day he loathed to-morrow. Scheme after scheme formed in his fertile brain, and jostled confusingly together. All in succession were pressed with enthusiasm. All at times were rejected with disdain. A temperament naturally neurotic had been aggravated by an acquired habit of smoking; and the General carried this to so great an extreme that he was rarely seen without a cigarette. His virtues are famous among men. His daring and resource might turn the tide of war. His energy would haw animated a whole people. His achievements are upon record, but it must also be set down that few more uncertain and impracticable forces than Gordon have ever been introduced into diplomacy.

Although the Egyptian Government might loudly proclaim their detestation of slavery, their behaviour in the Soudan was viewed with suspicion by the European Powers, and particularly by Great Britain. To vindicate his sincerity the Khedive Ismail in 1874 appointed Gordon to be Governor of the Equatorial Province in succession to Sir Samuel Baker. The name of the General was a sufficient guarantee that the slave trade was being earnestly attacked. The Khedive would gladly have stopped at the guarantee, and satisfied the world without disturbing 'vested interests.' But the mission, which may have been originally instituted as a pretence, soon became in Gordon's energetic hands very real. Circumstances enlisted the sympathies of the Egyptian Government on the side of their zealous agent. The slave dealers had committed every variety of atrocity for which the most odious traffic in the world afforded occasion. But when, under the leadership of Zubair Rahmana, they refused to pay their annual tribute it was felt in Cairo that their crimes had cried aloud for chastisement.

Zubair is sufficiently described when it has been said that he was the most notorious slave dealer Africa has ever produced. His infamy had spread beyond the limits of the continent which was the scene of his exploits to the distant nations of the north and west. In reality, his rule was a distinct advance on the anarchy which had preceded it, and certainly he was no worse than others of his vile trade. His scale of business was, however, more extended. What William Whiteley was in respect of goods and chattels, that was Zubair in respect of slaves—a universal provider. Magnitude lends a certain grandeur to crime; and Zubair in the height of his power, at the head of the slave merchants' confederacy, might boast the retinue of a king and exercise authority over wide regions and a powerful army.

It may be difficult for those who meet him, now that he is a pensioned prisoner in Cairo, to realise his former greatness.[10] Yet when he is asked to speak of the days when he conquered Darfur, the old man's face lights up, his eye glitters with triumphant memory, and, in spite of the incongruous frockcoat and shiny boots, the visitor may imagine the savage conqueror before whose golden couch chained leopards walked, and the wild peoples of the Soudan were made to bow in awe and fear.

As early as 1869 he was practically the independent ruler of the Bahr-el-Ghazal. The Khedive resolved to assert his rights. A small Egyptian force was sent to subdue the rebel slaver, who not only disgraced humanity but refused to pay tribute. Like most of the Khedivial expeditions the troops under Belial Bey met with ill-fortune. They came, they saw, they ran away. Some, less speedy than the rest, fell on the field of honour. The rebellion was open. Nevertheless it was the Khedive who sought peace. Zubair *apologised* for defeating the Viceregal soldiers and remained supreme in the Bahr-el-Ghazal. Thence he planned the conquest of Darfur, at that time an independent kingdom.

The Egyptian Government were glad to join with him in the enterprise. The man they had been unable to conquer, they found it expedient to assist. The operations were successful. The King of Darfur, who was distinguished no less for his valour than for his folly, was killed. The whole country was subdued. The whole population available after the battles became slaves. Zubair thus wielded a formidable power. The Khedivial Government, thinking to ensure his loyalty, created him a Pasha—a rank which he could scarcely disgrace—and the authority of the rebel was thus unwillingly recognised by the ruler. Such was the situation when Gordon first came to the Soudan.

10 Through the kindness of Sir Reginald Wingate I had the pleasure of a long and interesting conversation with Zubair in May 1899.

It was beyond the power of the new Governor of the Equatorial Province to at once destroy the slave-hunting confederacy. Yet he struck heavy blows at the slave trade, and when in 1877, after a short visit to England, he returned to the Soudan as Governor-General and with absolute power, he assailed it with redoubled energy. Fortune assisted his efforts, for the able Zubair was enticed to Cairo, and, once there, the Government refused to allow their faithful ally and distinguished guest to go back to his happy hunting grounds. Although the slave dealers were thus robbed of their great leader, they were still strong. Zubair's son, the brave Suliman, found a considerable following.

Furious at his father's captivity, and alarmed lest his own should follow, he meditated revolt. But the Governor-General, mounted on a swift camel and attired in full uniform, rode alone into the rebel camp and compelled the submission of its chiefs before they could recover from their amazement. The confederacy was severely shaken, and when, in the following year, Suliman again revolted, the Egyptian troops under Gessi Pasha were able to disperse his forces and induce him to surrender to terms. The terms were broken, and Suliman and ten of his companions suffered death by shooting.[11] The league of the slave dealers was thus destroyed.

Towards the end of 1879 Gordon left the Soudan. With short intervals he had spent five busy years in its provinces. His energy had stirred the country. He had struck at the root of the slave trade, he had attacked the system of slavery, and, as slavery was the greatest institution in the land, he had undermined the whole social system. Indignation had stimulated his activity to an extraordinary degree. In a climate usually fatal to Europeans he discharged the work of five officers. Careless of his methods, he bought slaves himself, drilled them, and with the soldiers thus formed, pounced on the caravans of the hunters. Traversing the country on a fleet dromedary—on which in a single year he is said to have covered 3,840 miles—he scattered justice and freedom among the astonished natives. He fed the infirm, protected the weak, executed the wicked. To some he gave actual help, to many freedom, to all new hopes and aspirations. Nor were the tribes ungrateful. The fiercest savages and cannibals

11 Slatin, *Fire and Sword*, p. 28.

respected the life of the strange white man. The women blessed him. He could ride unarmed and alone where a brigade of soldiers dared not venture. But he was, as he knew himself, the herald of the storm. Oppressed yet ferocious races had learned that they had rights. The misery of the Soudanese was lessened, but their knowledge had increased. The whole population was unsettled. The wheels of change began slowly to revolve, nor did they stop until they had accomplished a mighty revolution.

The part played by the second force is more obscure. Few facts are so encouraging to the student of human development as the desire, which most men and all communities manifest at all times, to associate with their actions at least the appearance of moral right. However distorted may be their conceptions of virtue, however feeble their efforts to attain even to their own ideals, it is a pleasing feature and a hopeful augury that they should wish to be justified. No community embarks on a great enterprise without fortifying itself with the belief that from some points of view its motives are lofty and disinterested. It is an involuntary tribute, the humble tribute of imperfect beings, to the eternal temples of Truth and Beauty.

The sufferings of a people or a class may be intolerable, but before they will take up arms and risk their lives, some unselfish and impersonal spirit must animate them. In countries where there is education and mental activity or refinement, this high and often ultra-human motive is found in the pride of glorious traditions, in a keen sympathy with surrounding misery, or in a philosophical recognition of the dignity of the species. Ignorance deprives savage nations of such incentives. Yet in the marvellous economy of nature this very ignorance is a source of greater strength. It affords them the mighty stimulus of fanaticism. The French Communists might plead that they upheld the rights of man. The desert tribes proclaimed that they fought for the glory of God. But although the force of fanatical passion is far greater than that exerted by any philosophical belief, its unction is just the same. It gives men something which they think is sublime to fight for, and this serves them as an excuse for wars which it is desirable to begin for totally different reasons. Fanaticism is not a cause of war. It is the means which helps savage peoples to fight. It is the spirit which enables them to combine the great common object before which all personal or tribal disputes become insignificant. What the horn is to the rhinoceros, what the sting is to the wasp, the Mohammedan faith was to the Arabs of the Soudan—a faculty of offence or defence.

It was all this and no more. It was not the reason of the revolt. It strengthened, it characterised, but it did not cause.[12] Those whose practice it is to regard their own nation as possessing a monopoly of virtue and common-sense, are wont to ascribe every military enterprise of savage peoples to fanaticism. They calmly ignore obvious and legitimate motives. The most rational conduct is considered mad. When simple persons are puzzled by some cunning and wonderful invention, they not infrequently endeavour to conceal their ignorance by explaining that it is all 'done by electricity.' In a similar vague way rebellions of natives goaded to fury by brutal oppression are airily set down to their fanaticism, and the question is dismissed as unworthy of further reflection. It has therefore been freely stated, and is to some extent believed, that the revolt in the Soudan was entirely religious.

If the greatest untruths are those that have some appearance of veracity, this impression must be very false indeed. It is, I believe, an historical fact that the revolt of a great population has never been caused solely or even mainly by religious enthusiasm. In every case social or racial causes have predominated. The rising of 1897 on the Indian Frontier—to take the most recent instance—was in character religious; but its cause was political. The *Mullahs* preached a holy war against the infidel; but they preached because they conceived their influence assailed by contact with the tolerant scepticism of the Indian Government; and the tribesmen were stirred by their preaching, because, having seen the forts and roads being made in their territory, they rightly thought their liberties were threatened by annexation. The high moral principle is used to excuse, not to explain, violent courses. It would scarcely be less absurd to contend that the revolt in the Soudan was caused by fanaticism, than to assert that the French Revolution was brought about by the great

12 'I do not believe that fanaticism exists as it used to do in the world, judging from what I have seen in this so-called fanatic land. It is far more a question of property, and is more like Communism under the flag of religion.'—General Gordon's *Journals at Khartoum*, bk. i. p. 13.

admiration which the French people had for the philosophy of the 'Contrat Social.'

The reasons which forced the peoples of the Soudan to revolt were as strong as the defence which their oppressors could offer was feeble. Looking at the question from a purely political standpoint, we may say that upon the whole there exists no record of a better case for rebellion than that which presented itself to the Soudanese. Their country was being ruined; their property was plundered; their women were ravished; their liberties were curtailed; even their lives were threatened. Aliens ruled the inhabitants; the few oppressed the many; brave men were harried by cowards; the weak compelled the strong. Here were sufficient reasons. Since any armed movement against an established Government can be justified only by success, strength is a cardinal revolutionary virtue. It was a virtue that the Arabs might boast. They were indeed far stronger than they, their persecutors, or the outside world had yet learned. All were soon to be enlightened.

The storm gathered and the waters rose. Three great waves impelled the living tide against the tottering house founded on the desert sand. The Arab suffered acutely from poverty, misgovernment, and oppression. Infuriated, he looked up and perceived that the cause of all his miseries was a weak and cowardly foreigner, a despicable 'Turk.' The antagonism of races increased the hatred sprung from social evils. The moment was at hand. Then and not till then the third wave came—the wave of fanaticism, which, catching up and surmounting the other waves, covered all the flood with its white foam, and, bearing on with the momentum of the waters, beat in thunder against the weak house so that it fell; and great was the fall thereof.

The chemist knows the difficulty and delicacy of quantitative analysis; and when, instead of a concrete substance, there are substituted the fluctuating passions of wild and savage men, the inquiry baffles human intelligence. To decide the relative strength of the different forces which together produced the rebellion of the Arab tribes would be an exercise more wearisome in the attempt than useful in the achievement. But if the causes are thus obscured, their results are most clearly apparent. Down to the year 1881 there was no fanatical movement in the Soudan. In their utter misery the hopeless inhabitants had neglected even the practices of religion. They were nevertheless prepared for any enterprise, however desperate, which might free them from the Egyptian yoke. All that delayed them was the want of some leader who could combine the tribes and restore their broken spirits. In the summer of 1881 the leader appeared. His subsequent career is within the limits of this account, and since his life throws a strong light on the thoughts and habits of the Arabs of the Soudan, I shall trace it from the beginning.

The man who was the proximate cause of the River War was born by the banks of the Nile, not very far from Dongola. His family were poor and of no account in the province. But as the Prophet had claimed a royal descent, and as a Sacred Example was sprung from David's line, Mohammed Ahmed asserted that he was of the 'Ashraf,'[13] and the assertion, since it cannot be disproved, may be accepted. His father was a humble priest; yet he contrived to give his son some education in the practices of religion, the principles of the Koran, and the art of writing. Then he died at Kerreri while on a journey to Khartoum, and left the future Mahdi, still a child, to the mercies of the world. Solitary trees, if they grow at all, grow strong; and a boy deprived of a father's care often develops, if he escape the perils of youth, an independence and vigour of thought which may restore in after life the heavy loss of early days. It was so with Mohammed Ahmed. He looked around ,for an occupation and subsistence. A large proportion of the population of religious countries pass their lives at leisure, supported by the patient labour of the devout. The young man determined to follow the profession for which he felt his talents suited, and which—since all great men are ambitious in their youth—would afford him the widest scope. He became a priest. A large proportion of the religious teachers of heathen and other countries are devoid of enthusiasm and turn their attention to the next world because doing so affords them an easy living in this.

Happily this is not true of all. It was not true of Mohammed. Even at an early age he manifested a zeal for God's service, and displayed a peculiar aptitude for learning the tenets and dogmas of

13 Descendants of the Prophet.

the Mohammedan belief. So promising a pupil did not long lack a master in a country where intelligence and enthusiasm were scarce. His aspirations growing with his years and knowledge, he journeyed to Khartoum as soon as his religious education was completed, and became a disciple of the renowned and holy Sheikh, Mohammed Sherif.

His devotion to his superior, to his studies and to the practice of austerities, and a strange personal influence he was already beginning to show, won him by degrees a few disciples of his own: and with them he retired to the Island of Abba. Here by the waters of the White Nile Mohammed Ahmed lived for several years. His two brothers, who were boatbuilders in the neighbourhood, supported him by their industry. But it must have been an easy burden, for we read that he 'hollowed out for himself a cave in the mud bank, and lived in almost entire seclusion, fasting often for days, and occasionally paying a visit to the head of the order to assure him of his devotion and obedience.'[14] Meanwhile his sanctity increased and the labour and charity of the brothers were assisted by the alms of godly travellers on the river.

This virtuous and frugal existence was disturbed and terminated by an untoward event. The renowned and holy Sheikh made a feast to celebrate the circumcision of his sons. That the merriment of the auspicious occasion and the entertainment of the guests might be increased, Sherif, according to the lax practice of the time, granted a dispensation from any sins committed during the festivities, and proclaimed in God's name the suspension of the rules against singing and dancing by which the religious orders were bound. The ascetic of Abba island did not join in these seemingly innocent dissipations. With all the recklessness of the reformer he protested against the demoralisation of the age, and loudly affirmed the doctrine that God alone could forgive sins. These things were speedily brought to the ears of the renowned Sheikh, and in all the righteous indignation that accompanies detected wrong-doing, he summoned Mohammed Ahmed before him. The latter obeyed. He respected his

14 I take this passage from *Fire and Sword in the Soudan*, by Slatin. His account is the most graphic and reliable of all known records of the Mahdi. He had terrible opportunities of collecting information. I have followed his version (chapter iv.) very closely on this subject.

superior. He was under obligations to him. His ire had disappeared as soon as it had been expressed. He submissively entreated forgiveness; but in vain. Sherif felt that some sort of discipline must be maintained among his flock. He had connived at disobedience to the divine law. All the more must he uphold his own authority. Rising in anger he drove the presumptuous disciple from his presence with bitter words, and forthwith expunged his name from the order of the elect.

Mohammed went home. He was greatly distressed. Yet his fortunes were not ruined. His sanctity was still a valuable and, unless he chose otherwise, an inalienable asset. The renowned Sheikh had a rival—nearly as holy and more enterprising than himself. There the young priest might expect a warm welcome. Nevertheless he did not yet abandon his former superior. Placing a heavy wooden collar on his neck, clad in sackcloth and sprinkled with ashes, he again returned to his spiritual leader, and in this penitential guise implored pardon. He was ignominiously ejected. Nor did he venture to revisit the unforgiving Sheikh. But it happened that in a few weeks Sherif had occasion to journey to the Island of Abba. His former disciple appeared suddenly before him, still clad in sackcloth and defiled by ashes. Careless of his plain misery, and unmoved by his loyalty, which was the more remarkable since it was disinterested, the implacable Sheikh poured forth a stream of invective. Among many insults, one went home; 'Be off, you wretched Dongolawi.'

Although the natives of the Dongola province were despised and disliked in the Southern Soudan, it is not at first apparent why Mohammed should have resented so bitterly the allusion to his birthplace. But abuse by category is a dangerous though effective practice. A man will perhaps tolerate an offensive word applied to himself, but will be infuriated if his nation, his class, or his profession are insulted. 'Soldier ' is an honourable term. 'Fool' is an abusive word. Yet a military officer would be more justly angered if he were told he was ' a thick-headed soldier' than if he were called a 'thick-headed fool.'

Mohammed Ahmed rose. All that man could do to make amends he had done. Now he had been publicly called 'a wretched Dongolawi.' Henceforth he would afflict Sherif with his repentance no longer. Beaching his house, he informed his disciples—for they had not abandoned him in all his trouble—that the Sheikh had finally cast him off, and that he would now take his discarded allegiance elsewhere. The rival, the Sheikh el Koreishi, lived near Mesalamia. He was jealous of Sherif and envied him his sanctimonious disciples. He was therefore delighted to receive a letter from Mohammed Ahmed announcing his breach with his former superior and offering his most devoted services. He returned a cordial invitation, and the priest of Abba island made all preparation for the journey.

This new development seems to have startled the unforgiving Sherif. It was no part of his policy to alienate his followers, still less to add to those of his rival. After all, the quality of mercy was high and noble. He would at last graciously forgive the impulsive but repentant disciple. He wrote him a letter to this effect. But it was now too late. Mohammed replied with grave dignity that he had committed no crime, that he sought no forgiveness, and that 'a wretched Dongolawi' would not offend by his presence the renowned Sheikh el Sherif. Although the scene is laid in the wilds of Africa, and the actors differ from us in colour, faith, and custom, the story will recall the personal experiences of many readers, and enable them to sympathise with Mohammed's satisfaction in writing this reply. After this indulgence he departed to Mesalamia.

But the fame of his doings spread far and wide throughout the land. 'Even in distant Darfur it was the principal topic of conversation.'[15] Barely had a *Fiki* been known to offend his superior; never to refuse his forgiveness. Mohammed did not hesitate to declare that he had done what he had done as a protest against the decay of religious fervour and the torpor of the times. Since his conduct had actually caused his dismissal, it appears that he was quite justified in making a virtue of necessity. At any rate he was believed, and the people groaning under oppression looked from all the regions to the figure that began to grow on the political horizon. His fame grew. Rumour, loud-tongued, carried it about the land that a great Reformer was come to purify the faith and break the stony apathy which paralysed the hearts of Islam. Whisperings added that a man was found who should break from off the necks of the tribes the

15 Slatin, *Fire and Sword.*

hateful yoke of Egypt. Mohammed now deliberately entered upon the path of ambition.

Throughout Nubia the Shukri belief prevails: some day, in a time of shame and trouble, a second great Prophet will arise—a *Mahdi* who shall lead the faithful nearer God and sustain the religion. The people of the Soudan always look inquiringly to any ascetic who rises to fame, and the question is often repeated, 'Art thou he that should come, or do we look for another?' Of this powerful element of disturbance, Mohammed Ahmed resolved to avail himself. He requested and obtained the permission of the Sheikh Koreishi to return to Abba, where he was well known, and with which island village his name was connected, and so came back in triumph to the scene of his disgrace. Thither many pilgrims began to resort. He received valuable presents, which he distributed to the poor, who acclaimed him as 'Zahed'—a renouncer of earthly pleasures. He journeyed preaching through Kordofan, and received the respect of the priesthood and the homage of the people. And while he spoke of the purification of the religion, they thought that the burning words might be applied to the freedom of the soil. He supported his sermons by writings, which were widely read. When a few months later the Sheikh Koreishi died, the priest of Abba proceeded forthwith to erect a tomb to his memory, directing and controlling the voluntary labours of the reverent Arabs who carried the stones.

While Mohammed was thus occupied, he received the support of a man, less virtuous than but nearly as famous as himself. Abdullahi was one of four brothers, the sons of an obscure priest; but he inherited no great love of religion or devotion to its observances. He was a man of determination and capacity. He set before himself two distinct ambitions, both of which he accomplished; to free the Soudan of foreigners, and to rule it himself. He seems to have had a queer presentiment of his career. This much he knew; there would be a great religious leader and he would be his lieutenant and his successor. When Zubair conquered Darfur, Abdullahi presented himself before him and hailed him as 'the expected Mahdi.' Zubair, however, protested with superfluous energy that he was no saint, and the impulsive patriot was compelled to accept his assurances. As soon as he saw Mohammed Ahmed rising to fame and displaying qualities of courage and energy, he hastened to throw himself at his feet and assure him of his devotion.

No part of Slatin Pasha's fascinating account of his perils and sufferings is so entertaining as that in which Abdullahi, then become Khalifa of the whole Soudan, describes his early struggles and adversity:—

'Indeed it was a very troublesome journey. At that time my entire property consisted of one donkey, and he had a gall on his back, so that I could not ride him. But I made him carry my water-skin and bag of corn, over which I spread my rough cotton garment, and drove him along in front of me. At that time, I wore the white cotton shirt, like the rest of my tribe. My clothes and my dialect at once marked me out as a stranger wherever I went; and when I crossed the Nile I was frequently greeted with "What do you want? Go back to your own country. There is nothing to steal here."'

What a life of ups and downs! It was a long stride from the ownership of one saddle-galled donkey to the undisputed rule of an empire. The weary wayfarer may have dreamed of this, for ambition stirs imagination nearly as much as imagination excites ambition. But further, he could not expect or wish to see. Nor could he anticipate as, in the complacency of a man who had done with evil days, he told the story of his rise to the submissive Slatin, that the day would come when he would lead an army of more than fifty thousand men to destruction, and that the night would follow when, almost alone, his empire shrunk again to the saddle-galled donkey, he would seek his home in distant Kordofan, while this same Slatin who knelt so humbly before him would lay the fierce pursuing squadrons on the trail.

Mohammed Ahmed received his new adherent kindly, but without enthusiasm. For some months Abdullahi carried stones to build the tomb of the Sheikh el Koreishi. Gradually they got to know each other. 'But long before he entrusted me with his secret,' said Abdullahi to Slatin, '1 knew that he was "the expected Guide."'[16] And though the world might think that the 'Messenger of God' was sent to lead men to happiness in heaven, Abdullahi attached to the phrase a significance of his own, and knew that he should lead him

16 Slatin, *Fire and Sword,* p. 131.

to power on earth. The two formed a strong combination. The Mahdi—for such Mohammed Ahmed had already in secret announced himself—brought the wild enthusiasm of religion, the glamour of a stainless life, and the influence of superstition into the movement. But if he was the soul of the plot, Abdullahi was the brain. He was the man of the world, the practical politician, the general.

There now commenced a great conspiracy against the Egyptian Government. It was fostered by the discontents and justified by the miseries of the people of the Soudan. The Mahdi began to collect adherents and to extend his influence in all parts of the country. He made a second journey through Kordofan, and received everywhere promises of support from all classes. The most distant tribes sent assurances of devotion and reverence, and, what was of more importance, of armed assistance. The secret could not be long confined to those who welcomed the movement. As the ramifications of the plot spread they were perceived by the renowned Sheikh Sherif, who still nursed his chagrin and thirsted for revenge. He warned the Egyptian Government.

They, knowing his envy and hatred of his former disciple, discounted his evidence and for some time paid no attention to the gathering of the storm. But presently more trustworthy witnesses confirmed his statements, and Raouf Pasha, then Governor-General, finding himself confronted with a growing agitation, determined to act. He accordingly sent a messenger to the Island of Abba, to summon Mohammed Ahmed to Khartoum to justify his behaviour and explain his intentions. The news of the despatch of the messenger was swiftly carried to the Mahdi. He consulted with his trusty lieutenant. They decided to risk everything, and without further delay to defy the Government. When it is remembered how easily an organised army, even though it be in a bad condition, can stamp out the beginnings of revolt among a population, the courage of their resolve must be applauded.

The messenger arrived. He was received with courtesy by Abdullahi, and forthwith conducted before the Mahdi. He delivered his message, and urged Mohammed Ahmed to comply with the orders of the Governor-General. The Mahdi listened for some time in silence, but with increasing emotion; and when the messenger advised him, as he valued his own safety, to journey to Khartoum, if only to justify himself, his passion overcame him. 'What!' he shouted, rising suddenly and striking his breast with his hand. 'By the grace of God and his Prophet, *I* am master of this country, and never shall I go to Khartoum to justify myself.'[17] The terrified messenger withdrew. The rebellion of the Mahdi had begun.

Both the priest and the Governor-General prepared for military enterprise. The Mahdi proclaimed a holy war against the foreigners, alike the enemies of God and the scourge of men. He collected his followers. He roused the local tribes. He wrote letters to all parts of the Soudan, calling upon the people to fight for a purified religion, the freedom of the soil, and God's holy prophet 'the expected Mahdi.' He promised the honour of men to those who lived, the favour of God,[18] to those who fell, and lastly that the land should be cleared of the miserable 'Turk.' 'Better,' he said, and it became the watchword of the revolt, 'thousands of graves than a dollar tax.'[19]

Nor was Raouf Pasha idle. He sent two companies of infantry with one gun by steamer to Abba to arrest the fanatic who disturbed the public peace. What followed is peculiarly Egyptian. Each company was commanded by a captain. To encourage their efforts, whichever officer captured the Mahdi was promised promotion. At sunset on an August evening in 1881 the steamer arrived at Abba. The promise of the Governor-General had provoked the strife, not the emulation of the officers. Both landed with their companies and proceeded by different routes under the cover of darkness to the village where the Mahdi abode.

Arriving simultaneously from opposite directions, they tired into each other, and, in the midst of this mistaken combat, the Mahdi rushed upon them with his scanty following and destroyed them impartially. A few soldiers succeeded in reaching the bank of the river. But the captain of the steamer would run no risks, and those who could not swim out to the vessel were left to their fate. With such tidings the expedition returned to Khartoum.

---

17 Slatin, *Fire and Sword*, p. 135.

18 He announced that all persons taking part in the religious war should earn the title of 'Emir el Aulia,' favourites of God.—Slatin, *Fire and Sword*, p. 136.

19 Ohrwalder, *Ten Years' Captivity in the Mahdi 's Camp.*

Mohammed Ahmed had been himself wounded in the attack, but the faithful Abdullahi bound up the injury, so that none might know that God's Prophet had been pierced by carnal weapons. The effect of the success was electrical. The news spread throughout the Soudan. Men with sticks had slain men with rifles. A priest had destroyed the soldiers of the Government. Surely this was the Expected One. The Mahdi, however, profited by his victory only to accomplish a retreat without loss of prestige. Abdullahi had no illusions. More troops would be sent. They were too near to Khartoum. Prudence counselled flight to regions more remote. But before this new *Hegira*[20] the Mahdi appointed his four Khalifas, in accordance with prophecy and precedent. The first was Abdullahi. Of the others it is only necessary at this moment to notice Ali-Wad-Helu, the chief of one of the local tribes, and among the first to rally to the standard of revolt.

Then the retreat began; but it was more like a triumphal progress. Attended by a considerable following, and preceded by tales of the most wonderful miracles and prodigies, the Mahdi retired to a mountain in Kordofan to which he gave the name of Jebel Masa, that being the mountain whence 'the expected Guide' is declared in the Koran sooner or later to appear. He was now out of reach of Khartoum, but within reach of Fashoda. The Egyptian Governor of that town, Rashid Bey, a man of more enterprise and even less military knowledge than is usual in his race, determined to make an attempt to seize the rebel and disperse his following. Taking no precautions, he fell on the 9th of December into an ambush, was attacked unprepared, and was himself, with fourteen hundred men, slaughtered by the ill-armed but valiant Arabs.

The whole country stirred. The Government, thoroughly alarmed by the serious aspect the revolt had assumed, organised a great expedition. Four thousand troops under Yusef, a Pasha of distinguished reputation, were sent against the rebels. Meanwhile the Mahdi and his followers suffered the extremes of want. Their cause was as yet too perilous for the rich to join. Only the poor flocked to the holy standard. All that Mohammed possessed he gave

20 Muhammad's departure from Mecca to Medina in AD 622, marking the consolidation of the first Muslim community. [Footnote to the new edition].

away, keeping nothing for himself, excepting only a horse to lead his followers in battle. Abdullahi walked. Nevertheless the rebels were half-famished, and armed with scarcely any more deadly weapons than sticks and stones. The army of the Government approached slowly. Their leaders anticipated an easy victory. Their contempt for the enemy was supreme. They did not even trouble themselves to post sentries by night, but slept calmly inside a slender thorn fence, unwatched save by their tireless foes. And so it came to pass that in the half-light of the early morning of the 7th of June the Mahdi, his ragged Khalifas and his 'almost naked' army,[21] rushed upon them, and slew them to a man.

The victory was decisive. Southern Kordofan was at the feet of the priest of Abba. Stores of arms and ammunition had fallen into his hands. Thousands of every class hastened to join his standard. No one doubted that he was the divine messenger sent to free them from their oppressors. The whole of the Arab tribes all over the Soudan rose at once. The revolt broke out simultaneously in Sennar and Darfur, and spread to provinces still more remote. The smaller Egyptian posts, the tax-gatherers and local administrators, were massacred in every district. Only the larger garrisons maintained themselves in the principal towns. They were at once blockaded. All communications were interrupted. All legal authority was defied. Only the Mahdi was obeyed.

It is now necessary to look for a moment to Egypt. The misgovernment which in the Soudan had caused the rebellion of the Mahdi, in Egypt produced the revolt of Arabi Pasha. As the people of the Soudan longed to be rid of the foreign oppressors—the so-called 'Turks'—so those of the Delta were eager to free themselves from the foreign regulators and the real Turkish influence. While men who lived by the sources of the Nile proclaimed that tribes did not exist for officials to harry, others who dwelt at its mouth protested that nations were not made to be exploited by creditors or aliens.

The ignorant south found their leader in a priest; the more educated north looked to a soldier. Mohammed Ahmed broke the Egyptian yoke; Arabi gave expression to the hatred of the Egyptians for the Turks. But although the hardy Arabs might scatter the effete

21 Slatin, *Fire and Sword n the Soudan*, p. 145.

Egyptians, the effete Egyptians were not likely to disturb the solid battalions of Europe. After much hesitation and many attempts at compromise, the Liberal Administration of Mr. Gladstone sent a fleet which reduced the forts of Alexandria to silence and the city to anarchy. The bombardment of the fleet was followed by the invasion of a powerful army. Twenty-five thousand men were landed in Egypt. The campaign was conducted with celerity and skill. The Egyptian armies were slaughtered or captured. Their patriotic, but commonplace leader was sentenced to death and condemned to exile, and Great Britain assumed the direction of Egyptian affairs.

The British soon restored law and order in Egypt, and the question of the revolt in the Soudan came before the English advisers of the Khedive. Notwithstanding the poverty and military misfortunes which depressed the people of the Delta, the desire to hold heir southern provinces was evident. The British Government, which at that time was determined to pursue a policy of non-interference in the Soudan, gave a tacit consent, and another great expedition was prepared to suppress the False Prophet, as the English and Egyptians deemed him— 'the expected Mahdi,' as the people of the Soudan believed.

A retired officer of the Indian Staff Corps and a few European officers of various nationalities were sent to Khartoum to organise the new field force. Meanwhile the Mahdi, having failed to take by storm, laid siege to El Obeid, the chief town of Kordofan. During the summer of 1883 the Egyptian troops gradually concentrated at Khartoum until a considerable army was formed. It was perhaps the worst army that has ever marched to war.[22] The officers and men who had been defeated fighting for their own liberties at Tel-el- Kebir were sent to be destroyed, fighting to take away the liberties of others in the Soudan. They had no spirit, no discipline, hardly any training, and in a force of over eleven thousand men there were scarcely a dozen capable officers. The two who were the most notable of these few—General Hicks who commanded, and Colonel Farquhar the Chief of the Staff—must be remarked.

---

22 One extract from General Hicks's letters will suffice. Writing on the 8th of June, 1883, to Sir E. Wood, he says incidentally: 'Fifty-one men of the Krupp battery deserted on the way here, although in chains.'

El Obeid had fallen before the ill-fated expedition left Khartoum. But the fact that Slatin Bey, an Austrian officer in the Egyptian service, was still maintaining himself in Darfur might provide it with object. On the 9th of September Hicks and his army[23] left Omdurman and marched to Duem. Although the actual command of the expedition was vested in the English officer, Ala-ed-Din Pasha, the Governor-General who had succeeded Raouf Pasha, exercised an uncertain authority. Differences of opinion were frequent, though all the officers were agreed in taking the darkest views of their chances. The miserable host toiled slowly onward towards its destruction, marching in a south-westerly direction through Shat and Eahad. Here the condition of the force was so obviously demoralised that a German servant[24] actually deserted to the Mahdi's camp. He was paraded in triumph as an English officer.

On the approach of the Government troops the Mahdi had marched out of El Obeid and established himself in the open country, where he made his followers live under military conditions and continually practised them in warlike evolutions. More than forty thousand men collected round his standard, and the Arabs were now armed with several thousand rifles and a few cannon, as well as a great number of swords and spears. To these proportions had the little band of followers who fought at Abba grown! The disparity of the forces was apparent before the battle. The Mahdi thereupon wrote to Hicks, calling on him to surrender and offering terms. His proposals were treated with disdain, although the probable result of an engagement was clear.

Until the expedition reached Kahad only a few cavalry patrols had watched its slow advance. But on the 1st of November the Mahdi left El Obeid and marched with his whole power to meet his adversary. The collision took place on the 3rd of November. All through that day the Egyptians struggled slowly forward, in great want of water, losing men continually from the fire of the Soudanese riflemen, and leaving several guns behind them. On the next morning they were confronted by the main body of the Arab army, and

23 The actual strength of the force was 7,000 infantry, 400 mounted Bashi-Bazooks, 500 cavalry, 100 Circassians, 10 mountain guns, 4 Krupps, 6 Nordenfeldt machine guns.

24 Gustave Klootz, the servant of Baron Seckendorf.

their attempts to advance further were defeated with heavy loss. The force began to break up. Yet another day was consumed before it was completely destroyed. Scarcely five hundred Egyptians escaped death; hardly as many of the Arabs fell.

The European officers perished fighting to the end, and the General met his fate sword in hand, at the head of the last formed body of his troops, his personal valour and amazing physical strength exciting the admiration even of the fearless enemy, so that in chivalrous respect they buried his body with barbaric honours. Mohammed Ahmed celebrated his victory with a salute of one hundred guns; and well he might, for the Soudan was now his, and his boast that, by God's grace and the favour of the Prophet, he was the master of all the land had been made good by force of arms.

No further attempt was made to subdue the country. The people of the Soudan had won their freedom by their valour and by the skill and courage of their saintly leader. It only remained to evacuate the towns and withdraw the garrisons safely. But what looked like the winding-up of one story was really the beginning of another, much longer, just as bloody, commencing in shame and disaster, but ending in triumph and, let us hope, in peace.

I desire for a moment to take a more general view of the Mahdi's movement than the narrative has allowed. The original causes were social and racial. But, great as was the misery of the people, their spirit was low, and they would not have taken up arms merely on material grounds. Then came the Mahdi. He gave the tribes the enthusiasm they lacked. The war broke out. It is customary to lay to the charge of Mohammed Ahmed all the blood that was spilled. To my mind it seems that he may divide the responsibility with the unjust rulers who oppressed the land, with the incapable commanders who muddled away the lives of their men, with the vacillating Ministers who aggravated the misfortunes. But, whatever is set to the Mahdi's account, it should not be forgotten that he put life and soul into the hearts of his countrymen, and freed his native land of foreigners. The poor miserable natives, eating only a handful of grain, toiling half-naked and without hope, found a new, if terrible magnificence added to life. Within their humble breasts the spirit of the Mahdi roused the fires of patriotism and religion.

Life became filled with thrilling, exhilarating terrors They existed in a new and wonderful world of imagination. While they lived there were great things to be done; and when they died, whether it were slaying the Egyptians or charging the British squares, a Paradise which they could understand awaited them. The materialist may deplore the loss of life, the interruption of trade, and the destruction of property; but the true philosopher, who realises that men's souls as well as their stomachs are capable of development, will view the tumult with impassive eye. There are many Christians who reverence the faith of Islam and yet regard the Mahdi merely as a commonplace religious impostor whom force of circumstances elevated to notoriety. In a certain sense, this may be true. But I know not how a genuine may be distinguished from a spurious Prophet, except by the measure of his success. The triumphs of the Mahdi were in his lifetime far greater than those of the founder of the Mohammedan faith; and the chief difference between orthodox Mohammedanism and Mahdism was that the original impulse was opposed only by decaying systems of government and society and the recent movement came in contact with a mighty civilisation and the machinery of science.

Recognising this, I do not share the popular opinion, and I believe that if in future years prosperity should come to the peoples of the Upper Nile, and learning and happiness follow in its train, then the first Arab historian who shall investigate the early annals of that new nation, will not forget, foremost among the heroes of his race, to write the name of Mohammed Ahmed.

CHAPTER III[1]
THE FATE OF THE ENVOY

Natural decay—The military spirit—The Arab inspiration—The policy of evacuation—British authority—Gordon—Zubair Pasha—Baring's view—The beginning: of the mission—The *Tanjore* memorandum—At Khartoum—The situation—Gordon and Zubair—The man on the spot—The case for Zubair—The decision of the Government—British responsibility—The quarrel between Gordon and the Government—The Eastern Soudan—'Baker's Teb'—The action of El Teb—Tamai—A flying column—Blockade of Khartoum—The defence of the city—The 'Journals at Khartoum'—Gordon and Slatin—Slatin's appeal—Its reception—The solitary man—Within besieged Khartoum—Gordon's troubles—His consolation—The maintenance of discipline, and of hope—Public Opinion—In Parliament—Mr. Gladstone—The Gordon Relief Expedition—The River Column—The Desert Column—Abu Klea—Abu Kru—'Too late'—Fall of Khartoum—The death of Gordon—His place in history—The excuse for the Government—Retreat of the expedition—Continental opinion—Daylight at last.

All great movements, every vigorous impulse that a community may feel, become perverted and distorted as time passes, and the atmosphere of the earth seems fatal to the noble aspirations of its peoples. A wide humanitarian sympathy in a nation easily degenerates into hysteria. A military spirit tends towards brutality. Liberty leads to licence, restraint to tyranny. The pride of race is distended to blustering arrogance. The fear of God produces bigotry and superstition. There appears no exception to the mournful rule, and the best efforts of men, however glorious their early results, have dismal endings; like plants which shoot and bud and put forth beautiful flowers, and then grow rank and coarse and are withered by the

1 Map, 'The Soudan,' page xiv.

GORDON'S PALACE IN KHARTOUM

winter. It is only when we reflect that the decay gives birth to fresh life, and that new enthusiasms spring up to take the places of those that die, even as the acorn is nourished by the dead leaves of the oak or the phoenix rose from the ashes of the pyre, that the hope strengthens, that the rise and fall of men and their movements are only the changing foliage of the ever-growing tree of life, while underneath a greater evolution goes on continually.

The movement which Mohammed Ahmed created did not escape the common fate of human enterprise. Nor was it long before the warm generous blood of a patriotic and religious revolt congealed into the dark clot of a military empire. With the expulsion or destruction of the foreign officials, soldiers, and traders, the racial element began to subside. The reason for its existence was removed. With the increasing disorders the social agitation dwindled; for communism pre-supposes wealth, and the wealth of the Soudan was greatly diminished. There remained only the fanatical fury which the belief in the divine mission of the Mahdi had excited. And as the necessity for a leader passed away, the belief in his sanctity grew weaker. But meanwhile a new force was making itself felt on the character of the revolt. The triumph no less than the plunder which had rewarded the Mahdi's victories had called into existence a military spirit distinct from the warlike passions of the tribesmen—the spirit of the professional soldier.

The siege of Khartoum was carried on while this new influence was taking the place of the original forces of revolt. There was a period when a neutral point was obtained and the Mahdist power languished. But the invasion of the Eastern Soudan by the British troops in the spring and the necessary advance of the relieving columns in the winter of 1884 revived the patriotic element. The tribes who had made a great effort to free themselves from foreign domination saw in the operations of Sir Gerald Graham and Lord Wolseley an attempt to bring them again under the yoke. The impulse which was given to the Mahdi's cause was sufficient to raise a fierce opposition to the invading forces. The delay in the despatch of the relief expedition had sealed the fate of Khartoum, and the fall of the town established the supremacy of the military spirit on which the Dervish Empire was afterwards founded.

All the warlike operations of Mohammedan peoples are characterised by fanaticism, but with this general reservation it may be said—that the Arabs who destroyed Yusef, who assaulted El Obeid, who annihilated Hicks, fought in the glory of religious zeal; that the Arabs who opposed Graham, Earle, and Stewart, fought in defence of the soil; and that the Arabs who were conquered by Kitchener fought in the pride of an army. Fanatics charged at Shekan;[2] patriots at Abu Klea; warriors at Omdurman.

In order to describe conveniently the changing character of the revolt, I have anticipated the story and must revert to a period when the social and racial influences were already weakening and the military spirit was not yet grown strong. If the defeat of Yusef Pasha decided the whole people of the Soudan to rise in arms and strike for their liberties, the defeat of Hicks satisfied the British Government that those liberties were won. The powerful influence of the desire to rule prompted the Khedive's Ministers to make still further efforts to preserve their country's possessions. Had Egypt been left to herself, other desperate efforts would have been made.[3] But the British Government had finally abandoned its policy of non-interference with Egyptian action in the Soudan. They 'advised' its abandonment. The protests of Cherif Pasha provoked Lord Granville to explain the meaning of the word 'advice.' The Khedive bowed to superior authority. The Minister resigned. The policy of evacuation was firmly adopted. 'Let us,' said the Ministers, 'collect the garrisons and come away.' It was simple to decide on the course to be pursued, but almost impossible to follow it. Several of the Egyptian garrisons, as in Darfur and El Obeid, had already fallen. The others were either besieged, like Sennar, Tokar, and Sinkat, or they were cut off from the north, as in the case of the Equatorial Province, by the area of rebellion. The capital of the Soudan was, however, as yet unmolested, and as its Egyptian population exceeded the aggregate of the provincial towns the first task of the Egyptian Government was obvious.

2 The scene of Hicks Pasha's disaster.—EDITOR.

3 'The idea of abandoning it [the Soudan] was intensely unpopular. . . . Had the Egyptian Ministry been left to themselves, there is no saying what new disasters their reluctance to look facts in the face might not have brought upon their country.'—Sir A. Milner, *England in Egypt*, chapter v.

Mr. Gladstone's Administration had repressed the revolt of Arabi Pasha. Through their policy the British were in armed occupation of Egypt. British officers were reorganising the army. A British official supervised the finances. A British plenipotentiary 'advised' the re-established Tewfik. A British fleet lay attentive before the ruins of Alexandria. The spectacle was one at which the Jingo might rejoice, for it was evident that Great Britain could annex the country in name as well as in fact. But Imperialism was not the object of the Radical Cabinet. Their aim was philanthropic and disinterested. As they were now determined that the Egyptians should evacuate the Soudan, so they had always been resolved that the British should evacuate Egypt.

Throughout this chapter it will be seen that the desire to get out of the country at once is the keynote of the British policy. Every act, whether of war or administration, is intended to be final. Every despatch is directed to breaking the connection between the two countries and winding up the severed strings. But responsibilities which had been lightly assumed clung like the shirt of Nessus. The ordinary practice of civilised nations demanded that some attempt should be made to justify interference by reorganisation. The British Government watched therefore with anxious solicitude the efforts of Egypt to evacuate the Soudan and bring the garrisons safely home. They utterly declined to assist with military force, but they were generous with their advice. Everybody at that time distrusted the capacities of the Egyptians.

The evacuation, it was thought, might be accomplished if it were entrusted to stronger and more honest men than were bred by the banks of the Nile. The Ministers looked about them, wondering how they could assist the Egyptian Government without risk or expense to themselves, and in an evil hour for their fame and fortunes someone—it is said, Mr. Stead—whispered the word 'Gordon.' Forthwith they proceeded to telegraph to Cairo: 'Would General Charles Gordon be of any use to you or to the Egyptian Government: and if so in what capacity?' The Egyptian Government replied through Sir Evelyn Baring that as the movement in the Soudan was partly religious they were 'very much averse' to the appointment of a Christian in high command.

The eyes of all those who possessed local knowledge were turned to a very different individual. There was one man who might stem the tide of Mahdism, who might perhaps restore the falling dominion of Egypt, who might at least save the garrisons of the Soudan. In their necessity and distress the Khedivial advisers and the British plenipotentiary looked to the man whose liberty they had curtailed, whose property they had confiscated, and whose son they had executed—Zubair Pasha. It was a desperate remedy.

This was the man for whom the Government of Egypt hankered. The idea was supported by all who were acquainted with the local conditions. A week after Sir Evelyn Baring had declined General Gordon's services he wrote: 'Whatever may be Zubair's faults, he is said to be a man of great energy and resolution. The Egyptian Government considers that his services may be very useful. . . . Baker Pasha is anxious to avail himself of Zubair Pasha's services.'[4]

It is certain that, had the Egyptian Government been a free agent, Zubair would have been sent to the Soudan as its Sultan, and assisted by arms, money, and perhaps men, to make head against the Mahdi. It is probable that at this particular period the Mahdi would have collapsed before a man whose fame was nearly equal to, and whose resources would have been much greater, than his own. But the British Ministry would countenance no dealings with such a man. They scouted the idea of Zubair, and by so doing increased their obligation to suggest an alternative. Zubair being rejected, Gordon remained. It is scarcely possible to conceive a greater contrast than that which these two men presented. It was a leap from the Equator to the North Pole.

When difficulties and dangers perplex all minds, it has often happened in history that many men different lines of thought arrive at the same conclusion. The choice may fall on some individual outside the circle of public life and engaged contentedly on his own affairs. Cincinnatus was ploughing his fields when he received the message of the Senate. Gordon was conferring with the King of the Belgians when everybody decided that he must go to the Soudan and bring the garrisons away. No complete record has yet been published of the telegrams which passed between the Government and

4 Sir Evelyn Baring, letter of December 9, 1883.

their agent at this juncture. The Blue Books preserve a disingenuous discretion. But it is known that from the very first Sir Evelyn Baring was bitterly opposed to General Gordon's appointment. No personal friendship existed between them, and the Administrator dreaded the return to the feverish complications of Egyptian politics of the man who had always been identified with unrest, improvisation, and disturbance. The pressure was, however, too strong for him to withstand. Nubar Pasha, Sir Evelyn Wood, the Foreign Office, the British public, everyone clamoured for the appointment. Had Baring refused to give way, it is probable that he would have been overruled. At length he yielded, and, having once withdrawn his opposition, he gave the General his heartiest support. As soon as Baring's consent had been obtained, the Government turned with delight to Gordon.

On the 17th of January Lord Wolseley requested him to come to England. On the 18th he met the Cabinet. That same night he started on the long journey from which he was never to return, but from which consequences would arise which would convulse his countrymen and excite the interest of the civilised world.

Gordon embarked on his mission in high spirits, sustained by that belief in personality which too often misleads great men and beautiful women. It was, he said, the greatest honour ever conferred upon him.

Everything smiled. The nation was delighted. The Ministers were intensely relieved. The most unbounded confidence was reposed in the envoy. His interview with the Khedive was 'very satisfactory.' His complete authority was proclaimed to all the notables and natives of the Soudan.[5] He was assured of the support of the Egyptian Government.[6] The London Foreign Office, having with becoming modesty admitted that they had not ' sufficient local knowledge,'[7] accorded him 'widest discretionary power.'[8] One hundred thousand pounds was placed to his credit, and he was informed that further sums would be supplied when this was exhausted. He was assured

5 Proclamation of the Khedive, January 26, 1884.
6 Sir E. Baring to Major-General Gordon, January 25, 1884.
7 Earl Granville to Sir E. Baring, January 22, 1884.
8 Sir E. Baring to Earl Granville, February 1, 1884.

that no effort would be wanting on the part of the Cairene authorities, whether English or Egyptian, to afford him all the support and co-operation in their power.[9] 'There is no sort of difference,' wrote Sir Evelyn Baring, 'between General Gordon's views and those entertained by Nubar Pasha and myself.'[10] Under these propitious auguries the dismal and disastrous enterprise began.

His task, though difficult and, as it ultimately proved, impossible, was clearly defined. 'You will bear in mind,' wrote Sir Evelyn Baring, that the main end to be pursued is the evacuation of the Soudan.' 'The object ... of your mission to the Soudan,' declared the Khedive, 'is to carry into execution the evacuation of those territories and to withdraw our troops, civil officials, and such of the inhabitants ... as may wish to leave for Egypt . . . and after the evacuation to take the necessary steps for establishing an organised Government in the different provinces.' Nor was he himself under any misconception. He drew up a memorandum when on board the *Tanjore* in which he fully acquiesced in the evacuation of the Soudan.[11] In a sentence which breathes the same spirit as Mr. Gladstone's famous expression, 'a people rightly struggling to be free,' he wrote 'I must say that it would be an iniquity to conquer these peoples and then hand them back to the Egyptians without guarantees of future good government.' Finally, he unhesitatingly asserted: 'No one who has ever lived in the Soudan can escape the reflection "What a useless possession is this land!"' And Colonel Stewart, who accompanied him and endorsed the memorandum, added: 'And what a huge encumbrance to Egypt!' Thus far there was complete agreement between the British envoys and the Radical Cabinet.

It is beyond the scope of these pages to describe his long ride across the desert from Korosko to Abu Hamed, his interview with the notables at Berber, or his proclamation of the abandonment of the Soudan, which some affirm to have been an important cause of his ruin. On the 22nd of February he arrived at Khartoum. He was received with rejoicing by the whole population

9 Sir E. Baring to Major-General Gordon, January 25, 1884.

10 Sir E. Baring to Earl Granville, February 1, 1884.

11 It is perhaps interesting to notice that this same memorandum was copied out for the General by the Editor of this book, then a subaltern officer en route for Egypt.

They recognised again their just Governor-General and their present deliverer. Those who had been about to fly for the north took fresh heart. They believed that behind the figure of the envoy stood the resources of an Empire. The Mahdi and the gathering Dervishes were perplexed and alarmed. Confusion and hesitancy disturbed their councils and delayed their movements. Gordon had come. The armies would follow. Both friends and foes were deceived. The great man was at Khartoum, but there he would remain—alone.

Whatever confidence the General had felt in the power of his personal influence had been dispelled on the journey to Khartoum. He had no more illusions. His experienced eye reviewed the whole situation. He saw himself confronted with a tremendous racial movement. The people of the Soudan had risen against foreigners. His only troops were Soudanese. He was himself a foreigner. Foremost among the leaders of the revolt were the Arab slave dealers, furious at the attempted suppression of their trade. No one, not even Sir Samuel Baker, had tried harder to suppress it than Gordon. Lastly, the whole movement had assumed a fanatical character. Islam marched against the infidel. Gordon was a Christian. His own soldiers were under the spell they were to try to destroy. To them their commander was accursed. Every influence was hostile, and particularly hostile to him personally. The combined forces of race, class, and religion were against him. He bowed before their irresistible strength. On the very day of his arrival at Khartoum, while the citizens were cheering his name in the streets and the batteries were firing joyful salutes, while the people of England thought his mission already accomplished and the Government congratulated themselves on the wisdom of their action, General Gordon sat himself down and telegraphed a formal request to Cairo for Zubair Pasha. The 'Christian hero' asked for the help of the 'abandoned ruffian.'

The whole story of his relations with Zubair is extremely characteristic. Zubair's son, Suliman, had been executed, if not by Gordon's orders, at least during his administration of the Soudan and with his complete approval. 'Thus,' he had said, 'does God make gaps in the ranks of His enemies.' He had hardly started from London on his new mission, when he telegraphed to Sir Evelyn Baring, telling him that Zubair was a most dangerous man and requesting that he might be deported to Cyprus. This was, of course, quite beyond the powers or intention of the British Agent. The General arrived in Cairo like a whirlwind close behind his telegram, and was very angry to hear that Zubair was still in Egypt. Before starting up the river he went to see Cherif Pasha. In the ex-Minister's anteroom he met the very man he had determined to avoid—Zubair. He greeted him with effusion. They had a long talk about the Soudan, after which Gordon hurried to the Agency and informed Sir Evelyn Baring that Zubair must accompany him to Khartoum at once. Baring was amazed. He did not himself disapprove of the plan. He had, in fact, already recommended it. But he thought the change in Gordon's attitude too sudden to be relied on. To-morrow he might change again. He begged the General to think more seriously of the matter. Gordon with his usual frankness admitted that his change of mind had been very sudden. He had been conscious, he said, of a 'mystic feeling' that Zubair was necessary to save the situation in the Soudan.

Gordon left Cairo still considering the matter. As soon as he made his formal demand from Khartoum for the assistance of Zubair it was evident that his belief in the old slave dealers usefulness was a sound conviction and not a mere passing caprice. Besides, he had now become 'the man on the spot,' and as such his words carried double force. Sir Evelyn Baring determined to support the recommendation with his whole influence. Never was so good a case made out for the appointment of so bad a man. The Envoy Extraordinary asked for him; Colonel Stewart, his colleague, concurred; the British Agent strongly urged the request; the Egyptian Government were unanimous; and behind all these were ranged every single person who had the slightest acquaintance with the Soudan. Nothing could exceed the vigour with which the demand was made. On the 1st of March General Gordon telegraphed: 'I tell you plainly, it is impossible to get Cairo *employés* out of Khartoum unless the Government helps in the way I told you. They refuse Zubair .... but it was the only chance.' And again on the 8th: 'If you do not send Zubair, you have no chance of getting the garrisons away.'

'I believe,' said Sir Evelyn Baring in support of these telegrams, 'that General Gordon is quite right when he says that Zubair Pasha is the only possible man. Nubar is strongly in favour of him. Dr.

Bohndorf, the African traveller, fully confirms what General Gordon says of the influence of Zubair.' The Pasha was vile, but indispensable.

Her Majesty's Government refused absolutely to have anything to do with Zubair. They declined to allow the Egyptian Government to employ him. They would not entertain the proposal. They scarcely consented to discuss it. Parliament and the nation approved their decision, and it has never since been impugned. It was in no degree a party matter. The position which all men assumed was, that great States cannot stoop to employ such agents.

The historians of the future may occupy their leisure and exercise their wits in deciding whether the Ministers and the people were right or wrong; whether they had a right to indulge their sensitiveness at so terrible a cost; whether they were not, more nice than wise; whether their dignity was more offended by what was incurred or by what was avoided. But, on whatever issue they meet, they will soon, revert to the old question, whether the end justifies the means, whether it is right to commit a smaller sin to avoid a greater wrong. They are welcome to the problem, which has teased and baffled all generations.

General Gordon has explained his views very clearly and concisely: 'Had Zubair Pasha been sent up when I asked for him, Berber would in all probability never have fallen, and one might have made a Soudan Government in opposition to the Mahdi. We choose to refuse his coming up because of his antecedents in the slave trade; granted that we had reason, yet, as we take no precautions as to the future of these lands with respect to the slave trade, the above opposition seems absurd. I will not send up A. because he will do this, but I will leave the country to B., who will do exactly the same.'[12]

But if the justice of the decision was doubtful, its consequences were obvious. Either the British Government were concerned with the Soudan, or they were not. If they were not, then they had no reason or right to prohibit the appointment of Zubair. If they were, they were bound to see that the garrisons were rescued. It was an open question whether Great Britain was originally responsible for the safety of the garrisons. General Gordon contended that we were

12 Major-General Gordon, *Journals at Khartoum.*

bound to save them at all costs, and he backed his belief with his life. Others may hold that Governments have no right to lay, or at any rate must be very judicious in the laying of, burdens on the backs of their own countrymen in order that they may indulge a refined sense of chivalry towards foreigners. England had not misgoverned the Soudan, had not raised the revolt, nor planted the garrisons. All that Egypt had a right to expect was commiseration. But the moment Zubair was prohibited, the situation was changed. The refusal to permit his employment was tantamount to an admission that affairs in the Soudan involved the honour of England as well as the honour of Egypt. When the British people—for this was not merely the act of the Government—adopted a high moral attitude with regard to Zubair, they bound themselves *ipso facto* to rescue the garrisons, peaceably if possible, forcibly if necessary. This is what the Government refused to recognise; and for this, among many other things, they will deserve the censures of posterity.

With their refusal to allow Zubair to go to the Soudan began the long and miserable disagreement between the Government and their envoy. Puzzled and disturbed at the reception accorded to his first request, Gordon cast about for other expedients. He had already stated that Zubair was 'the only chance.' But it is the duty of subordinates to suggest other courses when those they recommend are rejected; and with a whole-hearted enthusiasm and unreserved loyalty, the General threw himself into the affair and proposed plan after plan with apparent hope.

I do not purpose to chronicle all the pitiful details of the breach: yet some account is compelled by the course of the narrative. Gordon considered that he was personally pledged to effect the evacuation of Khartoum by the garrison and civil servants. He had appointed some of the inhabitants to positions of trust, thus compromising them with the Mahdi. Others had undoubtedly been encouraged to delay their departure by his arrival. He therefore considered that his honour was involved in their safety. Henceforward he was inflexible. Neither rewards nor threats could move him. Nothing that men could offer would induce him to leave Khartoum till its inhabitants were rescued. The Government on their side were equally stubborn, but since their firmness was unattended by personal danger, it has seemed less admirable to the nation. Nothing, however sacred, should induce them to send troops to Khartoum, or in any way involve themselves in the middle of Africa. The town might fall; the garrison might be slaughtered; their envoy— But what possibilities they were prepared to face as regards him, history will not be able to decide until all of this and the next generation are buried and forgotten.

The deadlock was complete. To some men the Foreign Office might have suggested lines of retreat, covered by the highest official praise, and leading to preferment and reward. Others would have welcomed an order to leave so perilous a post. But the man they had sent was the one man of all others who was beyond their control, who cared nothing for what they could give or take away. So events dragged on their wretched course. Gordon's proposals became more and more impracticable as the best courses he could devise were successively vetoed by the Government, and as his irritation and disappointment increased.

The editor of his *Journals* has enumerated them with indignant care. He had asked for Zubair. Zubair was refused. He had requested Turkish troops. Turkish troops were refused. He had asked for Mohammedan regiments from India. The Government regretted their inability to comply. He asked for a *Firman* from the Sultan to strengthen his position. It was 'peremptorily refused.' He proposed to go south in his steamers to Equatoria. The Government forbade him to proceed beyond Khartoum. He asked that two hundred British troops might be sent to Berber. They were refused. He begged that a few might be sent to Assuan. None were sent. He proposed to visit the Mahdi himself and try to arrange matters with him personally. Perhaps he recognised a kindred spirit. The Government in this case very naturally forbade him.

At last the quarrel is open. He makes no effort to conceal his disgust. 'I leave you,' he says, 'the indelible disgrace of abandoning the garrisons.'[13] Such abandonment is, he declares, 'the climax of meanness.'[14] He reiterates his determination to abide with the garrison

13 Major- General Gordon to Sir E. Baring (telegraphic), received at Cairo April 16.
14 *Ibid*, despatched April 8.

of Khartoum. 'I will not leave these people after all they have gone through.'[15] He tosses his commission contemptuously from him: 'I would also ask her Majesty's Government to accept the resignation of my commission.'[16]

The Government 'trust that he will not resign,'[17] and his offer remains in abeyance. Finally, in bitterness and vexation, thinking himself abandoned and disavowed, he appeals to Sir Evelyn Baring personally: 'I feel sure, whatever you may feel diplomatically, I have your support—and that of every man professing himself a gentleman—in private';[18] and as a last hope he begs Sir Samuel Baker to appeal to 'British and American millionaires 'to subscribe two hundred thousand pounds to enable him to carry out the evacuation without, and even in spite of, the Governments of Cairo and London; and Sir Samuel Baker writes a long letter to the *Times* in passionate protest and entreaty.

Such are the chief features in the wretched business. Even the Blue Books in their dry recital arouse in the reader painful and indignant emotions. But meanwhile other and still more stirring events were passing outside the world of paper and ink.

The arrival of Gordon at Khartoum had seriously perplexed and alarmed Mohammed Ahmed and his Khalifas. Their following was discouraged, and they themselves feared lest the General should be the herald of armies. His Berber proclamation reassured them, and as the weeks passed without reinforcements arriving, the Mahdi and Abdullahi, with that courage which in several great emergencies drew them to the boldest courses, determined to put a brave face on the matter and blockade Khartoum itself.

They were assisted in this enterprise by a revival of the patriotic impulse throughout the country and a consequent stimulus to the revolt. To discover the cause it is necessary to look to the Eastern Soudan, where the next tragedy, after the defeat of Hicks, is laid. The

---

15 Major-General Gordon to Sir E. Baring, Khartoum, July 30; received at Cairo October 15.

16 Major-General Gordon to Sir E. Baring (telegraphic), Khartoum, March 9.

17 Earl Granville to Sir E. Baring, Foreign Office, March 13.

18 Major-General Gordon to Sir E. Baring (telegraphic), received at Cairo April 16.

Hadendoa tribe, infuriated by oppression and misgovernment,[19] had joined the rebellion under the leadership of the celebrated, and perhaps immortal, Osman Digna. The Egyptian garrisons of Tokar and Sinkat were beleaguered and hard pressed. Her Majesty's Government disclaimed all responsibility. Yet, since these towns were not far from the coast, they did not prohibit an attempt on the part of the Egyptian Government to rescue the besieged soldiers. Accordingly an Egyptian force 3,500 strong marched from Suakin in February 1884 to relieve Tokar, under the command of General Baker, once the gallant colonel of the 10th Hussars. Hard by the wells of Teb they were, on the 5th of February, attacked by about a thousand Arabs.

'On the square being only threatened by a small force of the enemy . . . the Egyptian troops threw down their arms and ran, carrying away the black troops with them, and allowing themselves to be killed without the slightest resistance.'[20] The British and European officers in vain endeavoured to rally them. The single Soudanese battalion fired impartially on friend and foe. The General, with that unshaken courage and high military skill which had already on the Danube gained him a Continental reputation, collected some fifteen hundred men, 'mostly unarmed,'[21] and so returned to Suakin, Ninety-six officers and two thousand two hundred and fifty men were killed. Krupp guns, machine guns, rifles, and a large supply of ammunition fell to the victorious Arabs. Success inflamed their ardour to the point of madness. The attack of the towns was pressed with redoubled vigour. The garrison of Sinkat, eight hundred strong, sallied out and attempted to fight their way to Suakin. The garrison of Tokar surrendered. Both were destroyed.

The evil was done. The slaughter was complete. Yet the British Government resolved to add to it. The garrisons they had refused to rescue they now determined to avenge. In spite of their philanthropic professions, and in spite of the advice of General Gordon, who felt that his position at Khartoum would be still further com-

19 'As for the Hadendoa revolt, it would appear to have been caused by the robbery of Rashid Pasha and Ibrahim Bey.'—Major-General Gordon to Sir E. Baring, Assuan. February 1, 1884.

20 General Baker to Sir E. Baring, Feb. 6 (official despatch), telegraphic.

21 *Ibid.*

promised by operations on his only line of retreat,[22] a great military expedition, consisting of one cavalry and two infantry brigades, was sent to Suakin. The command was entrusted to General Graham. Troops were hurriedly concentrated. The 10th Hussars, returning from India, were stopped and mounted on the horses of the gendarmerie. With admirable celerity the force took the field. Within a month of the defeat at Teb they engaged the enemy almost on scene of the disaster. On the 4th of March, they slew three thousand Hadendoa and drove the rest in disorder from the ground. Four weeks later a second action was fought at Tamai. Again the success of the British troops was complete; again the slaughter of the Arabs was enormous. But neither victory was bloodless. El Teb cost 24 officers and 168 men; Tamai, 13 officers and 208 men. The effect of these operations was the dispersal of Osman Digna's gathering. That astute man, not for the first time, made a good retreat.

Ten thousand men had thus been killed in the space of three months in the Eastern Soudan. By the discipline of their armies the Government was triumphant. The tribes of the Red Sea shore cowered before them. But as they fought without reason, so they conquered without profit.

As soon as Gordon had been finally refused the assistance of Zubair Pasha, it was evident that the rescue of the garrisons was impossible. The General had been sent as the last hope. Rightly or wrongly, his recommendations were ignored. His mission was an admitted failure. After that the only question was how to bring him away as quickly as possible. It was certain that he would not come willingly. Force was necessary. Yet it was difficult to know how to apply it. After the victories in the Eastern Soudan the opportunity presented itself. The road was open. The local tribes were crushed. Berber had not then fallen. The Mahdi was himself still on the road from El Obeid to Khartoum. Sir Evelyn Baring saw the chance. He did not then occupy the formidable and imposing position in Egyptian politics that he has since attained. But with all his influence he urged the despatch of a small flying column to Khartoum. His idea

22 'I have received the following from General Gordon: "I think if Tokar has fallen Her Majesty's Government had better be quiet, as I see no advantage to be now gained by any action on their part."'—Sir E. Baring to Earl Granville, Cairo, February 23.

was simple. One thousand or twelve hundred men were to mount on camels and ride thither *viâ* Berber. Those who fell ill or whose camels broke down would have to take their chance by the roadside. Such was the plan; and both Lord Wolseley and Sir Evelyn Wood admitted its possibility. Sir Herbert Stewart begged to be allowed to make the attempt. It was true that a couple of hundred men would probably lose their lives; but still the rest would rescue Gordon. A far greater price was willingly paid later on. The scheme, however, broke down in the military detail. Everyone can understand a rough and-tumble dash until they become responsible for arranging it. Then all sorts of considerations obtrude themselves. One thousand men on camels might with loss have succeeded; but when this was turned into the language of scientific war, the fatuity of the idea was apparent. The doctors clamoured for much transport for medical stores. The various departments insisted on much more. The Signalling Corps, the Ordnance Store Corps, the Army Service Corps, the Army Pay Department, the Army Chaplains, must all be represented; otherwise the 'Flying Column' would not be a 'complete detached unit'; and the precious soldiers of civilisation would not be signalled to, armed, fed, paid, or prayed for as befitted the dignity of the nation to which they belonged. There must be so many camels to carry the accessories, that Asia and Africa could not meet the demand. The plan was rejected as impracticable. Only one honourable course remained—a regular military expedition. This the British Agent at once began to urge. This the Government obstinately refused to admit. Meanwhile time was passing.

The situation at Khartoum became grave even before the breach between General Gordon and Mr. Gladstone's Cabinet was complete. While the British Government was indulging in vengeful operations in the Eastern Soudan, the Mahdi advanced slowly but steadily upon the town with a following variously estimated at from fifteen to twenty thousand men. On the 7th of March Colonel Stewart telegraphed from Khartoum: 'The Mahdi has attempted to raise the people of Shendi by an emissary. . . . We may be cut off;'[23] and on the 11th Gordon himself reported: 'The rebels are four hours distant on the Blue Nile.'[24] Thereafter no more telegrams came, for on the

23 Lieut.-Col. Stewart to Sir E. Baring, March 7, 1884.

24 Major-Gen. Gordon to Sir E. Baring, March 11, 1884.

15th the wire was cut between Shendi and Berber, and the blockade had commenced.

The long and glorious defence of the town of Khartoum will always fascinate the historian. That one man, a European among Africans, a Christian among Mohammedans, should by his genius have inspired the efforts of 7,000 soldiers of inferior race, and by his courage have sustained the hearts of 30,000 inhabitants of notorious timidity, and with such materials and encumbrances have offered a vigorous resistance to the increasing attacks of an enemy who, though cruel, would yet accept surrender, during a period of 317 days is an event without parallel in history. But it may safely be predicted that no one will ever write an account which will compare in interest or in detail with that set forth by the man himself in the famous 'Journals at Khartoum.' Reading their pages, the soldier may draw instruction from the military events; the Christian will rejoice in the grandeur of his faith; the patriot may exult in the pride of nationality; and even the philosopher, perplexed by the unforeseen magnificence of a human soul, will find his mournful reasonings disturbed by a bright gleam of doubt.

The brief account has delighted thousands of readers in Europe and America. Perhaps it is because he is careless of the sympathy of men, that Charles Gordon so readily wins it. Before the first of the six parts into which the Journals were divided is finished, the reader has been won. Henceforth he sees the world through Gordon's eyes. With him he scoffs at the diplomatists; despises the Government; becomes impatient—unreasonably, perhaps—with a certain Major Kitchener in the Intelligence Branch, whose information miscarried or was not despatched; is wearied by the impracticable Shaiggia Irregulars; takes interest in the turkey-cock and his harem of four wives; laughs at the 'black sluts' seeing their faces for the first time in the mirror. With him he trembles for the fate of the 'poor little beast,' the *Husseinyeli,* when she drifts stern foremost on the shoal, 'a penny steamer under cannon fire,'; day after day he gazes through the General's powerful telescope from the palace roof down the long brown reaches of the river towards the rocks of the Shabluka Gorge, and longs for some sign of the relieving steamers; and when the end of the account is reached, no man of British birth can read the last words, 'Now mark this, if the Expeditionary Force—and I ask for no more than two hundred men—does not come within ten days, *the town may fall;* and I have done my best for the honour of our country. Good-bye,' without being thrilled with vain regrets and futile resolutions. And then the account stops short. Nor will the silence ever be broken. The sixth instalment of the Journals was despatched on the 14th of December; and when it . is finished, the reader, separated suddenly from the pleasant companionship, experiences a feeling of loss and annoyance. Imagination, long supported, is brushed aside by stern reality. Henceforward Gordon's perils were unrecorded.

I would select one episode only from the Journals as an example of the strength and the sternness of Charles Gordon's character—his behaviour towards Slatin. This Austrian officer had been Governor of Darfur with the rank in the Egyptian service of Bey. For four years he had struggled vainly against the rebellion. He had fought numerous engagements with varied success. He had been several times wounded. Throughout his province and even beyond its limits he bore the reputation of a brave and capable soldier. The story of his life of suffering and adventure, written by himself, is widely known, and he is thought by those who have read it to be a man of feeling and of honour. By those who enjoy his personal acquaintance this belief is unhesitatingly confirmed. He had, however, committed an act which deprived him of Gordon's sympathy and respect. During the fighting in Darfur, after several defeats, his Mohammedan soldiers were discouraged and attributed their evil fortune to the fact that their commander was an infidel under the curse of the Almighty. Slatin therefore proclaimed himself a follower of the Prophet, and outwardly at least adopted the faith of Islam. The troops, delighted at his conversion and cheered by the hope of success, renewed their efforts, and the resistance of the Governor of Darfur was prolonged. The end, however, was deferred, not averted. After the destruction of General Hicks's army Slatin was compelled to surrender to the Dervishes. The religion he had assumed to secure victory, he observed to escape death. The Arab leaders, who admired his courage, treated him at first with respect and kindness, and he was conducted to the Mahdi in his encampment before Khartoum. There during the siege he remained, close-

RUDOLPH P SLATIN

ly watched but not imprisoned. Thence he wrote letters to Gordon explaining his surrender, excusing his apostasy, and begging that he might be allowed—not even assisted—to escape to Khartoum. The letters are extant, and scarcely anyone who reads them, reflecting on the twelve years of danger and degradation that lay before this man, will refuse their compassion.

Gordon was inflexible. Before the arrival of the letters his allusions to Slatin are contemptuous:— 'One cannot help being amused at the Mahdi carrying all the Europeans about with him—nuns, priests, Greeks, Austrian officers—what a medley, a regular État-Major!'[25] He is suspicious of the circumstances of his surrender. 'The Greek .... says, Slatin had 4,000 ardebs of dour a, 1,500 cows, and plenty of ammunition: he has been given eight horses by the Mahdi.'[26]

He will not vouch for such a man; but he adds, with characteristic justice, 'all this information must be taken with reserve.'[27]

At length the letters came. At the peril of his life, when ordered to write and demand the surrender of the town, Slatin substituted an appeal to Gordon to countenance his escape. This is the uncompromising minute in the Journals:— 'Oct. 16. The letters of Slatin have arrived. I have no remarks to make on them, and cannot make out why he wrote them.' In the afternoon, indeed, he betrays some pity; but it is the pity of a man for a mouse. 'He is evidently not a Spartan .... he will want some *quarantine* .... one feels sorry for him.' The next day he is again inexorable and gives his reasons clearly. 'I shall have nothing to do with Slatin's coming here to stay, unless he has the Mahdi's positive leave, which he is not likely to get; his doing so would be the breaking of his parole, which should be as sacred when given to the Mahdi as to any other power, and it would jeopardise the safety of all these Europeans, prisoners with Mahdi.'[28]

Slatin's position, it should be observed, was not that of an officer released on parole, but of a prisoner of war in durance in the enemy's camp. Under such circumstances he was clearly entitled to escape at his own proper risk. If his captors gave him the chance,

25 *Journals at Khartoum.*
26 *Ibid.*
27 *Ibid.*
28 *Ibid.*

they had only themselves to blame. His position was not dissimilar from that of the black soldiers who had been captured by the Dervishes and were now made to serve against the Government. These deserted to Khartoum daily, and the General fully acquiesced in their doing so. As to Slatin's escape affecting the treatment of the other European prisoners, it must be observed that when at various times escapes were effected from Omdurman, and ultimately when Slatin himself escaped, no ill-treatment was inflicted on the rest of the prisoners; and even had such ill-treatment been the certain consequence of an escape, that need not have debarred a man, according to the customs of war, from attempting to regain his liberty. Nothing but his formal promise, obtained in return for favours received, can alienate that right. If the Mahdi chose to slaughter the remaining prisoners, the responsibility rested with the Mahdi; and by such act he would have excluded himself from the mercy of men and incurred the wrath of God .

Slatin was, however, in no position to argue his case. His correspondence with Gordon was discovered. For some days his life hung on a thread. For several months he was heavily chained and fed on a daily handful of uncooked doura, such as is given to horses and mules. Tidings of these things were carried to Gordon. 'Slatin,' he observes icily, 'is still in chains.' He never doubted the righteousness of the course he had adopted, never for an instant. The subject is one on which there is room for considerable difference of opinion. I have been unable to conceal mine. But few will deny that there were strong arguments on both sides. Many will assert that they were nicely balanced. Gordon must have weighed them carefully. He never wavered. Yet he needed Slatin. He was alone. He had no one in whose military capacity he could put the slightest confidence. Again and again in the Journals he expresses his want of trustworthy subordinates. He could not be everywhere, he said. 'Nearly every order has to be repeated two or three times. I am weary of my life.' 'What one has felt so much here is the want of men like Gessi, or Messodaglia, or Slatin, but I have no one to whom I could entrust expeditions. . .'

This was the man who would have employed Zubair and bowed to expediency. But Zubair had never 'denied his Lord.'

The actual defence of Khartoum is within the province of the Journals, nor shall I attempt a chronological account. After the 10th of September, when General Gordon sent Colonel Stewart and Messrs. Power and Herbin down the river in the ill-fated Abbas steamer, he was altogether alone. Many men have bowed to the weight of responsibility. Gordon's responsibility was undivided. There was no one to whom he could talk as an equal. There was no one to whom he could—as to a trusty subordinate—reveal his doubts. To some minds the exercise of power is pleasant, but few sensations are more painful than responsibility without control. The General could not supervise the defence. The officers robbed the soldiers of their rations. The sentries slumbered at their posts. The townspeople bewailed their misfortunes, and all ranks and classes intrigued with the enemy in the hope of securing safety when the town should fall. Frequent efforts were made to stir up the inhabitants or sap their confidence. Spies of all kinds pervaded the town. The Egyptian Pashas, despairing, meditated treason. Once an attempt was made to fire the magazine. Once no less than eighty thousand ardebs of grain were stolen from the arsenal. From time to time the restless and ceaseless activity of the commander might discover some plot and arrest the conspirators; or, checking some account, might detect some robbery; but he was fully aware that what he found out was scarcely a tithe of what he could not hope to know. The Egyptian officers were untrustworthy. Yet he had to trust them. The inhabitants were thoroughly broken by war, and many were disloyal. He had to feed and inspirit them. The town itself was scarcely defensible. It must be defended to the end. From the flat roof of his palace his telescope commanded a view of the forts and lines. Here he would spend the greater part of each day, scrutinizing the defences and the surrounding country with his powerful glass. When he observed that the sentries on the forts had left their posts, he would send over to have them flogged and their superiors punished. When his 'penny steamers' engaged the Dervish batteries he would watch, 'on tenter-hooks,' a combat which might be fatal to the defence, but which, since he could not direct it, must be left to officers by turns timid and reckless: and in the dark hours of the night he could not even watch. The Journals, the only receptacle of his confidences, display the bitterness of his sufferings no less than the greatness of his character. 'There is no contagion,' he writes, 'equal to that of fear. I have been rendered furious when from anxiety I could not eat, I would find those at the same table were in like manner affected.'

To the military anxieties were added every kind of worry which may weary a man's soul. The women clamoured for bread. The townsfolk heaped reproaches upon him. The quarrel with the British Government had cut him very deeply. The belief that he was abandoned and discredited, that history would make light of his efforts, would perhaps never know of them, filled his mind with a sense of wrong and injustice, which preyed upon his spirits. The miseries of the townsfolk wrung his noble, generous heart. The utter loneliness depressed him. And over all lay the shadow of uncertainty. To the very end the possibility that 'all might be well' mocked him with false hopes. The first light of any morning might reveal the longed-for steamers of relief and the red coats of British soldiers. He was denied even the numbing anaesthetic of despair.

Yet he was sustained by two great moral and mental stimulants: his honour as a man, his faith as a Christian. The first had put all courses which he did not think right, once and for all out of the question, and so allayed many doubts and prevented many vain regrets. But the second was the real source of his strength. He was sure that beyond this hazardous existence, with all its wrongs and inequalities, another life awaited him—a life which, if he had been faithful and true here upon earth, would afford him greater faculties for good, and wider opportunities for their use.

'Look at me now,' he once said to a fellow-traveller, 'with small armies to command and no cities to govern. I hope that death will set me free from pain, and that great armies will be given me, and that I shall have vast cities under my command.'[29] Such was his bright hope of immortality.

As the severity of military operations increases, so also must the sternness of discipline. The zeal of the soldiers, their warlike instincts, and the interests and excitements of war may ensure obedience of orders and the cheerful endurance of perils and hardships

29 Lieut.-Colonel N. Newnham Davis. 'Some Gordon Reminiscences,' published in *The Man of the World* newspaper, December 14, 1898.

during a short and prosperous campaign. But when fortune is dubious or adverse; when retreats as well as advances are necessary; when supplies fail, arrangements miscarry, and disasters impend; and when the struggle is protracted, men can only be persuaded to accept evil things by the lively realisation of the fact that greater terrors await their refusal. The ugly truth is revealed that fear is the foundation of obedience. It is certain that the influence of General Gordon upon the garrison and townspeople of Khartoum owed its greatest strength to that sinister element.

'It is quite painful,' he writes in his Journals in September, 'to see men tremble so, when they come and see me, that they cannot hold the match to their cigarette.' Yet he employed all other methods of inspiring their efforts. As the winter drew on, the sufferings of the besieged increased and their faith in their commander and his promises of relief diminished. To preserve their hopes—and, by their hopes, their courage and loyalty—was beyond the power of man. But what a great man in the utmost exercise of his faculties and authority might do, Gordon did.

His extraordinary spirit never burned more brightly than in these last, gloomy days. The money to pay the troops was exhausted. He issued notes, signing them with his own name. The citizens groaned under the triple scourge of scarcity, disease, and war. He ordered the bands to play merrily and discharged rockets. It was said that they were abandoned, that help would never come, that the expedition was a myth—the lie of a General who was disavowed by his Government.

Forthwith he placarded the walls with the news of victories and of the advance of a triumphant British army; or hired all the best houses by the river's bank for the accommodation of the officers of the relieving force. A Dervish shell crashed through his palace. He ordered the date of its arrival to be inscribed above the hole. For those who served him faithfully he struck medals and presented them with pomp and circumstance. Others less laudable he shot. And by all these means and expedients the defence of the city was prolonged through all the summer, autumn, and winter of 1884 and on into the year 1885. All this time the public anxiety in England had been steadily growing. If Gordon was abandoned, he was by no means forgotten. As his mission had been followed with intense interest throughout the whole country, so its failure had caused general despondency. Disappointment soon gave place to alarm. The subject of the personal safety of the distinguished envoy was first raised in the House of Commons on the 16th of March by Lord Randolph Churchill. Availing himself of the opportunities provided by Supply, he criticised the vacillating policy of the Government, their purposeless slaughter in the Eastern Soudan, and their failure to establish the Suakin-Berber route. He proceeded to draw attention to the perilous position of General Gordon at Khartoum.

'Colonel Coetlogon has stated that Khartoum may be easily captured; we know that General Gordon is surrounded by hostile tribes and cut off from communications with Cairo and London; and under these circumstances the House has a right to ask Her Majesty's Government whether they are going to do anything to relieve him. Are they going to remain indifferent to the fate of the one man on whom they have counted to extricate them from their dilemmas, to leave him to shift for himself, and not make a single effort on his behalf?'[30]

The Government remained impassive. Lord E. Fitzmaurice made an effective reply, and there were Ministerial cheers. But the subject, once raised, was not allowed to drop. Inspired and animated by the earnest energy of a young man, the Opposition were continually growing stronger. The conduct of Egyptian affairs afforded ample opportunity for criticism and attack. All through the summer months and almost every night Ministers were invited to declare, whether they would rescue their envoy or leave him to his fate.

Mr. Gladstone returned evasive answers. The Conservative Press took the cue. The agitation became intense. Even among the supporters of the Government there was dissatisfaction. But the Prime Minister was obdurate and unflinching. At length, at the end of the whole matter was brought forward in the gravest and most formal way by the moving of a vote of censure. The debate that followed Sir Michael Hicks Beach's motion was long and acrimonious. Mr. Gladstone's speech only increased the disquietude of his followers and the fury of the Opposition. Mr. Forster openly declared his disa-

30 *Hansard's Parliamentary Debates*, March 16. 1884.

greement with his leader; and although Lord Hartington in winding up the debate threw out some hopes of an expedition in the autumn, the Government majority fell on the division to twenty-eight. The House then adjourned, but the controversy was carried on with undiminished vigour outside the walls of Parliament, and the clamour in the country grew louder and louder.

It is usual to look upon Mr. Gladstone's conduct in the matter of the relief of Gordon as dictated by benevolent weakness. History may take another view. Strong and stubborn as was the character of the General, that of the Minister was its equal. If Gordon was the better man, Gladstone was incomparably the greater. It was easy for the First Minister of the Crown to despatch an expedition against savages. He was accustomed to the exercise of power. Compared with the resources of the Empire, the enterprise was insignificant. Few men have feared responsibility less than Gladstone. On the other hand, the expressed desire of the nation was a force to which he had always bowed, to which indeed he owed his political existence. Yet, in spite of the growing agitation throughout the land, he remained stern and silent. Most men do what is right, or what they persuade themselves is right; nor is it difficult to believe that Mr. Gladstone did not feel justified in involving the nation in operations in the heart of the Soudan for the purpose, not of saving the life of the envoy—for Gordon had but to embark on his steamers and come home—but simply in order to vindicate the personal honour of a man. And it is possible that a feeling of resentment against the officer whose intractable nature was bringing such odium upon the Government may have coloured his resolution with a darker tinge.

But for all his power and influence he was forced to give way. The Government which had long ignored the call of honour abroad, was driven to the Soudan by the cries of shame at home. Lord Hartington, at that time Secretary of State for War, must be dissociated from the general censure which his colleagues have incurred. He was the first to recognise the obligation which lay upon the Cabinet, and through the Cabinet upon the nation, and it was to his influence that the despatch of the relieving expedition was mainly due. The Commander-in-Chief and the Adjutant-General, who were fully alive to the critical position at Khartoum, added their recommendations. But even at the last moment Mr. Gladstone was induced to sanction the advance only by the belief that the scale of the operations would be small, and that only a single brigade would be necessary. The decision was taken forthwith, by the Ministry and announced to the nation. The Adjutant-General, however, asked for a very different force from that which the Government had anticipated, and the single brigade was expanded into an expedition of ten thousand men, selected from the whole army.

To reverse the decision was now however impossible, and the 'Gordon Relief Expedition' began. The commander to whom the conduct of the operations had been entrusted reviewed the situation. He saw himself confronted with a task which was easy and safe if it were undertaken at leisure, and which was doubtful and perilous if begun in haste. All the fruits of a long and successful career were staked on the result, and it is scarcely wonderful that he declined to be swift and reckless. Shrewdly estimating the military difficulties, he made his plans for a methodical and deliberate advance which should leave nothing to luck, and which resembles in character that afterwards carried out by Sir H. Kitchener. He excluded the idea of a wild glorious rush which might result in astonishing success or terrible disaster.

Troops and stores were steadily collected at Wady Halfa and along the Nile. The new Camel Corps, consisting of four regiments, practised their drills and evolutions. To pilot the boats up the Cataracts *voyageurs* were brought from Canada. At length, when all preparations were complete, the expedition started. The plan was simple. A strong column of infantry in boats was to work up the river. In case that should not arrive in time, the Camel Corps was to strike across the Bayuda Desert from Korti to Metemma. Having arrived there, a small detachment was to be thrown into Khartoum by Gordon's steamers to sustain the defence until the arrival of the main body in March or even April of 1885, when the town could be regularly relieved.

The dramatic character of the enterprise and its picturesque and original features fascinated the nation, and the advance was watched with breathless interest. The fortunes of the River Column have been graphically described by one who played no small part in their attempt. 'The Campaign of the Cataracts'[31] is a record of hard and unceasing toil. Day after day the long lines of soldiers hauled on the tow-ropes or pulled at the oars of the broad-bottomed boats. Night after night they camped on the banks amid the grim desolation of the Monassir Desert. Yet their monotonous labours were encouraged by the knowledge that as soon as the bend of the river at Abu Hamed was reached the strong north wind would carry them swiftly to Khartoum. And it seemed a strange and bitter irony that the order to turn back and the news that all had been in vain was announced to the troops on the very day when they had cleared the cataracts and were moving forward at five times their former speed.

The Desert Column started from Korti on the 30th of December. Their strength did not exceed 1,100 officers and men, but they were the flower of the army. Dropping their communications, they set forth along the caravan route towards Metemma. The knowledge which we have since gained of the resources of the Mahdists enables the peril of their desperate venture to be fully appreciated. Although the Dervishes were neither so well armed, nor trained as at a later date, they were nearly as numerous and equally devoid of fear. Their tactics, as will be explained in a future chapter, were more in accordance with modern conditions: their fanaticism was at its height. The British force, on the other hand, equipped with weapons scarcely comparable to those employed in the concluding campaigns. Instead of the powerful Lee-Metford rifle, with its smokeless powder, its magazine action, and its absence of recoil, they were armed with the. Martini-Henry, which possessed none of these advantages. In of the deadly Maxim there was the Gardner gun—the very gun that jammed at Tamai, and that jammed again at Abu Klea. The artillery was also in every respect inferior to that now in general use. Besides all this, the principles of fire-discipline and of scientific musketry were new, little understood, and hardly admitted. Nevertheless the Camel Corps went boldly forward, and engaged an enemy whose destruction ultimately required the strength of a better-armed and better-instructed army twelve times as strong.

On the 3rd of January they reached Gakdul Wells. A hundred miles of their march was accomplished. But they were now delayed

31 By Sir William Butler.

by the necessity of escorting a second column of supplies to Gakdul, and alter that until the arrival of reinforcements which raised their strength to 1,800 of all ranks. The interval was employed in building two small forts and establishing an advanced depôt; nor was it until the 13th that the march was resumed.[32] The number of camels was not sufficient for the necessities of the transport. The food of the camels was too poor for the work they had to perform. By the 16th, however, they had made fifty miles, and approached the wells of Abu Klea. Here their further advance was disputed by the enemy.

The news of the advance of the Desert Column had been duly reported to the Mahdi and his Arab generals. A small party of English, it was said, with camels and some cavalry were coining swiftly to the rescue of the accursed city. Their numbers were few, scarce 2.000 men. How should they hope to prevail against 'the expected Mahdi' and the conquering Ansar who had destroyed Hicks? They were mad; yet they should die; not one should escape. The delay in the advance afforded ample opportunity. A great force of Arabs was concentrated. Slatin relates how several thousand men under important Emirs were detached from the army before Khartoum and marched northward eager for the slaughter of the 'enemies of God.'

At Metemma the main strength of the Jaalin tribe was collected. With the reinforcements from Omdurman the total force of the Arabs actually at hand was not less than 10,000,[33] and behind were many thousands more. They permitted the little column to advance until their retreat, if defeated, was impossible, and then, confident of victory, they offered battle near the wells of Abu Klea.

The Camel Corps remained halted during the morning of the 16th, and built a small fort, in which they placed their reserve of stores, and made some arrangement for the reception of wounded. At one o'clock they moved leisurely forward, passed through the rocky defile which led into the valley of Abu Klea, and bivouacked. That night the camp was fired into and a few casualties occurred. Early the next morning the force moved out in square formation

32 The necessity for the halt at Gakdul had been foreseen by Lord Wolseley from the outset, and was alluded to in his orders. The insufficient number of camels rendered it inevitable.—EDITOR.

33 Between 9,000 and 11,000 according to Sir Charles Wilson.—EDITOR.

and advanced upon the enemy. The most savage and bloody action ever fought in the Soudan by British troops followed. Notwithstanding the numbers and the valour of the Arabs, that they penetrated the square, and that they inflicted on the troops a loss of nine officers and sixty-five men killed and nine officers and eighty-five men wounded—ten per cent, of the entire force—they were driven from the field with great slaughter, and the Desert Column camped at the wells.

On the morning of the 18th they rested, placed their wounded in the small fort they had built, and buried their dead. In the afternoon they continued their advance, marched all through the night, and, having covered twenty-three miles, halted exhausted, almost within sight of the river, at daylight on the 19th. Meanwhile the enemy had again collected in great strength, and an effective rifle fire was opened on the column. Sir Herbert Stewart received the wound of which a few weeks later he died. The command devolved upon Sir Charles Wilson. The position was desperate. Water was running short. The Nile was only four miles away; but the column were impeded by their wounded and store-, and between the river and the thirsty men lay the Dervish army, infuriated by their losses and fully aware of the sore straits to which their astonishing enemy was now reduced.

It now became necessary to divide the small force. Some must remain to guard the baggage and the wounded; the others must fight their way to the water. At three o'clock in the afternoon of the 19th, 900 men left the hastily made *zeriba* and marched towards the river. Without their camels or those of the transport they appeared insignificant, a mere speck on the broad plain of Metemma. The' Dervishes hastened to clinch the matter.

The square advances slowly and painfully over the stony ground, with frequent jerky halts to preserve order and to pick up the wounded. Little puffs of white smoke dot the distant sandhills. Here and there a gaudy flag waves defiantly. In front the green tops of the palm-trees by the Nile tantalise but stimulate the soldiers. On the left the great mud labyrinth of Metemma stretches indefinitely. Suddenly the firing: stops. The low scrub in front is alive with the swarming figures of the enemy. All the flags dance forward together. Ragged white figures spring up in hundreds. Emirs on horses appear as if by magic. Everywhere are men running swiftly forward, waving their spears and calling upon the Prophet of God to speed their enterprise. The square halts. The weary men begin to fire with thoughtful care. The Dervishes drop thickly. On then, children of the desert ! you are so many, they are so few. They are worn with fatigue and their throats are parched. You have drunk deeply of the Nile. One rush will trample the accursed under the feet of the faithful. The charge continues. A bugle sounds in the waiting square. The firing stops. What is this? They lose heart. Their ammunition is exhausted. On, then, and make an end. Again the smoke ripples along the line of bayonets and fire is reopened, this time at closer range and with far greater effect. The stubborn grandeur of the British soldier is displayed by desperate circumstances. The men shoot to hit. The attack crumples. The Emirs—horse and man—collapse. The others turn and walk—for they will not run sullenly back towards the town. The square starts forward. The road to the river is open. With dusk the water is reached, and never have victors gained a more precious prize. The Nile is won. Gordon remains.

Sir Charles Wilson, having collected his force, remained three days by the bank of the Nile before attempting any further advance on Khartoum. He has explained why this delay was necessary, to the satisfaction of most military critics. Nor is it possible to believe that men who had made such splendid efforts would have willingly lost a single moment. On the fourth day, he embarked on two of Gordon's steamers, which awaited the relieving column, and taking with him twenty British soldiers and a few blue-jackets set forth towards the Shabluka Gorge and the town that lay beyond. On the 27th of January the rescuers came in sight of Khartoum and under the fire of the enemy. Many of their perilous adventures seem to belong to romance rather than to reality: the tiny gimcrack boats struggling with the strong stream of the cataract, running the gauntlet of the Arab gnus, dropping disconsolately down the river with their terrible news or wrecked and stranded on the sandbank; Stuart-Wortley rowing to the camp before Metemma for help; Beresford starting in the remaining steamer; the bursting of the boiler by a Dervish shell: Benbow mending it in a single day; Wilson's rescue and the return to the entrenchment at Gubat. But the scene that appeals to the imagination above all the others is that where with both banks ablaze with musketry and artillery, the black smoke pouring through the shot-holes in the funnels, the water rising in spurts from the bullets, the men who had come far and braved so much, stared at the palace roof and, seeing no flag flying, knew that all was over and that they had come too late.

The news of the Dervish defeat at Abu Klea and Abu Kru impelled the Mahdi to a desperate venture. The English were but 120 miles away. They were few, but victorious. It was difficult to say what force could stop such men. In spite of the wrath of the true God and the valour of Islam they might prevail. The Mahdi depended on success for existence. The tremendous forces of fanaticism are exerted only in a forward direction. Retreat meant ruin. All must be staked on an immediate assault. And, besides, the moment was ripe. Thus the Arab chiefs reasoned, and wisely resolved to be reckless. Thus the night of the 25th of January arrived.

The band played as usual in the evening. Gradually the shadows fell and it became dark. The hungry inhabitants betook themselves to bed. The anxious but indomitable commander knew that the crisis impended, and knew, also that he was powerless to avert it. Perhaps he slept, satisfied that he had done his duty; and in the silence of the moonless night the savage enemy crawled stealthily towards the town. The weary and disheartened sentinels, weakened by famine and tired of war, maintained a doubtful vigilance along the ramparts. The subsiding waters of the river had left a bare gap between the White Nile and the wall. There may have been also treachery. If so, it was superfluous. On a sudden the loud explosion of musketry broke the stillness of the night and the slumbers of the people; and with a continual shouting thousands of Dervishes swarmed through the unprotected space and entered Khartoum.

There followed massacre, pillage, and confusion. The sack of a city is a spectacle which the world has often seen, but it belongs to other days. At the end of the nineteenth century it is an anachronism. Civilised humanity had done with such events. Yet here, with every ancient circumstance, was the unexpected horror—a foul thing raked out of the ashes of the past. One mob of Dervishes made their way to the palace. Gordon came out to meet them. The whole courtyard was filled with wild, harlequin figures and sharp, glittering blades. He attempted a parley. 'Where is your master, the Mahdi?' He knew his influence over native races. Perhaps he hoped to save the lives of some of the inhabitants. Perhaps in that supreme moment imagination flashed another picture before his eyes; and he saw himself confronted with the false prophet of a false religion, confronted with the European prisoners who had 'denied their Lord,' offered the choice of death or the Koran; saw himself facing that savage circle with a fanaticism equal to, and a courage greater than their own; like

Abdiel—

Among the faithless, faithful only he;
Among innumerable false unmoved,
Unshaken, unseduced, unterrified—

marching in all the pride of faith 'and with retorted scorn' to a martyr's death.

It was not to be. Mad with the joy of victory and religious frenzy, they rushed upon him and, while he disdained even to fire his revolver, stabbed him in many places. The body fell down the steps and lay—a twisted heap—at the foot. There it was decapitated. The head was carried to the Mahdi. The trunk was stabbed again and again by the infuriated creatures, till nothing but a shapeless bundle of torn flesh and bloody rags remained of what had been a great and famous man and the envoy of her Britannic Majesty. The blood soaked into the ground, and left a dark stain which was not immediately effaced. Slatin mentions that the Arabs used often to visit the place. Ohrwalder went himself, and more than six weeks after the capture of the town, saw 'black spots' upon the steps. But they have since been all wiped out.

Such, briefly, is the story of the fall of Khartoum and of the death of Gordon. The fact that the two steamers arrived only two days after the capture of the town, has given colour to the belief that, but for the three days' delay at Metemma, the catastrophe might have been averted. This view appears incorrect. The Arabs had long held Khartoum at their mercy. They hoped indeed to compel its surrender by famine and to avoid an assault, which after their experience at El Obeid they knew must cost them dear. Gordon has stated in his Journals that the town became defenceless by the middle of December. The arrival of twenty British soldiers and a few officers could not have materially affected the situation—could only, in fact, have increased the loss. Yet nearly everyone who reads the tale will wish—in spite of reason—that some help, however little, had reached the lonely man; that before the darkness fell he had grasped an English hand, and learned that his countrymen had not abandoned him, had not forgotten—would never forget.

The events thus briefly described are too recent, and the bitter controversies they excited are still too fresh in the minds of men, for an impartial and definite judgment to be passed on the character of the General or the conduct of the Government, But several features stand out with such prominence that, although the contemporaneous chronicler must ultimately bow to the historian, he is not altogether forbidden to pronounce? It may not be possible as yet to fix the exact place which Charles Gordon will occupy in English history. It is certainly a high one. Whether he will rank as a commander with Peterborough, Wolfe, and Clive, those who come after us must decide. From the lofty peaks of the future they will look out over the plain of the past, and may accurately appreciate the relative size and importance of the eminences that rise therefrom. We may, however, assert that he was a man of stainless honour and enduring courage, who in varied capacities displayed a fertile and abundant genius. He was careless alike of the honours and comforts of the world, and looked forward with firm faith to the reward- of a future state. The severity of his religion did not impair the amiability of his character. The uncertainty of his moods may have frequently affected the soundness of his opinions, but not often the justice of his actions. He perished with every heroic circumstance at the post of duty, lamented by his countrymen, who found in his life an example and in his memory an inspiration.

Gordon's statue, set up in the indignant grief of the nation in the space which is appropriated to the monuments of Great Captains by sea and land, claims the attention of the passer-by, not only because it is comparatively new. The figure, its pose, and its story are familiar to even the poorest citizens of London and to people from all parts of the United Kingdom. Amid the noise of the traffic, as formerly in that of the battle, the famous General seems still, with bowed head and thoughtful countenance, to revolve the problems of the dark Soudan and, inattentive to the clamour of men, inquires what is acceptable to God. It was easy to put up such a statue to Charles Gordon. It has since been possible to send an army corps thirteen hundred miles across the deserts and, beating down all opposition with the flaming sword of science, to celebrate his obsequies on the scene of his death. But though the might of a united people may repair many of the blunders of the past and has already repaired some, the noble life that was lost in the dark days of 1885 was not one that even the greatest Empire could spare.

The case against Mr. Gladstone's administration is so black that historians will be more likely to exercise their talents in finding explanations and excuses than in urging the indictment. Something may be said of grave difficulties; something of good intentions; something of human fallibility; something of ill-luck. But the real plea for oblivion is found in the fact that the conduct of affairs in Egypt by the Radical Government was in the spring of 1885 partly, and in the autumn of 1885 fully supported by the electorate at General Elections. A tremendous minority regarded their behaviour with horror and contempt. A majority voted for them. Here is their best defence at the bar of history; and since it can be sustained, that tribunal will be prevented from meting its most scathing censures and will only be able to pronounce that the Ministry were the representatives of the nation in an hour when its spirit was tame and sluggish, its courage and its fortunes low.

With the capture of the city and the death of the envoy the reason for the expedition disappeared. It remained only to withdraw the troops. The stores which had been brought across the desert at a terrible cost, were thrown hastily into the Nile. The battered steamers which had waited so long at Metemma were hurriedly dismantled. The Camel Corps, their extraordinary efforts futile and their camels killed, marched back on foot to Korti. Their retreat was pressed by the exultant enemy. The River Column, whose boast after months of labour had just cleared the Cataracts, and who had gained a success at Kirbekan, were carried back swiftly by the strong current against which they had hopefully struggled. The whole Expeditionary Force—Guards, Highlanders, sailors, Hussars, Indian soldiers, Canadian *voyageurs*, mules, camels, and artillery—trooped back forlornly over the desert sands, and behind them the rising tide of barbarism followed swiftly, until the whole vast region of the Soudan was submerged. For several months the garrison of Kassala under a gallant Egyptian maintained a desperate resistance, but at last famine forced them to surrender, and they shared the fate of the garrisons of El Obeid, Darfur, Sobat, Tokar, Sinkat, Sennar, and Khartoum. The evacuation of the Soudan was thus completed.

These events produced a profound feeling of despondency in Great Britain. The shame associated with the Soudan made its name odious to the whole people. The heavy losses in men and money caused all projects for the recovery of the territory to be unpopular. The nation was prepared to accept its humiliation and acquiesce in its defeat. The Ministers responsible for the disaster were again returned to power by a substantial majority, and when they lost office, it was on a matter wholly unconnected with foreign affairs. Abroad the military operations, in which four generals, seventy-five other officers, and 1,891 men had perished and, in consequence of which 303 officers and 6,560 men had been wounded or invalided, were severely criticised. The European opinion about Great Britain was not dissimilar from that lately held about Italy after the Abyssinian defeats, or about Spain since the Cuban war. It was not denied that the soldiers were brave. That was also admitted in the cases of Italy and Spain. They had failed, and Continental observers did not hesitate to declare that this failure was only the beginning of the end. And in a hopeless way the belief was widely shared in England.

Yet in this dark hour there dawned a brighter day. While the whole country cowered, a new and vigorous spirit was growing in the great towns of England and Scotland; and in the freshening breeze of Tory Democracy pride in the past and hope for the future came back to the British people.

Thus with the chapter the disasters end, and the tale is henceforth one of triumph.

CHAPTER IV
THE DERVISH EMPIRE[1]

Military dominion—The Dervish rule—Death of the Mahdi—The Khalifa Abdullahi—His triumph—His methods—A perilous prize—Soudan annals—Rival claimants—Treatment of the Ashraf—The military policy—The Taiasha Baggara—The balance of power—The quarrel with Abyssinia—Gallabat—Abu Anga—His deeds in Darfur and Kordofan—His justice—The great review—The invasion of Abyssinia—Sack of Gondar—Death of Abu Anga—King John of Abyssinia—Battle of Gallabat—Death of the Negus—A Pyrrhic victory—The Western revolts—Osman Wad Adam—'The Man of the Fig-tree'—Battle of El Fasher—The war with Egypt—Wad el Nejumi—Adjusting the balance—Famine—Plagues—The Arab capital—The weekly review—A Council of State—Trouble in the north.

The students of the more philosophical aspects of history have discovered that the larger the associations into which men form themselves, the surer and the swifter their progress usually becomes. The institution of the family has shaped all the mental and moral development of mankind. The most savage tribes must observe some rude code of justice and honour among themselves. The national and patriotic idea has given new opportunities to the generous impulses. The combination of millions is the foundation on which the stately palace of civilisation is raised. And there are many moderns who, perceiving the good results, would multiply the cause and, disdaining all racial distinctions, would strive only for the brotherhood of men.

It might, therefore, seem at first a great advantage that the peoples of the Soudan, instead of being a multitude of wild, discordant tribes, should unite of their own accord into one strong community,

1 Map, 'The Dervish Empire,' page 78.

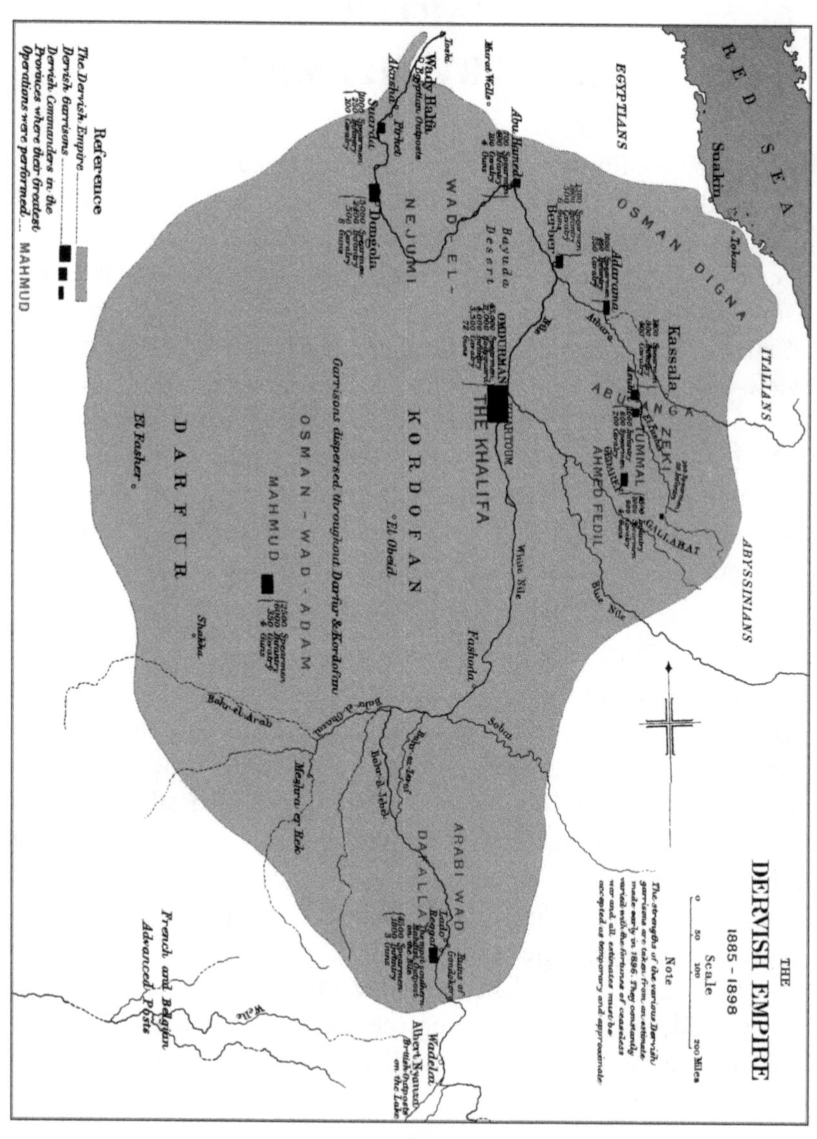
THE
DERVISH EMPIRE
1885 - 1898
Scale
Note
RED SEA
Suakin
Tokar
EGYPTIANS
ITALIANS
ABYSSINIANS
OSMAN DIGNA
Kassala
ABU ANGA
ZEKI
TUMMAL
AHMED FEDIL
GALLABAT
Abu Hamed
Berber
Adarama
Atbara
Bayuda Desert
OMDURMAN
KHARTOUM
THE KHALIFA
WAD-EL-NEJUMI
Dongola
Suarda
Wady Halfa
Akasha
Firket
Murat Wells
Toski
KORDOFAN
El Obeid
Garrisons dispersed throughout Darfur & Kordofan
OSMAN - WAD - ADAM
MAHMUD
DARFUR
El Fasher
Shakka
White Nile
Blue Nile
Fashoda
Sobat
Bahr-el-Arab
Bahr-el-Ghazal
Bahr-el-Jebel
Meshra-er-Rek
ARABI WAD DAFALLA
Lado
Rejaf
Wadelai
Albert Nyanza
French and Belgian Advanced Posts
Reference
The Dervish Empire
Dervish Garrisons
Dervish Commanders in the Provinces where their Greatest Operations were performed... MAHMUD

actuated by a common spirit, living under fixed laws, and ruled by a single sovereign. But there is one form of centralised Government which is almost entirely unprogressive and beyond all other forms costly and tyrannical—the rule of an army. Such a combination depends, not on the good faith and good will of its constituents, but on their discipline and almost mechanical obedience. Mutual fear, not mutual trust, promotes the co-operation of its individual members. History records many such dominations, ancient and modern, civilised or barbaric; and though education and culture may modify, they cannot change their predominant characteristics—a continual subordination of justice to expediency, an indifference to suffering, a disdain of ethical principles, a laxity of morals, and a complete ignorance of economics. The evil qualities of military hierarchies are uniform. The results of their rule are universally unfortunate. The degree may vary with time and place, but the political supremacy of an army always leads to the formation of a great centralised capital, to the consequent impoverishment of the provinces, to the degradation of the peaceful inhabitants through oppression and want, to the ruin of commerce, the decay of learning, and the ultimate demoralisation even of the military order through overbearing pride and sensual indulgence.

Of the military dominations which history records, the Dervish Empire was probably the worst. All others have displayed compensating virtues. A high sense of personal honour has counterbalanced a low standard of public justice. An ennobling patriotism may partly repair economic follies. The miseries of the people are often concealed by the magnificence of the army. The laxity of morals is in some degree excused by the elegance of manners. But the Dervish Empire developed no virtue except courage, a quality more admirable than rare. The poverty of the land prevented magnificence. The ignorance of its inhabitants excluded refinement. In the passage of years the Arabs might indeed have worked out their own salvation, as have the nations of Europe. The army, becoming effete, would wither and disappear, leaving behind it only the consciousness of nationality. A wise ruler might arise who should establish a more equitable and progressive polity. The natural course of development is long, but true. The British people have selected a shorter though more terrible road for the tribes to follow. The Dervish dominion was born of war, existed by war, and fell by war. It began on the night of the sack of Khartoum. It ended abruptly thirteen years later in the battle of Omdurman. Like a subsidiary volcano it was flung up by one convulsion, blazed during the period of disturbance, and was destroyed by the still more violent shock that ended the eruption.

After the fall of Khartoum and the retreat of the British armies the Mahdi became the absolute master of the Soudan. Whatever pleasures he desired he could command, and, following the example of the founder of the Mohammedan faith, he indulged in what would seem to Western minds gross excesses. He established an extensive harem for his own peculiar use, and immured therein the fairest captives of the war. The conduct of the ruler was imitated by his subjects. The presence of women increased the vanity of the warriors: nor was it long before the patched smock which had vaunted the holy poverty of the rebels developed into the gaudy *jibba* of the conquerors. Since the unhealthy situation of Khartoum amid swamps and marshes did not commend itself to the now luxurious Arabs, the Mahdi began to build on the western bank of the White Nile a new capital, which, from the detached fort which had stood there in Egyptian days, was called Omdurman. Among the first buildings which he set his subjects to construct were a mosque for the services of religion, an arsenal for the storage of military material, and a house for his benefit. But while he was thus entering at once upon the enjoyments of supreme power and unbridled lust, the God whom he had served, not unfaithfully, and who had given him whatever he had asked, required of Mohammed Ahmed his soul; and so all that he had won by his brains and bravery became of no more account to him.

In the middle of the month of June, scarcely five months after the completion of his victorious campaigns, the Mahdi fell sick. For a few days he did not appear at the mosque. The people were filled with alarm. They were reassured by remembering the prophecy that their liberator should not perish till he had conquered the earth. Mohammed, however, grew worse. Presently those who attended him could doubt no longer that he was attacked by typhus fever. The Khalifa Abdullahi watched by his couch continually. On the sixth day the inhabitants and the soldiers were informed of the serious nature of their ruler's illness, and public flayers were offered by all classes for his recovery. On the seventh day it was evident that he was dying. All those who had shared his fortunes—the Khalifas he had appointed, the chief priests of the religion he had reformed, the leaders of the armies who had followed him to victory, and his own family whom he had hallowed—crowded the small room. For some hours he lay unconscious or in delirium, but as the end approached he rallied a little, and, collecting his faculties by a great effort, declared his faithful follower and friend the Khalifa Abdullahi his successor, and adjured the rest to show him honour. 'He is of me, and I am of him; as you have obeyed me, so you should deal with him. May God have mercy upon me!'[2] Then he immediately expired. Thus died, at the age of thirty-seven, the most remarkable Mohammedan of modern times, and one of the most famous Africans the world has yet seen.

If the merits of a ruler are to be judged by the affection of his subjects, the position of Mohammed Ahmed is rare and estimable. Grief and dismay filled the city. In spite of the emphatic prohibition by law of all loud lamentations, the sound of 'weeping and wailing arose from almost every house.'[3] The whole people, deprived at once of their acknowledged sovereign and spiritual guide, were shocked and affrighted. Only the Mahdi's wives, if we may credit Slatin, 'rejoiced secretly in their hearts at the death of their husband and master,' and, since they were henceforth to be doomed to an enforced and inviolable chastity, the cause of their satisfaction is as obscure, as its manifestation was unnatural.

The body of the Mahdi, wrapped in linen, was reverently interred in a deep grave dug in the floor of the room in which he had died, nor was it disturbed until after the capture of Omdurman by the British forces in 1898, when by the orders of Sir H. Kitchener the sepulchre was opened and the corpse exhumed. The Khalifa Abdullahi had been declared by the Mahdi's latest breath his successor. He determined to have the choice ratified once for all by the popular vote. Hurrying to the pulpit in the courtyard of the mosque, he addressed the assembled multitude in a voice which trembled

2 Slatin, *Fire and Sword.*

3 *Ibid.*

with intense excitement and emotion. His oratory, his reputation as a warrior, and the Mahdi's expressed desire aroused the enthusiasm of his hearers, and the oath of allegiance was at once sworn by thousands. The ceremony continued long after it was dark. With an amazing endurance he harangued till past midnight, and when the exhausted Slatin, who had attended him throughout the crisis, lay down upon the ground to sleep, he knew that his master's succession was assured; for, says he, 'I heard the passers-by loud in their praises of the late Mahdi, and assuring each other of their firm resolve to support his successor.'

Few men are satisfied with the mere accomplishment of their ambitions, and, although the efforts nearly always give more pleasure than the prize, they hold tenaciously to what they have won. The Khalifa Abdullahi had achieved his not inconsiderable desires. His country was at his feet. He had obtained the supreme authority in the Soudan. It remained, however, to preserve it. Like Macbeth he reflected, 'To be thus is nothing; but to be safely thus—' And all the actions of his reign were directed to the strengthening of his own position. He ruled a turbulent people who had learnt their power, tigers who had tasted blood. The nice methods of constitutional Government were scarcely suited to such a task. Sterner and bloodier measures were necessary. Nor was Abdullahi the man to shrink from the harshest or the most treacherous expedients. His cruelty indeed may escape notice in a land where all men hold life cheap and regard suffering with callous indifference; but his low and unscrupulous cunning must excite the disgust and indignation even of the most tolerant chronicler. He was a crafty, vain, and savage man, faithless in all respects save one. His unswerving loyalty to the Mahdi must be credited to him as a single virtue. His talents were, however, indisputable. He understood affairs of peace and war; had studied the characters of his countrymen; and knew exactly how he might avail himself of their fanaticism. He could take advantage of their weaknesses and utilise their strength. With punctilious care he fostered their religious prejudices. His sensual passions were discreetly veiled from the public eye, and the Arabs were impressed by the appearance of a sovereign who always preserved that dignified gravity which has distinguished the noblest of their race. His tyrannical and despotic actions were cloaked with the forms of legality, and the Khalifa bowed before the judgment of the courts which were his instruments, or paid an 'exaggerated respect to judges whom he effectively controlled by fear and bribery.

The exercise of despotic power never improves the ruler and rarely gratifies the subjects. As the years pass, their vexation increases and the spectacle of their dissatisfaction provokes the suspicion and the cruelty of the sovereign. Abdullahi was an evil man when he succeeded the Mahdi. His vices grew with his age until he presented a deplorable spectacle, and the Soudan groaned beneath an oppression as terrible as that of the Egyptians. A just sense of proportion must, however, be cultivated. The Khalifa is not rightly judged by the standards of European civilisation. To find his peers we must look to barbaric potentates. His methods and his manners were not widely different from those which prevail throughout the dominions of the Shah of Persia, or in the territories of ' our ally ' the Amir of Afghanistan. No execution which he ordered at Omdurman was more terrible than those which, with the approval of the British Government, accompanied the suppression of the Indian Mutiny. His chastisement of rebellious tribes was less brutal than the massacres of Armenians, and far more rational than the anti-Semitism from which even the most polite nations have not purged themselves. His morals compared not unfavourably with those of several Asiatic Princes, and his treatment of the European captives was admirable by contrast with that suffered by some of the Italian prisoners in Abyssinia, and not much worse than the methods of keeping French prisoners of war practised in England within the present century.

The sovereignty that Abdullahi had obtained must be held, as it had been won, by the sword. The passionate agitation which the Mahdi had excited, survived him. The whole of the Soudan was in a ferment. The success which had crowned rebellion encouraged rebels. All the turbulent and fanatical elements were aroused. As the various provinces had been cleared of the Egyptians, the new Executive had appointed military governors by whom the country was ruled and taxed, subject to the pleasure of Mohammed Ahmed. His death was the signal for a long series of revolts of all kinds—military, political, and religious. Garrisons mutinied; Emirs plotted;

prophets preached. Nor was the land torn only by internal struggles. Its frontiers were threatened. On the east the tremendous power of Abyssinia loomed terrible and menacing. There was war in the north with Egypt and around Suakin with England. The Italians must be confronted from the direction of Massowa. Far to the south Emin Pasha still maintained a troublesome resistance. Yet the Khalifa triumphed over nearly all his enemies: and the greatest spectacle which the Soudan presented from 1885 to 1898 was of this strong, capable ruler bearing up against all reverses, meeting each danger, overcoming each difficulty, arid offering a firm front to every foe.

It is unlikely that any complete history of these events will ever be written in a form and style which will interest a later generation. The complications of extraordinary names and the imperfection of the records might alone deter the chronicler. The universal squalor of the scenes and the ignorance of the actors add discouragements. Nor, upon the other hand, are there great incentives. The tale is one of war of the cruellest, bloodiest, and most confused type. One savage army slaughters another. One fierce general cuts his rival's throat. The same features are repeated with wearying monotony. When one battle is understood, all may be imagined. Above the tumult the figure of the Khalifa rises stern and solitary, the only object which may attract the interest of a happier world. Yet even the Khalifa's methods were oppressively monotonous. For although the nature or course of the revolts might differ with the occasion, the results were invariable; and the heads of all his chief enemies, of many of his generals, of most of his councillors, met in the capacious pit which yawned in Omdurman. I shall not therefore attempt any chronological account. It will be sufficient to select from the confusion one or two striking events illustrating main characteristics, and, if they can be found, a few striking figures. The reader may glance at the general colouring of the picture; nor must he complain if much of the canvas is left unpainted.

During the thirteen years of his reign Abdullahi tried nearly every device by which Oriental rulers have sought to fortify their perilous sovereignty. He shrank from nothing. Self-preservation was the guiding principle of his policy, his first object and his only excuse. Among many wicked and ingenious expedients three main methods are remarkable. Firstly, he removed or rendered innocuous all real or potential rivals. Secondly, he pursued what Sir Alfred Milner has called 'a well-considered policy of military concentration.' Thirdly, he maintained among the desert and riverain peoples a balance of power on the side of his own tribe. All these three methods merit some attention or illustration.

The general massacre of all possible claimants usually follows the accession of a usurper to an Oriental throne. The Khalifa was able to avoid this extreme measure. Nevertheless he took precautions. Availing himself of the grief and terror that had followed Mohammed Ahmed's death, he had extorted the oath of allegiance from the two other Khalifas and from the 'Ashraf' or relations of the Prophet.[4] But these complaisant men soon repented of their submission. Each Khalifa boasted his independence. Each marched attended by a numerous retinue. Each asserted his right to beat his own great copper drum. Both the unsuccessful Khalifas combined against Abdullahi. But while they had been busy with the beating of war-drums and the preparation of pageants, that sagacious ruler had secured the loyalty of the Baggara tribe, to a section of which he belonged, and of a considerable force of black riflemen. At length matters reached a climax. Both parties prepared for war. Abdullahi drew up his array without the city, and challenged his rivals to the utmost proof. The combined forces of the ousted Khalifas were the more numerous. But the fierce Baggara waved their swords, and the Soudanese riflemen were famous for their valour. For some hours a bloody struggle appeared imminent. Then the confederacy broke up. The Khalifa Ali-Wad-Helu, a prudent man, talked of compromise and amity. The Khalifa Sherif, thus seriously weakened, hastened to make peace while time remained. Eventually both bowed to the superior force of the ruler and the superior courage of his followers. It was a barbaric *plebiscite*, with swords for voting-papers. Once they had submitted, their power was gone. Abdullahi reduced their forces to a personal escort of fifty men each, deprived them of their flags and their war-drums—the emblems of royalty—and they became for the future the useful supporters of a Government they were unable to subvert.

4 The Mahdi had superseded the original Mohammed His relations consequently became the 'Ashraf.'

To other less powerful or more stubborn enemies he showed a greater severity. The Mahdi's two uncles, named respectively Abdel Kerim and Abdel Kader, were thrown chained into prison, their houses were destroyed, and their wives and other property confiscated. The numerous persons who claimed to be of the 'Ashraf,' found the saintly honour a burden upon earth; for, in order to keep them out of mischief, the Khalifa enjoined them to attend five times every day at the prayers in the mosque. Eighteen months of the devotions, declares the Christian chronicler, were considered 'the highest punishment.'[5] Still more barbarous was the treatment meted out to the unfortunate Emir who had charge of the Treasury. Ahmed Wad Suliman had been accustomed under the Mahdi's mild rule to keep no public accounts, and consequently he had amassed a large fortune. He was actively hostile to Abdullahi, and proclaimed his sympathy with the Ashraf. Whereupon the Khalifa invited him to give an account of his stewardship. This he was, of course, unable to do. He was then dismissed from his appointment. His private property was taken to fill the deficiencies of the State, and the brutal population of Omdurman applauded his punishment as 'an act of justice.'[6]

Although the Khalifa might establish his authority by such atrocities, its maintenance depended on the military policy which he consistently pursued. The terrible power of a standing army may usually be exerted by whoever can control its leaders, as a mighty engine is set in motion by the turning of a handle. Yet to turn the handle some muscular force is necessary. Abdullahi knew that to rule the Soudan he must have a great army. To make the great army obedient he must have another separate force; for the influences which keep European armies in subjection were not present among the Dervishes. For some years, indeed, he was compelled to leave much to chance or the loyalty of his officers. But latterly, when he had perfected his organisation, he became quite independent and had no need to trust anyone. By degrees and with astonishing ability he carried out his schemes. He invited his own tribe, the Taiasha section of the Baggara Arabs, to come and live in Omdurman. 'Come,' he wrote in numerous letters to them, ' and take possession of the

5 Ohrwalder, *Ten Years' Captivity.*

6 Slatin, *Fire and Sword.*

lands which the Lord your God has given you.' Allured by the hopes of wealth and wives and the promise of power, the savage herdsmen came to the number of 7,000 warriors. Their path was made smooth and easy. Granaries were erected along the route. Steamers and sailing-vessels waited on the Nile. Arrived at the capital, all were newly clothed at the expense of the State. An entire district of the city was forcibly cleared of its inhabitants for the accommodation of the strangers.

What the generosity of the Khalifa forgot or refused, the predatory habits of his clansmen procured; and they robbed, plundered, and swindled with all the arrogance and impunity of royal favourites. The populace of the city returned a bitter hatred for these injuries; and the Khalifa's object was attained. He had created a class in Omdurman who were indissolubly attached to him. Like him, they were detested by the local tribes. Like him, they were foreigners in the land. But, like him, they were fierce and brave and strong. His dangers, his enemies, his interests were their own. Their lives depended on their loyalty.

Here was the motor muscle which animated the rest. The Taiasha Baggara controlled the black *Jehadia*, once the irregular troops of the Egyptians, now become the regulars of the Khalifa. The black Jehadia overawed the Arab army in the capital. The army in the capital dominated the forces in the provinces. The forces in the provinces subdued the inhabitants. The centralisation of power was assured by the concentration of military material. Cannon, rifles, stores of ammunition, all the necessities of war were accumulated in the arsenal. Only the armies on the frontiers, the Taiasha tribe, and the Khalifa's personal bodyguard habitually carried firearms and cartridges. The enormous population of Omdurman was forced to be content with spears and swords.

Rifles were issued to the Soudanese whenever safe and necessary; cartridges only when they were about to be used. Thus several millions of warlike and savage people, owning scarcely any law but that of might, and scattered about a vast roadless territory, were brought the firm grip of a single man.

The third principle of government which the Khalifa was compelled, or inclined, to adopt was to keep the relative power of the various tribes and classes conveniently proportioned. If an Emir rose to great influence and wealth, he became a possible rival, and suffered forthwith death, imprisonment, or spoliation. If a tribe threatened the supremacy of the Taiasha it was stricken down while its menace was vet a menace. The regulation of classes and tribes was a far more complicated affair than the adjustment of individuals. Yet for thirteen years the Khalifa held the balance, and held it exact until the very end. Such was the statecraft of a savage from Kordofan.

His greatest triumph was the Abyssinian war. It is not likely that two great barbaric kingdoms living side by side, but differing in race and religion, will long continue at peace; nor was it difficult to discover a cause of the quarrel between the Dervishes and the Abyssinians. After the fall of Khartoum and the retreat of the British army the garrison of Kassala still continued to hold out. The well-considered proposal of a British officer[7] to relieve the town by a small Indian brigade operating from Massowa was disdained, in spite of the heroic spectacle which the resistance of the Mudir presented.[8] Mr. Gladstone's Government, however, made attempts to induce the Abyssinians to undertake the relief. While these negotiations were dragging on, the Ministry changed, and the Conservatives, coming into power, carried them to their abortive result. The Abyssinian expedition failed. The town was taken and the garrison slaughtered. There, as far as Great Britain was concerned, the matter ended. But the Abyssinians had thus been placed in direct antagonism to their Dervish neighbours. Frontier raids were planned and resisted by both sides.

For some time a harassing and desultory warfare disturbed the border. At length in 1885 a Dervish—half-trader, half-brigand—sacked an Abyssinian church. Eas Adal, the Governor of the Amhara province, demanded that this sacrilegious robber should be surrendered to justice. The Arabs haughtily refused. The response was swift. Collecting an army which may have amounted to 30,000 men, the Abyssinians invaded the district of Gallabat and marched

7 Captain Speedy to Mr. Egerton, August 31, 1884.

8 There is extant a very pathetic telegram from Captain Speedy to Nubar Pasha, describing the Mudir's defence.

on the town. Against this host the Emir Wad Arbab could muster no more than 6,000 soldiers. But, encouraged by the victories of the previous four years, the Dervishes accepted battle, in spite of the disparity of numbers. Neither valour nor discipline could withstand such odds. The Moslems, broken by the fierce onset and surrounded by the overwhelming numbers of their enemies, were destroyed, together with their intrepid leader. Scarcely any escaped. The Abyssinians indulged in all the triumphs of savagery. The wounded were massacred: the slain were mutilated: the town of Gallabat was sacked and burnt. The women were carried into captivity. All these tidings came to Omdurman. Under this heavy and unexpected blow the Khalifa acted with prudence and promptitude. He opened negotiations with King John of Abyssinia for the ransom of the captured wives and children, and at the same time he sent the Emir Yunes with a large force to Gallabat. The immediate necessities having thus been dealt with, Abdullahi prepared for revenge.

Of all the Arab leaders which fifteen years of continual war and tumult throughout the Soudan produced, none displayed higher ability, none obtained greater successes, and none were more honourable, though several were more famous, than the man whom the Khalifa selected to avenge the destruction of the Gallabat army. Abu Anga had been a slave in Abdullahi's family long before the Mahdi had preached at Abba island and while Egypt yet oppressed the country. After the revolt had broken out, his adventurous master summoned him from the distant Kordofan home to attend him in the war, and Abu Anga came with that ready obedience and strange devotion for which he was always distinguished. Nominally as a slave, really as a comrade, he fought by Abdullahi's side in all the earlier battles of the rebellion. Nor was it until after the capture of El Obeid, that he rose suddenly to power and place. The Khalifa was a judge of men. He saw very clearly that the black Soudanese troops, who had surrendered and were surrendering as town after town was taken, might be welded into a powerful weapon. And in Abu Anga he knew a man who could not only fashion the blade, but would hold it ever loyally at his master's disposal. The former slave threw himself into the duties of his command with extraordinary energy. His humble origin pleased the hardy blacks, who recognised in their leader their equal in birth, their superior in prowess. More than any other Emir, Abu Anga contributed to the destruction of Hicks's army. The *Jehadia*, as his soldiers were called because they had joined in the *Jehad*[9]—were armed with Remington rifles, and their harassing fire inflicted heavy losses on the struggling column until it was finally brought to a standstill, and the moment for the spearmen to charge arrived. Henceforward the troops of Abu Anga became famous throughout the land for their weapons, their courage, and their cruelty. Their numbers at first did not exceed 5,000; but as more towns were taken and more slaves were turned into soldiers they increased, until at one time they reached the formidable total of 15,000 men.

During the siege of Khartoum the black riflemen distinguished themselves by the capture of Omdurman fort, but their violent natures and predatory instincts made them an undesirable garrison even for the Dervish capital, and they were despatched under their general to Kordofan, where they increased their reputation by a series of bloody fights with the Nubas, an aboriginal mountain people who cared for nothing but their independence.

While the general and his valiant riflemen were thus warring in Kordofan, events occurred which increased his own authority and the Khalifa's obligations. A mutiny broke out in El Obeid. Some 200 black soldiers, formerly belonging to the Egyptian Government, now in the service of the Khalifa and disgusted with their treatment, revolted. Beating down the Arab Emir and his forces, they marched in triumph to the Nuba mountains under the leadership of an ex-officer of the Khedivial army named Beshir. The Nubas welcomed the reinforcement with enthusiasm. Abu Anga was eager to attack. The Khalifa had, however, a still more important duty for him to perform. A great Sheikh in Darfur was meditating revolt. He had already collected a force of 3,000 riflemen and 1,000 horse, supported by a numerous armed rabble. Secret orders reached Abu Anga. Marching swiftly to the scene, he arrived while the rebellion was yet in embryo and surrounded the camp of the Sheikh. The morning light revealed to the revolutionists both the situation and its hopelessness. Their leader was sent in chains to Omdurman. His army swelled the force under Abu Anga, who now turned his at-

9 *Jehad* (Arabic) = 'Holy War.'—EDITOR.

tention from the rebels to the mutineers. He offered Beshir terms. They were rejected. On the next day therefore Abu Anga attacked with a large part of his force. He was, as usual, victorious. Beshir was killed, and his followers were 'forced to accept the pardon offered them'[10]—a mild punishment, considering their offence. Slatin's old servant, who was among the prisoners, was returned to him with a polite letter by the princely slave. After these affairs had been disposed of, the Khalifa summoned his faithful general to Omdurman, instructing him to bring his whole army and leave only a small detachment in Darfur. Abu Anga complied forthwith; yet I desire to relate two incidents which occurred before he started, that the reader may form some estimate of the character of this remarkable barbarian.

A poor woman complained that a soldier had robbed her of some milk which he drank. The culprit protested his innocence. The general was perplexed. At length a solution occurred to him. 'Rip open the man's stomach,' he said. 'If milk be found, he is justly punished; if not, let the woman die.' The operation was immediately performed, and the presence of the milk confirmed the justice of the judgment and vindicated the woman's testimony.[11] Otherwise the man would, of course, have been acquitted and the false witness slain. The milk was in any case spilt beyond recall.

The second incident reveals a loftier strain, since the prostitution of public authority to personal vengeance must always be censured. A certain Emir named Madibbo was convicted of treasonable practices and sentenced to death. Furious at being condemned by one of servile origin, the proud criminal broke out: 'A slave like you can never become noble. The traces of the lashes of my whip can still be seen on your back and were well deserved.'[12] Neither the memory of his old flogging nor the bitter taunts moved the just and inexorable Anga, and, although he could at his pleasure have inflicted the most frightful tortures, he abstained from interfering with the ordinary course of the law. Madibbo met his fate with composure, by a method in strict accordance with constitutional practice.

---

10 Slatin, *Fire and Sword*, p. 399.

11 Ohrwalder, *Ten Years' Captivity*, p. 246.

12 Slatin, *Fire and Sword*, p. 398.

At the end of June Abu Anga reached Omdurman with an army variously estimated at from 22,000 to 31,000 men, of whom at least 10,000 were armed with Remington rifles. The Khalifa received him with the utmost honour. After a private interview, which lasted for several hours, a formal entry into the town was arranged. At daybreak on the following morning the whole force marched into the city and camped along the northern suburbs, applauded and welcomed alike by the population and their ruler. A few days after this a great review was held under the Kerreri hills, on the very ground where the Dervish Empire was doomed to be shattered. But the fateful place oppressed the Khalifa with no forebodings. He exulted in his power: and well he might, for after the cannon had thundered indefinite salutes, no less than 100,000 armed men defiled to the music of the war-drums and the *Ombyas*[13] before the famous Black Flag.

The spectacle of the enormous numbers provoked their enthusiasm. The triumphant Khalifa was cheered by his mighty host, who pressed upon him in their exuberant loyalty until he was almost crushed. It was indeed a stirring scene. The whole plain was filled with the throng. Banners of every hue and shape waved gaily in the breeze, and the sunlight glinted from innumerable spearpoints. The swarming Dervishes displayed their bright parti-coloured *jibbas*. The wild Baggara cavalry circled on the flanks of the array. The brown dome of the Mahdi's Tomb, rising above the city, seemed to assure the warriors . of supernatural aid. Abdullahi was at the summit of his power. The movement initiated by the priest of Abba island had attained its climax. Behind, in the plain, the frowning rocks of Surgham Hill rose ragged and gloomy, as if their silence guarded the secrets of the future .

After the feast of Bairam had been celebrated on a gigantic scale, Abu Anga was despatched to Gallabat with his army and considerable reinforcements from the troops in Omdurman, and it became evident that war with Abyssinia was imminent. The great leader relieved the Emir Yunes, much to his disgust, of the chief command, and, since the strong Gallabat garrison was added to his own force, Abu Anga might take the field at the head of 15,000 riflemen, 45,000

13 War-horns made from the hollowed tusks of elephants.—EDITOR.

spearmen, and 800 horse.[14] The Khalifa had embarked on a great venture in planning the invasion of Abyssinia. The vast strength of the Negus was known to the Dervishes, and has since been proved to the world. The Mahdi had forbidden such a war. An ill-omened prophecy further declared that the King of Abyssinia would tether his horse to a solitary tree by Khartoum, while his cavalry should ride through the city, fetlock deep in blood. But Abdullahi feared neither God nor man. He reviewed the political situation, and determined at all risks to maintain his frontiers inviolate. His Emir Wad Arbab had been killed. Blood must settle the matter.

The Abyssinians had not watched the extensive hostile preparations apathetically. Ras Adal had collected an army which in numbers actually exceeded that of the Dervishes. But the latter were far superior in rifles, and the black infantry were of invincible valour. Nevertheless, confident in his strength and relying on his powerful cavalry, the Abyssinian general allowed the Arabs to toil through all the mountainous country, to traverse the Mintik Pass, and to debouch unmolested on to the plain of Debra Sin. Abu Anga neglected no precaution. He knew that since he must fight in the heart of Abyssinia, with the mountains behind him, a defeat would involve annihilation.

He drew up his army swiftly and with skill. Then the Abyssinians attacked. The rifle fire of the Soudanese repulsed them. The onset was renewed with desperate gallantry. It was resisted with equal valour and superior weapons. After frightful losses the Abyssinians wavered, and the wise Arab seized the moment for a counterstroke. In spite of the devotion of his cavalry Eas Adal was driven from the field. Great numbers of his army were drowned in the river in front of which he had recklessly elected to fight. His camp was captured, and a valuable spoil rewarded the victors, who also gratified their passions with a wholesale slaughter of the wounded—a practice commonly followed by savages. The effect of the victory was great. The whole of the Amhara province submitted to the invaders, and Abu Anga was able to advance without further fighting to the capture and sack of Gondar, the ancient capital of Abyssinia.

14 The cavalry were wisely reduced in number, on account of the hilly nature of the Abyssinian Highlands.—EDITOR.

Meanwhile the Khalifa had been anxiously expecting tidings of his army. The long silence of thirty days which followed their plunge into the mountains filled him with fear, and Ohrwalder relates that he 'aged visibly' during that period. But his judgment was proved by the event, and the arrival of a selected assortment of heads turned doubt to triumph. The Dervishes did not long remain in Abyssinia, as they suffered from the climate. In December the army returned to Gallabat, which they commenced to fortify, and their victorious general followed his grisly, but convincing despatch to Omdurman, where he received the usual welcome accorded by warlike peoples to military heroes. But the famous and faithful slave may have been more gratified by the tears of joy which his master and sovereign shed on beholding him again safe and successful.

The greater struggle was still to come. The whole of Abyssinia was convulsed with fury, and King John in person prepared to take the field and settle the quarrel for ever. He assembled a mighty host, which is said to have amounted to 130,000 foot and 20,000 horsemen. The rumours of this formidable concentration reached Gallabat and Omdurman, and in spite of the recent victory caused deep alarm. The Khalifa saw his frontiers—even his existence—menaced, for King John had declared that he would sweep the Dervishes from off the face of the earth: and in the hour of need the General on whom so much depended died of some poisonous medicine with which he had endeavoured to cure himself of indigestion. Abu Anga was buried in his red-brick house at Gallabat amid the lamentations of his brave black soldiers, and gloom pervaded the whole army. But, since the enemy were approaching, the danger had to be faced. The Khalifa appointed Zeki Tummal, one of Anga's lieutenants, to the command of the forces at Gallabat, which by strenuous exertions he brought up to a total of 85,000 men. King John sent word that he was coming, lest any should afterwards say that he had come secretly thief. The Dervishes resolved to remain on the defensive, and fortified themselves in an enormous *zeriba* around the town. Then they awaited the onslaught.

At dawn on the 9th of March the Abyssinians came within sight of their enemies, and early the next morning the battle began. Great clouds of dust obscured the scene, and all intelligible sounds were lost in the appalling din. The Abyssinians, undaunted by the rifle fire of the Soudanese, succeeded in setting the *zeriba* alight. Then, concentrating all their force on one part of the defence, they burst into the enclosure and town. The division of Wad Ali, a fourth part of the entire Dervish army, which bore the brunt of this attack, was almost completely destroyed. The interior of the *zeriba* was crowded with women and children, who were ruthlessly butchered by the exultant Abyssinians. The assailants scattered in all directions in search of plunder, and they even had time to begin to disinter the body of Abu Anga, which they were eager to insult in revenge for Gondar. The Dervishes wavered. Their ammunition began to fail. Suddenly a rumour spread about among the Abyssinians that the King was killed. Seizing what booty they could snatch, the victorious army began a general retreat and the *zeriba* was soon cleared. The Arabs were too exhausted to pursue, but when on the following day the attack was not renewed they learned, to their surprise, that they were the victors and that their enemy was falling back towards the Atbara river. Zeki Tummal resolved to pursue, and his army were further incited to the chase by the fact that the Abyssinians had carried off with them a large number of Dervish women, including the harem of the late beloved Abu Anga. Two days after the battle the Dervishes overtook the enemy's rearguard, and, surprising their camp, inflicted severe loss and captured much booty. The temporary Negus who had been appointed to fill the vacancy caused by the death of King John, was among the killed. The body of that courageous monarch fell into the hands of the Dervishes, who struck off the head and sent it—a tangible proof of victory—to Omdurman. The Abyssinians, still formidable, made good their retreat: nor did Zeki Tummal venture to follow into the mountains. Internal strife within his dominions prevented the new Negus from resuming the offensive, and thus the Dervish-Abyssinian war dwindled down to, as it had arisen out of, frontier raids.

The arrival in Omdurman of King John's head intoxicated the Khalifa with joy. Abyssinia was regarded throughout the Soudan as a far greater power than Egypt, and here was its mighty ruler slain and decapitated. But the victory had been dearly purchased. The two great battles had been fought with indescribable ferocity by both sides, and the slaughter was appalling. No reliable statistics are available, but it may be reasonably asserted that neither side sustained a loss in killed during the war of less than 30,000 fighting men. The flower of the Dervish army, the heroic blacks of Abu Anga, were almost destroyed. The Khalifa had won a Pyrrhic triumph. Never again was he able to put so great a force in the field, and, although the army which was shattered at Omdurman was better armed and better drilled, it was less formidable than that which broke the might of Abyssinia. I am drawn to the conclusion that even this small world is large enough for its inhabitants by the reflection that these tremendous battles with their prodigious slaughter excited no more interest in Europe than did the Franco-German war in the Soudan.

Next in importance after the Abyssinian war among the military undertakings of the Khalifa was the suppression of the western revolts. When Abu Anga was summoned to Omdurman to command the army at Gallabat he left his cousin, Osman-Wad-Adam, as his representative in El Obeid. This Emir, whose reputation had been made by his complete destruction of the Kabbabish or camel-breeding Arabs, was a man of little talent but great brutality. He harried and oppressed the population until they thought the Egyptian days were come back again. Every rope has its breaking strain; every liquid its boiling point. As soon as the troubles of life outweigh the fear of death a maddened people need only a leader to rise in revolt. As usual in the East, the leader was a fanatic. A young man sat under a fig-tree and preached, prayed, and fasted. His influence rapidly increased. Soon all admitted his miraculous powers. He could produce milk from his finger-tips. From a single plateful of food he could feed hundreds. Within the space of one hour he had raised a fruitful palm-tree from the desert sand. Is it quite wise to call such men impostors? These wild enthusiasts for the most part care nothing for the pains and pleasures of earthly life. They rise above a scene of misery and despair, and vaguely point to the promise of better things beyond the sky. They come to distressed peoples in their bitter hour of need, even as the Judges came to Israel and Judah. Behind them follows the fury of rebellion. Tyrants tremble and oppressors quake before the passions they arouse. And there be some who think they hear above the shrill fury of wronged thousands the heavy menace of an angered God.

From being a worker of miracles it was but a step to the command of an army: nor was it long before 'The Man of the Fig-tree,' Abu Gemaiza, headed a formidable revolt against Mahdism. Careless of consequences, he declared merciless war against all who wore the patched *jibba* and believed that Mohammed Ahmed was a holy Prophet. The Western Soudan seethed and fermented. Thousands flocked to the standard of the new deliverer. The forces which Osman-Wad-Adam despatched against him were annihilated, and that bloody man was closely penned in El Fasher. The Khalifa, who was at the same time confronted by the Abyssinian perils, sent him positive orders to remain on the defensive. But death terminated the career of the victorious 'Man of the Fig-tree,' and in the beginning of 1889, while still blockading El Fasher, he died of smallpox. The confidence of the rebels was destroyed: the inspiration had departed. The elated Osman sallied out of the town in which he had so long been beleaguered, and in a fierce battle under its walls on the 22nd of February, 1889, dispersed the besiegers. A great slaughter accompanied the struggle: a greater massacre followed the victory. The skull of the 'Man of the Fig-tree'—exhumed according to the customs of savages—met that of the Negus in the pit at Omdurman. The Khalifa, delighted at his general's success, prepared a special house for Osman near the mosque. But before the triumphant Emir could enjoy the honours he had won, he was summoned to answer for the crimes he had committed, and he died in the year of his victory near its scene at El Fasher.

During the progress of the struggle with Abyssinia the war against Egypt languished. The Mahdi, counting upon the support of the population, had always declared that he would free the Delta from 'the Turks,' and was already planning its invasion, when he and his schemes were interrupted by death. His successor inherited all the quarrel, but not all the power. Much of Mohammed Ahmed's influence died with him.

Alive, he might conquer the Moslem world; dead, he was only a saint. All fanatical feeling in Egypt soon subsided. Nevertheless the Khalifa persisted in the enterprise. He always feared the danger in the north. He felt the weight of a stronger hand; and, besides, war was a condition of his existence. The military operations—the trouble at Suakin, the actions of Ginniss, Gemaiza, Argin and Toski—will be noticed in the next chapter from the Egyptian point of view.

I will avoid repetition by examining only the Dervish motives. The success of the Abyssinian war encouraged and enabled the Khalifa to resume the offensive on his northern frontier, and he immediately ordered Wad-el-Nejumi, who commanded in Dongola, to march with his scanty force to the invasion of Egypt. The mad enterprise ended, as might have been foreseen, in the destruction of both Emir and army.

The Khalifa received the news with apparent grief, but it is difficult to avoid suspecting him of dark schemes. He was far too clever to believe that Egypt could be conquered by five thousand men. He knew that besides the Egyptians there was a strange white tribe of men, the same that had so nearly saved Khartoum. 'But for the English,' he exclaimed on several occasions, 'I would have conquered Egypt.' Yet, knowing of the British occupation, he deliberately sent an army to its inevitable ruin. It is difficult to reconcile such conduct with the character for sagacity and intelligence which Abdullahi has deserved. There is no doubt that he wanted to conquer Egypt. Possibly by some extraordinary chance Wad-el-Nejumi might succeed, even with his small force. If so, then the glory of God and the power of the Khalifa would advance together. If not and herein lies the true reason for the venture—the riverain tribes would have received a crippling blow.

The terrible slaughter of the Abyssinian war had fallen mainly on the Jehadia and the eastern Arabs. The jealous tribes in the north had not suffered. The balance of power was in need of readjustment. The Jaalin and Barabra were fast becoming dangerous. Nejumi's army was recruited almost entirely from these sources. The reinforcements sent from Omdurman consisted of men selected from the flag of the Khalifa Sherif, who was growing too powerful, and of the Batahin tribe, who had shown a mutinous spirit.[15] The success of such an army in Egypt would be glorious. Its destruction anywhere would be convenient. Whatever Abdullahi's motives may have been, his advantage was certain. But the life of the empire thus compelled to prey upon itself must necessarily be short.

15 Ohrwalder, *Ten Years' Captivity*.

Other forces were soon added to the work of exhaustion. The Tear following the end of the Abyssinian war was marked by a fearful famine. Slatin and Ohrwalder vie with each other in relating its horrors—men eating the raw entrails of donkeys; mothers devouring their babies; scores dying in the streets; all the more ghastly in the bright sunlight; hundreds of corpses floating down the Nile—these are among the hideous features. The depopulation caused by the scarcity was even greater than that produced by the fighting. Nature, more wholesale than any human engine of destruction, takes, when she is roused, a terrible vengeance.[16] The famine area extended over the whole Soudan and ran along the banks of the river as far as Lower Egypt. The deserted villages, which excited the indignation of the soldiers of the British expedition and have been made a heavy accusation against the Dervishes, protest the severity of Nature rather than the cruelty of man.

The effects of the famine were everywhere appalling. Entire districts between Omdurman and Berber became wholly depopulated. In the salt regions near Shendi almost all the inhabitants died of hunger. The camel breeding tribes ate their she-camels. The riverain peoples devoured their seed-corn. The population of Gallabat, Gedaref, and Kassala was reduced by nine-tenths, and these once considerable towns shrank to the size of hamlets. Everywhere the deserted mud houses crumbled back into the plain. The frightful mortality, general throughout the whole country, may be gauged by the fact that Zeki Tummal's army, which before the famine numbered not less than 87,000 could scarcely muster 10,000 men in the spring of 1890.

The new harvest came only in time to save the inhabitants of the Soudan from becoming extinct. The remnant were preserved for further misfortunes. War, scarcity, and oppression there had always been. But strange and mysterious troubles began to afflict the tortured tribes. The face of Heaven was pitiless or averted. In 1890 innumerable swarms of locusts descended on the impoverished soil.

16 I cannot help reflecting that in this town (Bangalore) in which I write the present chapter, no fewer than 6,500 persons have perished in four months of plague—an unnoticed slaughter nearly as great as that at Omdurman. The machinery of modern war is still defective. Someday science make call the mighty *bacillus* into the disputes of nations.

The multitude of their red or yellow bodies veiled the sun and darkened the air, and although their flesh, tasting when roasted like fried fish, might afford a delicate meal to the natives, they took so heavy a toll of the crops that the famine was prolonged and scarcity became constant. Since their first appearance the locusts are said to have returned annually.[17] Their destructive efforts were aided by millions of little red mice, who destroyed the seeds before they could grow. So vast and immeasurable was the number of these tiny pests that after a heavy rain the whole country was strewn with, and almost tinted by the squirrel-coloured corpses of the drowned.

Yet, in spite of all the strokes of fate, the Khalifa maintained his authority unshaken. The centralisation which always occurs in military States was accelerated by the famine. The provincial towns dwindled; thousands and tens of thousands perished; but Omdurman continually grew, and its ruler still directed the energies of a powerful army. Thus for the present I would leave the Dervish Empire. Yet the gloomy city of blood, mud, and filth that arose by the confluence of the Niles deserves a final glance while still in the pride of independent barbarism.

It is early morning, and the sun, lifting above the horizon, throws the shadows of the Khartoum ruins on the brimful waters of the Nile. The old capital is solitary and deserted. No sound of man breaks the silence of its streets. Only memory broods in the garden where the Pashas used to walk, and the courtyard where the Imperial envoy fell. Across the river miles of mud houses, lining the banks as far as Khor Shambat, and stretching back into the desert and towards the dark hills, display the extent of the Arab metropolis.

As the sun rises, the city begins to live. Along the road from Kerreri a score of camels pad to market with village produce. The north wind is driving a dozen sailingboats, laden to the water's edge with merchandise, to the wharfs. One of Gordon's old steamers lies moored by the bank. Another, worked by the crew that manned it in Egyptian days, is threshing up the Blue Nile, sent by the Khalifa to Sennar on some errand of State. Ear away to the southward the dust of a Darfur caravan breaks the clear-cut skyline with a misty blur. The prolonged beating of war-drums and loud booming notes

17 Ohrwalder, *Ten Years' Captivity in the Soudan.*

of horns chase away the silence of the night. It is Friday, and after the hour of prayer all grown men must attend the review on the plain without the city. Already the streets are crowded with devout and obedient warriors. Soon the great square of the mosque—for no roof could shelter so many thousand worshippers—is filled with armed men, kneeling in humble supplication to the stern God of Islam and his most holy Mahdi. It is finished. They rise and hurry to the parade. The Emirs plant their flags, and all form in the ranks. Woe to the laggard; and let the speedy see that he wear his newest *jibba*, and carry a sharp sword and at least three spears. Presently the array is complete.

A salute of seven guns is fired. Mounted on a fine camel, which is led by a gigantic Nubian, and attended by perhaps two hundred horsemen in chain armour, the Khalifa rides on to the ground and along the ranks. It is a good muster. Few have dared absent themselves. Yet his brow is clouded. What has happened? Is there another revolt in the west? Do the Abyssinians threaten Gallabat? Have the black troops mutinied; or is it only some harem quarrel?

The parade is over. The troops march back to the arsenal. The rifles are collected and the warriors disperse to their homes. Many hurry to the market-place to make purchases, to hear the latest rumour, or to watch the executions—for there are usually executions. Others stroll to the Suk-er-Rekik and criticise the points of the slave girls as the dealers offer them for sale. But the Khalifa has returned to his house, and his council have been summoned. The room is small, and the ruler sits cross-legged upon an *angarib*.[18] Before him squat the Emirs and Kadis. Yakub is there, with Ali-Wad-Helu and the Khalifa Sherif. Only the Sheikh-ed-Din is absent, for he is a dissolute youth and much given to drinking.

Abdullahi is grave and anxious. A messenger has come from the north. The Turks are on the move. Advancing beyond their frontier, they have established themselves at Akasha. Wad Bishara fears lest they may attack the faithful *Ansar*[19] who hold Firket. In itself this is but a small matter, for all these years there has been frontier fighting. But what follows is full of menacing significance. The 'enemies

18 A native bed, identical with the Indian *charpoy*.

19 *Ansar* = helpers in the Holy War.

of God' have begun to repair the railway—have repaired it, so that the train already runs beyond Sarras. Even now they push their iron road out into the desert towards their position at Akasha and to the south. What is the object of their toil? Are they coming again? Will they bring those terrible white soldiers who broke the hearts of the Hadendoa and almost destroyed the Degheim and Kenana? What should draw them up the Nile? Is it for plunder, or in sheer love of war; or is it a blood feud that brings them? True, they are now far off. Perchance they will return, as they returned before. Yet the iron road is not built in a day, nor for a day. Of a surety there are war-clouds in the north.

CHAPTER V
THE YEARS OF PREPARATION

Weariness—A transformation scene—'England in Egypt'—Regeneration—The Egyptian army—The European system—The Egyptian soldier—The test of war—Increase of the army—'Sambo'—The defence of the frontier—Suakin—The lean years—The sword of re-conquest—Herbert Kitchener—His education—He learns Arabic—Kitchener in 1882—A military crime—Its reward—Kitchener in the Nile expedition—Gordon's complaints—Governor of Suakin—Handub—Adjutant-General—The post of Sirdar—Colonel Wode- house—Cromer's choice—The Intelligence Department—Fugitives from Omdurman—Change of public opinion in England—Sentimental, fanatical, and political causes—The opinion of the Cabinet—Adowa—The immediate cause—Some diplomatic arrangements—The Egyptian point of view—War or water—The beginning of the expedition—A financial digression—The fetters of Egypt—The Caisse de la Dette—Political justice—'Extraordinary expenses'—The French action—Their triumph—An unexpected development—Decline of French influence.

In the summer of 1886, when all the troops had retreated to Wady Halfa and all the Soudan garrisons had been massacred, the British people averted their eyes in shame and vexation from the valley of the Nile. A long succession of disasters had reached their disgraceful culmination. The dramatic features added much to the bitterness and nothing to the grandeur of the tragedy. The cost was heavy. Besides the pain produced by the death of General Gordon, the heavy losses in officers and men, and the serious expenditure of public money, the nation smarted under failure and disappointment, and were, moreover, deeply sensible that they had been humiliated before the whole world. The situation in Egypt was scarcely more pleasing. The reforms initiated by the British Administrators had as yet only caused unpopularity. Baring's interference galled the Khedive and his Ministers. Vincent's parsimony excited contempt. Moncrieft's energy had convulsed the Irrigation Department. Wood's army was the laughing-stock of Europe. Among and beneath the rotten weeds and garbage of old systems and abuses the new seed was being sown. But England saw no signs of the crop; saw only the stubborn husbandmen begrimed with the dust and dirt, and herself hopelessly involved in the Egyptian muddle: and so in utter weariness and disgust, stopping her ears to the gibes and cat-calls of the Powers, she turned towards other lands and other matters.

Great and impressive are the effects of contrast. A prosperous man fallen into poverty, a happy man become miserable, a beautiful woman grown suddenly ugly, are woeful spectacles. And on the other hand when evil things give place to good, besides the subtraction of the pain and the addition of the pleasure, there is an extra delight—the joy of relief. When the attention of the nation was again directed to Egypt the scene was transformed. It was as though at the touch of an angel the dark morasses of the Slough of Despond had been changed to the breezy slopes of the Delectable Mountains. The Khedive and his Ministers lay quiet and docile in the firm grasp of the Consul-General. The bankrupt State was spending surpluses upon internal improvement. The disturbed Irrigation Department was vivifying the land. The derided army held the frontier against all comers.

Astonishment gave place to satisfaction, and satisfaction grew into delight. The haunting nightmare of Egyptian politics ended. Another dream began—a bright if vague vision of Imperial power, of trans-continental railways, of African Viceroys, of conquest and commerce. The interest of the British people in the work of regeneration grew continually. The fascination of doing good began to appeal to men of many classes. Each new reform was hailed with applause. Each annual Budget was scrutinised with pride. England exulted in the triumph of failure turned into success. There was a general wish to know more about Egypt and the men who had done these great things. In 1893 this desire was satisfied and yet stimulated by the publication of Sir Alfred Milner's 'England in

Egypt.' His skilful pen displayed what had been overcome, no less than what was accomplished. By explaining the difficulties he enhanced the achievement. He showed how, while Great Britain was occupied elsewhere, her brilliant, persevering sons had repeated on a lesser scale in Egypt the marvellous evolution which is working out in India. Smaller systems circulate more rapidly. The Administrators were guided by experience. The movement had been far swifter. The results were more surprising. Such was the wonderful story, and it was told in a happy moment. The audience were eager and sympathetic. The subject was enthralling. The story-teller had a wit and a style that might have brightened the dullest theme. In these propitious circumstances the book was more than a book. The words rang like the trumpet-call which rallies the soldiers after the parapets are stormed, and summons them to complete the victory.

The summons was not unheeded. If there had been a change in Egypt since 1880, there had also been a change in England. The idea of Imperial Democracy—a great empire ruled under the crown by a greater people—was no longer a philosophic dream. The spark which had fallen in the principal towns and centres of thought and action had been fanned into a flame which burned bright and steady during the years of recovery following the Home Rule crisis of 1886; and though in 1892 the flame flickered in the breath of Mr. Gladstone's eloquence, it blazed all the brighter when that terrible power was withdrawn. And it came to pass that men looked towards Egypt, and so remembered the lost provinces and the tragedy with which the name 'Khartoum' must, despite all later successes, be for ever associated.

The regeneration of Egypt is not a theme which would fall within the limits of this account, even if it had not been fully—though, I hope, not finally—dealt with by Sir Alfred Milner. But the reorganisation of the Egyptian army, the forging of the weapon of reconquest, is an essential feature. I would willingly transcribe whole pages of 'England in Egypt' on this subject, were it not incongruous to patch the garb of a wayfarer with the raiment of a king. But though I choose my own words, the ground covered is the same.

On the 20th of December, 1882, the old Egyptian army—or, rather, such parts as had escaped destruction was disbanded by a single sentence of a British decree. The sure foundation of society is force, and it was evident that some military body must replace that which had been swept away. To try to make soldiers of the Egyptians seemed a task better suited to the students of Laputa than to ordinary men. It appeared easier to draw sunbeams out of cucumbers than to put courage into the *fellah*. All sorts of schemes for the employment of foreign legions or Turkish janissaries were devised. But Lord Dufferin—to his honour—adhered firmly to the principle of entrusting the defence of a country to its inhabitants. It was determined to form a new Egyptian army. The poverty of the Government, no less than the apparent folly of the experiment, demanded that the new army should be small. The force was intended only for the preservation of internal order and the defence of the eastern and western frontiers of Egypt against the Bedouin Arabs. The Soudan still slumbered out its long nightmare. Six thousand men was the number originally drawn by conscription—for there are no volunteers in Egypt—from a population of more than 6,000,000. Twenty-six British officers—either poor men attracted by the high rates of pay, or ambitious allured by the increased authority—and a score of excellent drill-sergeants undertook the duty of teaching the recruits to fight. Sir Evelyn Wood directed the enterprise, and became the first British *Sirdar* of the Egyptian army. The work began and immediately prospered. Within three months of its formation the army had its first review. The whole 6,000 paraded in their battalions and marched past the Khedive and their country's flair. Their bearing and their drill extorted the half-contemptuous praise of the indifferent spectators. Experienced soldiers noticed other points. Indeed, the new army differed greatly from the old. In the first place, it was paid. The recruits were treated with justice. Their rations were not stolen by the officers. They were given leave to go to their villages from time to time. When they fell sick, they were sent to hospital instead of being flogged. In short, the European system was substituted for the Oriental. That of itself was a complete revolution. Still the difficulties appeared insuperable; for it is beyond dispute that the Egyptian is not a fighting animal.

It was hardly possible that the fertile soil and enervating climate of the Delta would have evolved a warrior race. Ages of oppression and poverty rarely produce proud and warlike spirits. Patriotism

A SOUDANESE PIPER.

does not grow under the 'Kourbash.' The *fellah* soldier lacks the desire to kill. Even the Mohammedan religion has failed to excite his ferocity. He may be cruel. He is never fierce. Yet he is not without courage—a courage which bears pain and hardship in patience, which confronts ill-fortune with indifference, and which looks on death with apathetic composure. It is the courage of down-trodden peoples, and one which stronger breeds may often envy, though they can scarcely be expected to admire. He has other military virtues. He is obedient, honest, sober, well-behaved, quick to learn, and above all physically strong. Generations of toiling ancestors, though they could not brace his nerves, have braced his muscles. Under the pressure of local circumstances there has been developed a creature who can work with little food, with little incentive, very hard for long hours under a merciless sun. Throughout the river campaigns, if the intellect of the army, if the spirit of the troops, have come from without, Egypt herself has provided the sinews of war.

Such was the material out of which the British officers have formed the new Egyptian army. At first, indeed, their task was embittered by the ridicule of their comrades in the British and Indian services; but as the drill and bearing of the force improved, the thoughtless scorn would have been diverted from the Englishmen to fall only upon the Egyptian soldiers. But this was not allowed. The British officers identified themselves with their men. Those who abused the *fellah* soldier were reminded that they insulted English gentlemen. Thus a strange bond of union was established between the officers and soldiers of the Egyptian service; and although material forces may have accomplished much, without this moral factor the extraordinary results would never have been achieved.

It was not long before the new military organisation was exposed to the stern test of war. The army that was raised to preserve internal order was soon called upon to guard the frontier. The revolt in the Soudan, which in its earlier stages seemed the least of the Egyptian difficulties, speedily dwarfed all the rest.

The value of the new force was soon recognised. In June 1883 we find General Hicks preparing for his fatal march, writing to Sir Evelyn Wood: 'Send me four battalions of your new army, and I shall be content.' But fortune protected the infant organisation from such a disastrous beginning.

The 'new army' remained for a space in Cairo; and although during the Nile expedition of 1884–85 the Egyptians were employed guarding the lines of communication, it was not until the British troops had been withdrawn from Dongola, that they received at Ginniss their baptism of fire. Henceforth their place was on the frontier, and from 1886 onward the Egyptian troops proved equal to the task of resisting the northward pressure of the Dervishes.

The numbers of the army grew with its responsibilities. Up to the end of 1883 the infantry still consisted of eight *fellahin* battalions. In 1884 the first Soudanese battalion was raised. The black soldier was of a very different type from the *fellahin*. The Egyptian was strong, patient, healthy, and docile. The negro was in all these respects his inferior. His delicate lungs, slim legs, and loosely knit figure contrasted unfavourably with the massive frame and iron constitution of the peasant of the Delta. Always excitable and often insubordinate, he required the strictest discipline. At once slovenly and uxorious, he detested his drills and loved his wives with equal earnest-

SAMBO'S' WIFE.

ness. Often his teeth carefully sharpened into points, betrayed the cannibal habits of his ancestral tribe; and altogether 'Sambo'—for such is the Soudanese equivalent of 'Tommy'—was a lazy, fierce, disreputable child. But he displayed two tremendous military virtues. To the faithful loyalty of a dog he added the heart of a lion. He loved his officer, and feared nothing in the world. With the introduction of this element the Egyptian army became a formidable military machine. Chance or design has placed the blacks ever in the forefront of the battle, and in Lord Kitchener's campaigns on the Nile the losses in the six Soudanese battalions have exceeded the aggregate of the whole of the rest of the army.

It was well that the Egyptian troops were strengthened by these valiant auxiliaries, for years of weary war lay before them. Sir Reginald Wingate, in his exhaustive account of the struggle of Egypt with the Mahdist power,[1] has described the successive actions which accompanied the defence of the Wady Halfa frontier and of Suakin. I shall not attempt to do more than recapitulate them. After the re-

1 *Mahdism and the Egyptian Soudan.* Sir Reginald Wingate.

treat of the British expedition in 1885 the Dervishes pressed steadily northward. They soon came in contact with the frontier force, and at Ginniss, on the last day but one of the year, they sustained a severe repulse at the hands of Sir Frederick Stephenson. Three years of raids and reprisals followed; while the Khalifa, in the intervals of his Abyssinian wars, was preparing for the invasion of Egypt. In 1889 this hopeless enterprise began. Wad-el-Nejumi, the Emir who had defeated Hicks and led the assault on Khartoum, started from Dongola with about 5,000 warriors. The Sirdar, at that time General Grenfell, awaited him. Colonel Wodehouse, the commander of the frontier force, hung on his flank, headed him from the river, and on the 2nd of July defeated a strong detachment of his army in the small but brilliant action of Argin. The Dervish main body, however, marched resolutely on, and on the 3rd of August were practically destroyed by General Grenfell at Toski. Wad-el-Nejumi, and with him whatever designs the Khalifa may have had upon Egypt, perished. The Wady Halfa frontier became again the scene of raids and desultory skirmishes; but all danger of a Dervish invasion of Egypt passed away.

The fighting round Suakin was the cause of greater loss of life and of less satisfaction. In 1885, after the fall of Khartoum, and while the idea of re-conquering the Soudan was cherished by the Liberal Administration, an expedition of 13,000 British and Indian troops had been sent to Suakin.[2] At Hashin (March 20), Tofivk (March 22), and Tamai (April 3) this force engaged the Dervishes under Osman Digna, without other result than the heavy loss of valuable lives. The growing unpopularity of the disastrous warfare in the Soudan and the difficulty with Russia in Afghanistan obliged or persuaded the Radical Ministers to abandon the attempt. The railway was broken up; the expedition, having lost nearly 800 men killed and wounded, was re-embarked; and Suakin settled down into a permanent state of blockade. In 1888 the Dervish activity increased and Osman Digna advanced upon the town. The action of Handub followed, and lighting continued throughout the year. In December Sir Francis Grenfell was sent from Cairo with a single British battalion and some Egyptian reinforcements. A successful, though purposeless

2 Map, 'Around Suakin.' Page 141.

engagement was fought at Geniaiza, outside Suakin, on the 20th of December. The disturbances continued actively until in 1891 Colonel Holled Smith, defeating the Dervishes at Afafit, occupied Osman Digna's base in the Tokar delta. This was a serious blow to the influence of the Emir, and, although the country around Suakin was freely raided by the Dervishes, no important operations were thereafter attempted on either side.

The ten years that elapsed between Ginnis and the first movements of the expedition of re-conquest were the dreary years of the Egyptian army. The service was hard and continual. Though the operations were petty, an untiring vigilance was imperative.

The public eye was averted. A pitiless economy was everywhere enforced. The British officer was deprived of his leave and the Egyptian private of his rations, that a few pounds might be saved to the Egyptian Treasury. The clothing of the battalions wore thin and threadbare, and sometimes their boots were so bad that the soldiers' feet bled from the cutting edges of the rocks, and the convoy escorts left their trails behind them. But preparation was ever going forward. The army improved in efficiency, and the constant warfare began to produce, even among the *fellahin* infantry, experienced soldiers. The officers, sweltering at weary Wady Halfa and Suakin, looked at the gathering resources of Egypt and out into the deserts of the declining Dervish Empire and knew that some day their turn would come. The sword of re-conquest which Evelyn Wood had forged, and Grenfell had tested, was gradually sharpened; and when the process was almost complete, the man who was to wield it presented himself.

Horatio Herbert Kitchener, the eldest son of a lieutenant-colonel, was born in 1850, and, after being privately educated, entered in 1869 the Royal Military Academy at Woolwich as a cadet of the Royal Engineers. He passed through the ordinary routine of a military training without attracting the attention of his comrades or instructors either by promise in study or prowess in athletics. In the spring of 1871 he obtained his commission, and for the first ten years of his military service remained an obscure officer, performing his duties with regularity, but giving no promise of the talents and character which he was afterwards to display. One powerful weapon, however, he acquired in this time of waiting. In 1874 accident or instinct led him to seek employment in the surveys that were being made of Cyprus and Palestine, and in the latter country he learned Arabic. For six years the advantage of knowing a language with which few British officers were familiar brought him no profit. For procuring military preferment Arabic was in 1874 as valueless as Patagonian. All this was swiftly changed by the surprising course of events. The year 1882 brought the British fleet to Alexandria, and the connection between England and Egypt began to be apparent

Kitchener did not neglect his opportunity. Securing leave of absence, he hurried to the scene of crisis. The delays which preceded actual hostilities devoured his leave, though at his earnest request it was once extended, and while Arabi was still strengthening his fortifications the time when Kitchener must return to the crashing routine of ordinary duty arrived. But the political climax was also approaching. The British residents in Alexandria were advised to embark in refuge ships. On a steamer in the harbour the future martinet meditated disobedience of orders. Should he break his leave or not? As a last chance he applied for a further extension. He felt that it would be refused, and it was at the suggestion of a newspaper correspondent that he added that he would assume it granted unless he was recalled by telegraph. The telegram came with promptness, but it fell into the hands of the friendly newspaper correspondent, who did not manage to deliver it until the weekly Cyprus mail had left, and compliance with its orders was for the time being impossible.

Thus a week was gained. Much might happen before the week was out. The event was fortunate.

Four days later Alexandria was bombarded. Detachments from the fleet were landed to restore order. The British Government decided to send an army to Egypt. British officers and soldiers were badly wanted at the seat of the war; an officer who could speak Arabic was indispensable.

Thus Kitchener came to Egypt and set his feet firmly on the high road to fortune. It is strange that the soldier who is at this moment the bitterest opponent of the Press that modern militarism has yet produced in England, should have received much material assistance at the turning-point of his life from a 'special correspondent,' and that the General who, in the interests of regularity, has opposed—always uncompromisingly, though sometimes unsuccessfully —the enterprising subaltern, should have based his success upon an act of pardonable indiscipline. But it is his work and not his character that now claims our attention. He came to Egypt when she was plunged in misery and shame, when hopeless ruin seemed already the only outcome of the public disasters, and when even greater misfortunes impended. He remained to see her prosperous and powerful; to restore empire to her people, peace to her empire, honour to her army; and among those clear-minded men of action by whom the marvellous work of regeneration has been accomplished, Herbert Kitchener will occupy certainly the third, and possibly even the second place.

Lord Wolseley on his arrival soon found employment for the active officer who could speak Arabic. As a major of Egyptian cavalry he served through the campaign of 1882. He joined the new army which was formed at the conclusion of the war, as one of the original twenty-six officers. In the Nile expedition of 1885 Arabic again led him to the front, and in the service of the Intelligence Department he found ample opportunity for his daring and energy. His efforts to communicate with Gordon in Khartoum did not, however, meet with much success, and the 'Journals' bristle with so many sarcastic comments that their editor has been at pains to explain in his preface that there was really no cause for complaint. One incident is scarcely covered by this assurance. It is best related in Gordon's own laconic words:—

'A curious thing has happened; my friend Kitchener sent up the post; he wrapped the letters in some old newspapers (he gave me no news in his letter), the old newspapers were thrown out in the garden: there a clerk who knew some English found them blowing about, and gave them to the apothecary of the hospital, who knows English. The doctor found him reading them, saw date 15th *September*, and secured them for me; they are like gold, as you may imagine, since we have had no news since 24th February, 1884!'[3]

Major Kitchener, however, gave satisfaction to his superiors in Cairo, if not to the exacting General at Khartoum, and in 1886 he

3 *Gordon's Journals at Khartoum*, November 5, 1884.

was appointed Governor of Suakin. This post, always one of responsibility and danger, did not satisfy Kitchener, whose ambition was now taking definite form. Eager for more responsibility and more danger, he harried and raided the surrounding tribes; he restricted and almost destroyed the slender trade which was again springing up, and in consequence of his measures the neighbourhood of Suakin was soon in an even greater ferment than usual. This culminated at the end of 1887 in the re-appearance and advance of Osman Digna. The movements of the Dervishes were, however, uncertain. The defences of the town had been greatly strengthened and improved by the skill and activity of its new Governor.[4]

Osman Digna retreated. The 'friendlies' were incited to follow, and Kitchener, although he had been instructed not to employ British officers or Egyptian regulars in offensive operations, went out in support. At Handub on the morning of the 17th of January, 1888, the friendlies attacked the camp of Osman Digna. They were at first successful; but while they dispersed to plunder, the enemy rallied and, returning, drove them back with loss. Kitchener arrived on the field with the support, to find a defeat instead of a victory awaiting him. He bravely endeavoured to cover the retreat of the friendlies, and in so doing was severely—as it as it first seemed dangerously—wounded in the jaw.

The loss among the friendlies and the support amounted to twenty men killed and two British officers, and twenty-eight men wounded. The Governor returned in great pain and some discomfiture to Suakin. In spite of his wound and his reverse he was impatient to renew the conflict, but this was definitely forbidden by the British Government. Colonel Kitchener's military conduct was praised, but his policy was prevented.

'The policy which it is desirable to follow ... in the Eastern Soudan,' wrote Sir Evelyn Baring on the 14th of March, in measured rebuke, 'should consist in standing purely on the defensive against any hostile movement or combination of the Arab tribes, in avoid-

4 See dispatch from Major General Dormer to War Office, Cairo, April 22nd 1888: 'With regard to the military works and defences of this town, I was much struck with the great improvement that has been affected by Colonel Kitchener since my last visit to Saukin in the autumn of 1884.'

ing any course of action which might involve the ultimate necessity of offensive action, and in encouraging legitimate trade by every means in our power.'[5]

The Governor could scarcely be expected to carry out a policy so much at variance with his views and inclinations, and in the summer of 1888 he was transferred to a purely military appointment and became Adjutant-General of the Egyptian army. For the next four years he worked busily in the War Office at Cairo, effecting many useful reforms and hard economies, and revealing strange powers of organisation, which, although not yet appreciated by his comrades in the Egyptian service, were noticed by one vigilant eye. In 1892 Sir F. Grenfell resigned the post of Sirdar, and the chief command of the Egyptian army was vacant. Two men stood out prominently as candidates—Colonel Wodehouse, who held the command of the Halfa Field Force, and- the Adjutant-General.

Colonel Wodehouse had undoubtedly the greater claims. He had been for several years in command of a large force in continual contact with the enemy. He had won the action of Argin, and was known throughout the Soudan as 'the conqueror of Wad-el-Nejumi.' He had conducted the civil administration of the frontier province with conspicuous success, and he was popular with all ranks of the Egyptian army.

Kitchener had little to set against this. He had shown himself a brave and active soldier. He was known to be a good official. But he had been a failure in civil administration, and was moreover little known to and less liked by his brother officers. Sir Evelyn Baring's influence, however, turned the scale. To the astonishment—indeed, to the disgust—of the Egyptian army, Kitchener was promoted Sirdar. Wodehouse retired from the Khedivial service, and, having commanded 7,000 men in war, became the officer in charge of a single battery of Horse Artillery. He carried with him to India, however, the regrets of his comrades-in-arms and a high reputation, which, in spite of an unfortunate wound, he fully maintained in the Frontier War.

Lord Cromer had found the military officer whom he considered capable of re-conquering the Soudan when the opportunity should

5 Sir E. Baring to Consul Cameron, March 14, 1888.

come. He set his opinion against many facts and considerations. But it must be owned that time has justified his choice. The support which he gave to Kitchener at this important crisis in his career has been continued to the present day. In many moments of doubt and difficulty the General looked towards the British Agent, and always found confidence and encouragement, 'Whatever you do, and whatever may happen, I will support you. You are the best judge of the situation.' Such was the telegram that preceded the battle of the Atbara; and as it describes the attitude of the great Administrator to his subordinates, so in some measure it explains the wonderful work they have done.

The years of preparation, wasted by no one in Egypt, were employed by no department better than by the Intelligence Branch. The greatest disadvantage from which Lord Wolseley had suffered was the general ignorance of the Soudan and its peoples. The British soldiers had to learn the details of Dervish fighting by bitter experience. But the experience, once gained, was carefully preserved. The Intelligence Branch of the Egyptian army rose under the direction of Colonel (now Sir Reginald) Wingate to an extraordinary efficiency. For ten years the history, climate, geography, and inhabitants of the Soudan were the objects of a ceaseless scrutiny. The sharp line between civilisation and savagery was drawn at Wady Halfa; but beyond that line, up the great river, within the great wall of Omdurman, into the arsenal, into the treasury, into the mosque, into the Khalifa's house itself, the spies and secret agents of the Government—disguised as traders, as warriors, or as women—worked their stealthy way. Sometimes the road by the Nile was blocked, and the messengers must toil across the deserts to Darfur, and so by a tremendous journey creep into Omdurman. At others a trader might work his way from Suakin or from the Italian settlements. But by whatever route it came, information—whispered at Halfa, catalogued at Cairo—steadily accumulated, and the diaries of the Intelligence Department grew in weight and number, until at last every important Emir was watched and located, every garrison estimated, and even the endless intrigues and brawls in Omdurman were carefully recorded. In the centre of the elaborate system of investigation which he had created sat Sir Reginald Wingate, a military Lecoq, applying to the perplexing masses of detail a keen intelligence, guided

REGINALD WINGATE

by profound study and experience; and thus throughout the years of preparation the increasing exhaustion of the Dervish Empire was silently contemplated by its inexorable foes.

The reports of the spies were at length confirmed and amplified by two most important witnesses. At the end of 1891 Father Ohrwalder made his escape from Omdurman and reached the Egyptian territory. Besides giving the Intelligence Department much valuable information, he published a thrilling account of his captivity,[6] which created a wide and profound impression in England. In 1895 a still more welcome fugitive reached Assuan. Early on the 16th of March a weary, travel-stained Arab, in a tattered *jibba* and mounted on a lame and emaciated camel, presented himself to the Commandant. He was received with delighted wonder, and forthwith conducted to the best bath-room available. Two hours later a little Austrian gentleman stepped forth, and the telegraph hastened to tell the news that Slatin, sometime Governor of Darfur, had escaped from the Khalifa's clutches. Here at last was a man who knew everything that concerned the Dervish Empire—Slatin, the Khalifa's trusted and confidential servant, almost his friend, who had lived with him, who was even permitted to dine with him alone, who had heard all his counsels, who knew all his Emirs, and moreover Slatin, the soldier and administrator, who could appreciate all he had learned, was added with the rank of Pasha to the staff of the Intelligence Department. While his accurate knowledge confirmed the belief of the Egyptian authorities that the Dervish power was declining, his tale of 'Fire and Sword in the Soudan' increased the horror and anger of thoughtful people in England at the cruelties of the Khalifa. Public opinion began to veer towards the policy of re-conquest.

I shall not try to trace the course of the gradual change that took place. Its characteristics may, however, be noted. There had always been the military spirit, which regarded the evacuation of the Soudan with shame and horror, and was eager now, as on all other occasions, to at once restore the honour and extend the frontiers of the Empire. This may not be a very broad, but it is a very powerful, influence —for it is ceaselessly applied. It is, moreover, often exerted by men of capacity, possessed of expert information,

6 *Ten Years' Captivity in the Mahdi's Camp*, Father Ohrwalder.

occupying responsible positions, and enjoying the power of giving official expression to their views in reports, despatches, and Blue Books. This military spirit was aroused no less by the memory of Khartoum than by that of Majuba Hill. But in the former case it received a great accession of strength from the emotions which the closing scenes in the life of General Gordon had excited. The personal character of 'the Christian hero' had produced a profound impression upon the people of Great Britain. His death at the hands of infidel savages transformed him into something like a martyr. There was an earnest desire on the part of a pious nation to dissociate his name from failure.

The idea of revenge, ever attractive to the human heart, appeared to receive the consecration of religion. What community is altogether free from fanaticism? The spirit of the Crusaders stirred beneath the surface of scientific civilisation; and as the years passed by, there continued in England a strong undercurrent of public opinion which ran in the direction of 'a holy war.' The publication of the books of Ohrwalder and Slatin added a third to these already powerful forces. The misery of the Dervish dominions appealed to that great volume of generous humanitarian feeling which sways our civilised State. Extremes of thought met. Jingoism found—not for the first time—support at Exeter Hall. The name of Gordon fused the military, the fanatical, and the philanthropic spirits into one strong and moving influence; to this were added the impulse of the national pride in the regeneration of Egypt and the momentum of modern Imperialism; and these three forces—the sentimental, the intellectual, and the political—gradually overcame the fear and hatred of Soudan warfare which a long series of profitless campaigns had created in the mind of the average taxpayer. The re-conquest of the Soudan became again, as far as British public opinion was concerned, a practical question.

The year 1895 brought in a Conservative and Unionist Administration. A Government came into office supported by a majority which was so strong that there seemed little reason to expect a transference of power for five or six years. Ministers were likely to be able to carry to a definite conclusion any projects they might devise. They belonged chiefly to that party in the State which had consistently assailed Mr. Gladstone's Egyptian policy. Here was an opportunity of repairing the damage done by their Radical opponents. The comparisons that would follow such an accomplishment were self-evident and agreeable even to anticipate. The idea of re-conquering the Soudan presented itself indefinitely, but not unpleasingly, alike to the Government and the people of Great Britain. The unexpected course of events crystallised the idea into a policy.

On the 1st of March, 1896, the battle of Adowa was fought, and Italy at the hands of Abyssinia sustained a crushing defeat. Two results followed which affected other nations. Firstly, a great blow had been struck at European prestige in North Africa. It seemed probable that the Abyssinian success would encourage the Dervishes to attack the Italians at Kassala. It was possible that they might also attack the Egyptians at Suakin or on the Wady Halfa frontier. Secondly, the value of Italy as a factor in European politics was depreciated. The fact that her defeat had been assisted by the arms and munitions of war which had been supplied to the Abyssinians from French, and Russian sources complicated the situation. The Triple Alliance was concerned. The third partner had been weakened. The balance might be restored if Great Britain would make some open sign of sympathy. Germany looked towards England. The precise form of the negotiations is shrouded in mystery. England and Italy had long been on the most friendly terms; but the London Cabinet required from Germany some substantial return for their intervention on behalf of a partner of the Triple Alliance. Perhaps they asked for the detachment of Germany from the South African Republic. But whatever they may have asked, they received enough to make it worth their while to show by definite action their sympathy with Italy.

The expectations of the Egyptian military authorities had been fulfilled. The Dervishes threatened Kassala as soon as the news of Adowa reached them, and indeed there were signs of increased activity in Omdurman itself. Under these circumstances the British Government determined to assist Italy by making a demonstration on the Wady Halfa frontier. They turned to Egypt. It had always been recognised that the recovery of the lost provinces was a natural and legitimate aspiration. 'The doubtful point was to decide the time when the military and financial resources of the country were sufficiently developed to justify an assumption of the offensive.'[7]

From a purely Egyptian point of view the best possible moment had not yet arrived. A few more years of recuperation were needed. The country would fight the Soudan campaigns more easily if first refreshed by the great reservoirs which were projected. For more than two years both projects had been pressed upon the Government of His Highness the Khedive—or, to write accurately, upon Lord Cromer. At regular intervals Sir Herbert Kitchener and Sir William Garstin would successively visit the British Agency (it would be treason to call it 'Government House ')—the one to urge the case for a war, the other to plead for a reservoir. The reservoir had won. Only a few weeks before the advance to Dongola was ordered Garstin met Kitchener returning from the Agency. The engineer inquired the result of the General's interview. 'I'm beat,' said Kitchener abruptly; 'you've got your dam'—and Garstin went on his way rejoicing.

The decision of the British Government came therefore as a complete surprise to the Cairene authorities. The season of the year was unfavourable to military operations. The hot weather was at hand. The Nile was low. Lord Cromer's report, which had been published in the early days of March, had in no wise foreshadowed the event. The frontier was tranquil. With the exception of a small raid on a village in the Wady Halfa district and an insignificant incursion into the Tokar Delta the Dervish forces had during the year maintained 'a strictly defensive attitude.'[8] Lord Cromer, however, realised that while the case for the reservoirs would always claim attention, the re-conquest of the Soudan might not receive the support of a Radical Government. The increasing possibility of French intrigues upon the Upper Nile had also to be considered. All politics are series of compromises and bargains, and while the historian may easily mark what would have been the best possible moment for any great undertaking, a good moment must content the Administrator. Those who guarded the interests of Egypt could hardly consent to an empty demonstration on the Wady Halfa frontier at her expense,

7 Lord Cromer's Reports: Egypt, No. 2, 1869.

8 Egypt, No. 1, 1896.

and the original intention of the British Government was at once extended to the re-conquest of the Dongola province—a definite and justifiable enterprise which must in any case be the first step towards the recovery of the Soudan.

Such were the circumstances under which the River War began. The discussions had been brief, and the decision was sudden. England as well as Egypt was astonished by the news. The Radical leaders at once denounced the project in scathing terms. But the nation, influenced by the forces that have been described, acquiesced timidly. The diplomatist said: 'It is to please the Triple Alliance.' The politician said: 'It is to triumph over the Radicals.' The polite person said: 'It is to restore the Khedive's rule in the Soudan.' But the man in the street—and there are many men in many streets—said: 'It is to avenge General Gordon.' And thereafter all awaited the outcome of the expedition.

* * * * *

It will be convenient, before embarking upon the actual chronicle of the military operations, to explain how the money was obtained to pay for the war. I desire to avoid the intricate though fascinating tangles of Egyptian finance. Yet even when the subject is treated in the most general way the difficulties which harass and impede the British Administrators and insult the sovereign power of Egypt—the mischievous interference of a vindictive nation, the galling and almost intolerable financial fetters in which a prosperous country is bound—may arouse in the sympathetic reader a Hush of annoyance, or at any rate a smile of pitying wonder.

About half the revenue of Egypt is devoted to the development and government of the country, and the other half to the payment of the interest on the debt and other external charges; and, with a view of preventing in the future the extravagance of the past, the London Convention in 1885 prescribed that the annual expenditure of Egypt shall not exceed a certain sum. When the expenditure exceeds this amount, for every pound that is spent on the government or development of Egypt, another pound must be paid to the Commissioners of the Debt; so that, after the limit is readied, for every pound that is required to promote Egyptian interests, two pounds must be raised by taxation from an already heavily taxed community. But the working of this law was found to be so severe that, like all laws which exceed the human conception of justice, it has been somewhat modified. By an arrangement which was effected in 1888, the Caisse de la Dette is empowered, instead of devoting *their* surplus pound to the sinking fund, to pay it into a general reserve fund, from which the Commissioners may make grants to meet 'extra-ordinary expenses'; those expenses, that is to say, which may be considered 'once for all' (capital) expenditure and not ordinary annual charges.

The Dongola expedition was begun, as has been said, without reference to the immediate internal condition of Egypt. The moment was a good one, but not the best. It was obviously impossible for Egypt to provide for the extraordinary expenses of the military operations out of revenue. The Ministry of Finance therefore appealed to the Caisse de la Dette for a grant from the general reserve fund. Here was an obvious case of 'extraordinary expenses.' The Egyptian Government asked for £E500,000.

The Caisse met in council. Six Commissioners representing England, France, Russia, Germany, Austria, and Italy—duly discussed the application. Four Commissioners considered that the grant should be made. Two Commissioners, those representing France and Russia, voted against it. The majority decided. The grant was made. The money was handed to the Egyptian Government and devoted to the prosecution of the war.

Egypt as a sovereign power had already humbly begged to be allowed to devote part of the surplus of her own revenues to her own objects. A greater humiliation remained. The Commissioners of France and Russia, who had been out-voted, brought an action against their colleagues on the grounds that the grant was *ultra vires*; and against the Egyptian Government for the return of the money thus wrongly obtained.

Other actions were brought at French instigation by various people purporting to represent the bondholders, who declared that their interests were threatened. The case was tried before the Mixed Tribunals, an institution which exists in Egypt superior to and independent of the sovereign rights of that country. On the part of the Egyptian Government and the four Commissioners it was contended that the Mixed Tribunals had no competency to try the case; that the attacking parties had no right of action; that the Egyptian Government had, in applying, done all that the law of liquidation required; and that the act of sovereignty was complete as soon as the Caisse, which was the legal representative of the bondholding interest, had pronounced its decision.

The argument was a strong one; but had it been ten times as strong, the result would have been the same. The Mixed Tribunals, an international institution, delivered its judgment on strictly political grounds, the judges taking their orders from the different countries they represented. It was solemnly pronounced that war expenses were not ' extraordinary expenses.' The proximate destruction of the Khalifa's power was treated quite as a matter of everyday occurrence. A state of war was apparently regarded as usual in Egypt. On this wise and philosophic ground the Egyptian Government was condemned to pay back £E500,000 together with interest and costs.

After a momentary hesitation as to whether the hour had not come to join issue on the whole subject of the financial restrictions of Egypt, it was decided to bow to this iniquitous decision. The money had now to be refunded. It had already been spent. More than that, other sums were needed for the carrying on of the war. The army was by then occupying Dongola, and was in actual expectation of a Dervish counter-attack, and it was evident that the military operations could not be suspended or arrested. It was impossible to stop; yet without money it seemed impossible to go on; and, besides, it appeared that Egypt would be unable to repay the £E500,000 which she had been granted, and of which she was now deprived.

Such was the painful and difficult situation which a friendly nation, in the utmost exercise of her wit and the extreme compass of her legal rights, had succeeded in producing in a country for whose welfare she had always professed an exaggerated regard. Such was the effect of French diplomacy.

But there is a Nemesis that waits on international malpractices, however clever. Now, as before and since, the very astuteness of the French Ministers and is to strike a terrible blow at French interests and French influence in Egypt. At this period France still exercised a considerable force on Egyptian politics. One Egyptian party, the weaker, but still by no means insignificant, looked towards her for support. The news of the French success cheered their hearts and raised their spirits. Orientals appreciate results. The result was a distinct reverse to the British. The conclusion to the native mind was obvious. Great Britain had been weighed in the European balances and found wanting. In all Eastern countries a large proportion of the population fluctuate uncertainly, eager only to be on the winning side. All this volume of agitation and opinion began to glide and flow towards the stronger Power, and when the Egyptian Government found their appeal from the decision of the Court of First Instance of the Mixed Tribunals to the International Court of Appeal at Alexandria quashed and the original decision confirmed, the defeat of the British was no less complete than the triumph of the French.

But meanwhile the Consul-General acted. On the 2nd of December he telegraphed to Lord Salisbury, reporting the judgment of the Court of Appeal and asking that he might be 'authorised to state directly that Her Majesty's Government will be prepared to advance the money on conditions to be hereafter arranged.' The reply was prompt, though guarded. 'You are authorised,' said Lord Salisbury, 'by the Chancellor of the Exchequer to state that though of course the primary liability for the payment of the £E500,000 rests with the Egyptian Government, Her Majesty's Government will hold themselves prepared to advance, on conditions to be decided hereafter, such a sum as they feel satisfied that the Egyptian Treasury is powerless to provide.'[9] This obvious development does not seem to have been foreseen by the French diplomatists, and when on the 3rd of December it was rumoured in Cairo that Great Britain was prepared to pay the money, a great feeling of astonishment and of uncertainty was created. But the chances of the French interference proving effective still seemed good. It was known that the English Government would not be in a position to make an advance to the Egyptian Government until funds had been voted by Parliament for the purpose. It was also thought that Egypt would be utterly unable to find the immediate money. In the meantime the position of Egypt

9 The original £500,000 was afterwards increased to £800,000; which sum was paid by the British Exchequer to the Egyptian Government, at first as a loan, and later as a gift.

was humiliating. France conceived herself mistress of the situation. A complete disillusionment, however, awaited the French Government. The taxes in Egypt, as in other countries, are not collected evenly over the whole year. During some months there is a large cash balance in the Exchequer. In others the money drains in slowly. It happened at this period of the year, after the cotton crop had been gathered, that a considerable balance had accumulated in the Treasury, and on the guarantee of the English Government being received, to the effect that they would ultimately assist Egypt with regard to the expenses of the expedition, Lord Cromer determined to repay the money at once.

The event was foreshadowed. On the 5th of December the Egyptian Council of Ministers, presided over in person by the Khedive, decided on their own initiative to despatch an official letter expressing in warm terms their gratitude for the financial help offered them by Her Majesty's Government. 'I am desired,' said Boutros, 'to beg your lordship to be good enough to convey to his lordship the Marquess of Salisbury the expression of the lively gratitude of the Khedive and the Egyptian Government for the great kindness which her Majesty's Government has shown to them on this occasion.'[10]

On the 6th of December £E500,000, together with £E15,600 interest and costs, in gold, were conveyed in boxes in a cart from the Egyptian Treasury to the offices of the Caisse de la Dette. The effect was tremendous. All Cairo knew of the difficulty. All Cairo witnessed the manner in which it had been overcome. The lesson was too plain to be lost on the native mind. The reverse of the French diplomacy was far greater even than its success had appeared. For many years French influence in Egypt had not received so heavy a blow; yet even in the short space of time which this story covers it was to receive a still more terrible wound.

---

10 Egypt, No. 1, 1897.

CHAPTER VI
THE BEGINNING OF THE WAR

The advance to Akasha—The concentration on the frontier—The communications—Suakin—A miserable town—The fortifications—Osman Digna—Politics on the Bed Sea shore—The Suakin Field Force—The plan of action—The affairs of Teroi Wells—And of Khor Wintri—The casualties—A triumphant return—The Indian contingent—An unnecessary dispute—Arrival of the Indian troops—The squabble with the Egyptian authorities—Troubles of the contingent—Scurvy—Return to India—On the Upper Nile—Wady Halfa—Sarras—Akasha—A lucky shot—Arrival of the Sirdar—The cavalry fight on the 1st of May—The scrimmage in the ravine—The concentration at Akasha—The eve of Firket.

Shortly before midnight on the 12th of March 1896, the Sirdar received instructions from Lord Cromer authorising an expedition into the Dongola province and directing him to occupy Akasha.[1] The next morning the news was published in the *Times*, ostensibly as coming from its correspondent in Cairo: and the Egyptian Cabinet was convened to give a formal assent by voting the decree. Throughout the day the military department was a scene of frantic activity. On the 14th the reserves were called out. On the 15th the Khedive reviewed the Cairo garrison: and at the termination of the parade Sir H. Kitchener[2] informed him that the earliest battalions would start for the front that night.

The Egyptian frontier force had always been kept in a condition of immediate readiness by the restless activity of the enemy. The beginning of the long-expected advance was hailed with delight by the British officers sweltering at Wady Halfa and Sarras. On Sunday, the

1 Map. 'The Advance to Akasha,' p. 154.

2 Brevet Colonel with local and temporary rank of Major-General, Sir H. H. Kitchener, K.C.M.G., C.B., Royal Engineers and Egyptian army

15th of March, three days after the Sirdar had received his orders and before the first reinforcements had started from Cairo, Colonel Hunter,[3] who commanded on the frontier, formed a column of all arms to seize and hold Akasha. The force consisted of the XIIIth Soudanese under Major Collinson,[4] two squadrons of cavalry under Captain Broad wood,[5] one company of the Camel Corps, No. 2 Field Battery, and two Nordenfeldts.[6] The mounted troops started on the afternoon of the 16th, and, camping for the night at Gemai, reached Semna the next day. Here they were overtaken by the infantry, who had been railed from Halfa to Sarras, and had marched on from the rail-head. At dawn on the 18th the column started for Akasha, and the actual invasion of the territory which for ten years had been abandoned to the Dervishes began.

The route lay through a wild and rocky country—the debateable ground, desolated by years of war—and the troops straggled into a long procession, and had several times for more than an hour to move in single file over passes and through narrow defiles strewn with the innumerable boulders from which the 'Belly of Stones' has derived its name. The right of their line of march was protected by the Nile, and although it was occasionally necessary to leave the bank, to avoid difficult ground, the column camped each night by the river. The cavalry and the Camel Corps searched the country to the south and east; for it was expected that the Dervishes would resist the advance; no living enemy was, however, seen. Creeping along the bank, and prepared at a moment's notice to stand at bay at the water's edge, the small force proceeded on its way. Wady Atira was reached on the 18th, Tanjore on the 19th, and on the 20th the column marched into Akasha.

The huts of the mud village were crumbling back into the desert sand. The old British fort and a number of storehouses—relics of the Gordon Relief Expedition—were in ruins. The railway from Sarras

---

3 Brevet Colonel A. Hunter, D.S.O., Royal Lancaster Regiment and Egyptian army.

4 Major J. Collinson, Northamptonshire Regiment and Egyptian army.

5 Capt. R. G. Broadwood, 12th Lancers and Egyptian army.

6 The batteries of the Egyptian army, though in some ways more like Mountain Batteries, the guns being carried by mules, are always called Field Batteries.—EDITOR.

had been pulled to pieces. Most of the sleepers had disappeared, but the rails lay scattered along the track. All was deserted: yet one grim object proclaimed the Dervish occupation. Beyond the old station and near the river a single rail had been fixed nearly upright in the ground. From one of the holes for the fish-plate bolts there dangled a rotten cord, and on the sand beneath this improvised, yet apparently effective, gallows lay a human skull and bones, quite white and beautifully polished by the action of sun and wind. Half-a-dozen friendly Arabs, who had taken refuge on the island below the cataract, were the only inhabitants of the district.

The troops began to place themselves in a defensive position without delay. On the 22nd the cavalry and Camel Corps returned with the empty convoy to Sarras to escort to the front a second and larger column, under the command of Major MacDonald,[7] and consisting of the XIth and XIIth Soudanese, one company of the 3rd Egyptians (dropped as a garrison at Ambigole Wells), and a heavy convoy of stores numbering six hundred camels. Starting from Sarras on the 24th, the column, after four days' marching, arrived without accident or attack, and MacDonald assumed command of the whole advanced force.

Akasha was now converted into a strong entrenched camp, in which an advanced base was formed. Its garrison of three battalions, a battery, and the mounted troops, drew their supplies by camel transport from Sarras. The country to the south and east was continually patrolled, to guard against a turning movement, and the communications were further strengthened by the establishment of fortified posts at Semna, Wady Atira, and Tanjore. The friendly Arab tribes—Bedouin, Kabbabish, and Foggara—ranged still more widely in the deserts and occupied the scattered wells. All this time the Dervishes watched supinely from their position at Firket, and although they were within a single march of Akasha they remained inactive and made no attempt to disturb the operations.

Meanwhile the concentration of the Egyptian army on the frontier was proceeding.[8] Before the expedition the distribution of troops was as follows:—At Cairo four and a half battalions (the 2nd,

7 Major H. A. MacDonald, D.S.O., Royal Fusiliers and Egyptian army.

8 Map, 'The Nile from Cairo to Wady Halfa,' p. 135.

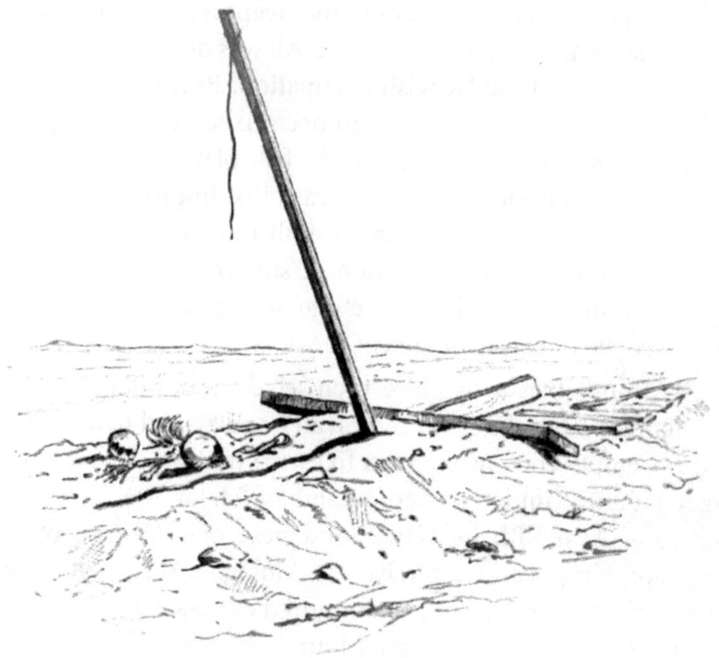

A NEW USE FOR RAILWAY IRON

4th, half the 5th,[9] 6th, and XIVth); at Suakin three battalions (the 1st, IXth, and Xth); at Wady Halfa six battalions (the 3rd, 7th, 8th, XIth, XIIth, and XIIIth).[10] The reservists obeyed the summons to the colours of their own free-will and with gratifying promptness, instead of being tardily dragged from their homes in chains as in the days of Ismail. All the battalions of the army were brought up to war strength. Two new battalions of reservists were formed, the 15th and 16th. The 15th was placed at Assnan and Korosko on the line of communications. The 16th was despatched to Suakin to release the two battalions in garrison there for service on the Nile. The 1st battalion of the North Staffordshire Regiment was moved up the river from Cairo to take the place of the Wady Halfa garrison of six battalions, which had moved on to Sarras and Akasha. A Maxim battery of four guns was formed from the machine-gun sections of the

9 The rest of the 5th battalion was at Suakin.—EDITOR.

10 For convenience throughout the text and maps the Arabic numerals are used for the Egyptian battalions and the Roman for the Soudanese, thus: 3rd Egyptians, IXth Soudanese.

Staffordshires and Connaught Rangers and hurried south. The 2nd, 4th, 5th, 6th, and XIVth Egyptian battalions from Cairo were passed in a continual succession along the railway and river to the front. In all this busy and complicated movement of troops the Egyptian War Office worked smoothly, and clearly showed the ability with which it was organised.

The line of communications from Cairo, the permanent base, to the advanced post at Akasha was 825 miles in length. But of this distance only the section lying south of Assnan could be considered as within the theatre of war. The ordinary broad-gauge railway ran from Cairo to Balliana where a river base was established. From Balliana to Assuan reinforcements and supplies were forwarded by Messrs. Cook's fleet of steamers, by barges towed by small tugs, and a number of native sailing craft. A stretch of seven miles of railway avoids the First Cataract, and joins Assuan and Shellal. Above Shellal a second flotilla of gunboats, steamers, barges, and Nile-boats was collected to ply between Shellal and Halfa. The military railway ran from Halfa to Sarras. South of Sarras supplies were forwarded by camels. To meet the increased demands of transport, 4,500 camels were purchased in Egypt and forwarded in boats to Assuan, whence they marched *viâ* Korosko to the front. The British Government had authorised the reconstruction of the military railway to Akasha, and a special railway battalion was collected at Assuan, through which place sleepers and other material at once began to pass to Sarras. The strategic railway construction will, however, form the subject of a later chapter, which I shall not anticipate.

By the 1st of April, less than three weeks from the commencement of the advance, the whole line of communications had been organised and was working efficiently, although still crowded with the concentrating troops. It was the first and not the least remarkable instance of Sir H. Kitchener's strange powers of rapid and comprehensive arrangement.

As soon as the 16th battalion of reservists arrived at Suakin, the IXth Soudanese were conveyed by transports to Kossier, and marched thence across the desert to Kena. The distance was 120 miles, and the fact that in spite of two heavy thunderstorms—rare phenomena in Egypt—it was covered in four days is a notable example of the marching powers of the black soldiers. It had been determined that the Xth Soudanese should follow at once, but circumstances occurred which detained them on the Red Sea littoral and must draw the attention of the reader thither.[11]

CONVOY DUTY

The aspect and history of the town and port of Suakin may afford a useful instance to the political cynic. The majority of the houses stand on a small barren island which is connected with the mainland by a narrow causeway. At a distance the tall buildings of white coral, often five storeys high, present an imposing appearance, and the prominent chimneys of the condensing machinery—for there is scarcely any fresh water—seem to surest manufacturing activity. But a nearer view reveals the melancholy squalor of the scene. A large part of the town is deserted. The narrow streets wind among tumbled-down and neglected houses. The quaintly carved projecting windows of the façades are boarded up. The soil exhales an odour of stagnation and decay. The atmosphere is rank with memories of waste and failure. The scenes that meet the eye intensify these impressions. The traveller who lands on Quarantine Island is first confronted with the *débris* of the projected Suakin-Berber Railway. Two or three locomotives that have neither felt the pressure

11 Map, 'Around Suakin,' page 146

of steam nor tasted oil for a decade, lie rusting in the ruined workshops. Huge piles of railway material rot, unguarded and neglected, on the shore. Boiling stock of all kinds—carriages, trucks, vans, and ballast waggons—are strewn or heaped near the sheds, and the initials H.B.W.R.R. painted distinctly upon them show that they were originally part of the stock of the bankrupt Hull and Barnsley Railway, and have hence played their part in disasters of peace as well as of war. The Christian cemetery alone shows a decided progress, and the long lines of white crosses which mark the graves of British soldiers and sailors who lost their lives in action or by disease during the various campaigns, no less than the large and newly enclosed areas to meet future demands, increase the depression of the visitor. The numerous graves of Greek traders—a study of whose epitaphs may conveniently refresh a classical education—protest that the climate of the island is pestilential. The high loopholed walls declare that the desolate scrub of the mainland is inhabited only by fierce and valiant savages, who love their liberty.

For eleven years all trade had been practically stopped, and the only merchants remaining were those who carried on an illicit traffic with the Arabs or, with Eastern apathy, were content to wait for better days. Being utterly unproductive, Suakin had been wisely starved by the Egyptian Government, and the gloom of the situation was matched by the poverty of its inhabitants. The condensers, which alone of Suakin institutions continued to do useful work, were capable of supplying 50,000 gallons of fresh, but unwholesome water a day. The harbour, though not very capacious, is good. The water is deep. There is no tide. There is scarcely any place where a ship cannot draw up within forty feet of the shore. The bottom is hard and firm, and, as there is no silt, no dredging is required. The wooden piers which had been built for the disembarkation of the British troops in 1884 are in the last stage of disrepair, and, since the submarine insects have devoured the piles flush with the water, they half hang-over and half float upon its surface. But fresh and durable stages could easily be built with cast-iron screw piles, and, as Suakin is a natural outlet of Soudan trade, this will probably be an undertaking of the next few years. It is impossible, however, to contemplate this miserable spot in its present forlorn condition without remembering with a thrill of indignation the gallant lives and hard-earned millions that have been recklessly squandered to preserve it as an Egyptian possession.

The island on which the town stands is joined to the mainland by a causeway, at the further end of which is an arched gateway of curious design called 'the Gate of the Soudan.' Upon the mainland stands the crescent-shaped suburb of El Kaff. It comprises a few mean coral-built houses, a large area covered with mud huts inhabited by Arabs and fishermen, and all the barracks and military buildings. The whole is surrounded by a strong wall a mile and a half long, fifteen feet high, six feet thick, with a parapet pierced for musketry and strengthened at intervals by bastions armed with Krupp guns. Standing upon this wall, the traveller may refresh his memory by an extensive view of the surrounding country. All around the suburb, at the distance of 2,000 yards, there is drawn a ring of small redoubts. Upon a high embankment to the westward the outlines of the right and left water forts are clearly seen, and beyond it is possible to distinguish the green patch of verdure near the wells and solitary fig-tree from which the action of Gemaiza derived its name. To the northward rises the black rock of Hashin. To the south-west lie Tofrek and Tamai. The whole scene and all its memories are framed by the dark circle of hills, which at a distance of seven miles terminate the view.

Three strong detached posts complete the defences of Suakin. Ten miles to the northward, on the scene of Sir H. Kitchener's unfortunate enterprise, is the fort of Handub. Tambuk is twenty-five miles inland and among the hills. Situate upon a high rock, and consisting only of a store, a formidable block-house and a look-out tower, this place is safe from any enemy unprovided with artillery. Both Handub and Tambuk were at the outset of the campaign provisioned for four months. The latter may be the site of a reservoir for a future Suakin water-supply.

The hills, which near the fort are scarcely 300 yards apart, open into a wide valley stretching away towards Berber; and it is possible that so lame a catchment area would make it worth while to construct a dam to store even the small annual rainfall. The third post, Tokar Fort, lies fifty miles along the coast to the south. Its function is to deprive the Arabs of a base in the fertile delta of the Tokar river.

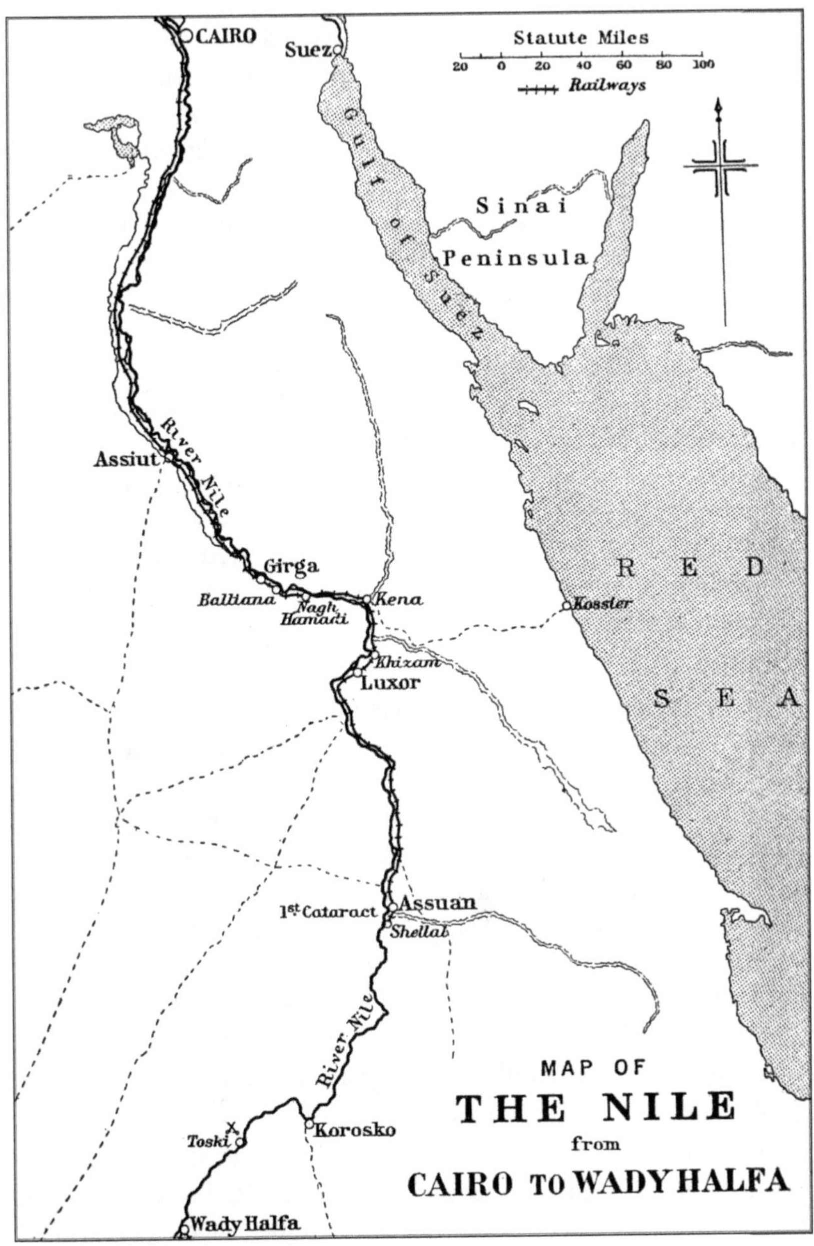
CAIRO
Suez
Statute Miles
20 0 20 40 60 80 100
Railways
Gulf of Suez
Sinai
Peninsula
River Nile
Assiut
Girga
Balliana
Nagh Hamadi
Kena
Kosseir
RED
SEA
Khizam
Luxor
1st Cataract
Assuan
Shellal
River Nile
Toski
Korosko
Wady Halfa
MAP OF
THE NILE
from
CAIRO TO WADY HALFA

The fort is strong, defended by artillery, and requires for its garrison an entire battalion of infantry.

No description of Suakin would be complete without some allusion to the man to whom it owes its fame. Osman Digna had been for many years a most successful and enterprising Arab slave-dealer. The attempted suppression of his trade by the Egyptian Government drove him naturally into opposition. He joined in the revolt of the Mahdi, and by his influence roused the whole of the Hadendoa and other powerful tribes of the Red Sea shore. The rest is upon record. Year after year, at a horrid sacrifice of men and money, the Imperial Government and the old slaver fought like wolves over the dry bone of Suakin. Baker's Teb, El Teb, Tamai, Tofrek, Hashin, Handub, Gemaiza—such were the fights of Osman Digna, and through all he passed unscathed. Often defeated, but never crushed, the wily Arab might justly boast to have run further and fought more than any Emir in the Dervish armies. Nor are his deeds forgotten; and to this day, if the name of Osman Digna be whispered in Pall Mall, the Generals begin to talk of brigades and divisions, and the whole War Office buzzes like a bee-hive.

It had scarcely seemed possible that the advance on Dongola could influence the situation around Kassala, yet the course of events encouraged the belief that the British diversion in favour of Italy had been effective; for at the end of March—as soon, that is to say, as the news of the occupation of Akasha reached him—Osman Digna separated himself from the army threatening Kassala, and marched with 300 cavalry, 70 camelry, and 2,500 foot towards his old base in the Tokar Delta. On the first rumour of his advance the orders of the Xth Soudanese to move *viâ* Kossier and Kena to the Nile were cancelled, and they remained in Garrison at Tokar. At home the War Office, touched in a tender spot, quivered apprehensively, and began forthwith to make plans to strengthen the Suakin garrison with powerful forces:

The state of affairs in the Eastern Soudan has always been turbulent. The authority of the Governor of the Red Sea littoral was not at this time respected beyond the extreme range of the guns of Suakin. The Hadendoa and other tribes who lived under the walls of the town professed loyalty to the Egyptian Government, not from any conviction that their rule was preferable to that of Osman Digna, but simply for the sake of a quiet life. As their distance from Suakin increased, the loyalty of the tribesmen became even less pronounced, and at a radius of twenty miles all the Sheikhs oscillated alternately between Osman Digna and the Egyptian Government, and tried to avoid, open hostilities with either. Omar Tita, Sheikh of the district round about Erkowit, found himself situated on this fringe of intriguing neutrality. Although he was known to have dealings with Osman, it was believed that if he had the power to choose he would side with the Egyptian Government. Early in April Omar Tita reported that Osman Digna was in the neighbourhood of Erkowit with a small force, and that he, the faithful ally of the Government, had on the 3rd of the month defeated him with a loss of four camels. He also said that if the Egyptian Government would send up a force to fight Osman, he, the aforesaid ally, would keep him in play until it arrived.

After a few days of hesitation and telegraphic communication with the Sirdar, Colonel Lloyd,[12] the Governor of Suakin, who was then in very bad health, decided that he had not enough troops to justify him in taking the risk of going up to Erkowit to fight Osman. Around Suakin, as along the Indian frontier, a battle is always procurable on the shortest notice. When a raid has taken place, the Government may choose the scale of their reprisals. If they are poor, they will arrange a counter-raid by means of ' friendlies,' and nothing more will be heard of the affair. If they are rich, they will mobilise two or three brigades, and make an expedition or fight a pitched battle, so that another glory may be added to the annals of the British army. In the present instance the Egyptian Government was poor, and as the British Government did not desire to profit by the opportunity, it was determined to have only a small-scale operation. The Governor therefore arranged a plan for a demonstration at the foot of the hills near Khor Wintri by means of combined movements from Suakin and Tokar. The garrison of Suakin consisted of the 1st and half the 5th Egyptian battalions; the 16th Egyptian reservists, who had just replaced the IXth Soudanese, and were as yet hardly formed into a military body; one squadron of cavalry,

12 Major (temporary Lieut.-Colonel) G. E. Lloyd, D.S.O., South Staffordshire Regiment and Egyptian army.

one company of Camel Corps, and some detachments of artillery. The garrison of Tokar consisted of the Xth Soudanese and a few gunners. From these troops there was organised in the second week in April, with all due ceremony, a 'Suakin Field Force'[13] composed as follows:—

SUAKIN COLUMN

Commanding: Lieutenant-Colonel Lloyd

Egyptian cavalry, 8th squadron
Two guns
Camel Corps, 1 company
1st Egyptians, 3 companies
5th Egyptians, 3 companies
One company formed from the depôts of the IXth and Xth Soudanese
Mule Transport, 1 company

TOKAR COLUMN

Commanding: Major Sidney[14]

Xth Soudanese, 3 companies
Tokar Camel Transport

The plan of campaign was simple. Colonel Lloyd was to march out from Suakin and effect a junction with the 'Tokar Column' at Khor Wintri, where the Erkowit road enters the hills. It was then hoped that Osman Digna would descend and fight a battle of the required dimensions in the open; after which, if victorious, the force would return to Suakin and Tokar. In order to make the Suakin Column as mobile as possible, the whole force was mounted on camels, of which more than 1,000 were requisitioned, as well as 60 mules and 120 donkeys. Two hundred Arabs accompanied the column to hold these beasts when necessary. Six days' forage and rations, one day's reserve of water, 200 rounds per man, and 100 shell per gun were carried. At five o'clock on the afternoon of Tuesday, the 14th of April, the troops paraded outside the walls of Suakin, and bivouacked in the open ready to march at daylight.

---

13 See Appendix A, vol. ii., for Staff, &c.

14 Captain (temporary Major) H. M. Sidney, Duke of Cornwall's Light Infantry and Egyptian army.

The next morning the column, which numbered about 1,200 men of all arms, started. After marching for four or five hours in the direction of Khor Wintri the cavalry, who covered the advance, came in contact with the Dervish scouts. The force thereupon assumed an oblong formation: the mixed Soudanese company and the two guns in front, three Egyptian companies on each flank, the Camel Corps company in the rear, and the transport in the centre. The pace was slow, and, since few of the camels had ever been saddled or ridden, progress was often interrupted by their behaviour and by the broken and difficult nature of the country.

Nevertheless at about four o'clock in the afternoon, Teroi wells, eight miles from Khor Wintri, were reached; and here, having marched nineteen miles, Colonel Lloyd determined to halt. While the infantry were making the *zeriba,* the cavalry were sent on under Captain Fenwick[15] (an infantry officer employed on the Staff) to gain touch with the Tokar force, who were expected to have already reached the rendezvous. Apparently, under the belief that Omar Tita and his Arabs would give timely notice of an attack, the cavalry appear to have neglected many of the usual precautions, and in consequence at about five o'clock, when approaching Khor Wintri, they found themselves suddenly confronted with a force of about 200 Dervish horsemen supported by a large body of infantry. The squadron wheeled about with promptitude, and began to retire at a trot. The Dervish horsemen immediately pursued.

The result was, that the Egyptians began a disorderly flight at a gallop through the thick and treacherous scrub and over broken, dangerous ground. Sixteen horses fell; their riders were instantly speared by the pursuers. The undisturbed courage of the British officer alone saved the situation. Rallying by his personal efforts thirty-eight troopers, Captain Fenwick seized a rocky hillock, and dismounting with the natural instinct of an infantry soldier, prepared to defend himself to the last. The remainder of the squadron continued its flight, and thirty-two troopers under an Egyptian officer (whose horse is said to have bolted) arrived at the Teroi *zeriba* with the news that their comrades had been destroyed, or had perhaps 'returned to Suakin,' and that they themselves had been closely fol-

15 Captain M. A. C. B. Fenwick, Royal Sussex Regiment and Egyptian army.

lowed by the enemy. The news caused the gravest anxiety, which was not diminished when it was found that the bush around the zeriba was being strongly occupied by Dervish spearmen. Two mounted men, who volunteered for the perilous duty, were sent to make their way through this savage cordon, and try to find either the remainder of the cavalry or the Tokar Column. Both were hunted down and killed. The rest of the force continued in hourly expectation of an attack.

Their suspense was terminated towards midnight, when the Dervishes began to approach the *zeriba*. In the darkness what was thought to be a body of horsemen were seen moving along a shallow *khor* opposite the right face of the defence. At the same moment a loud yell was raised by the enemy on the other side. An uncontrolled musketry fire immediately broke out. The guns fired blindly up the valley; the infantry wildly on all sides. The fusillade continued furiously for some time, and when by the efforts of the British officers the troops were restrained, it was found that the Dervishes had retired, leaving behind them a single wounded man. Occasional shots were fired from the scrub until the morning, but no fresh attack was attempted by the Dervishes.

Meanwhile Captain Fenwick maintained his solitary and perilous position on the hillock. He was soon surrounded by considerable bodies of the enemy, and as soon as it became dark he was sharply attacked. But the Dervishes fortunately possessed few rifles, and the officers and troopers, by firing steady volleys, succeeded in holding their ground and repulsing them. The sound of the guns at Teroi encouraged the Egyptians, and revealed the direction of their friends. With the daylight the Dervishes, who seem throughout the affair to have been poor-spirited fellows, drew off, and the detachment remounting made haste to rejoin the main body.

The force, again united, pursued its way to Khor Wintri where they found the column from Tokar already arrived. Marching early on the 15th, Major Sidney with 250 men of the Xth Soudanese, the only really trustworthy troops in the force, had readied Khor Wintri the same afternoon. He drove out the small Dervish post occupying the khor, and was about to bivouac, when he was sharply attacked by a force of Arabs said to have numbered 80 horsemen and 500 foot. The Soudanese fought with their usual courage, and the Dervishes were repulsed, leaving thirty dead upon ground. The regulars had three men wounded.

Up to this point Colonel Lloyd's plan had been successfully carried out. The columns from Suakin and Tokar had effected a junction at Khor Wintri on the Erkowit road. It now remained to await the attack of Osman Digna, and inflict a heavy blow upon him. It was decided, however, in view of what had occurred, to omit this part of the scheme, and both forces returned together without delay to Suakin, which they reached on the 18th. The casualties were as follows:—British officers, *nil;* Egyptian soldiers, killed 18, wounded 3.

Their arrival terminated a period of anxious doubt as to their fate. The town, which had been almost entirely denuded of troops, was left in charge of Captain Ford-Hutchinson.[16] At about two o'clock in the afternoon of the 16th a few stragglers from the Egyptian cavalry with half-a-dozen riderless horses knocked at the gates, and vague but sinister rumours spread on all sides. The belief that a disaster had overtaken the Egyptian force greatly excited the Arabs living within the walls, and it appeared that they were about to rise, plunder the town, and massacre the Christians. Her Majesty's ship *Scout* was, however, by good fortune in the harbour. Strong parties of blue-jackets were landed to patrol the streets. The guns of the warship were laid on the Arab quarter. These measures had a tranquillising effect, and order reigned in Suakin until the return of the Field Force, when their victory was celebrated with appropriate festivities.

It was announced that as a result of the successful operations the Dervish enterprise against the Tokar Delta had collapsed, and that Osman Digna's power was for ever broken. In order, however, that no unfortunate incident should mar the triumph, the Xth Soudanese were sent back to Tokar by sea *viâ* Trinkitat, instead of marching direct; and the garrison of Suakin confined themselves henceforward strictly to their defences. Osman Digna remained in the neighbourhood and raided the friendly villages. On the arrival of the Indian contingent he was supposed to be within twelve miles of

---

16 Captain G. H. Ford-Hutchinson, Connaught Rangers and Egyptian army.

the town, but thereafter he retired to Adarama on the Atbara river, where he remained during the Dongola campaign. The fact that no further offensive operations were undertaken in the Eastern Soudan prevented all fighting, for the Dervishes were, of course, unable to assail the strong permanent fortifications behind which the Egyptians took shelter. They nevertheless remained in actual possession of the surrounding country, until the whole situation was altered by the successful advance of powerful forces behind them along the Nile and by the occupation of Berber.

After the affair of Khor Wintri it was evident that it would not be possible to leave Suakin to the defence only of the 16th battalion of reservists. On the other hand, Sir H. Kitchener required every soldier the Egyptian army could muster to carry out the operations on the Nile. It was therefore determined to send Indian troops to Suakin to garrison the town and forts, and thus release the Xth Soudanese and the Egyptian battalions for the Dongola Expedition. Accordingly early in the month of May the Indian Army authorities were ordered to prepare a brigade of all arms for service in Egypt. The request caused the greatest excitement throughout military circles in the Eastern Empire. The British officer serving in India has always looked with longing eyes towards the land of the Nile as a happy hunting-ground for decorations and distinction. Conscious that his countrymen can neither understand nor appreciate the stern and bloody conflicts of the mountains, he aspires to participate in the easier warfare of the river. The Indian soldier, no less than his officer, keenly enjoys being sent to fight beyond the seas. His adventurous and conquering spirit exults in the prospect of war in other lands and against new enemies. The fact that he has made foreign campaigns will, when the Sikh returns to his native village, procure him the deference of his inferiors and the respect of his equals. Nor is the Indian Government insensible to the improvement in recruiting which usually follows the return to their homes of the soldiers from across the sea with strange medals and stranger stories.

Under these circumstances the dispute which arose about the payment of the expenses was unfortunate. The decision of the Secretary of State was sensible and not unjust. The amount which the force would have cost had it remained in India—about 5,000*l.* a month—was to be paid by India. The extraordinary expenses necessitated by the expedition were to be defrayed by the British Government. No extra strain was placed upon the finances of India, and her troops were furthermore ordered on a service which might have increased their own experience and the popularity of the army. It seems strange that this fair and convenient arrangement should have aroused a violent outcry. The protest of the Council of the Governor-General was supported by the influence of the *Times*. For some days, and until the public attention was distracted, the gross injustice to India in compelling her to pay the ordinary expenses, while her troops were abroad, was a popular theme. Ministers were reminded by the Opposition that the Indian Empire was not 'a large barrack beyond the seas' from which a worn-out Mother Country might draw thousands of soldiers to prosecute her misguided enterprises; and they were, moreover, warned of the fate of States that put their sole trust in mercenary troops. They replied with vigour, and I think with force, that Her Majesty's Government had an undoubted right to use the armed forces of the Empire as they thought fit; that the position of Egypt, on the high road to the East, interested India in the event; that India's financial loss was nothing; that the diminution of her internal security, consequent upon the temporary reduction of her native army, was insignificant; that they did not wholly confide in mercenaries; and that the enterprise was not misguided nor the Mother Country worn out.

Meanwhile the Indian Army authorities were swiftly preparing the brigade. They looked around for the soldiers and a General to do honour to the army from which they came. The troops selected were as follows:—26th Bengal Infantry, 35th Sikhs, 1st Bombay Lancers, 5th Bombay Mountain Battery, two Maxim guns, one section Queen's Own (Madras) Sappers and Miners—in all about 4,000 men. The command was entrusted to Colonel Egerton, of the Corps of Guides, a soldier worthy of the regiment that produced him.[17]

On the 30th of May the dreary town of Suakin was enlivened by the arrival of the first detachments, and during the following week the whole force disembarked at the rotten piers and assumed the duties of the defence. It is mournful to tell how this gallant bri-

17 Colonel C. C. Egerton, C.B., D.S.O., Indian Staff Corps.

gade, which landed so full of high hope and war-like enthusiasm, and which was certainly during the summer the most mobile and efficient force in the Soudan, was reduced in seven months to the sullen band who returned to India wasted by disease, embittered by disappointment, and inflamed by feelings of resentment and envy. It is easy to understand how a jealous dislike might spring up between the British officers of the Indian and Egyptian armies. Perhaps the newcomers were scarcely conciliatory. They despised the Egyptian soldiers, saw none of their virtues, and remembered only the dark tales of the past. Their contempt was returned with interest by the officers in the Khedive's service, and a long, petty, and miserable disagreement began.

The Indian contingent landed in the full expectation of being immediately employed against the enemy. After a week, when all the stores had been landed, officers and men spent their time speculating when the order to march would come. It was true that there was no transport in Suakin, but that difficulty was easily overcome by rumours that 5,000 camels were on their way from the Somali coast to enable the force to move on Kassala or Berber. As these did not arrive, General Egerton[18] sent in a proposed scheme to the Sirdar, in which he undertook to hold all the advanced posts up to the Kokreb range, if he were supplied with 1,000 camels for transport. A characteristic answer was returned, to the effect that it was not intended to use the Indian contingent as a mobile force. They had come as a garrison for Suakin, and a garrison for Suakin they should remain. This information was not, however, communicated to the troops, who continued to hope for orders to advance until the fall of Dongola.

The heat when the contingent arrived was not great, but as the months wore on the temperature rose steadily, until in August and September the thermometer rarely fell below 103° during the night, and often rose to 115° by day. Dust-storms were frequent. A veritable plague of flies tormented the unhappy soldiers. The unhealthy climate, the depressing inactivity, and the scantiness of fresh meat or the use of condensed water, provoked an outbreak of scurvy. At one time nearly all the followers and fifty per cent, of the troops were

18 He held temporary rank of Brigadier.—EDITOR.

affected. Several large drafts were invalided to India. The symptoms were painful and disgusting open wounds, loosening of the teeth, curious fungoid growths on the gums and legs. The cavalry horses and transport animals suffered from *bursati,* and even a pin-prick expanded into a large open sore. It is doubtful whether the brigade could have been considered fit for active service after September. All the Europeans suffered acutely from prickly heat. Malarial fever was common. There were numerous cases of abscess on the liver. Twenty-five per cent, of the British officers were invalided to England or India, and only six escaped a stay in hospital. The experiences of the battalion holding Tokar Fort were even worse that those of the troops in Suakin.

At length the longed-for time of departure arrived. With feelings of relief and delight the Indian contingent shook the dust of Suakin off their feet and returned to India. The last ship, with the Headquarters Staff of the brigade on board, sailed on the 9th of December, and the Egyptian authorities terminated a policy of studied slights by neglecting to give the farewell salute, which the customs and courtesies of military service prescribed.

It is with satisfaction that I turn from the dismal narrative of events in the Eastern Soudan to the successful campaign on the Nile.[19] By the middle of April the concentration on the frontier was completed. The communications were cleared of their human freight, and occupied only by supplies and railway material, which continued to pour south at the utmost capacity of the transport. Eleven thousand troops had been massed at and beyond Wady Halfa. But no serious operations could take place until a strong reserve of stores had been accumulated at the front. Meanwhile the army waited, and the railway grew steadily. The battalions were distributed in three principal fortified camps—Halfa, Sarras, and Akasha and detachments held the chain of small posts which linked them together.

Including the North Staffordshire Regiment, the garrison of Wady Halfa numbered about 3,000 men. The town and cantonment, nowhere more than 400 yards in width, straggle along the river-bank, squeezed in between the water and the desert for nearly

19 Map, 'The Advance to Akasha, page 154.

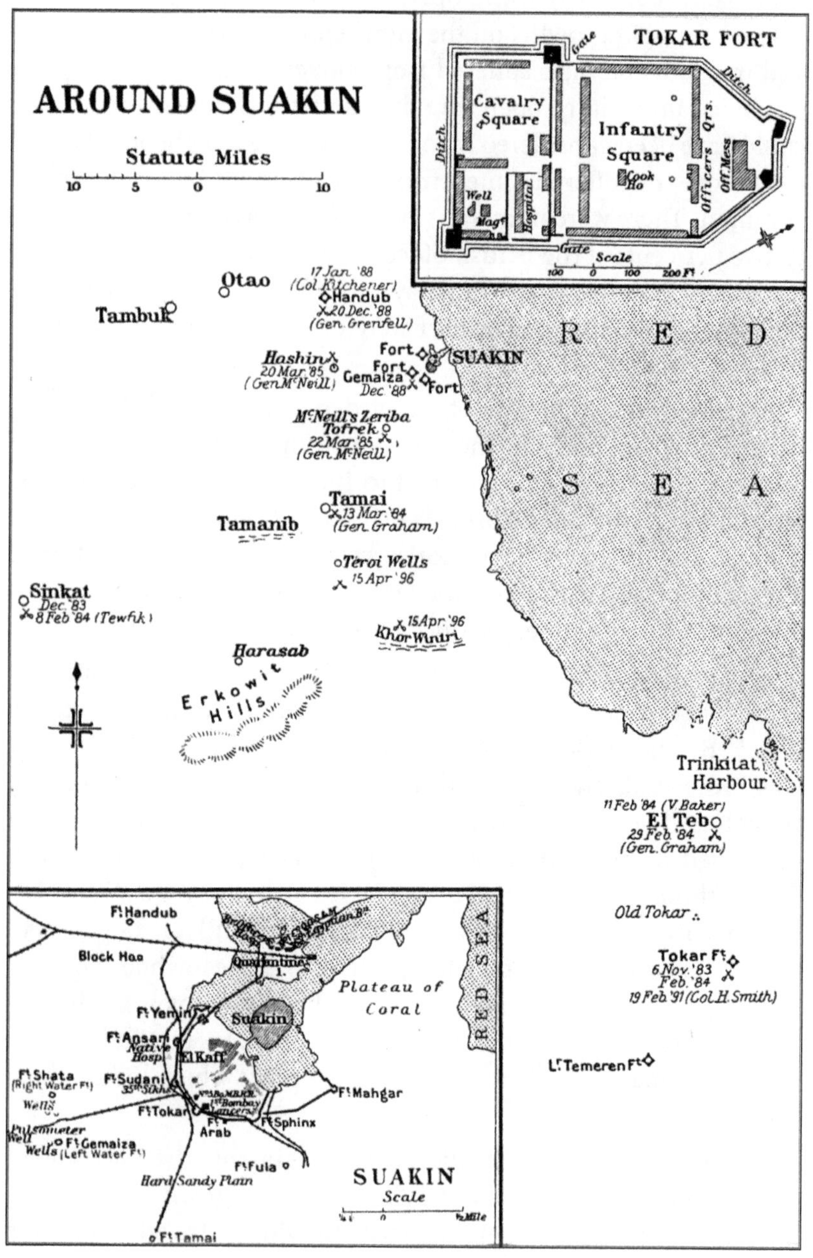
AROUND SUAKIN
Statute Miles
10 5 0 10
TOKAR FORT
Gate
Ditch
Cavalry Square
Infantry Square
Officers Qrs.
Off. Mess
Cook Ho
Well
Hospital
Scale
100 0 100 200 Ft
Otao
Tambuk
17 Jan. '88 (Col. Kitchener)
Handub
20 Dec. '88 (Gen. Grenfell)
Hashin
20 Mar. '85 (Gen. McNeill)
Fort
SUAKIN
Gemaiza
Dec. '88
McNeill's Zeriba
Tofrek
22 Mar. '85 (Gen. McNeill)
RED SEA
Tamai
13 Mar. '84 (Gen. Graham)
Tamanib
Teroi Wells
15 Apr. '96
Sinkat
Dec. '83
8 Feb. '84 (Tewfik)
15 Apr. '96
Khor Wintri
Harasab
Erkowit Hills
Trinkitat Harbour
11 Feb. '84 (V. Baker)
El Teb
29 Feb. '84 (Gen. Graham)
Old Tokar
Tokar Ft.
6 Nov. '83
Feb. '84
19 Feb. '91 (Col. H. Smith)
Lt. Temeren Ft.
Ft. Handub
Block Ho.
Quarantine
Plateau of Coral
RED SEA
Ft. Yemin
Suakin
Ft. Ansar
Native Hosp.
El Kaff
Ft. Shata (Right Water Ft.)
Ft. Sudani
35th Sikhs
Wells
Ft. Tokar
Ft. Arab
Ft. Sphinx
Ft. Mahgar
Ft. Gemaiza (Left Water Ft.)
Wells
Ft. Fula
Hard Sandy Plain
SUAKIN
Scale
½ 0 ½ Mile
Ft. Tamai

three miles. The houses, offices, and barracks are all built of mud, and the aspect of the place is brown and squalid. A few buildings, however, attain to the dignity of two storeys. At the northern end of the town a group of fairly well-built houses occupy the river-front, and a distant view of the clusters of palm-trees, of the white walls, and the minaret of the mosque refreshes the weary traveller from Korosko or Shellal with the hopes of civilised entertainment. The hospital, which enjoys a significant importance—for Halfa is not a health resort—displays glass windows; but the rest of the buildings, though shaded by deep verandahs, have shutters, so that when the dust-storm rages, which is a frequent occurrence—the occupants must be content to shut out the daylight with the dust. Along the river-bank a row of *shadoofs*[20] enables the inhabitants to draw their water, and a single steam-pump at the southern end of the town proclaims and rewards the enterprise of an agriculturist, who is by this means assured even in the most sultry summers of a regular and abundant supply. Beneath the shade of a palm-tree near the hospital is buried the head of King John of Abyssinia. The trophy which Zeki Tummal sent to Omdurman as a proof of victory had become the Khalifa's gage of battle to the Khedive, and at last, after much wandering, found peace at Wady Halfa.[21] The whole town is protected towards the deserts by a ditch and mud wall; and heavy Krupp field-pieces are mounted on little bastions where the ends of the rampart rest upon the river. Five small detached forts strengthen the land front, and the futility of an Arab attack at this time was evident.

The North Staffordshire Regiment was accommodated in the barracks, and from the account of an officer who served with them[22] we learn that the days passed slowly and tediously. The great heat, the discomfort, and, above all, the uncertainty whether they would be employed at the front, or held in garrison like the Indian contingent, preyed upon the troops, and in some measure explained the large proportion of sick. The Egyptian and Soudanese battalions

20 *Shadoof*'= an ancient contrivance of rope, lever, and bucket whereby the water is scooped up from the Nile and brought to the crop.

21 Here it has recently been joined by the head of the Mahdi, which had also experienced vicissitudes.

22 *The Egyptian Soudan: its Loss and Recovery*, Alford and Sword.

had strong drafts of recruits who drilled daily outside the walls, and the place resounded during the cool hours of the morning with the stentorian tones of the British sergeant-instructors. The only diversion was to be found at the Egyptian Army Mess— 'The Club' as it was called; and here the officers and the press correspondents, of whom ten had already arrived, bewailed the monotony of the station and the delay of the advance.

Halfa had now become the terminus of a railway, which was rapidly extending; and the continual arrival and despatch of tons of material, the building of sheds, workshops, and storehouses, lent the African slum the bustle and activity of a civilised city. Officers and rumours passed up and down the line with frequency and speed. Daily trains carried supplies forward to Sarras and construction plant to Bail-head. Sarras Fort is an extensive building, perched on a crag of black rock rising on the banks of the Nile about thirty miles south of Halfa. During the long years of preparation it had been Egypt's most advanced outpost and the southern terminus of the military railway. The beginning of the expedition swelled it into an entrenched camp, holding nearly 6,000 men. From each end of the black rock on which the fort stood a strong stone wall and wire entanglement ran back to the river. The space thus enclosed was crowded with rows of tents and lines of animals and horses; and in the fort Colonel Hunter, commanding the district known as 'Sarras and the South,' had his headquarters.

From Sarras the army seemed to have chosen a double line of advance. The railway reconstruction followed the old track which had been prepared through the desert in 1885. The convoy route wound along by the river. Both were protected from attack. The 7th Egyptians guarded Rail-head, while the chain of small posts secured the road by the Nile. It was four days' march to Akasha. The advanced base grew during the months of April and May into a strong position. It lay in a small half-circle of hills rising in the distance to precipitous peaks of dark reddish rock. The broken and confused nature of the ground, commanded by high and often inaccessible rocks, and intersected by frequent small *khors,* which afforded good lines of approach to an enemy, made Akasha a difficult place to defend. Indeed, Colonel Wingate, writing six years before, had called it 'an impossible military position .... surrounded on all sides by hills . . . and quite untenable.'[23] But the Dervish force at Firket was known to be neither very numerous nor enterprising, and the troops holding Akasha were a powerful and well-equipped body. By dint of hard and judicious work an efficient outpost line was formed, strengthened by numerous detached posts and small forts. Towards the end of April the force under Colonel MacDonald was reinforced by the IXth Soudanese, another squadron, and the Maxim Battery; and there is no reason to believe that the advanced depôt was ever in any danger. Only once during the two months did the Arabs venture to approach within artillery range. A small body of horse and camel-men made a sort of haphazard reconnaissance, and being seen from the outpost line were fired on at a great distance by a field-gun. They fell back immediately, but it was believed that the range was too great for the projectile to have harmed them, and it was not until two days later that the discovery on the spot of a swollen, blistering corpse, clad in bright *jibba,* apprised the delighted gunners of the effect of their fire. Warned by this lucky shot the Dervishes came no more, or came unseen.

The Sirdar, accompanied by Colonel Rundle,[24] his Chief of Staff, had left Cairo on the 22nd of March, and after a short stay at Assuan reached Wady Halfa on the 29th Here he remained during the month of April, superintending and pressing the extension of the railroad and the accumulation of supplies. On the 1st of May he arrived at Akasha, with a squadron of cavalry under Major Burn-Murdoch,[25] as his escort. It happened that a convoy had come in the previous day, so that there were two extra cavalry squadrons at the advanced post.

Almost at the same moment that Sir H. Kitchener entered the camp, a party of friendly Arabs came in with the news that they had been surprised some four miles to the eastward by a score of Dervish camelmen, and had only succeeded in escaping with the loss of two of their number. In the belief that the enemy in the immediate vicinity were not in force, the Sirdar ordered the three squadrons of

23 *Mahdism and the Egyptian Soudan*, p. 296.
24 Colonel H. M. L. Rundle, C.M.G., D.S.O., R.A. and Egyptian army.
25 Major J. F. Burn-Murdoch, *p.s.c,* 1st Royal Dragoons.

AN EGYPTIAN PATROL

Egyptian cavalry, supported by the XIth Soudanese, to go out and reconnoitre towards Firket and endeavour to cut off hostile patrols that might be found. Captain Broadwood, who knew the ground to the southward thoroughly, had started with a couple of troopers on one of his frequent reconnaissances of the Dervish position. Under cover of the darkness he had crossed the river and was already moving along the west bank. The reconnoitring squadrons were thus deprived of the officer best acquainted with the country. At ten o'clock, however, Major Burn-Murdoch started with four British officers, and 240 lances. After moving for seven or eight miles among the hills which surround Akasha, the cavalry passed through a long, sandy defile, flanked on either side by rocky peaks and impracticable ravines. As the head of the column was about to debouch from this, the advanced scouts reported that there was a body of Dervishes in the open ground in front of the defile.

The cavalry commander rode forward to look at them, and found himself confronted, not, as he had expected, by a score of camel-men, but by a strong force of Dervishes, numbering at least 1,500 foot and 250 horse. The cavalry, by trotting, had left the supporting infantry some distance behind them. The appearance of the enemy was threatening. The horsemen, who were drawn up scarcely 300 yards away, were already advancing to the attack, their right flank protected by a small force of camelry: and behind was the solid array of the spearmen. Major Burn-Murdoch determined to fall back on his infantry support and escape from the bad ground. He gave the order, and the squadrons wheeled about by troops and began to retire. Forthwith the Dervish horse charged, and galloping furiously into the defile attacked the cavalry in rear. Both sides were crowded in the narrow space. The wildest confusion followed, and the dust raised by the horses' hoofs hung over all like a yellow London fog, amid which the bewildered combatants discharged their pistols and thrust at random. The Egyptian cavalry, thus highly tried, showed at first no disposition to turn to meet the attack. The tumult drowned all words of command. A disaster appeared imminent. But the British officers, who had naturally been at the head of the column during its advance, were now at the rear and nearest the enemy. Collecting a score of troopers, they made such an astonishing resistance with their swords and revolvers that they actually held the defile and beat back the Dervish horse, who retired on their infantry, leaving a dozen dead upon the ground. Two of the Egyptian squadrons continued to retreat until clear of the defile, a distance of 700 yards; but the third and rearmost was compelled by the British officers to face about, and galloping with this force down the ravine, Major Burn-Murdoch drove the Arabs pell-mell out of it.

The cloud of dust prevented a clear view, and the squadron, pursuing blindly, was astonished by a sharp fire from the Dervish infantry. The other two squadrons had now returned, and the whole force dismounted, and, taking up a position among the sand-hills near the mouth of the defile, opened fire with their carbines. The repulse of their cavalry seemed to have disheartened the Dervishes, for they made no attempt to attack the dismounted troopers, and contented themselves with maintaining a desultory fire, which was so ill-aimed that but little loss was caused. Captain Fitton,[26] who had accompanied the reconnaissance, was slightly wounded. The heat of the weather was terrific, and both men and horses suffered acutely from thirst. The squadron which had escorted the Sirdar had performed a long march before the reconnaissance and was exhausted. The cavalry, however, held their position among the sandhills and easily defeated a feeble attempt to turn their right. At noon they were joined by Captain Broad wood. From the other side of the river he had seen that the enemy's camp was unusually empty, and had ridden hurriedly back to Akasha to report. He now caught up the reconnaissance and had the opportunity of witnessing the end of

26 Captain H. Gr. Fitton, *p.s.c*, Royal Berkshire Regiment.

the skirmish. At a quarter past twelve the Dervishes began to retire slowly and deliberately, and by one o'clock, when the XIth Soudanese arrived, eager and agog, the last Arab had disappeared. The force then returned to camp, bearing many spears and leading six captured horses as trophies of victory. The intensity of the heat may be gauged by the fact that one of the Soudanese soldiers—that is to say, an African negro—died of actual sunstroke. Such was the affair of the 1st of May, and it is pleasing to relate that in this fierce fight the loss was not severe. One British officer was slightly wounded. One native soldier was killed; one was mortally and eight severely wounded.

During May the preparations for the advance on the Dervish position at Firket continued, and towards the end of the month it became evident that they were nearly complete. The steady accumulation of stores at Akasha had turned that post into a convenient base from which the force might operate for a month without drawing supplies of any kind from the north. The railway, which had progressed at the rate of about half a mile a day, had reached and was working to Ambigole Wells, where a four-gun fort and entrenchment had been built. The distance over which convoys must plod was reduced by half, and the business of supply was doubly accelerated. By degrees the battalions and squadrons began to move forward towards Akasha. Sarras, deprived of its short-lived glory, became again the solitary fort on a crag. The camp was gone, and the space enclosed by the walls and the river was deserted.

The garrison had shrunk from 6,000 regulars to 300 reservists, armed only with Remington rifles. It was no longer the railway terminus, but only a station on the line and the depôt for the construction plant which had been collected to extend the line beyond Akasha as soon as Firket should be seized. Wady Halfa was also deserted, and, except for the British battalion in garrison, could scarcely boast a soldier. Both the Egyptian battalions from Suakin had arrived on the Nile. The Xth Soudanese were on their way. The country beyond Akasha had been thoroughly reconnoitred and mapped to within three miles of the Dervish position. Everything was ready. The actual concentration may be said to have begun on the 1st of June, when the Sirdar started for the front from Halfa, whither he had returned after the cavalry skirmish. Construction work on the railway came to a full stop. The railway battalions, dropping their picks and shovels, shouldered their Remington rifles and became the garrisons of the posts on the line of communications. On the 2nd of June the correspondents were permitted to proceed to Akasha. On the 3rd the Xth Soudanese passed through Ambigole and marched south. The Horse battery from Halfa followed. The Egyptian battalions and squadrons which had been camped along the river at convenient spots from Ambigole to Akasha marched to a point opposite Okma. Between this place and the advanced post an extensive camp, stretching three miles along the Nile bank, arose with magic swiftness. On the 4th the 7th Egyptians moved from rail-head, and with these the last battalion reached the front. Nine thousand men with ample supplies were collected within striking distance of the enemy.

All this time the Dervishes at Firket watched in senseless apathy the deliberate, machine-like preparations for their destruction. They should have had good information, for although the Egyptian cavalry patrolled ceaselessly, and the outpost line was impassable to scouts, their spies, as camel-drivers, water-carriers, and the like, were in the camp. They may not, perhaps, have known the exact moment of the intended blow, for the utmost secrecy was observed. But though they must have realised that it was imminent, they did nothing. There was, indeed, no course open to them but retreat. Once the army was concentrated with sufficient supplies at Akasha, their position was utterly untenable. The Emir-in-Chief, Hammuda, then had scarcely 3,000 men around his flag. Their rifles and ammunition were bad; their supplies scanty. Nor could the valour of fifty-seven notable Emirs sustain the odds against them. There was still time to fall back on Kosheh, or even on Suarda—anywhere outside the sweep of their terrible enemy's sword. They would not budge. Obstinate and fatuous to the last, they dallied and paltered on the fatal ground, until sudden, blinding, inevitable catastrophe fell upon them from all sides at once, and swept them out of existence as a military force. On the afternoon of the 6th of June the Expeditionary Force was warned that the Dervish position would be attacked at daylight. The operation which followed deserves a chapter of its own.

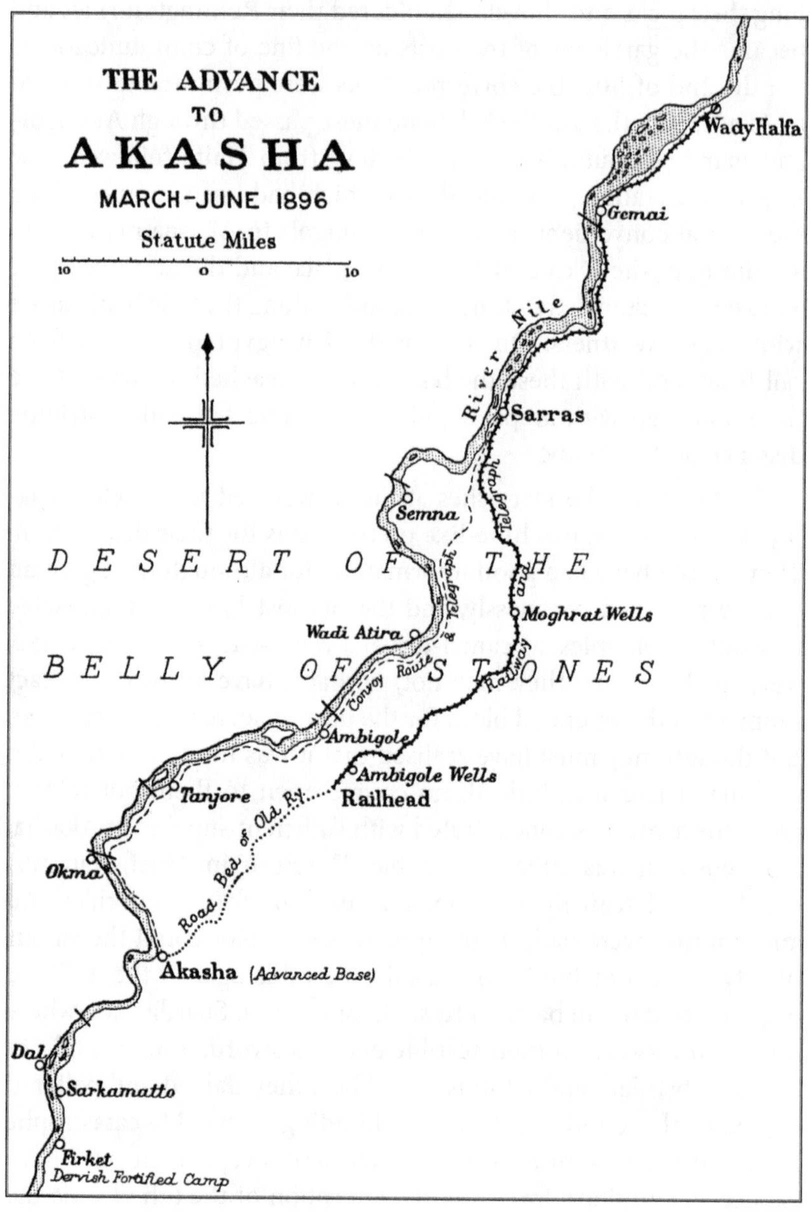
THE ADVANCE
TO
AKASHA
MARCH-JUNE 1896
Statute Miles
10
0
10
Wady Halfa
Gemai
River Nile
Sarras
Semna
Telegraph
Railway and Telegraph
DESERT OF THE
BELLY OF STONES
Moghrat Wells
Wadi Atira
Convoy Route & Telegraph
Ambigole
Ambigole Wells
Railhead
Tanjore
Road Bed of Old Ry.
Okma
Akasha (Advanced Base)
Dal
Sarkamatto
Firket
Dervish Fortified Camp

CHAPTER VII

FIRKET[1]

June 7, 1896

The Dervish Emirs—A change of leadership—Osman Azrak—Composition of the force—The desert column—The main force—Sarkamatto—A false alarm—The first shot—Firket village—The deployment—MacDonald's brigade—Capture of the village—The pursuit—Casualties—Comments

Since the end of 1895 the Dervish force in Firket had been under the command of the Emir Hammuda, and it was through the indolence and neglect of this dissipated Arab that the Egyptian army had been able to make good its position at Akasha without any fighting. Week after week the convoys had straggled unmolested through the difficult country between Sarras and the advanced base. No attack had been made upon the brigade in Akasha. No enterprise was directed against its communications. This fatal inactivity did not pass unnoticed by Wad Bishara, the Governor of Dongola; but although he was nominally in supreme command of all the Dervish forces in the province, he had hardly any means of enforcing his authority. His rebukes and exhortations, however, gradually roused Hammuda, and during May two or three minor raids were planned and executed, and the Egyptian position at Akasha was several times reconnoitred.

Bishara remained unsatisfied, and at length, despairing of infusing energy into Hammuda, he ordered his subordinate, Osman Azrak, to supersede him. Osman was a Dervish of very different type. He was a fanatical and devoted believer in the Mahdi and a loyal follower of the Khalifa. For many years he had served on the northern frontier of the Dervish Empire, and his name was well known to

1 Map, 'The Action at Firket,' page 166.

the Egyptian Government as the contriver of the most daring and the most brutal raids. His cruelty to the wretched inhabitants of the border villages had excluded him from all hope of mercy, should he ever fall into the hands of the enemy. His crafty skill however protected him, but among the Emirs gathered at Firket there was none whose death would have given greater satisfaction to the military authorities than the man who was now to replace Hammuda.

Whether Osman Azrak had actually assumed command on the 6th of June is uncertain. It seems more likely that Hammuda declined to admit his right, and that the matter still stood in dispute. But in any case Osman was determined to justify his appointment by his activity, and about midday he started from the camp at Firket, and, accompanied by a strong patrol of camel-men, set out to reconnoitre Akasha. Moving cautiously, he arrived unperceived within sight of the position at about three o'clock in the afternoon. The columns which were to storm Firket at dawn were then actually parading. But the clouds of dust which the high wind drove across or whirled about the camp obscured the view, and the Dervish could distinguish nothing unusual. He therefore made the customary pentagonal mark on the sand to ensure good luck, and so returned to Firket to renew his dispute with Hammuda, bearing the reassuring news that 'the Turks lay quiet.'

The force which the Sirdar had concentrated for the capture of Firket amounted to about 9,000 men, and was organised as follows:—

Commander-in-Chief: THE SIRDAR

The Infantry Division: Colonel Hunter *Commanding*

1st Brigade	*2nd Brigade*	*3rd Brigade*
Major Lewis*	Major MacDonald	Major Maxwell**
3rd Egyptians	IXth Soudanese	2nd Egyptians
4th Egyptians	XIth Soudanese	7th Egyptians
Xth Soudanese	XIIth Soudanese	8th Egyptians
	XIIth Soudanese	
*Major D. F. Lewis, Cheshire Regiment and Egyptian army.		** Major J. G. Maxwell, Black Watch and Egyptian army.

Mounted Forces: Major Burn-Murdoch

Egyptian Cavalry . . . . 7 squadrons
Camel Corps . . . . .8 companies

Artillery

Horse Artillery..1 Battery
Field Artillery...2 Batteries
Maxim Guns..1 Battery

Two roads led from Akasha to Firket—one by the bank of the river, the other inland and along the projected railway line. The Sirdar determined to avail himself of both. The force was therefore divided into two columns. The main column, under command of the Sirdar, was to move by the river road, and consisted of the infantry division, the Field Artillery, and the Maxim guns. The Desert Column, under command of Major Burn-Murdoch, consisted of the mounted forces, the Horse Artillery, and one battalion of infantry (the XIIth Soudanese, under Major Townshend[2]), drawn from MacDonald's brigade and mounted upon camels: in all about two thousand men.

Very precise orders were given to the smaller column, and Burn-Murdoch was instructed to occupy the hills to the south-east of the centre of Firket village by 4.30 a.m.; to dispose his force facing west, with the cavalry on the left, the Camel Corps in the centre, and the XIIth Soudanese on the right. The only point left to his discretion was the position to be occupied by the Horse battery. He was especially warned not to come under the fire of the main infantry force. As soon as the enemy should be routed, the XIIth Soudanese were to return to the Sirdar The cavalry, camelry, and Horse Artillery were to pursue—their objective being, firstly, Koyeka, and, secondly, Suarda.[3]

The infantry column began to march out of Akasha at 3.30 in the afternoon of the 6th, and trailed southwards along the track by the river in the following order: Lewis's brigade, with the Xth Soudanese leading; two Maxim guns and the artillery; MacDonald's brigade; Maxwell's brigade; and lastly, the field hospitals and a half-battal-

2 Major C.V.F. Townshend, C.B., Indian Staff Corps and Egyptian army.

3 Map, 'The Capture of Dongola,' page 193.

A DERVISH SCOUT

ion forming rearguard. The Sirdar marched behind the artillery. The rear of the long column was clear of the camp by 4.30, and about two hours later the mounted force started by the desert road. The River Column made good progress till dark, but thereafter the advance was slow and tedious. The track led through broken rocky ground, and was so narrow that it nowhere allowed a larger front to be formed than of four men abreast. In some places the sharp rocks and crumbling heaps of stone almost stopped the gun-mules altogether, while the infantry tripped and stumbled painfully. The moon had not risen, and the darkness was intense. Still the long procession of men, winding like a whiplash between the jagged hills, toiled onward through the night, with no sound except the tramping of feet and the rattle of accoutrements. At half-past ten the head of Lewis's brigade debouched into a smooth sandy plain about a mile to the north of Sarkamatto village.

This was the spot—scarcely three miles from the enemy's position—where the Sirdar had decided to halt and bivouac. The bank and foreshore of the river were convenient for watering; all bottles and skins were filled, and soldiers and animals drank deeply. A little food was eaten, and then battalion by battalion, as the force arrived at the halting-place, they lay down to rest. The tail of Maxwell's brigade reached the bivouac about midnight, and the whole column was then concentrated.

Meanwhile the mounted force was also on its way. Like the River Column, they were disordered by the broken ground, and the XIIth Soudanese, who were unused to camel-riding and mounted only on transport saddles, were soon wearied. After one o'clock many men, both in the Camel Corps and in the battalion, fell asleep on their camels, and the officers had great difficulty in keeping them awake. However, the force reached their point of concentration—about three miles to the south-east of Firket—at a quarter to three. Here the XIIth Soudanese dismounted from their camels and became again a fighting unit. Leaving the extra camels under a guard, Major Burn-Murdoch then advanced towards his appointed position on the hills overlooking Firket.

The Sirdar moved on again with the infantry at 2.30. The moon had risen over the rocks to the left of the line of march, but it was only a thin crescent and did not give much light. The very worst part of the whole track was encountered immediately the bivouac was left, and the column of nearly 6,000 men had to trickle through one narrow place in single file. There were already signs of the approach of dawn; the Dervish camp was near; the Sirdar and his Staff began to look anxious. He sent many messages to the leading battalions to hurry; and the soldiers, although now very weary, ran and scrambled through the difficult passage like sheep crowding through a gate. By four o'clock the leading brigade had cleared the obstacle, and the most critical moment seemed to have passed.

Suddenly, a mile to the southward, rose the sound of the beating of drums. Everyone held their breath. The Dervishes were prepared. Perhaps they would attack the column before it could deploy. Then the sound died away, and but for the clatter of the marching columns all was again silent. It was no alarm, but only the call to the morning prayer; and the Dervishes, still ignorant that their enemies approached and that swift destruction was upon them, trooped from their huts to obey the pious summons.

The great mass of Firket mountain, still dark in the half-light, now rose up upon the left of the line of march. Between it and the river stretched a narrow strip of scrub-covered ground; and here, though obstructed by the long grass, bushes, palm-trees, and holes, the leading brigade was ordered to deploy.[4] There was, however, as yet only room for the Xth Soudanese to form line, and the 3rd and 4th Egyptians contented themselves with widening to column of companies—the 3rd in rear of the right of the Xth, the 4th in rear of the centre. The force now began to emerge from the narrow space between the hills and the river, and debouch into open country. As the space widened No. 1 field battery came into line on the left, and No. 2 on the right of the Xth Soudanese. A swell of ground hid Firket village, though it was known to be within a mile and it was now daylight. Still there was no sign that the Dervishes were prepared. It seemed scarcely possible to believe that the advance had not yet been discovered. The silence seemed to forebode some unexpected attack. The leading brigade and guns halted for a few minutes to allow MacDonald to form his battalions from 'fours' into column of companies. Then at five o'clock the advance was resumed, and at this moment from the shoulder of Firket mountain there rang out a solitary shot. The Dervish outposts had at last learned their danger. Several other shots followed in quick succession, and were answered by a volley from the Xth, and then from far away to the south-east came the report of a field-gun. The Horse Artillery battery had come into action. The operation of the two columns was simultaneous: the surprise of the enemy was complete.

The great object was now to push on and deploy as fast as possible. The popping of musketry broke out from many points, and the repeated explosions of the Horse battery added to the eager excitement of the troops. For what is more thrilling than the sudden and swift development of an attack at dawn ? The Dervish outpost which had fired the alarm fled towards the rocky hills to the left front of Lewis's brigade losing two of their number by the way, but waited to fire several shots, by one of which Captain Fitton's horse was killed.

The Xth Soudanese had now reached the top of the rise which had hidden Firket, and the whole scene came into view. To the right front the village of Firket stretched by the side of the river—a confusion of mud houses nearly a mile in length and perhaps 300

4 Map, 'The Action at Firket,' page 166.

yards broad. On the landward side the tents and straw shelters of the Dervish force showed white and yellow. A system of mud wall- and loop-holed houses strengthened the northern end of the village. Behind it as a background stood lines and clusters of palm-trees, through which the broad river and the masts of the Arab boats might be seen. In front of the troops, but a little to their left, rose a low rocky ridge surmounted with flags and defended by a stone breastwork running along its base. Across the open space between the village and the hill hundreds of Dervishes on horse and on foot were hurrying to man their defences, and others scrambled up the rocks to see for themselves the numbers of the enemy. Scores of little puffs of smoke already speckled the Mack rocks of the ridge and the brown houses of the village.

The attack developed very rapidly. The narrow passage between the mountain and the river poured forth its brigades and battalions, and the firing-line stretched away to the right and left with extraordinary speed. The Xth Soudanese opened fire on the village as they topped the rise. The 3rd and 4th Egypt deployed on the right and left of the leading regiment, two companies of the 4th extending down on to the foreshore below the steep river-bank. Peake's[5] battery (No. 1) and the Maxim guns, coming into action from a spur of Firket mountain, began to fire over the heads of the advancing infantry.

The whole of Lewis's brigade now swung to the right and attacked the village; MacDonald's, coming up at the double in line of battalion columns, deployed to the left, inland, round the shoulder of the mountain, and, bearing away still more to the left, advanced swiftly upon the rocky ridge. The ground in MacDonald's front was much broken by boulders and scrub, and a deep *khor* delayed the advance. The enemy, though taken at obvious disadvantage, maintained an irregular fire: but the Soudanese, greatly excited, pressed on eagerly towards the breastworks. When the brigade was still 200 yards from the ridge, about fifty Dervish horsemen dashed out from among the rocks and charged the left flank. All were immediately shot down by a wild but heavy independent fire. With joyful yells the blacks broke into a run and carried the breastworks at the bayonet. The Dervishes did not await the shock. As soon as they saw their horsemen—

5 Major M. Peake, R.A. and Egyptian army.

among whom was the Emir Hammuda himself and Yusef Angar, Emir of the *Jehadia*—swept away, they abandoned the first ridge and fell back on another which lay behind. The Soudanese followed closely, and pursued the outnumbered enemy up one, and down the other side of the rocky hills, up again and down again, continually shouldering and bringing round the left of the brigade, until at last the hills were cleared of all except the dead, and the fugitives were running towards the river-bank. Then the scattered battalions re-formed facing west, and the panting soldiers looked about them.

Whilst MacDonald's brigade was storming the hills, Lewis's had advanced on the village and the Dervish camp. The Arabs from their loopholed houses made a stubborn resistance, and the 4th battalion by the river-bank were sharply engaged, their commanding officer, Captain Sparkes,[6] having his horse shot in four places. Encouraged by their enormous superiority in number and weapons, the Egyptians showed considerable zeal in the attack, and their conduct on this occasion was regarded as a very happy augury for the war, of which this was the first general engagement.

As Lewis's brigade had swung to its right, and MacDonald's had borne away to the left, a wide gap had opened in the centre of the attack. This was immediately filled by Maxwell's brigade, so that the whole force was now formed in one line, which curved and wheeled continually to the right until, by the time the rocky hills had been taken, all three brigades practically faced west and were advancing together towards the Nile. The Dervishes—penned between the river and the enemy, and unable to prevent remorseless advance, which every moment restricted them to narrower limits—now thought only of flight, and they could be seen galloping hither and thither seeking for some means of escape. The foreshore of the river at the southern end of Firket is concealed from a landward view by the steep bank, and by this sandy path the greater number of the fugitives found safety.

The position of the Desert Column would have enabled the XIIth Soudanese, by moving down to the river, to cut off this line of retreat; but the Sirdar, doubtless fearing lest they should come under the fire of his main force, failed to take this advantage. The battalion,

6 Captain W. S. Sparkes, Welsh Regiment and Egyptian army.

forbidden to advance, remained the idle spectators of the Dervish flight. The cavalry and the Camel Corps, instead of cutting at the flank, contented themselves with making a direct pursuit after the enemy had crossed their front, and in consequence several hundred Arabs made good their escape to the south. Others swam the river and fled by the west bank. The wicked Osman Azrak, his authority now no longer disputed, for his rival was a corpse galloped from the field and reached Suarda. The rest of the Dervish force held to the houses, and prepared to fight to the death or surrender to their conquerors.

The three brigades now closed upon the village and, clearing it step by step, advanced to the water's edge. MacDonald's brigade did not indeed stop until they had crossed the swampy isthmus and occupied the island. The Arabs, many of whom refused quarter, resisted desperately, though without much effect, and more than eighty corpses were afterwards found in one group of buildings. By 7.20 o'clock all firing had ceased; the entire Dervish camp was in the hands of the Egyptian troops, and the engagement of Firket was over.

The Sirdar now busied himself with the pursuit, and proceeded with the mounted troops as far as Mograka, five miles south of Firket. The whole cavalry force, with the Camel Corps and Horse Artillery, pressed the retreat vigorously to Suarda. Osman Azrak, however, succeeded in transporting the women and children and some stores, with a sufficient escort, to the west bank before the arrival of the troops.

On the approach of the cavalry he retired along the east bank, with a small mounted force, without fighting. The Emir in charge of the escort on the other side delayed, and was in consequence shelled at long range by the Horse battery. The local inhabitants, tired of the ceaseless war which had desolated the frontier province for so long, welcomed their new masters with an appearance of enthusiasm. The main pursuit stopped at Suarda, but a week later two squadrons and sixteen men of the Camel Corps, under Captain Mahon,[7] were pushed out twenty miles further south, and an Arab store of grain was captured.

7 Captain B. T. Mahon, 8th Hussars and Egyptian army.

The Dervish loss in the action was severe. More than 800 dead were left on the field, and there were besides 500 wounded and 600 prisoners. The casualties in the Egyptian army were chiefly among the mounted forces:—

British Officer Wounded Captain Legge, 7 Egyptian Cavalry[8] *Native Ranks*		
	Killed	Wounded
Cavalry	3	18
Artillery	—	1
Camel Corps	2	18
2nd Egyptians	—	1
3rd Egyptians	3	3
4th Egyptians	5	15
IXth Soudanese	3	14
Xth Soudanese	—	2
XIth Soudanese	2	5
XIIth Soudanese	1	6
Medical Corps	1	—
Total	20	83

Firket is officially classed as a general action: special despatches were written, and a special clasp struck. The reader will have formed his own estimate of the magnitude and severity of the fight. The whole operation was well and carefully planned, and its success in execution was complete. The long and difficult night march, the accurate arrival and combination of the two columns, the swift deployment, the enveloping movement, proved alike the discipline and training of the troops and the skill of their officers. The only point on which criticism may be made is the failure of the Desert Column to intercept the flying Dervishes. There are two reasons which may excuse the neglect. Firstly, with modern rifles it is very dangerous

8 Captain N. Legge, 20th Hussars and Egyptian army.

to make attacks from several directions at once, and it is said that the XIIth Soudanese in advancing would probably have come under the fire of the main force. But the reader, by looking at the plan of the action, will at once perceive that as soon as MacDonald's wheel to the right was completed, the whole force was practically facing west, and the XIIth, in advancing to the river, would merely have prolonged the line.

The second explanation is perhaps the more convincing. As it is so much cheaper to kill men in flight, than when they are 'cornered,' it is usually expedient to leave some line of escape to an enemy.

If this was the Sirdar's reason for forbidding the XIIth Soudanese to close on the foreshore, then it must be observed that this cautious policy, when the Dervishes were already outnumbered by more than three to one, besides being under a terrible disadvantage in weapons, shows how little confidence was at this time placed in the Egyptian troops. The brilliant aspect of the affair, however, caused great satisfaction in England, and the further prosecution of the campaign was looked for with increasing interest.

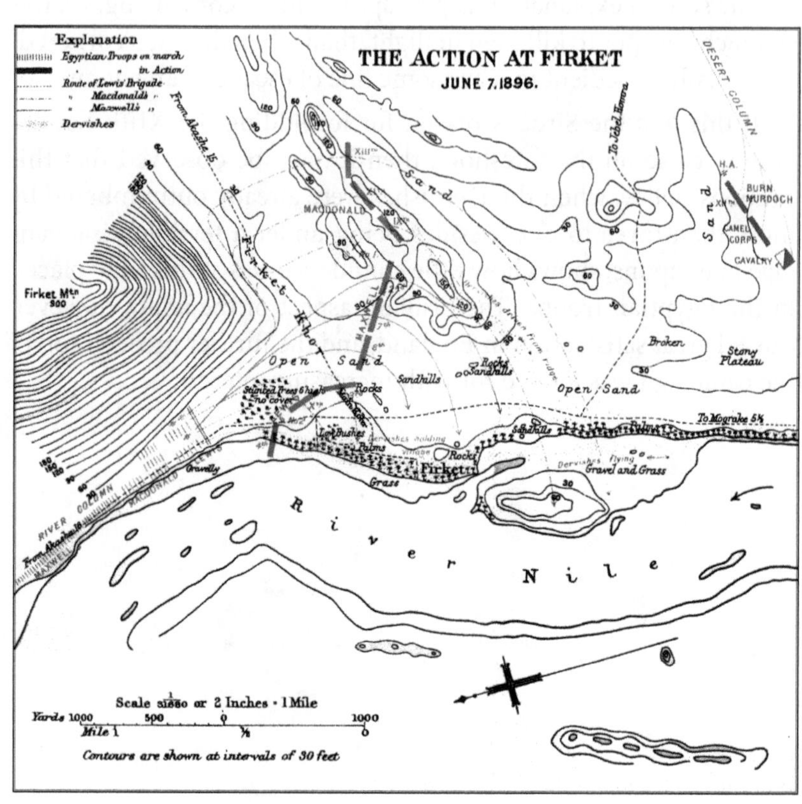
THE ACTION AT FIRKET
JUNE 7.1896.
Explanation
Egyptian Troops on march
in Action
Route of Lewis' Brigade
Macdonald's
Maxwell's
Dervishes
DESERT COLUMN
RIVER COLUMN
Firket Mtn
Firket Khor
Open Sand
Sandhills
Rocks
Firket
Gravel and Grass
River Nile
Broken
Stony Plateau
To Mograke 5½
BURN MURDOCH
CAMEL CORPS
CAVALRY
MACDONALD
MAXWELL
Scale or 2 Inches = 1 Mile
Yards 1000 500 0 1000
Mile 1 ½ 0
Contours are shown at intervals of 30 feet

CHAPTER VIII
THE RECOVERY OF THE DONGOLA PROVINCE[1]

The element of chance—Ill luck—The flotilla—Extension of the railway—The move to Kosheh—The new gunboats—Cholera—A time of trouble—The north wind—The Second Cataract—The gunboats ascend it—The luck turns—The advance on Dongola—Occupation of Absarat—'The Death March'—A time of crisis—The Sirdar's power—Composition of the Expeditionary Force—An explosion—Resumption of the advance—The enemy—Wad Bishara—He inspirits his soldiers—Hafir, September 19th—The river action—A striking scene—Artagasha island—Retreat of the Dervishes—The casualties—The Sirdar crosses the Nile—Bombardment of Dongola—The advance of the army—Its array—Unequal forces—Capture of Dongola—The pursuit of the enemy—Occupation of the Dongola province—Losses and rewards of the campaign.

Countless and inestimable are the chances of war. Those who read the story, and still more those who share the dangers, of a campaign feel that every incident is surrounded with a host of possibilities, any one of which, had it become real, would have changed the whole course of events. The influence of Fortune is powerfully and continually exerted. In the flickering light of conflict the outlines of solid fact throw on every side the vague shadows of possibility. We live in a world of 'ifs.' 'What happened,' is singular; 'What might have happened,' legion. But to try to gauge the influence of this uncertain force were utterly futile, and it is perhaps wise, and indisputably convenient to assume that the favourable and adverse chances equate, and then eliminate them both from the calculation.

1 Map, 'The Capture of Dongola,' page 193.

The 'Sirdar's luck' has become almost proverbial in the Soudan. As the account progresses numerous instances will suggest themselves. It was lucky that the Dervishes did not harass the communications, or assail Akasha before it was fortified. It was lucky that they fought at Firket; that they retired from Berber; that Mahmud did not advance in January; that he advanced in March; that he did not retire before the battle of the Atbara; that the Khalifa did not hold the Shabluka; that he did not attack on the night before Omdurman, and that he did attack at dawn.

We instinctively try to explain astonishing success. But had the expedition been disastrous it would have been no less easy—though perhaps less congenial—to collect an array of opposite chances. 'By ill luck this or that happened, or did not happen.' It appears, however, to the unprejudiced student, that, in the River War, fortune played a comparatively unimportant part. Much depended on forethought: much on machinery; little was left to chance. I shall, further on, examine the peculiar military facilities that Sir H. Kitchener enjoyed in his campaigns. They were undoubtedly tremendous. But, as far as luck was concerned, the balance of advantage throughout the war was insignificant, and in the earlier stages fortune was distinctly adverse.

After Firket all things were contrary. One unexpected misfortune succeeded another. Difficulties were replaced by others as soon as they had been overcome. The autumn of 1896 was marked by delay and disappointment. The state of the Nile, the storms, the floods, the cholera, and many minor obstacles, vexed but did not weary the commander. The victory at Firket was succeeded by a long pause in the operations. The army had made one spring forward. It must now gather energy for another. The preparations, however, proceeded rapidly. A strong camp was formed at Firket. MacDonald's brigade occupied Suarda two days after the fight, and this place now became the advanced post, just as Akasha had been in the first phase of the campaign. The accumulation of stores at Firket and Suarda began forthwith. Owing to the arrangements which had been made before the engagement it was possible to collect within one week of the action two months' supplies at Suarda for the garrison of 2,000 men, and one month at Firket for the 7,000 troops encamped there.

Thereafter, however, the necessity of hurrying the railway construction and the considerable daily demands of 9,000 men only allowed this margin to be increased very gradually.

The army had now passed beyond the scope of a camel, or other pack-animal, system of supply, except for very short distances, and it was obvious that it could only advance in future along either the railway or a navigable reach of the river, and preferably along both. From the Dal Cataract near Kosheh there is a clear waterway at high Nile to Merawi. To Kosheh, therefore, the railway must be extended before active operations could recommence. A third condition had also to be observed. For the expulsion of the Dervishes from Kerma and Dongola it was desirable that a flotilla of gunboats should co-operate with the land forces. Four of these vessels: the *Tamai, El Teb*, the *Metemma,* and the *Abu Klea*; and three steamers: the *Kaibar, Dal*, and *Akasha,* which it was proposed to arm, had, since 1885, patrolled the river from Assuan to Wady Halfa, and assisted in protecting the frontier from Dervish raids. All seven were now collected at the foot of the Second Cataract, and awaited the rise of the river to attempt the passage. To strengthen the flotilla three new and very powerful gunboats had been ordered in England. These were to be brought in sections over the railway to a point above the Second Cataract, and be fitted together there. It was thus necessary to wait,

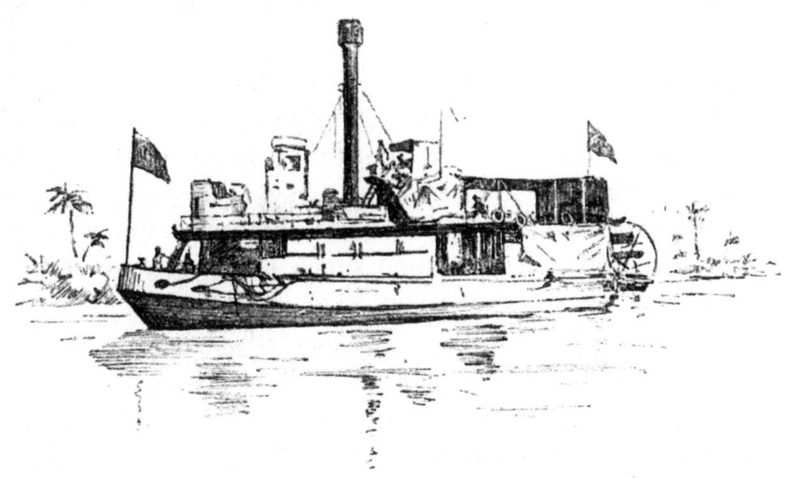

GUNBOATS: THE 1885 CLASS

firstly, for the railway to reach Kosheh; secondly, for the Nile to rise; thirdly, for the old gunboats to ascend the Cataract; fourthly, for the new gunboats to be launched on the clear waterway; and, fifthly, for the accumulation of supplies. With all of these matters the Sirdar now busied himself.

The reconstruction of the railway to Akasha and its extension beyond this place towards Kosheh was pressed forward. By the 26th of June Akasha was reached. Thenceforward the engineers no longer followed an existing track, but were obliged to survey, and to make the formation for themselves. Strong fatigue parties from the Egyptian and Soudanese battalions were, however, employed on the embankments, and the line grew daily longer. On the 24th of July the first train ran across the battlefield of Firket; and on the 4th of August the railway was working to Kosheh.

Kosheh is six miles south of Firket, and consists, like most places in the 'Military Soudan,' of little more than a name and few ruined mud-huts which were once a village. On the 5th July the whole camp was moved thither from the scene of the action. The reasons were clear and apparent.

Kosheh is a point on the river above the Dal Cataract whence a clear waterway runs at high Nile to beyond Dongola. The camp at Firket had become foul and insanitary. The bodies of the dead, swelling and decaying in their shallow graves, assailed, as if in revenge, the bodies of the living. The dysentery which had broken out was probably due to the 'green' water of the Nile; for during the early period of the flood what is known as 'the false rise washes the filth and sewage off the foreshore all along the river, and brings down the green and rotting vegetation from the spongy swamps of Equatoria. The water is then dangerous and impure. There was nothing else for the army to drink; but it was undesirable to aggravate the evil by keeping the troops in a dirty camp.

The earliest freight which the railway carried to Kosheh was the first of the new stern-wheel gunboats. Train after train arrived with its load of steel and iron, or with the cumbrous sections of the hull and a warship in pieces—engines, armaments, fittings, and stores—soon lay stacked by the side of the river. An improvised dockyard, equipped with powerful twenty-ton shears and other appliances, was established, and the work—complicated as a Chinese puzzle—of fitting and riveting together the hundreds of various parts proceeded swiftly. Gradually the strange heaps of parts began to evolve a mighty engine of war. The new gunboats were in every way remarkable. The old vessels had been 90 feet long.. These were 140 feet. Their breadth was 24 feet, They steamed 12 miles per hour. They had a command of 30 feet. Their decks were all protected by steel plates, and prepared by loopholed shields for musketry. Their armament was formidable. Each carried one twelve-pounder quick-firing gun forward; two six-pounder quick-firing guns in the central battery, and four Maxim guns. Every modern improvement— such as ammunition hoists, telegraphs, search-lights, and steam-winches—was added. Yet with all this they drew only thirty-nine inches of water.

The design and construction of these vessels was entirely British. They were planned by Mr. Thubron, of the Nile Engine Works, Cairo, a north countryman, and not, as was stated, a German. The order to build them was given to Messrs. John Stewart and Son, Limited—a London firm. The contract specified that they should be delivered at Alexandria by the 5th of September, but, by extraordinary exertions, the first boat, the *Zafir*, reached Egypt on the 23rd of July, having been made in eight weeks, and in time to have assisted in the advance on Dongola. The vessels and machinery had been constructed and erected in the works in London; they were then marked, numbered, and taken to pieces, and after being shipped to Alexandria and transported to the front were finally put together at Kosheh. Although in a journey of 4,000 miles they were seven times transhipped, not a single important piece was lost.

The London firm sent out three engineers to supervise the re-erection at Kosheh. Of these the chief, Mr. F. W. L. Shaw, was killed at Balliana by a piece of machinery falling on him when superintending the transportation there. The second, Mr. M. Nicholson, a Newcastle man, died from cholera at Wady Halfa. The third of these brave citizens, Mr. McDonald, completed the undertaking, and remained at the front during the campaign.

The convenience of Kosheh on the clear waterway, and the dirty condition of Firket, were in themselves sufficient reasons for the change of camp; but another and graver cause lay behind. During the month of June an epidemic of cholera began to creep up the Nile from Cairo. On the 29th there were some cases at Assuan. On the 30th it reached Wady Halfa. In consequence of this the North Staffordshire Regiment marched into camp at Gemai. Their three months' occupation of the town had not improved their health or their spirits. Lieutenant Sword's account dwells with a persistence that is almost unsoldierly on the hardships and privations to which his regiment was exposed throughout the campaign—hardships which, although undoubtedly severe, did not bear comparison with those suffered by the regiments in the expedition to Tirah, and were no greater than those experienced the British Brigade before the Atbara. But of all their misfortunes the cholera was undoubtedly the worst. During the sixteen-mile march along the railway track to Gemai the first fatal case occurred, and thereafter the sickness clung to the regiment until the middle of August, causing continual deaths.

The cholera spread steadily southward up the river, claiming successive victims in each camp. In the second week of July it reached the new camp at Kosheh, whence all possible precautions to exclude it had proved vain. The epidemic was at first of a virulent form. As is usual, when it had expended its destructive energy, the recoveries became more frequent. But of the first 1,000 cases between Assuan and Suarda nearly 800 proved fatal. Nor were the lives thus lost to be altogether measured by the number.[2] To all, the time was one of trial, almost of terror. The violence of the battle may be cheaply braved, but the insidious attacks of disease appal the boldest. Death moved continually about the ranks of the army—not the death they had been trained to meet unflinchingly, the death in high enthusiasm and the pride of life, with all the world to weep or cheer; but a silent, unnoticed, almost ignominious summons, scarcely less sudden and far more painful than the bullet or the sword-cut. The Egyptians, in spite of their fatalistic creed, manifested profound depression. The English soldier was moody and ill-tempered. Even the light-hearted

2 The attacks and deaths from cholera in the Dongola Expeditionary Force were as follow:

	Attacks	Deaths
British troops	24	19
Native troops	406	260
Followers	788	640

WATER TRANSPORT

Soudanese lost their spirits; their merry grins were seen no longer; their laughter and their drums were stilled. Only the British officers preserved a stony cheerfulness, and ceaselessly endeavoured by energy and example to sustain the courage of their men. Yet they suffered most of all. Their education had developed their imaginations; and imagination, elsewhere a priceless gift, is amid such circumstances a dangerous burden.

It was, indeed, a time of sore trouble. To find the servant dead in the camp kitchen; to catch a hurried glimpse of blanketed shapes hustled quickly to the desert on a stretcher; to hold the lantern over the grave into which a friend or comrade—alive and well six hours before—was hastily lowered, even though it was still night; and through it all to work incessantly at pressure in the solid, roaring heat, with a mind ever on the watch for the earliest of the fatal symptoms and a thirst that could only be quenched by drinking of the deadly and contaminated Nile: all these things combined to produce an experience which those who endured are unwilling to remember, but unlikely to forget. One one some of the best of the field army and the communication staff were stricken down. Gallant Fenwick, of whom they used to say that he was 'twice a V.C. without a Gazette'; Polwhele,[3] the railway subaltern, whose strange knowl-

3 Lieut. R. Polwhele, R.E. and Egyptian army.

edge of the Egyptian soldiers had won their stranger love; Trask,[4] an heroic doctor, indifferent alike to pestilence or bullets; Mr. Vallom, the chief superintendent of engines at Halfa; Farmer,[5] a young officer already on his fourth campaign; Mr. Nicholson, the London engineer; long, quaint, kind-hearted 'Roddy' Owen[6] all filled graves in Halfa cemetery or at the foot of Firket mountain. Gradually the epidemic burnt itself out, and by the middle of August it had practically ceased to be a serious danger. But the necessity of enforcing quarantine and other precautions had hampered movement up and down the line of communications, and so delayed the progress of the preparations for an advance.

Other unexpected hindrances arose. Sir H. Kitchener had clearly recognised that the railway, equipped as it then was, would be at the best a doubtful means for the continual supply of a large force many miles ahead of it. He therefore organised an auxiliary boat service and passed *gyassas* and *nuggurs*[7] freely up the Second Cataract. During the summer months, in the Soudan, a strong north wind prevails, which not only drives the sailing-boats up against the stream—sometimes at the rate of twenty miles a day—but also gratefully cools the air. This year, for forty consecutive days, at the critical period of the campaign, the wind blew hot and adverse from the south. The whole auxiliary boat service was thus practically arrested. But in spite of these aggravating obstacles the preparations for the advance were forced onwards. It soon became necessary for the gunboats and steamers to be brought on to the upper reach of the river.

The Second Cataract has a total descent of sixty feet, and is about nine miles long. For this distance the Nile flows down a rugged stairway formed by successive ledges of black granite.

The flood river deeply submerges these steps, and rushes along above them with tremendous force, but with a smooth though swirling surface. As the Nile subsides, the steps begin to show, until the river tumbles violently from ledge to ledge, its whole surface for

4 Surg.-Captain J. E. Trask, A.M.S.

5 Lieut. H. H. F. Farmer, 60th Rifles and Egyptian army.

6 Brevet-Major E. R. Owen, D.S.O., Lancashire Fusiliers.

7 Native sailing craft.

miles churned to the white foam of broken water, and thickly studded with black rocks. At the Second Cataract, moreover, the only deep channel of the Nile is choked between narrow limits, and the stream struggles furiously between stern walls of rock. These dark gorges present many perils to the navigator. The most formidable, the Bab-el-Kebir, is only thirty-five feet wide.

The river here takes a plunge of ten feet in seventy yards, and drops five feet at a single bound. An extensive pool above, formed by the junction of two arms of the river, increases the volume of the water and the force of the stream, so that the 'Gate' constitutes an obstacle of difficulty and danger which might well have been considered insurmountable.

It had been expected that in the beginning of July enough water would be passing down the Second Cataract to enable the gunboats and steamers waiting below to make the passage. Everything depended upon the rise of the river, and in the perversity of circumstances, the river this year rose much later and slower than usual. By the middle of August, however, the attempt appeared possible. On the 14th the first gunboat, the *Metemma,* approached the Cataract . The North Staffordshire Regiment from Gemai, and the 6th and 7th Egyptian battalions from Kosheh, marched to the 'Gate ' to draw the vessel bodily up in spite of the current.

The best native pilots had been procured. Colonel Hunter and the naval officers under Commander Colville directed the work. The boat had been carefully prepared for the ordeal. To reduce, by raising the freeboard, the risk of swamping, the bows were heightened and strengthened, and stout wooden bulwarks were built running from bow to stern. Guns and ammunition were then removed, and the vessel lightened by every possible means.

A strop of wire rope was passed completely round the hull, and to this strong belt the five cables were fastened—two on each side and one at the bow. So steep was the *slope of the water* that it was found necessary to draw all the fires, and the steamer was thus dependent entirely upon external force. It was luckily possible to obtain a direct pull, for a crag of black rock rose above the surface of the pool opposite the 'Gate.' On this a steel block was fixed, and the hawser was led away at right angles until it reached the east bank, where a smooth stretch of sand afforded a convenient place for the hauling parties. Two thousand men were then set to pull at the cables, yet such was the extraordinary force of the current that, although the actual distance in which these great efforts were necessary was scarcely one hundred yards, the passage of each steamer occupied an hour and a half, and required the most strenuous exertions of the soldiers. No accident, however, occurred, and the six other vessels accomplished the ascent on successive days. In a week the whole flotilla steamed safely in the open water of the upper reach.

And now for a moment it seemed that the luck of the expedition had returned. The cholera was practically extinct. The new gunboat *Zafir* was nearly ready at Kosheh, and her imposing appearance delighted and impressed the army. On the 23rd of August all the seven steamers which had passed the Cataract arrived in a stately procession opposite the camp. Almost at the same time the wind changed to the north, and a cool and delicious breeze refreshed the weary men and bore southward to Suarda a whole fleet of sailing boats laden with supplies, which had been lying weather-bound during the previous six weeks at the head of the rapids. The preparatory orders for the advance tinkled along the telegraph. The North Staffordshire Regiment were, to the intense relief of officers and men, warned to hold themselves in readiness for an immediate move.

The mounted troops had already returned to the front from the camps in which they had been distributed. At last the miserable delay was over. From Kosheh to Kerma, the first Dervish position, the distance by river is 127 miles. A study of the map shows that by land marches this can be shortened by nearly 41 miles; 30 miles being saved by cutting across the great loop of the Nile from Kosheh to Sadin Fanti, and 11 miles by avoiding the angle from Fereig to Abu Fatmeh. From Kerma to Dongola, which latter town was the objective of the expedition, a further distance of 35 miles must be traversed, making a total of 120 miles by land or 101 by river. The long desert march from Kosheh to Sadin Fanti was the only natural difficulty by land.

Although the river from Kosheh to Kerma is broken by continual rapids, it is, with one interval, freely navigable at half Nile. The Amara Cataract, ten miles beyond Kosheh, is easily ascended by sailing boats with a fair wind, and by steamers without assistance. From Amara to the Kaibar Cataract stretches a reach of sixty-five miles of open water. The Kaibar Cataract is, during the flood, scarcely any hindrance to navigation; but at Hannek, about thirty miles further on, the three miles of islands, rocks, rapids, and broken water which are called the Third Cataract are, except at high Nile, a formidable barrier. Once this is passed, there is open water for more than 200 miles at all seasons to Merawi. The banks of the river, except near Sadin Fanti, where .the hills close in, are flat and low.

The Eastern bank is lined with a fringe of palmtrees and a thin strip of cultivation, which constitutes what is called 'the fertile province of Dongola.' On the other side the desert reaches the water's edge. Along the right bank of this part of the river the army was now to move.

The first act of the advance was the occupation of Absarat, and on the 23rd of August MacDonald's brigade marched thither from Suarda, cutting across the desert to Sadin Fanti, and then following the bank. The march of twenty-one miles proved most painful to the troops. The day was intensely hot. The soldiers were in heavy marching order. All the remaining camels of the army—for hundreds had died during the campaign were absorbed by the Transport. Economy had forbidden the purchase of more, and, in consequence, the soldiers had only such water as they could carry in their bottles, and the column was not accompanied by camels laden with water-skins. The brigade suffered terribly from thirst. Although the battalions were Soudanese there were twenty-nine cases of heat apoplexy, two of which proved immediately fatal. Great numbers of men fell out, and all struggled into camp in an exhausted condition.

The occupation of Absarat covered the next movement. On the 26th Lewis's brigade was ordered to march across the loop from Kosheh to Sadin Fanti and reinforce the brigade at Absarat. The distance of thirty-seven miles was far too great to be accomplished without a system of watering-places. This the Sirdar rapidly organised. Water-depôts were formed by carrying tanks and water-skins on camels to two points in the desert, and replenishing them by daily convoys. But now a heavy calamity descended on the arrangements of the General and the hopes of the troops.

During the afternoon of the 25th the wind veered suddenly to the south, and thereupon a terrific storm of sand and rain, accompanied by thunder and lightning, burst over the whole of the Nubian desert, and swept along the line of communications from Suarda to Halfa. On the next day a second deluge delayed the march of Lewis's brigade. But late on the 27th they started, with disastrous results. Before they had reached the first watering-place a third tempest, preceded by its choking sandstorm, overtook them. Nearly 300 men fell out during the early part of the night, and crawled and staggered back to Kosheh. Before the column reached Sadin Fanti 1,700 more sank exhausted to the ground. Out of one battalion 700 strong, only 60 men marched in. Nine deaths and eighty serious cases of prostration occurred, and the movement of the brigade from Kosheh to Absarat was grimly called 'The Death March.'

It would perhaps be scarcely just to accuse the Sirdar of having caused the misfortune by the neglect of any precaution. The fact that on subsequent days the other brigades made the march without great suffering proves the sufficiency of his arrangement when not upset by such phenomenal occurrences as these fearful storms. It was imperative that the advance, once begun, should be rapid. It was desirable to avoid the loop of the river and save a thirty-mile detour. The desert march was therefore not unnecessary. The disaster can fairly be described as an 'Act of God.'

Doubtless the original conception of this phase of the campaign contemplated the infliction on the troops of arduous and severe marches. Such circumstances will often occur in war.[8] They were in this case aggravated by the pitiless economy which was enforced; for which the Sirdar cannot be held alone responsible, and which was the necessary condition to the recovery of the Soudan until the British nation became interested in the enterprise. The whole of the Camel Corps, the officers' chargers, every available animal was sent out into the desert to pick up the wretched stragglers; and the promptitude with which the General acted minimised the evil results. But the 'Death March' was the least of the misfortunes caused by the storms. The violent rains produced floods, such as had not

8 I am reminded of the march of the 35th Sikhs to the relief of the Malakand on the 30th July, 1897. Eighteen men in this one battalion fell down dead by the roadside between Jalala and Dargai.

been seen in the Soudan for fifty years. The water, pouring down the broad valleys, formed furious torrents in the narrower gorges. More than twelve miles of the railway were washed away. The rails were twisted and bent; the formation entirely destroyed. The telegraph wires were broken. The work of weeks was lost in a few hours. The advance was stopped as soon as it had been begun. At the moment when every military reason demanded speed and suddenness, a hideous delay became inevitable.

In this time of crisis the success of the whole campaign hung in the balance. Sir Herbert Kitchener did not then possess that measure of the confidence and affection of his officers which his military successes have since compelled. Public opinion was still undecided on the general question of the war. The initial bad luck had frightened many. All the croakers were ready. 'A Jingo Government' — 'An incapable General' — 'Another disaster in the Soudan' —such were the whispers. A check would be the signal for an outcry. The accounts of 'The Death March' had not yet reached England; but the correspondents, irritated—not without reason—at being 'chained to Headquarters,' were going to see about that. And, besides all this, there was the army to feed and the Dervishes to fight. In this serious emergency, which threatened to wreck his schemes, the Sirdar's organising talents shone more brilliantly than at any other moment in this account. Travelling swiftly to Moghrat, he possessed himself of the telephone, which luckily still worked. All depended on him. But his grasp of detail and power of arrangement were never better displayed. He knew the exact position of every soldier, coolie, camel, or donkey at his disposal. In a few hours, in spite of his crippled transport, he concentrated 5,000 men on the damaged sections of the line, and thereafter fed them until the work was finished. In seven days traffic was resumed. The advance had been delayed, but it was not prevented.

On the 5th of September the 1st (Lewis) and 2nd (MacDonald) brigades moved to Dulgo, and at the same time the remainder of the army began to march across the loop from Kosheh by Sadin Fanti to Absarat. Every available soldier had been collected for the final operation of the campaign.

The Expeditionary Force was organised as follows:—

Commander-in-Chief: The Sirdar

The Infantry Division: Colonel Hunter Commanding

1st Brigade	*2nd Brigade*	*3rd Brigade*	*4th Brigade*
Major Lewis	Major MacDonald	Major Maxwell	Major David*
3rd Egyptians	XIth Soudanese	2nd Egyptians	1st Egyptians
4th Egyptians	XIIth Soudanese	7th Egyptians	5th Egyptians
IXth Soudanese	XIIth Soudanese	8th Egyptians	15th Egyptians
Xth Soudanese			

Cavalry Brigade and Mounted Forces: Major Burn-Murdoch

Cavalry. . . . . .8 Squadrons

Camel Corps . . . . .6 Companies

Horse Artillery . . . . 1 Battery

Artillery: Major Parsons**

Field Artillery . . . . .2 Batteries

Maxims . . . . 1 Battery (British)

Divisional Troops: Major Currie***

North Staffordshire Regiment . . . . 1st Battalion

The Flotilla: Commander Colville****

Gunboats. . . . . *Zafir, Tamai, Abu Klea, Metemma, El Teb*

Armed Steamers . . . . *Kaibar, Dal, Akasha*

Total: 15.000 men, 8 war-vessels, and 36 guns

Thus thirteen of the sixteen battalions of the Egyptian army were employed at the front. Two others, the 6th and XIth, were disposed along the line of communication, holding the various fortified posts. The 16th battalion of reservists remained at Suakin. The whole native army was engaged in the war, and the preservation of domestic order in the capital and throughout the Khedive's dominions was left entirely to the police and to the British Army of Occupation. By the 9th all four brigades had reached the rendezvous at Dulgo; on the 10th the British regiment, which it was determined

* Major E. F. David, R.M.L.I. and Egyptian army.

** Major C. S. B. Parsons, R.A. and Egyptian Army.

*** Major T. Currie, North Staffordshire Regiment.

**** Commander Hon. S. C. G. Colville, R.N.

to send up in the steamers, was moved to Kosheh by rail from Sarras and Gemai. The Sirdar prepared to start with the flotilla on the 12th.

But a culminating disappointment remained. By tremendous exertions the *Zafir* had been finished in time to take part in the operations. The Sirdar had watched the vessel grow day by day with a strange attention. She became his toy, his pet. Throughout the army it was expected that the *Zafir* would be the feature of the campaign. At length the work was finished, and the *Zafir* floated, powerful and majestic, on the waters of the Nile. On the afternoon of the 11th of September many officers and men came to witness her trial trip. The bank was lined with spectators. Colville took command. The Sirdar and his Staff embarked. Flags were hoisted and amid general cheering the moorings were cast off.

But the stern paddle had hardly revolved twice when there was a loud report, like that of a heavy gun, clouds of steam rushed up from the boilers, and the engines stopped. Sir H. Kitchener and Commander Colville were on the upper deck. The latter rushed below to learn what had happened, and found that she had burst her low-pressure cylinder, a misfortune impossible to repair until a new one could be obtained from Halfa and fitted. The Sirdar was still waiting on the deck, expecting to hear of some trifling accident, when the naval officer returned. 'She has burst her cylinder,' he said. A slight flush passed over the General's face. 'How many days,' he asked, ' will it take to repair her?' 'To repair her is impossible. You will have to wait until a new one is sent up.' 'Then she is absolutely useless, and put out of action?' 'Absolutely.'

The Sirdar stood immovable, while everyone, remembering all the disappointments and misfortunes, watched and expected another explosion of a different kind. His face was impassive, and only a slight twitching of the eyes betrayed his intense emotion. There was a long and unpleasant silence. Then he said: ' By God, Colville, I don't know which of us it's hardest luck on—you or me. Well, get her guns out at once and put them on board the other steamers;' and with that he left the ship. Within a quarter of an hour of the accident the guns were being dismantled, and before night the *Zafir*—proudly named the *Victorious*—was cleared of everything. The Sirdar in bitterness and vexation shut himself in the cabin of the *Dal* steamer, figuring out his calculations again and estimating his forces, now deprived of so powerful a factor. It was not until the next day that he reappeared, and only the passionate telegrams which he had despatched to Cairo revealed the depth of his emotions.

The advance was now finally begun. On the 13th the 1st. 2nd, and 3rd brigades occupied Kaderma. Here the flotilla overtook them, and henceforward the boats on the river kept pace with the army on the bank. Fareig was reached on the 14th, and as the numerous palms by the water afforded a pleasant shade a halt of two days was ordered. On the 16th the 4th brigade arrived, and the concentration of the force was then complete.

Meanwhile the reader has heard nothing of the enemy, for the enemy in this phase of the Dongola campaign were the smallest part of the Sirdar's difficulties. The cholera, the adverse winds, the floods, were redoubtable antagonists. Beside them the Dervishes appeared insignificant. Yet it is necessary to consider them, for although it was certain that, once the army was within striking distance, their destruction or rout would follow, they add a pleasing excitement to the labours of the troops and a romantic interest to the account of the campaign.

After the annihilation of his strong advanced post Firket, the Dervish Emir, Wad Bishara, concentrated his remaining forces in Dongola. Here during the summer he had waited, and in the middle of August some small reinforcements under one Emir of low rank reached him from Omdurman. The Khalifa, indeed, promised that many more should follow, but his promises long remained unfulfilled, and the greatest strength that Bishara could muster was 900 Jehadia, 800 Baggara Arabs, 2,800 spearmen, 450 camel-men, 650 cavalry—in all 5,600 men, with six small brass cannon and one mitrailleuse gun. To augment in numbers, if not in strength, this small force of regular soldiers, he impressed a large number of the local tribesmen; but as these were, for the most part, anxious to join the Government troops at the first opportunity, their effect in the conflict was inconsiderable.

The army was small, but the spirit of its leader placed it above contempt; for among the later commanders of the Dervish forces it is difficult to find a better type of Arab than Bishara. Although only thirty-two, he had risen to a high place in the Khalifa's service. He was a Baggara of Baggaras, and the fact that he belonged to Abdullahi's particular clan, the Taiasha, may explain, as his conduct justified, his rapid promotion. His military experience had been gained in Darfur, where he had commanded a *rub* or brigade under Osman-Wad-Adam throughout the revolt of the 'Man of the Fig-tree.' On the death of Osman Bishara for some time held the supreme command of the Army of the West, He was in due course superseded by Mahmud, a relation of the Khalifa, and a man of whom this story must later take much notice.

The cruelty, the sensuality, and the incapacity of his new chief disgusted the chaste and valiant Bishara, and, having incautiously expressed himself on the subject, he was degraded by Mahmud from the position of second in command of the army to that of the commander of a simple *rub*. After this, the breach between the two being open, the Khalifa, who seems to have had some regard for Bishara, recalled him to Omdurman, and appointed him to the command of a brigade of his own guard or *mulazemin*.

The vice which was at this time unhappily rampant in the capital soon assailed the virtue of the young Emir, and in the giddy whirl of Omdurman society he fell from his high standard of austerity: nor was he able to regain it when he was sent to take command of the army in Dongola after the recall of Yunes, and we read that he lived in the town surrounded by singing-girls and concubines. His courage and his talents were, however, undoubted. He was the first to recover from the general consternation that followed in Dongola the news of the disaster at Firket. His determination restored the firmness of the others.

The delay in the advance raised their hopes: and they were further cheered by the tidings of the floods and cholera by which their enemies were afflicted, and which seemed to prove to them that God would defend the right. Some of the Emirs, indeed, desired to send their wives and families to Metemma; but Bishara, fearing lest they themselves should follow, decided to keep the women at the front a sort of sheet-anchor to his nervous but uxorious warriors. To further fortify their resolution he informed them in July that pestilence and famine had dispersed the army of 'the Turks'; that the

'God-forsaken Sirdar' had retired to a small island, attended only by his cook; and that, the cook having died, the impious general was about to starve. Nor did he neglect military precautions, and as soon as his Dervishes had regained their courage he ordered Osman Azrak to reoccupy Hafir and Kerma. During the month of August rumours that the advance was about to recommence reached him, and he thereupon marched north with his whole force and his whole harem, and began to fortify Kerma, as if finally determined to abide the issue there.

The first sign that the forces were drawing closer was the cutting of the telegraph-wire by a Dervish patrol on the 6th of September. On the 10th the Sirdar heard that Kerma was strongly held. On the 15th of September the Egyptian cavalry first established contact with the Dervish scouts, and a slight skirmish took place. On the 18th the whole force advanced to Sardek, and as Bishara still held his position at Kerma it looked as if an action was imminent. It was resolved to attack the Dervish position at Kerma at dawn. Although it seemed that only four miles separated the combatants, the night passed quietly. With the first light the army began to move, and when the sun rose the spectacle of the moving masses of men and artillery, with the gunboats on the right, was inspiring.

The soldiers braced themselves for the expected action. But no sooner were the village and fort of Kerma visible than the report passed along the ranks that it was deserted. Rumour was soon merged in certainty, for on reaching Kerma it was found that the Dervishes had evacuated the place, and only the strong, well-built mud fort attested the recent presence of Bishara. Whither had he gone? The question was not left unanswered.

Half a mile to the southward, on the opposite bank of the river, among the groves of palm-trees ran a long and continuous line of shelter trenches and loopholed walls. The flanks of this new position rested on the deep morasses which extend from the river both on the north and south sides of Hafir. A small steamer, a fleet of large *gyassas* and other sailing vessels moored to the further shore explained what had happened.

Conscious of his weakness, the prudent Emir had adroitly transported himself across the river, and had thus placed that broad flood between his troops and their destruction. Meanwhile the three gunboats—all that now remained of the armed flotilla, for the *Teb* had run on a rock in the Hannek Cataract—were steaming gradually nearer the enemy, and the army swung to the right, and, forming along the river bank, became spectators of a scene of fascinating interest. At half-past six the Horse battery unlimbered at the water's edge, and began to fire obliquely up and across the river. As soon as the first few shells had reached the Arab entrenchment the whole line of shelter trenches was edged with smoke, and the Dervishes replied with a heavy rifle fire. The distance was, however, too great for their bad rifles and inferior ammunition, and their bullets, although they occasionally struck the ground on which the infantry were drawn up, did not during the day cause any loss to the watching army.

The Dervish position was about half a mile in length. As the gunboats approached the northern end they opened fire with their guns, striking the mud entrenchments at every shot, and driving clouds of dust and splinters into the air. The Maxim guns began to search the parapets, and two companies of the Staffordshire Regiment on board the unarmoured steamers *Dal* and *Akasha* fired long-range volleys. Now, as on other occasions throughout the war, the Dervishes by their military behaviour excited the admiration of their enemies. Encouraged by the arrival in the morning of a reinforcement from Omdurman of 1,000 Black *Jehadia* and 500 spearmen under Abdel Baki, the Dervish gunners stood to their guns and the riflemen to their trenches, and, although suffering severely, maintained a formidable fire.

The gunboats continued to advance, beating up slowly against the strong current. As they came opposite Hafir, where the channel narrows to about 600 yards, they were received by a very heavy fire from guns placed in cleverly screened batteries, and from the riflemen sheltered in deep pits by the water's edge or concealed amid the foliage of the tops of the palm-trees. These aerial skirmishers commanded the decks of the vessels, and the shields of the guns were thus rendered of little protection. All the water round the gunboats was torn into foam by the projectiles. The bullets pattered against their sides, and, except where they were protected by steel plates, penetrated. One shell struck the *Abu Klea* on the water-line, and entered the magazine. Luckily it did not explode, the Dervishes having forgotten to set the fuse. Three shells struck the *Metemma*. On board the *Tamai*, which was leading, Commander Colville was severely wounded in the wrist; Armourer-Sergeant Richardson was killed at his Maxim gun, and on each boat some casualties occurred. So hot was the fire that it was thought doubtful whether to proceed with the bombardment, and the *Tamai* swung round, and hurried down the river with the current and at full steam to report to the Sirdar. The other gunboats remained in action, and continued to shell the Dervish defences. The *Tamai* soon returned to the fight, and, steaming again up the river, was immediately hotly re-engaged.

The sight which the army witnessed was thrilling. Beyond the flood waters of the river, backed against a sky of staring blue and in the blazing sunlight, the whole of the enemy's position was plainly visible. The long row of shelter trenches was outlined by the white smoke of musketry and dotted with the bright-coloured flags waving defiantly in the wind and with the still brighter flashes of the guns. Behind the entrenchments and among the mud houses and enclosures strong bodies of the *jibba*-clad Arabs were arrayed. Still further back in the plain a large force of cavalry—conspicuous by the gleams of light reflected from their broad-bladed spears—wheeled and manoeuvred.

By the Nile all the tops of the palmtrees were crowded with daring riflemen, whose positions were indicated by the smoke-puffs of their rifles or when some tiny black figure fell, like a shot rook, to the ground. In the foreground the gunboats, panting and puffing up the river, surrounded on all sides by spouts and spurts of water, thrown up by the shells and bullets, looked like portly gentlemen pelted by schoolboys. It was, however, a more dangerous game. Again the flotilla drew near the narrow channel; again the watching army held their breath; and again they saw the leading boat, the *Metemma*, turn and run down stream towards safety, pursued by the wild cheers of the Arabs. It was evident that the gunboats were not strong enough to silence the Dervish fire, and it was too perilous to run the gauntlet without having at least subdued it. The want of the terrible *Zafir* was acutely felt.

The firing had lasted two hours and a half, and the enemy's resistance was no less vigorous than at the beginning of the action. The Sirdar now altered his plans. He saw that his flotilla could not hope to silence the Dervishes. He therefore ordered De Rougemont—who had assumed the command after Colville was wounded—to run past the entrenchments without trying to crush their fire, and steam on to Dongola. To support and cover the movement, the three batteries of artillery under Major Parsons were brought into action from the swampy island of Artagasha, which was connected at this season with the right bank by a shoal. At the same time three battalions of infantry were moved along the river until opposite the Arab position. At 9 a.m. the eighteen guns on the island opened a tremendous bombardment at 1,200 yards range on the entrenchments, and at the same time the infantry and a rocket detachment concentrated their fire on the tops of the palm-trees. The artillery now succeeded in silencing three of the five Dervish guns and in sinking the little Dervish steamer *Tahra,* while the infantry by a tremendous long-range fire drove the riflemen out of the palms. Profiting by this, the gunboats at ten o'clock moved up the river in line, and, disregarding the fusillade which the Arabs still stubbornly maintained, passed by the entrenchment and steamed on towards Dongola. After this the firing on both sides became intermittent, and the fight may be said to have ended.

Both forces remained during the day facing each other on opposite sides of the river, and the Dervishes, who evidently did not admit a defeat, brandished their rifles and waved their flags, and their shouts of loud defiance floated across the water to the troops. But they had suffered very heavily. Their brave and skilful leader was severely wounded by the splinters of a shell. The wicked Osman Azrak had been struck by a bullet, and more than 200 Ansar had fallen, including several Emirs. Moreover, a long train of wounded was seen to start during the afternoon for the south. It is doubtful, however, whether Bishara would have retreated, if he had not feared being cut off. He seems to have believed that the Sirdar would march along the right bank at once to Dongola, and cross there under cover of his gunboats. Like all Moslem soldiers, he was nervous about his line of retreat. Nor, considering the overwhelming force against him, can we wonder. There was, besides this strategic reason for retiring, a more concrete cause. All his supplies of grain were accumulated in the *gyassas* which lay moored to the west bank. These vessels were under the close and accurate fire of the artillery and Maxim guns on Artagasha island. Several times during the night the hungry Dervishes attempted to reach their store; but the moon was bright and the gunners watchful. Each time the enemy exposed themselves, a vigorous fire was opened and they were driven back. When morning dawned, it was found that Hafir was evacuated, and that the enemy had retreated on Dongola.

Wad Bishara's anxiety about his line of retreat was unnecessary, for the Sirdar could not advance on Dongola with a strong Dervish force on his line of communications: and it was not desirable to divide the army and mask Hafir with a covering force. But as soon as the Dervishes had left their entrenchments the situation was simplified. At daybreak all the Arab boats were brought over to the right bank by the villagers, who reported that Bishara and his soldiers had abandoned the defence and were retreating to Dongola. Thereupon the Sirdar, relieved of the necessity of forcing the passage, transported his army peacefully to the other bank. The operation afforded scope to his powers of organisation, and the whole force—complete with cavalry, camels, and guns—was moved across the broad, rushing river in less than thirty-six hours and without any apparent difficulty.

The casualties on the 19th were not numerous, in a force of nearly 15,000 men they appeared insignificant. Commander Colville was wounded. One British sergeant and one Egyptian officer were killed. Eleven native soldiers were wounded. The total—fourteen—amounted to less than one per thousand of the troops engaged. Nevertheless, this picturesque and bloodless affair has been solemnly called the 'Battle of Hafir.' Special despatches were written for it. It is officially counted in records of service as a 'general action.' Telegrams of congratulation were received from Her Majesty and the Khedive. A special clasp was struck. Of all the instances of cheaply bought glory which the military history of recent years affords, Hafir is the most remarkable.

The 20th and part of the 21st were occupied by the passage of the army across the Nile. The troops were still crossing when the gunboats returned from Dongola. The distance of this place by water from Hafir is about 36 miles, and the flotilla had arrived opposite the town during the afternoon of the 19th. A few shells expelled the small Dervish garrison, and a large number of sailing vessels were captured. The results of the movement of the gunboats to Dongola must, however, be looked for at Hafir. In consequence of the Sirdar's manoeuvre that place was evacuated and the unopposed passage of the river secured.

Bishara continued his retreat during the 20th, and, marching all day, reached Dongola in the evening. Wounded as he was, he re-occupied the town and began forthwith to make preparations for the defence of its considerable fortifications. The knowledge of his employment was not hidden from his enemy, and during the 21st a gunboat under Lieutenant Beatty,[9] R.N., arrived with the design of keeping him occupied. Throughout the day a desultory duel was maintained between the entrenchments and the steamer. Although the Dervish artillery was repeatedly dismounted, they continued to reply to the fire, and, changing their brass guns from one embrasure to the other with great rapidity, puzzled the gunboat. But their aim was bad. The ten Egyptian artillerymen who had been forced to serve in the batteries at Hafir had now escaped from their long captivity. The Dervishes themselves had no skill in shooting, and although they were firing at intervals for two days they did not once hit their target.

At daylight on the 22nd, Beatty was reinforced by another gunboat, and an unceasing bombardment was made on the town and its defences. Notwithstanding that the army did not finish crossing the river until the afternoon of the 21st, the Sirdar determined to continue his advance without delay, and the force accordingly marched twelve miles further south and camped opposite the middle of the large island of Argo. At daybreak the troops started again, and before the sun had attained its greatest power reached Zowarat. This place was scarcely six miles from Dongola, and, as it was expected that an action would be fought the next day, the rest of eighteen hours was welcomed by the weary soldiers. All day long the army remained halted by the palms of the Nile bank. Looking through their glass-

9 The *Abu Klea*, Lieut. D. Beatty, R.N.

es up the river, the officers might watch the gunboats methodically bombarding Dongola, and the sound of the guns was clearly heard. At intervals during the day odd parties of Dervishes, both horse and foot, approached the outpost line and shots were exchanged. All these things, together with the consciousness that the culmination of the campaign was now at hand, raised the excitement of the army to a high pitch, and everyone lay down that night warmed by keen anticipations. An atmosphere of unrest hung over the bivouac, and few slept soundly. At three o'clock the troops were aroused, and at half-past four the final advance on Dongola had begun.

It was still night. The full moon, shining with tropical brilliancy in a cloudless sky, vaguely revealed the rolling plains of sand and the huge moving mass of the army. As long as it was dark the battalions were closely formed in quarter columns. But presently the warmer, yellower light of dawn—as different from the moonlight as is the flush of youth from the pallor of a corpse—began to grow across the river and through the palms. Gradually, as the sun rose and it became daylight, the dense formation of the army was extended to an array more than two miles long. On the left, nearest the river, marched Lewis's brigade—three battalions in line and the fourth in column as a reserve. Next in order Maxwell's three battalions prolonged the line. The artillery were in the centre, supported by the North Staffordshire Regiment.

The gunners of the Maxim battery had donned their tunics, so that the lines and columns of yellow and brown were relieved by a single flash of British red. MacDonald's brigade was on the right. David's brigade followed in rear of the centre as a reserve. The cavalry, the Camel Corps, and the Horse Artillery watched the right flank. On the left the gunboats steamed along the river, and all who looked towards them experienced a feeling of delighted confidence when they saw that a fresh vessel had joined the flotilla. The *Zafir* her new cylinder fitted by extra-ordinary exertions, had arrived in time to be 'in at the death.' It is strange to reflect that this fine force of 15,000 bayonets and sabres and the strong flotilla which together advanced swiftly upon the enemy were commanded by a British colonel. Such are the rewards which the Egyptian service has given to capable men.

For two hours the army was the only living thing visible on the smooth sand, but at seven o'clock a large body of Dervish horse appeared on the right flank. The further advance of half a mile displayed the Arab forces. Their numbers were less than those of the Egyptians, but their white uniforms, conspicuous on the sand, and the rows of flags of many colours lent an imposing appearance to their array. Their determined aspect, no less than the reputation of Bishara, encouraged the belief that they were about to charge.

The disparity of the forces was, however, too great; and as the Egyptian army steadily advanced, the Dervishes slowly retired. Their retreat was cleverly covered by the Baggara horse, who, by continually threatening the desert flank, delayed the progress of the troops. Bishara did not attempt to re-enter the town, on which the gunboats were now concentrating their fire, but continued to retire in excellent order towards the south and Debba.

The Egyptian infantry halted in Dongola, which when they arrived they found already in the hands of detachments from the flotilla. The red flag with the crescent and star waved once again from the roof of the Mudiria. The garrison of 400 black *Jehadia* had capitulated, and were already fraternising with their Soudanese captors whose comrades-in-arms they were soon to be. While the infantry occupied the town the cavalry and Camel Corps were despatched in pursuit. The Baggara horse, however, maintained a firm attitude, and attempted several charges to cover the retreat of their infantry. In one of these an actual collision occurred, and Captain Adams's[10] squadron of Egyptian cavalry inflicted a loss of six killed on the enemy at a cost to themselves of eight men wounded.

The cavalry and Camel Corps had about twenty casualties in the pursuit. But although the Dervishes thus withdrew in an orderly manner from the field, the demoralising influence of retreat soon impaired their discipline and order, and many small parties, becoming detached from the main body, were captured by the pursuers. The line of retreat was strewn with weapons and other effects, and so many babies were abandoned by their parents that an artillery waggon had to be employed to collect and carry them. Wad Bishara, Oman Azrak, and the Baggara horse, however, made good

10 Captain R. H. Adams, Scots Greys and Egyptian army.

PRISONERS OF WAR

their flight across the desert to Metemma, and, in spite of terrible sufferings from thirst, retained sufficient discipline to detach a force to hold Abu Klea Wells in case the retreat was followed. The Dervish infantry made their way along the river to Abu Hamed, and were much harassed by the gunboats until they reached the Fourth Cataract, when the pursuit was brought to an end.

The Egyptian losses in the capture of Dongola and in the subsequent pursuit were:—British, *nil.* Native ranks: killed, 1; wounded, 25. Total, 26.

The occupation of Dongola terminated the campaign of 1896. About 900 prisoners, mostly the Black Jehadia, all the six brass cannon, large stores of grain, and a great quantity of flags, spears, and swords fell to the victors, and the whole of the province, said to be the most fertile in the Soudan, was restored to the Egyptian authority. The existence of a perpetual clear waterway from the head of the

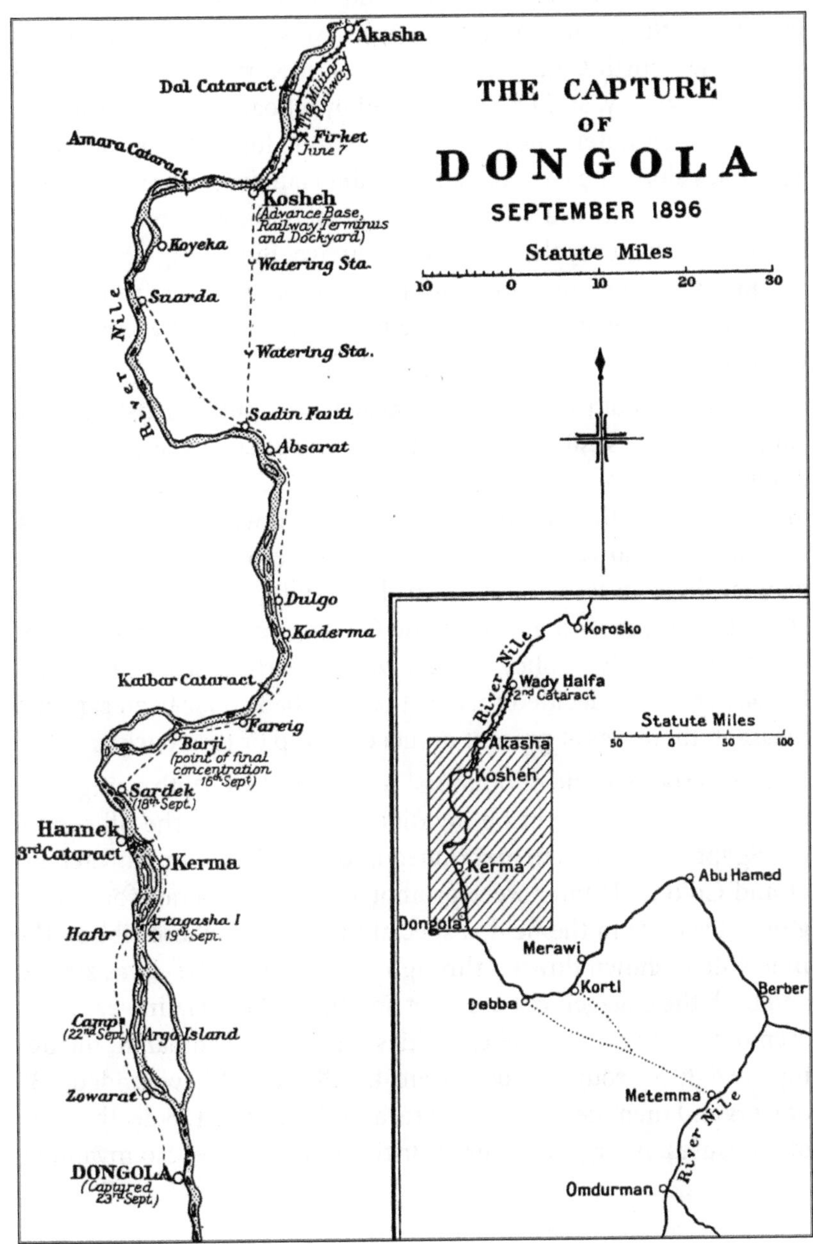
THE CAPTURE
OF
DONGOLA
SEPTEMBER 1896
Statute Miles
10 0 10 20 30
Akasha
Dal Cataract
The Military Railway
Firket
June 7
Amara Cataract
Kosheh
(Advance Base, Railway Terminus and Dockyard)
Koyeka
Watering Sta.
Suarda
River Nile
Watering Sta.
Sadin Fanti
Absarat
Dulgo
Kaderma
Kaibar Cataract
Fareig
Barji
(point of final concentration 16th Sept)
Sardek
(18th Sept.)
Hannek
3rd Cataract
Kerma
Artagasha I
Hafir
19th Sept.
Camp
(22nd Sept)
Argo Island
Zowarat
DONGOLA
(Captured 23rd Sept.)
Korosko
River Nile
Wady Halfa
2nd Cataract
Statute Miles
50 0 50 100
Akasha
Kosheh
Kerma
Abu Hamed
Dongola
Merawi
Korti
Debba
Berber
Metemma
River Nile
Omdurman

Third Cataract to Merawi enabled the gunboats to at once steam up the river for more than 200 miles, and in the course of the following month the greater part of the army was established in Merawi below the Fourth Cataract, at Debba or at Korti, drawing supplies along the railway, and from Bail-head by a boat service on the long reach of open water. The position of a strong force at Merawi—only 120 miles along the river bank from Abu Hamed, the northern Dervish post—was, as will be seen, convenient to the continuance of the campaign whenever the time should arrive. But a long delay in the advance was now inevitable, and nearly a year was destined to pass without any collision between the forces of the Khedive and those of the Khalifa.

The success of the operations caused great public satisfaction in England. The first step had been taken. The Soudan was re-entered. After ten years of defensive war the Dervishes had been attacked, and it was clear that when they were attacked with adequate forces, they were not so very terrible after all. The croakers were silent. A general desire was manifested in the country that the operations should continue, and although the Government did not yet abandon their tentative policy, or resolve to utterly destroy the Khalifa's power, it was decided that, as the road had so far been safe and pleasant, there was at present no need to stop or turn back.

A generous gazette of honours[11] was published. With a single exception, which it would be invidious to specify, all the officers of the Egyptian army were mentioned in despatches.[12] Sir H. Kitchener and Colonel Hunter were promoted Major-Generals for distinguished service in the field; a special medal—on whose ribbon the Blue Nile is shown flowing through the yellow desert—was struck; and both the engagement at Firket and the affair at Hafir were commemorated by clasps. The casualties during the campaign, including the fighting round Suakin, were 43 killed and 139 wounded; 130 officers and men died from cholera; and there were 126 deaths from other causes. A large number of British officers were also invalided.

11 Appendix C, vol. ii.
12 Appendix B, vol. ii.

CHAPTER IX
THE DESERT RAILWAY

The stem of the flower—The waterway—The Dongola campaign—The Dongola railway—A battalion of the line—Education—The floods—The extension to Kerma—The line of advance—The strategy of the war—Via Abu Hamed—The Desert Railway—Questions—Water—Into the wilderness—The town of Rail-head—The daily trains—The daily work—A peculiar peril—Abu Hamed at last—The cost—Wells of water—Breaking the record—Babel—A matter of trade—England and America—Further extensions—The country—The business of supply—The victualling yard—The Akasha phase—Dongola—Abu Hamed—The Berber difficulties—Arrival of the railway—The subalterns' victory.

It often happens that in prosperous public enterprises the applause of the nation and the rewards of the sovereign are bestowed on those whose offices are splendid and whose duties have been dramatic. Others whose labours were no less difficult, responsible, and vital to success are unnoticed. If this be true of men, it is also true of things. In a tale of war the reader's mind is filled with the fighting. The battle—with its vivid scenes, its moving incidents, its plain and tremendous results—excites imagination and commands attention. The eye is fixed on the fighting brigades as they move amid the smoke; on the swarming figures of the enemy; on the General, serene and determined, mounted in the middle of his Staff. The long trailing line of communications is unnoticed. The fierce glory that plays on red, triumphant bayonets dazzles the observer; nor does he care to look behind to where, along a thousand miles of rail, road, and river, the convoys are crawling to the front in uninterrupted succession. Victory is the beautiful, bright-coloured flower. Transport is the stem without which it could never have blossomed. Yet even the military student, in his zeal to master the fascinating com-

A BEAST OF BURDEN

binations of the actual conflict, often forgets the far more intricate complications of supply.

It cannot be denied that a battle, the climax to which all military operations tend, is an event which is not controlled by strategy or organisation. The scheme may be well planned, the troops well fed, the ammunition plentiful, and the enemy entangled, famished, or numerically inferior. The glorious uncertainties of the field can yet reverse everything. The human element in defiance of experience, probability, and logic—may produce a wholly irrational result, and a starving, outmanoeuvred army may win food, safety, and honour by their bravery. But such considerations apply with greater force to wars where both sides are equal in equipment and discipline. In savage warfare in a flat country the power of modern machinery is such that flesh and blood can scarcely prevail, and the chances of battle are reduced to a minimum. Fighting the Dervish was primarily a matter of transport. The Khalifa was conquered on the railway.

Hitherto, as the operations have progressed, it has been convenient to speak of the railway in a general manner as having been laid or extended to various points, and to merely indicate the direction of the lines of communication. The reader is now invited to take a closer view. This chapter is concerned with boats, railways, and pack animals, but particularly with railways. The details are important, for from them great events depend; nor would the pen of Rudyard Kipling search vainly for the element of romance.

Throughout the Dongola campaign in 1896 the Nile was the main channel of communication between the Expeditionary Force and its base in Egypt. All supplies were brought to the front as far as possible by water transport. Wherever the Nile was navigable, it was used. Other means of conveyance—by railways and pack animals—though essential, were merely supplementary. Boats carry more and cost less than any other form of transport. The service is not so liable to interruption; the plant needs only simple repair; the waterway is ready-made. But the Nile is not always available. Frequent cataracts obstruct its course for many miles. Other long reaches are only navigable when the river is in flood. To join the navigable reaches, and thus preserve the continuity of the communications, a complex system of railways and caravans was necessary.[1]

In the expedition to Dongola a line of railway was required to connect the two navigable reaches of the Nile which extend from Assuan to Wady Halfa, and from Kerma to Merawi. Before the capture of Dongola, however, this distance was shortened by the fact that the river at high Nile is navigable between the Third Cataract and Kerma. In consequence it was at first only necessary to construct the stretch of 108 miles between Wady Halfa and Kosheh. During the years when Wady Halfa was the southernmost garrison of the Egyptian forces a strong post had been maintained at Sarras. In the Nile expeditions of 1885 the railway from Halfa had been completed through Sarras and as far as Akasha, a distance of eighty-six miles. After the abandonment of the Soudan the Dervishes destroyed the line as far north as Sarras.

The old embankments were still standing, but the sleepers had been burnt and the rails torn up, and in many cases bent or twisted. The position in 1896 may, in fact, be summed up as follows: The section of 33 miles from Wady Halfa to Sarras was immediately

1 Map, 'Rail and River,' page 219.

available and in working order. The section of 53 miles from Sarras to Akasha required partial reconstruction. The section of 32 miles from Akasha to Kosheh must, with the exception of 10 miles of embankment completed in 1885, at once be newly made. And, finally, the section from Kosheh to Kerma must be completed before the Nile flood subsided.

The first duty therefore which the Engineer officers had to perform was the reconstruction of the line from Sarras to Akasha. No trained staff or skilled workmen were available. The lack of men with technical knowledge was doubtfully supplied by the enlistment of a 'Railway Battalion' 800 strong. These men were drawn from many tribes and classes. Their only qualification was capacity and willingness for work. They presented a motley appearance. Dervish prisoners, released but still wearing their *jibbas*, assisted stalwart Egyptians in unloading rails and sleepers. Dinkas, Shillooks, Jaalin, and Barabras shovelled contentedly together at the embankments. One hundred civilian Soudanese—chiefly time-expired soldiers—were also employed; and these, since they were trustworthy and took an especial pride in their work, soon learned the arts of spiking rails and sleepers, fishing rails together, and straightening. To direct and control the labours of these men of varied race and language, but of equal inexperience, some civilian foremen platelayers were obtained at high rates of pay from Lower Egypt. These, however, with very few exceptions were not satisfactory, and they were gradually replaced by intelligent men of the 'Railway Battalion,' who had learned their trade as the line progressed. The projection, direction, and execution of the whole work was entrusted to a few subalterns of Engineers, of whom the best-known was Edouard Girouard.[2]

Work was begun south of Sarras at the latter end of March. At first the efforts of so many unskilled workmen, instructed by few experienced officers, were productive of results ridiculous rather than important. Gradually, however, the knowledge and energy of the young director and the intelligence and devotion of still more youthful subordinates began to take effect. The pace of construction increased, and the labour was lightened by the contrivances of experience and skill.

2 Lieut. E. P. C. Girouard, R.E. and Egyptian army.

As the line grew longer, native officers and non-commissioned officers from the active and reserve lists of the Egyptian army were appointed station-masters. Intelligent non-commissioned officers and men were converted into shunters, guards, and pointsmen. Traffic was controlled by telephone. To work the telephone, men were discovered who could read and writ e—very often who could read and write only their own names, and even that with such difficulty that they usually preferred a seal. They developed into clerks by a simple process of selection. To improve their education, and to train a staff in the office work of a railway, two schools were instituted at Halfa. In these establishments, which were formed by the shade of two palm-trees, twenty pupils received the beginnings of knowledge. The simplicity of the instruction was aided by the zeal of the students, and learning grew beneath the palm-trees more quickly perhaps than in the more magnificent schools of civilisation.

The rolling stock of the Halfa-Sarras line was in good order and sufficient quantity, but the eight locomotives were out of all repair, and had to be patched up again and again with painful repetition. The regularity of their breaks-down prevented the regularity of the road, and the Soudan military railway gained a doubtful reputation during the Dongola expedition and in its early days. Nor were there wanting those who employed their wits in scoffing at the undertaking and in pouring thoughtless indignation on the engineers. Nevertheless the work went on continually.

The initial difficulties of the task were aggravated an unexpected calamity. On the 26th of August the violent cyclonic rain-storm of which some account has been given in the last chapter broke over the Dongola province.

A writer on the earlier phases of the war[3] has forcibly explained why the consequences were so serious:

'In a country where rain is an ordinary event the engineer lays his railway line, not in the bottom of a valley, but at a higher level on one slope or the other Where he passes across branching side valleys, he takes care to leave in all his embankments large culverts to carry off flood-water. But here, in what was thought to be the rainless Soudan, the line south of Sarras followed for mile after mile

3 Hilliard Atteridge, *Towards Khartoum.*

the bottom of the long valley of Khor Ahrusa, and no provision had been made, or had been thought necessary, for culverts in the embankments where minor hollows were crossed. Thus, when the flood came, it was not merely that the railway was cut through here and there by the rushing deluge. It was covered deep in water, the ballast swept away, and some of the banks so destroyed that in places rails and sleepers were left hanging in the air across a wide gap.'

Nearly fourteen miles of track were destroyed. The camp of the construction gangs was wrecked and flooded. Some of the rifles of the escort—for the conditions of war were never absent—were afterwards recovered from a depth of three feet of sand. In one place, where the embankment had partially withstood the deluge, a great lake several miles square appeared. By extraordinary exertions the damage was repaired in a week.

As soon as the line as far as Kosheh was completed, the advance towards Dongola began. After the army had been victorious at Hafir the whole province was cleared of Dervishes, and the Egyptian forces pushed on to Merawi. Here they were dependent on river transport. But the Nile was falling rapidly, and the army was soon in danger of being stranded by the interruption of river traffic between the Third Cataract and Kernia. The extension of the line from Kosheh to Kerma was therefore of vital importance. The survey was at once undertaken, and a suitable route was chosen through the newly acquired and unmapped territory. Of the ninety-five miles of extended track, fifty-six were through the desert, and the constructors here gained the experience which was afterwards of value on the great desert railway from Wady Halfa to the Atbara. Battalions of troops were distributed along the line and ordered to begin to make the embankments. Track-laying commenced south of Kosheh on the 9th of October, and the whole work was carried forward with feverish energy. As it progressed, and before it was completed, the reach of the river from the Third Cataract to Kerma ceased to be navigable. The army was now dependent for its existence on the partly finished railway, from the head of which supplies were conveyed by an elaborate system of camel transport. Every week the line grew, the Rail-head moved forward, and the strain upon the pack animals diminished. But the problem of feeding the field army

. without interfering with the railway construction was one of extraordinary intricacy and difficulty. The carrying capacity of the line was strictly limited. The worn-out engines frequently broke down. On many occasions only three were in working order, and the other five undergoing 'heavy repairs' which might secure them another short span of usefulness. Three times the construction had to be suspended to allow the army to be revictualled. Every difficulty was, however, overcome. By the beginning of May the line to Kerma was finished, and the whole of the Railway Battalion, its subalterns and its director, turned their attention to a greater enterprise.

In the first week in December the Sirdar returned from England with instructions or permission to continue the advance towards Khartoum, and the momentous question of the route to be followed arose. It may at first seem that the plain course was to continue to work along the Nile, connecting its navigable reaches by sections of railway. But from Merawi to Abu Hamed the river is broken by continual cataracts, and the broken ground of both banks made a railway nearly an impossibility. The movements of the French expeditions towards the Upper Nile counselled speed. The poverty of Egypt compelled economy. The Nile route, though sure, would be slow and very expensive. A short cut must be found. Three daring and ambitious schemes presented themselves:—(1) The line followed by the Desert Column in 1884 from Korti to Metemma; (2) the celebrated, if not notorious, route from Suakin to Berber; (3) across the Nubian desert from Korosko or Wady Halfa to Abu Hamed.

The question involved the whole strategy of the war. No more important decision was ever taken by Sir Herbert Kitchener, whether in office or in action. The request for a British division, the attack on Mahmud's *zeriba*, the great left wheel towards Omdurman during that battle, the treatment of the Marchand expedition, were matters of lesser resolve than the selection of the line of advance. The known strength of the Khalifa made it evident that a powerful force would be required for the destruction of his army and the capture of his capital. The use of railway transport to some point on the Nile whence there was a clear waterway was therefore imperative. Berber and Metemma were known, and Abu Hamed was believed to fulfil this condition. But both Berber and Metemma were important strategic points. It was improbable that the Dervishes would abandon these keys to Khartoum and the Soudan without severe resistance. It seemed likely, indeed, that the Khalifa would strongly reinforce both towns, and desperately contest their possession. The deserts between Korti and Metemma, and between Suakin and Berber, contained scattered wells, and small raiding parties might have cut the railway and perhaps have starved the army at its head. It was therefore too dangerous to project the railway toward either Berber or Metemma until they were actually in our hands. The argument is circular. The towns could not be taken without a strong force; so strong a force could not advance until the railway was made; and the railway could not be made till the towns were taken.

Both the Korti-Metemma and the Suakin-Berber routes were therefore rejected. The resolution to exclude the latter was further strengthened by the fact that the labour of building a railway over the hills behind Suakin would have been very great.

The route *viâ* Abu Hamed was selected by the exclusion of the alternatives. But it had distinct and apparent advantages. Abu Hamed was within striking distance of the army at Merawi. It was not a point essential to the Dervish defences, and not therefore likely to be so strongly garrisoned as Berber or Metemma. It might, therefore, be captured by a column marching along the river, and sufficiently small to be equipped with only camel transport. The deserts through which the railway to Abu Hamed would pass contain few wells, and therefore it would be difficult for small raiding parties to cut the line or attack the construction gangs; and before the line got within reach of the Dervish garrison at Abu Hamed, that garrison would be dislodged and the place seized.

The plan was perfect, and the argument in its favour conclusive. It turned, however, on one point: Was the Desert Railway a possibility? With this question the General was now confronted. He appealed to expert opinion. Eminent railway engineers in England were consulted. They replied with unanimity that, having due regard to the circumstances, and remembering the conditions of war under which the work must be executed, it was impossible to construct such a line. Distinguished soldiers were approached on the subject. They replied that the scheme was not only impossible, but absurd. Many other persons who were not consulted volunteered the opinion that the whole idea was that of a lunatic, and predicted ruin and disaster to the expedition. Having received this advice, and reflected on it duly, the Sirdar ordered the railway to be constructed without more delay.[4]

A further question immediately arose: Should the railway to Abu Hamed start from Korosko or from Wady Halfa? There were arguments on both sides. The adoption of the Korosko line would reduce the river stage from Assuan by forty-eight hours upstream.

The old caravan route had been from Korosko *viâ* Murat wells to Abu Hamed. It was by this road that General Gordon had travelled to Khartoum on his last journey. On the other hand, many workshops and appliances for construction were already existing at Wady Halfa. It was the northern terminus of the Dongola railway. This was an enormous advantage. Both routes were reconnoitred; that from Wady Halfa was selected. The decision having been taken, the enterprise was at once begun.

Lieutenant Girouard, to whom everything was entrusted, was told to make the necessary estimates. Sitting in his hut at Wady Halfa, he drew up a comprehensive list. Nothing was forgotten. Every want was provided for; every difficulty was foreseen; every requisite was noted. The questions to be decided were numerous and involved. How much carrying capacity was required? How much rolling stock? How many engines? What spare parts How much oil? How many lathes? How many cutters? How many punching and shearing machines? What arrangements of signals would be necessary? How many lamps? How many points? How many trolleys? What amount of coal should be ordered? How much water would be wanted? How should it be carried? To what extent would its carriage affect the hauling power and influence all previous calculations? How much railway plant was needed? How many miles of rail? How many thousand sleepers? Where could they be procured at such short notice? How many fish-plates were necessary? What

4 It is, however, only fair to state that in 1884 Sir Evelyn Wood had recorded his opinion that the only route from Egypt to the Soudan was *viâ* Abu Hamed—EDITOR.

tools would be required? What appliances? What machinery? How much skilled labour was wanted? How much of the class of labour available? How were the workmen to be fed and watered? How much food would they want? How many trains a day must be run to feed them and their escort? How many must be run to carry plant? How did these requirements affect the estimate for rolling stock? The answers to all these questions, and to many others with which I will not afflict the reader, were set forth by Lieutenant Girouard in a ponderous volume several inches thick; and such was the comprehensive accuracy of the estimate that the working parties were never delayed by the want even of a piece of brass wire.

Under any circumstances the task would have been enormous. It was, however, complicated by five important considerations:—It had to be executed with military precautions. There was apparently no water along the line. The feeding of 2,000 platelayers in a barren desert was a problem in itself. The work had to be completed before the winter. And, finally, the money voted was not to be outrun. The Sirdar attended to the last condition.

Girouard was sent to England to buy the plant and rolling stock. Fifteen new engines and two hundred trucks were ordered. The necessary new workshops were commenced at Halfa. Experienced mechanics were procured to direct them. Fifteen hundred additional men were enlisted in the Railway Battalion and trained. Then the water question was dealt with. The reconnoitring surveys had reported that though the line was certainly 'good and easy' for 110 miles—and, according to Arab accounts, for the remaining 120 miles—no drop of water was to be found, and only two likely spots for wells were noted. Camel transport was, of course, out of the question. Each engine must first of all haul enough water to carry it to Rail-head and back, besides a reserve against accidents. It was evident that the quantity of water required by any locomotive would continually increase as the work progressed and the distance grew greater, until finally the material trains would have one-third of their carrying power absorbed in transporting the water for their own consumption. The amount of water necessary is largely dependent on the grades of the line. The 'flat desert' proved to be a steady slope, up to a height of 1,600 feet above Halfa, and the calculations were further complicated. The difficulty had, however, to be faced, and a hundred 1,500-gallon tanks were procured. These were mounted on trucks and connected by hose; and the most striking characteristic of the trains of the Soudan military railway was the long succession of enormous boxes on wheels, on which the motive power of the engine and the lives of the passengers depended.

The first spadeful of sand of the Desert Railway was turned on the first day of 1897; but until May, when the line to Kerma was finished, no great efforts were made, and only forty miles of track had been laid. In the meanwhile the men of the new Railway Battalion were being trained; the plant was steadily accumulating; engines, rolling stock, and material of all sorts had arrived from England. From the growing workshops at Wady Halfa the continual clatter and clang of hammers and the black smoke of manufacture rose to the African sky. The malodorous incense of civilisation was offered to the startled gods of Egypt. All this was preparation; nor was it until the 8th of May that track-laying into the desert was begun in earnest. The whole of the construction gangs and railroad staff were brought from Kerma to Wady Halfa, and the daring pioneers of modern war started on their long march through the wilderness, dragging their railway behind them—a safe and sure road which infantry, cavalry, guns, and gunboats might follow with speed and convenience.

It is scarcely within the power of words to describe the savage desolation of the regions into which the line and its constructors plunged. A smooth ocean of bright-coloured sand spread far and wide to distant horizons. The tropical sun beat with senseless perseverance upon the level surface until it could scarcely be touched with a naked hand, and the filmy air glittered and shimmered as over a furnace. Here and there huge masses of crumbling rock rose from the plain, like islands of cinders in a sea of fire. Alone in this vast expanse stood Rail-head—a canvas town of 2,500 inhabitants, complete with station, store-, post-office, telegraph-office, and canteen, and only connected with the living world of men and ideas by two parallel iron streaks, three feet six inches apart, growing dim and narrower in a long perspective until they were twisted and blurred by the mirage and vanished in the indefinite distance.

Every morning in the remote nothingness there appeared a black speck growing larger and clearer, until with a whistle and a welcome clatter, amid the aching silence of ages, the 'material' train arrived, carrying its own water and 2,500 yards of rails, sleepers, and accessories. At noon came another speck, developing in a similar manner into a supply train, also carrying its own water, food and water for the half-battalion of the escort and the 2,000 artificers and platelayers, and the letters, newspapers, sausages, jam, whiskey, soda, and cigarettes which enable the Briton to conquer the world without discomfort. And presently the empty trains would depart, reversing the process of their arrival, and vanishing gradually along a line which appeared at last to turn up into the air and run at a tangent into an unreal world.

The life of the strange and lonely town was characterised by a machine-like regularity, born perhaps of the iron road from which it derived its nourishment. Daily at three o' clock in the morning the 'camp-engine' started with the 'bank parties.' With the dawn the 'material' train arrived, the platelaying gangs swarmed over it like clusters of flies, and were carried to the extreme limit of the track. Every man knew his task, and knew, too, that he would return to camp when it was finished, and not before. Forthwith they set busily to work without the necessity of an order. A hundred yards of material were unloaded. The sleepers were arranged in a long succession. The rails were spiked to every alternate sleeper, and then the great 80-ton engine moved cautiously forward along the unballasted track, like an elephant trying a doubtful bridge.

The operation was repeated continually through the hours of the burning day. Behind the train there followed other gangs of platelayers, who completed the spiking and ballasting process; and when the sun sank beneath the sands of the western horizon, and the engine pushed the empty trucks and the weary men home to the Railhead camp, it came back over a finished and permanent line. There was a brief interval while the camp-fires twinkled in the waste, like the lights of a liner in mid-ocean, while the officers and men chatted over their evening meal, and then the darkness and silence of the desert was unbroken till morning brought the glare and toil of another long day.

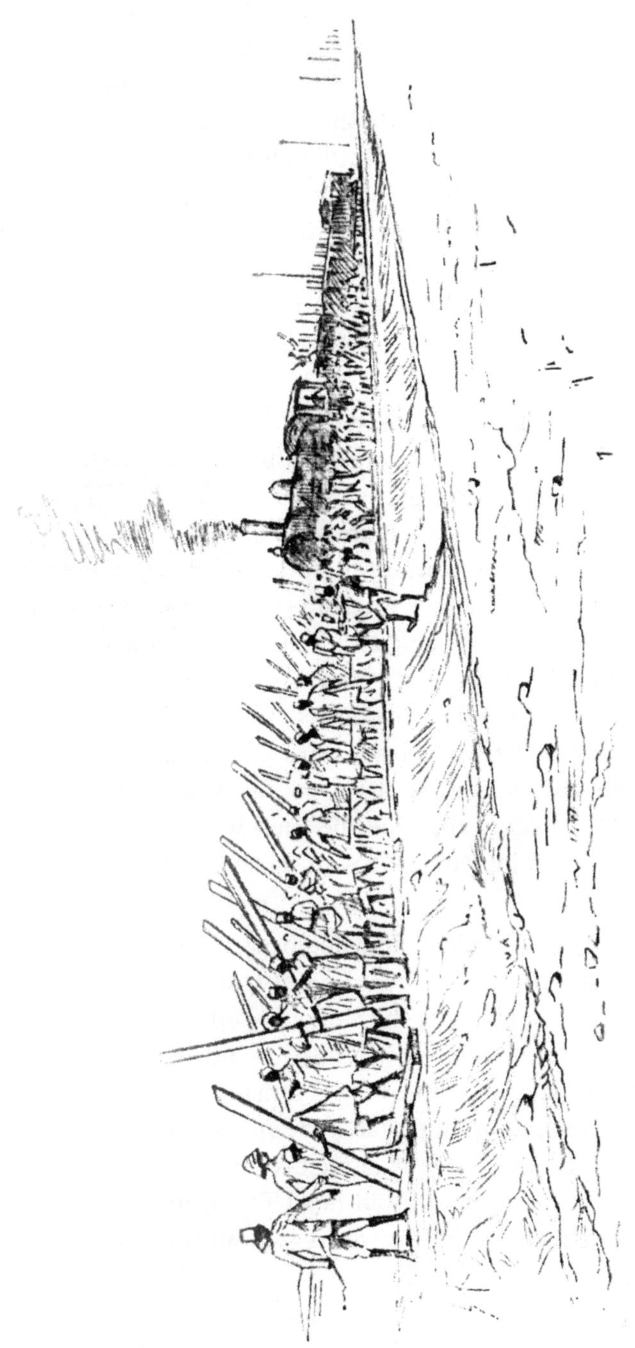

INTO THE WILDERNESS

So week in, week out, the work went on. Every few days saw a further advance into the wilderness. The scene changed and remained unaltered— 'another, yet the same.' As Wady Halfa became more remote and Abu Hamed grew near, an element of danger, the more appalling since it was peculiar, was added to the strange conditions under which the inhabitants of Rail-head lived. What if the Dervishes should cut the line behind them? They had three days' reserve of water. After that, unless the obstruction were removed and traffic restored, all must wither and die in the sand, and only their bones and their cooking-pots would attest the folly of their undertaking.

By the 20th of July a hundred and thirty miles of had been finished, and it became too dangerous to advance further until Abu Hamed had been cleared of the Dervish force. They were still a hundred miles away, but camels travel fast and far, and the resources of the enemy were uncertain. It appeared that progress would be checked, but on the 7th of August General Hunter, marching from Merawi along the river bank, attacked and took Abu Hamed. The operation will be described hereafter. Work was at once resumed with renewed energy. The pace of construction now became remarkable; As much as 5,300 yards of track were surveyed, embanked, and laid in a single day. On the 1st of November Abu Hamed was reached, and by the banks of the Nile the men who had fought their way across the desert joined hands with those who had fought their way along the river.

The strain and hardship had not, however, been without its effect on the constructors. Two of the Engineer subalterns[5] out of the eight concerned in the laving of the Dongola and the Desert railways had died. Their places were eagerly filled by others. Of the men of the construction gangs but little record remains. They were accustomed to the local conditions; the heat of the sun did not sap their strength. Nevertheless there are many nameless mounds in the desert, which mark the changing sites of Rail-head Town, and show that nothing good is ever achieved in this world without someone having to pay the cost.

---

5 Lieut. R. Polwhele, R.E. and Egyptian army; Lieut. E. M. S. Cator. R.E. and Egyptian Army.

The completion of the line was accelerated by nearly a month by the fortunate discovery of water. At the beginning of July a well was sunk in what was thought to be a likely place at 'No. 4 Station,' 77 miles from Halfa. After five weeks' work water was found at a depth of 90 feet in abundance. A steam-pump was erected, and the well yielded a continual supply. In October a second well was sunk at 'No. 6 Station,' 55 miles further on, whence water was obtained in still greater quantity. These discoveries modified, though they did not solve, the water question. They substantially increased the carrying capacity of the line. They reduced the danger to which the construction gangs were exposed. The sinking of the wells, an enterprise at which the friendly Arabs scoffed, was begun by Lieutenant Gorringe, R.E.,[6] on the Sirdar's personal initiative; but the chronicler must impartially observe that the success was won by luck as much as by calculation, for, since the first two wells were made, eight others of greater depth have been bored and in no case has water been obtained.

As the railway had been made, the telegraph-wire had, of course, followed it. Every consignment of rails and sleepers had been accompanied by their proportion of telegraph-poles, insulators, and wire. Another subaltern of Engineers, Lieutenant Manifold,[7] who managed this part of the military operations against the Arabs, had also laid a line from Merawi to Abu Hamed, so that immediate correspondence was effected round the entire circle of rail and river.

On the 3rd of November Sir Herbert Kitchener had the satisfaction of travelling over the line which owed its existence to his judgment, and the rapidity of its construction to the influence of his personality. He accomplished in sixteen hours a journey which had previously consumed ten days. At the end of the war, when he returned from Fashoda, the enthusiastic subalterns improved on this record by running his train from Atbara Fort to Wady Halfa—384 miles—in thirteen hours without breaking his neck.

The labours of the Railway Battalion and its officers did not end with the completion of the line to Abu Hamed. The Desert Railway was made. It had now to be maintained, worked, and rapidly

6 Lieut. G. F. Gorringe, R.E. and Egyptian army.

7 Lieut. M. G. E. Manifold, R.E. and Egyptian army.

extended. The terminus at Halfa had become a busy town. A mud village was transformed into a miniature Crewe. The great workshops that had grown with the line were equipped with diverse and elaborate machines. Plant of all kinds purchased in Cairo or requisitioned from England, with odds and ends collected from Ismail's scrap heaps, filled the depôts with an extraordinary variety of stores. Foundries, lathes, dynamos, steam-hammers, hydraulic presses, cupola furnaces, screw-cutting machines, and drills had been set up and were in continual work. They needed constant attention. Every appliance for repairing each must be provided. To haul the tonnage necessary to supply the army and extend the line nearly forty engines were eventually required. Purchased at different times and from different countries, they included ten distinct patterns; each pattern needed a special reserve of spare parts. The permutations and combinations of the stores were multiplied. Some of the engines were old and already worn out. These broke down periodically. The frictional parts of all were affected by the desert sand, and needed ceaseless attention and repair. The workshops were busy night and day for seven days a week.

To the complication of machinery was added the confusion of tongues. Natives of various races were employed as operatives. Foremen had been obtained from Europe. No fewer than seven separate languages were spoken in the shops. Wady Halfa became a second Babel. Yet the undertaking prospered. The Engineer officers displayed qualities of tact and temper. Their director was cool and indefatigable. Over all the Sirdar exercised a regular control. Usually ungracious, rarely impatient, never unreasonable, he moved among the workshops and about the line, satisfying himself that all was proceeding with economy and despatch. The sympathy of common labour won him the affection of the subalterns. Nowhere in the Soudan was he better known than on the railroad. Nowhere was he so ardently believed in. That he deserved the confidence is beyond dispute. That he reciprocated the affection is more doubtful.

As the army at Rail-head increased, the strain upon the line grew. New engines had to be ordered. The director, being patriotic, looked to England and sent his order. But in England all the operatives were busily engaged in the great strike in the engineering trade and had no time to spare to manufacture locomotives. There were, however, a number of engines which had been made by Messrs. Neilson, in Scotland, for the Bulawayo Railway. The matter was urgent. It was decided to ask the President of the South African line to allow the Egyptian army to purchase two or three of these engines in order to prevent a breakdown in the communications. The request was accordingly made. The President, who happened to be Mr. Cecil Rhodes, gave an amiable and immediate assent. Five locomotives which might have traversed the South African *veldt* now run by the banks of the Nile. Nevertheless, they may reach Cape Town some day.

The continued paralysis of the engineering trade made it necessary to give a further order for three engines to the United States. The money which should have refreshed the industries of Britain, stimulated those of America. The order, though small, was eagerly accepted and promptly executed. The new locomotives were delivered without delay, and it may be instructive to institute a comparison between the products of the great commercial rivals.

As the British engines were designed for goods traffic, and the American for passenger service, no examination of their relative speeds and hauling powers is possible. But it is necessary to remark that the American engines were sooner delivered and 1,000*l* cheaper. They broke down rarely. All their similar parts were interchangeable. If two engines had been disabled, the third might have supplied the material for the repairs. The fact that they were considerably faster soon won them a good reputation on the railway, and the soldier who travelled to the front was as anxious to avoid his country's locomotives as to preserve its honour.

'They were,' said one of the subalterns, 'the products of a higher class of labour than that employed in England. They represented greater talent, though less toil. While appearance was not neglected, no "finish" was wasted on unnoticeable parts. Thus economy was increased and efficiency preserved.' There is no pleasure in recording these facts. They have not, unfortunately, even the merit of being new. Let us return to the railway and the war.

It is now necessary to anticipate the course of events. As soon as the railway reached Abu Hamed, General Hunter's force, which was holding that place, dropped its slender camel communications with Merawi and drew its supplies along the new line direct from Wady Halfa. After the completion of the desert line there were still left seventeen miles of material for construction, and the railway was consequently at once extended to Dakhesh, sixteen miles south of Abu Hamed. Meanwhile Berber was seized, and military considerations compelled the concentration of a larger force to maintain that town. The four battalions which had remained at Merawi were floated downstream to Kerma, and, there entraining, were carried by Halfa and Abu Hamed to Dakhesh—a journey of 450 miles.

When the railway had been begun across the desert, it was believed that the Nile was always navigable above Abu Hamed. In former campaigns it had been reconnoitred and the waterway declared clear. But as the river fell it became evident that this was untrue. With the subsidence of the waters cataracts began to appear, and to avoid these it became necessary first of all to extend the railway to Bashtinab, later on to Abadia, and finally to the Atbara. To do this more money had to be obtained, and the usual financial difficulties presented themselves. Finally, however, the matter was settled, and the extension began at the rate of about a mile a day. The character of the country varies considerably between Abu Hamed and the Atbara river. For the first sixty miles the line ran beside the Nile, at the edge of the riparian belt.

On the right was the cultivable though mostly uncultivated strip, long neglected and silted up with fine sand drifted into dunes, from which scattered, scraggy *dôm*-palms and prickly-mimosa bushes grew. Between the branches of these sombre trees the river gleamed, a cool and attractive flood. On the left was the desert, here broken by frequent rocks and dry watercourses. From Bashtinab to Abadia another desert section of fifty miles was necessary to avoid some very difficult ground by the Nile banks. From Abadia to the Atbara the last stretch of the line runs across a broad alluvial expanse from whose surface plane-trees of mean appearance, but affording welcome shade, rise, watered by the autumn rains. The fact that the railway was approaching regions where rain is not an almost unknown phenomenon increased the labour of construction. To prevent the embankments from being washed away in the watercourses, ten bridges and sixty culverts had to be made; and this involved the transport over the railway of more than 1,000 tons of material in addition to the ordinary plant.[8]

By the arrival of the reinforcements at Berber the fighting force at the front was doubled: doubled also was the business of supply. The task of providing the food of an army in a desert, a thousand miles from its base, and with no apparent means of subsistence at the end of the day's march, is less picturesque, though not less important than the building of railways along which that nourishment is drawn to the front. Supply and transport stand or fall together; history depends on both; and in order to explain the Commissariat aspect of the River War, I must again both repeat and anticipate the account. The Sirdar exercised a direct and personal supervision over the whole department of supply, but his action was restricted almost entirely to the distribution of the rations. Their accumulation and regular supply were the task of Colonel Rogers,[9] and this officer, by three years of exact calculation and unfailing allowance for the unforeseen, has well deserved his high reputation as a feeder of armies.

The first military necessity of the war was, as has been described, to place the bulk of the Egyptian army at Akasha. Under ordinary circumstances this would not have been a serious Commissariat problem. The frontier reserves of food were calculated to meet such an emergency. But in 1895 the crops in Egypt had been much below the average. At the beginning of 1896 there was a great scarcity of grain. When the order for the advance was issued, the frontier grain stores were nearly exhausted. The new crops could not be garnered until the end of April. Thus while the world regarded Egypt as a vast granary, her soldiers were obliged to purchase 4,000 tons of *doura* and 1,000 tons of barley from India and Russia on which to begin the campaign.

The chief item of a soldier's diet in most armies is bread. In several of our wars the health, and consequently the efficiency, of the troops have been impaired by bad bread or by the too frequent sub-

8 The regular feeding of the working parties, with rails and sleepers and other material, was throughout a business vital to the success of the whole enterprise. All the credit belongs to three officers at different Major J. G. Maxwell, D.S.O., at Wady Halfa; Captain O. H. Pedley, p.s.c, at Assuan; and Captain W. Staveley Gordon, at Cairo—EDITOR.

9 Lieut.-Colonel J. Rogers, A.S.C. and Egyptian army.

stitution of hard biscuit. For more than a year the army up the river ate twenty tons of flour daily, and it is easy to imagine how bitter under ordinary circumstances would have been the battle between the Commissariat officers, whose duty it was to insist on proper quality, and the contractors—often, I fear, meriting the epithet 'rascally' intent only upon profit. But in the well-managed Egyptian service no such difficulties arose. The War Department had in 1892 converted one of Ismail Pasha's gun factories near Cairo into a victualling-yard. Here were set up their own mills for grinding flour, machinery for manufacturing biscuit to the extent of 60,000 rations daily, and even for making soap. Three great advantages sprang from this wise arrangement. Firstly, the good quality of the supply was assured. Complaints about bread and biscuit were practically unknown, and the soap—since the soldier, in contrast to the mixture of rubble and grease with which the contractors had formerly furnished him, could actually wash himself and his clothes with it—was greatly prized. Secondly, all risk of contractors failing to deliver in time was avoided. Lastly, the funds resulting from the economy had been utilised to form a useful corps of 150 bakers. And thus, although the purchase of foreign grain added to the expense, the beginning of the war found the Commissariat of the Egyptian army in a thoroughly efficient state.

Vast reserves of stores were quickly accumulated at Assuan. From these not an ounce of food was issued without the Sirdar's direct sanction. At the subsidiary depôt, formed at Wady Halfa, the same rule prevailed. The man who was responsible to no one, took all the responsibility; and the system whereby a Chief of the Staff is subjected to the continual bombardment of heads of departments was happily avoided. Sufficient supplies having been accumulated at Akasha to allow for a forward movement, Firket was fought. After Firket the situation became difficult, and the problem of the Supply officers was to keep the troops alive without delaying the progress of the railway with the carriage of their food. A small quantity of provisions was painfully dragged, with an average loss of fifty per cent, from theft and water damage, up the succession of cataracts which obstruct the river-way from Halfa to Kosheh. Camel convoys from Rail-head carried the rest. But until the line reached Kosheh the resources of the Transport were terribly strained, and at one time it was even necessary to send the mounted troops north to avoid actual famine. The apparent inadequacy of the means to the end reached a climax when the army moved southward from Dulgo, The marches and halts to Dongola were estimated to take ten days, which was the utmost capacity of camel and steam transport. A few boat-loads of grain might be captured; a few handfuls of dates might be plucked but scarcely any local supplies would be available. The sailing-boats, which were the only regular means of transport, were all delayed by the adverse winds. Fortune returned at the critical moment. By good luck on the first day of the march the north wind began to blow, and twelve days' supplies, over and above those moved by camel and steamer, reached Dongola with the troops. With this reserve in hand, the occupation of the province was completed, and, although the army only existed from hand to mouth until the railway reached Kerma, no further serious difficulty was experienced in supplying them.

The account of the Commissariat is now complete to the end of the Dongola Expedition; but it may conveniently be carried forward with the railway construction. In the Abu Hamed phase the supplies were so regulated that a convoy travelling from Murat Wells along the caravan route arrived the day after the fight; and thereafter communications were opened with Merawi. The unexpected occupation of Berber, following Abu Hamed, created the most difficult situation of the war. Until the railway was forced on to Berber a peculiarly inconvenient line of supply had to be used; and strings of camels, scattering never less than thirty per cent, of their loads, meandered through the rough and thorny country between Merawi and Abu Hamed. This line was strengthened by other convoys from Murat and the approaching Rail-head, and a system of boats and camel portages filtered the supplies to their destination.

Even when the railway had reached Dakhesh the tension was only slightly relaxed. The necessities of supplying the large force at Berber, 108 miles from the Rail-head, still required the maintenance of a huge and complicated system of boat and camel transport. Of course, as the railway advanced, it absorbed stage after stage of river and portage, and the difficulties decreased. But the reader may gain some idea of their magnitude by following the progress of a box of biscuits from Cairo to Berber in the month of December 1897. The route was as follows:—From Cairo to Nagh Hamadi (340 miles) by rail; from Nagh Hamadi to Assuan (205 miles) by boat; from Assuan to Shellal (6 miles) by rail; from Shellal to Halfa (226 miles) by boat; from Halfa to Dakhesh (Rail-head)—248 miles—by military railway; from Dakhesh to Shereik (45 miles) by boat; from Shereik by camel (13 miles) round a cataract to Bashtinab; from Bashtinab by boat (25 miles) to Omsheyo; from Omsheyo round another impracticable reach (11 miles) by camel to Geneinetti, and thence (22 miles) to Berber by boat. The road taken by this box of biscuits was followed by every ton of supplies required by 10,000 men in the field. The uninterrupted working of the long and varied chain was vital to the welfare of the army and the success of the war. It could only be maintained if every section was adequately supplied and none were either choked or starved.

This problem had to be solved correctly every day by the Transport officers, in spite of uncertain winds that retarded the boats, of

A GYASSA

camels that grew sick or died, and of engines that repeatedly broke down. In the face of every difficulty a regular supply was maintained. The construction of the railway was not delayed nor the food of the troops reduced.

The line continued to grow rapidly, and as it grew the difficulties of supply decreased. The weight was shifted from the backs of the camels and the bottoms of the sailing-boats to the trucks of the iron road. The strong hands of steam were directed to the prosecution of the war, and the swiftness of the train replaced the toilsome plodding of the caravan. The advance of the Dervishes towards Berber checked the progress of the railway. Military precautions were imperative. Construction was delayed by the passage of the 1st British Brigade from Cairo to the front, and by the consequently increased volume of daily supplies. By the 10th of March, however, the line was completed to Bashtinab. On the 5th of May it had reached Abadia. On the 3rd of July the whole railway from Wady Halfa to the Atbara was finished, and the southern terminus was established in the great entrenched camp at the confluence of the rivers.

The question of supply was then settled once and for all. In less than a week stores sufficient for three months were poured along the line, and the exhausting labours of the Commissariat officers ended. Their relief and achievement were merged in the greater triumph of the Railway Staff.

The director and his subalterns had laboured long, and their efforts were crowned with complete success. All had displayed high qualities of resource and invention. Their perseverance had been magnificent. Their energy was tireless. They endured hardship unrelieved by adventure, and danger which was not exciting. All the pomp and circumstance of war passed through their hands reduced to *avoirdupois*.[10] Scarcely anyone has appreciated their work. It is pleasing to note that among the discriminating few is the commander who directed and inspired their enterprise. Girouard has since been placed at the head of the Railway Administration in Egypt, and in that important office may find still fuller scope for the remarkable qualities he is known to possess. The subalterns have received the Distinguished Service Order—a reward which, though

10 A system of weights based on pounds and ounces. [Note to new edition].

better suited to their rank than to their services, may yet help them to fresh opportunities, the best prize that a soldier can desire. Besides their decoration they were granted a holiday. The last train south from Halfa, the last steamer from the Atbara encampment, bore the Railway Staff to the front; and as gallopers to the various Brigadiers they were afforded every chance of losing their lives and of witnessing the great event for the accomplishment of which they had worked so long and worked so well.[11]

On the day that the first troop train steamed into the fortified camp at the confluence of the Nile and the Atbara rivers the doom of the Dervishes was sealed. It had now become possible, with convenience and speed, to send into the heart of the Soudan great armies independent of the season of the year and of the resources of the country; to supply them not only with abundant food and ammunition, but with all the variegated paraphernalia of scientific war; and to support their action on land by a powerful flotilla of gunboats, which could dominate the river and command the banks, and could at any moment make their way past Khartoum even to Sennar, Fashoda, or Sobat. Though the battle was not yet fought, the victory was won. The Khalifa, his capital, and his army were now within the Sirdar's reach. It remained only to pluck the fruit in the most convenient hour, with the least trouble and at the smallest cost.

11 For names of Railway and Supply Staff, see Appendix A, vol. ii.

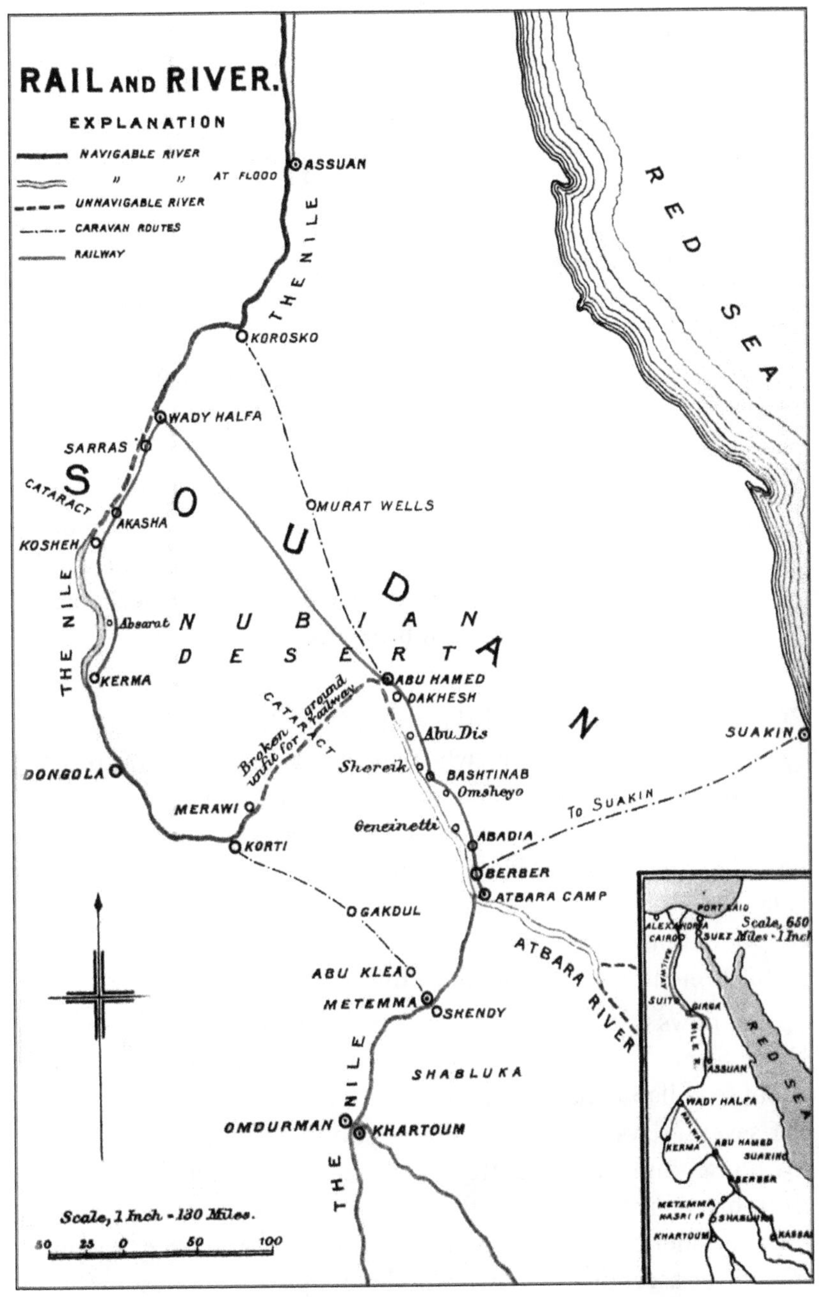
RAIL AND RIVER.
EXPLANATION
NAVIGABLE RIVER
" " AT FLOOD
UNNAVIGABLE RIVER
CARAVAN ROUTES
RAILWAY
ASSUAN
THE NILE
RED SEA
KOROSKO
WADY HALFA
SARRAS
CATARACT
AKASHA
KOSHEH
SOUDAN
MURAT WELLS
THE NILE
Absarat
NUBIAN DESERT
KERMA
ABU HAMED
DAKHESH
CATARACT
Broken ground unfit for railway
Abu Dis
SUAKIN
DONGOLA
Shereik
BASHTINAB
Omsheyo
MERAWI
To SUAKIN
Geneinetti
ABADIA
KORTI
BERBER
ATBARA CAMP
GAKDUL
ATBARA RIVER
ABU KLEA
METEMMA
SHENDY
THE NILE
SHABLUKA
OMDURMAN
KHARTOUM
Scale, 1 Inch - 130 Miles.
50 25 0 50 100
PORT SAID
ALEXANDRIA
CAIRO
SUEZ
Scale, 650 Miles - 1 Inch
RAILWAY
SUIT
GIRGA
NILE R.
ASSUAN
RED SEA
WADY HALFA
RAILWAY
KERMA
ABU HAMED
SUAKIN
BERBER
METEMMA
KHARTOUM

CHAPTER X
ABU HAMED

The Khalifa's harangue—Dervish concentration upon Omdurman—The riverain tribes—The Khalifa's plans—The patrol to Salamat—Cavalry action of the 1st of June—The Jaalin—Their revolt against the Khalifa—Two letters—Mahmud at Metemma—The hour of advance—The Flying Column—Sir Archibald Hunter—The march from Kassingar to Abu Hamed—Description of the village—Storm of Abu Hamed, August 7th—A determined man—Casualties—An idle tale—Consternation in Berber—The gunboats ascend the Fourth Cataract—The loss of the *Teb*—A wonderful escape—Capture of Berber—A decisive step—The critical period of the war begins.

The last chapter carried the account of the war forward at express speed. The reader, who had already on the railway reached the Atbara encampment and was prepared for the final advance on Khartoum, must allow his mind to revert to a period when the Egyptian forces are distributed along the river in garrisons at Dongola, Debba, Korti, and Merawi; when the re-organisation of the conquered province has been begun; and when the Desert Railway is still stretching steadily forward towards Abu Hamed.

The news of the fall of Dongola created a panic in Omdurman. Great numbers of Arabs, believing that the Khalifa's power was about to collapse, fled from the city. All business was at a standstill. For several days there were no executions. Abdullahi himself kept his house, and thus doubtfully concealed his vexation and alarm from his subjects. On the fifth day, however, having recovered his own confidence, he proceeded to the mosque, and after the morning prayer ascended his small wooden pulpit and addressed the assembled worshippers. After admitting the retreat of the Dervishes under Wad Bishara, he enlarged on the losses the 'Turks ' had sustained and described their miserable condition. He deplored the fact that certain of the *Jehadia* had surrendered, and reminded his listeners with a grim satisfaction of the horrible tortures which it was the practice of the English and Egyptians to inflict upon their captives. He bewailed the lack of faith in God which had allowed even the meanest of the Ansar to abandon the *Jehad* against the infidel, and he condemned the lack of piety which disgraced the age. But he proclaimed his confidence in the loyalty of his subjects and his enjoyment of the favour of God and the counsels of the late Mahdi; and having by his oratory raised the fanatical multitude to a high pitch of excitement he thus concluded his long harangue: 'It is true that our chiefs have retired from Dongola. Yet they are not defeated. Only they that disobeyed me have perished. I instructed the faithful to refrain from fighting and return to Metemma. It was by my command that they have done what they have done. For the angel of the Lord and the spirit of the Mahdi have warned me in a vision that the souls of the accursed Egyptians and of the miserable English shall leave their bodies between Dongola and Omdurman, at some spot which their bones shall whiten. Thus shall the infidels be conquered.' Then, drawing his sword, he cried with a loud voice: 'Ed din mansur! The religion is victorious! Islam shall triumph!' Whereupon the worshippers, who to the number of 20,000 filled the great quadrangle—although they could not all hear his voice—saw his sword flashing in the sunlight, and with one accord imitated him, waving their swords and spears and raising a mighty shout of fury and defiance. When the tumult had subsided, the Khalifa announced that those who did not wish to remain faithful might go where they liked, but that he for his part would remain, knowing that God would vindicate the faith. Public confidence was thus restored.

In order that the divine favour might be assisted human effort, Abdullahi adopted every measure or precaution that energy or prudence could suggest. At first he seems to have apprehended that the Sirdar's army would advance at once upon Omdurman, following the route of the Desert Column in 1885 from Korti to Metemma. He therefore ordered Osman Azrak—in spite of his severe wound—to hold Abu Klea wells with the survivors of his flag. Bishara, who had rallied and reorganised the remains of the Dongola army, was instructed to occupy Metemma in concert with the Jaalin, who had lately made that town their headquarters. Messengers were despatched to the most distant garrisons to arrange for a general concentration upon Omdurman. The Emir Ibrahim Khalil was recalled from the Ghezira, or the land between the Blue and White Niles, and with his force of about 4,000 Jehadia and Baggara soon reached the city. Another chief, Ahmed Fedil, who was actually on his way to Gedaref, was ordered to return to the capital. Thither also Osman Digna repaired from Adarama. But it appears that the Khalifa only required the advice of that wily councillor, for he did not reduce the number of Dervishes in the small forts along the line of the Atbara—Ed Darner, Adarama, Asubri, El Fasher—and after a short visit and a long consultation Osman Digna returned to his post at Adarama. Last of all, but not least in importance, Mahmud, who commanded the 'Army of the West,' was ordered to leave very reduced garrisons in Kordofan and Darfur, and march with his whole remaining force, which may have numbered 10,000 fighting men, to the Nile, and so to Omdurman. Mahmud, who was as daring and ambitious as he was conceited and incapable, received the summons with delight, and began forthwith to collect his troops.

The Khalifa saw very clearly that he could not trust the riverain tribes. The Jaalin and Barabra were discontented. He knew that they were weary of his rule and of war. In proportion as the Egyptian army advanced, so their loyalty and the taxes they paid decreased. He therefore abandoned all idea of making a stand at Berber. The Emir Yunes—who, since he had been transferred from Dongola in 1895, had ruled the district—was directed to collect all the camels, boats, grain, and other things that might assist an invading army and send them to Metemma. The duty was most thoroughly performed. The inhabitants were soon relieved of all their property and of most of their means of livelihood, and their naturally bitter resentment at this merciless treatment explains to some extent the astonishing events which followed the capture of Abu Hamed. This last place Abdullahi never regarded as more than an outpost. Its garrison was not large, and although it had now become the most northerly Dervish position, only a slender reinforcement was added to the force under command of Mohammed-ez-Zein.

The power of the gunboats and their effect in the Dongola campaign were fully appreciated by the Arabs; and the Khalifa, in the hopes of closing the Sixth Cataract, began to construct several forts at the northern end of the Shabluka gorge. The *Bordein*, one of Gordon's old steamers, plied busily between Omdurman and Wad Hamed, transporting guns and stores; and Ahmed Fedil was sent with a sufficient force to hold the works when they were made. But the prophecy of the Mahdi exercised a powerful effect on the Khalifa's mind, and while he neglected no detail he based his hopes on the issue of a great battle on the plains of Kerreri, when the invaders should come to the walls of the city. With this prospect continually before him he drilled and organised the increasing army at Omdurman with the utmost regularity, and every day the savage soldiery practised their evolutions upon the plain they were presently to strew with their bodies.

But after a while it became apparent that the 'Turks' were not advancing. They tarried on the lands they had won. The steamers went

ON VEDETTE

no further than Merawi. The iron road stopped at Kerma. Why had they not followed up their success? Obviously because they feared the army that awaited them at Omdurman. At this the Khalifa took fresh courage, and in January 1897 he began to revolve schemes for taking the offensive and expelling the invaders from the Dongola province .

The army drilled and manoeuvred continually on the plains of Kerreri. Great numbers of camels were collected at Omdurman. Large stores of dried *kisru* or 'Soudan biscuit,' the food of Dervishes on expeditions, were prepared.

The Sirdar did not remain in ignorance of these preparations. The tireless enterprise of the Intelligence Branch furnished the most complete information; and preparations were made to concentrate the troops in Dongola on any threatened point, should the enemy advance. Regular reconnaissances were made by the cavalry both into the deserts towards Gakdul Wells and along- the river. Towards the end of May it was reported that the Emir Yunes had crossed the Nile and was raiding the villages on the left bank below Abu Hamed. In consequence the Sirdar ordered a strong patrol under Captain Le Gallais, and consisting of three squadrons of cavalry under Captain Mahon, three companies of the Camel Corps, and of 100 men of the IXth Soudanese on camels with one Maxim gun, to reconnoitre up the Nile through the Shukuk Pass and 'as far as Salamat.[1]

The force started at daylight on the 31st of May, the cavalry scouting ten miles in front, and the Camel Corps and mounted infantry acting as a support. Bivouacking at a convenient spot, they pushed on the next morning, and by three o' clock in the afternoon the support had arrived on the old battlefield of Kirbeckan and the cavalry had reconnoitred several miles beyond Salamat. Not an enemy was to be seen. The officers climbed the hills that rose above the level and scanned the whole horizon. The wilderness contained no moving thing except the Nile, which rambled along among the dark rocks and sandy shoals of the Monassir Desert—the most barren and dismal stage of its long journey to the sea.

The object of the reconnaissance accomplished, and the reports of the Dervish movements being apparently disproved, the order

1 Map, 'The Nile from Merawi to Abu Hamed,' page 241.

was given to return. The support had already cleared the Shukuk Pass, and the cavalry were watering about two miles on the homeward side of Salamat, when the enemy appeared. Two squadrons were dismounted to feed and water. The third, under Captain Peyton,[2] was acting as rearguard. All of a sudden the last squadron perceived that ten Dervish horsemen were watching them at scarcely a hundred yards' distance.

Thereupon the young Egyptian officer who commanded the rear troop, with a recklessness so rare in his nation that it may be pardoned, wheeled about and galloped wildly off in pursuit. The ten Arabs fled in the direction of Salamat. The Egyptian troop followed. As they approached the village, with their horses blown by the long gallop across the sand, there rushed from behind the houses more than ninety mounted Dervishes, who were uniformly dressed in red and white *jibbas*, and who savagely assailed the rash officer and his confiding troop.

To so unequal a combat there could only have been one end. But as soon as he saw his rear troop galloping off in pursuit without his orders, Peyton had determined to follow and support them with the rest of the squadron. His arrival on the scene was almost simultaneous with that of the Dervish reinforcement. He immediately charged to extricate the troop. A disordered scrimmage ensued, in which Peyton, who is said to have killed three Dervishes in personal combat, was very severely wounded by a spear which pierced his lungs. Finding his strength failing him, the officer felt himself unable to continue the fight, and the squadron, having been worsted in the encounter, galloped away, leaving nine men on the ground, to a small rocky knoll, where they dismounted and opened fire with their carbines. While this was passing the other two squadrons, who had mounted their horses in great haste, came up at a gallop, led by Captain Mahon. Thus outnumbered, the Dervishes fled, waiting only to destroy the wounded troopers who had fallen into their hands. The cavalry pursued for four miles, and then returned to Salamat. The Dervishes left fifteen killed and no wounded on the scene of the fight, and this curious proportion is perhaps best explained by the stern law of reprisals.

2 Captain W. E. Peyton, 15th Hussars and Egyptian army.

A. Bassano photo. Walter L. Colls ph. sc.

Sir Archibald Hunter.

The cavalry then fell back very slowly towards the Shukuk Pass, at the Abu Hamed end of which they found the support. They were delayed by the wounded, and did not return to Merawi till the 3rd of June. In the skirmish nine men were killed, one man was mortally wounded, Captain Peyton and two men were severely wounded—a total of thirteen casualties. It being now known that the Dervishes were on the move, the greatest vigilance was exercised in all the Dongola garrisons.

At the end of May, Mahmud with his army arrived at Omdurman. The Khalifa received him with delight, and several imposing reviews were held outside the city. Mahmud himself was eager to march against the 'Turks.' He had no experience of modern rifles, and felt confident that he could easily destroy or at least roll back the invading forces. Partly persuaded by the zeal of his lieutenant, and partly by the wavering and doubtful attitude of the Jaalin, the Khalifa determined early in June to send the Kordofan army to occupy Metemma, and thereby either to awe the tribe into loyalty, or force them to revolt while the Egyptian troops were still too distant to assist them. He summoned the chief of the Jaalin, Abdalla-Wad-Saad, to Omdurman, and informed him that the Jaalin territories were threatened by the Turks. In the goodness of his heart, therefore, and because he knew that they loved the Mahdi and practised the true religion, he was resolved to protect them from their enemies. The chief bowed his head. The Khalifa continued that the trusty Mahmud with his army would be sent for that purpose; Abdalla might show his loyalty in furnishing them with all supplies and accommodation. He intimated that the interview was over. But the Jaalin chief had the temerity to protest. He assured the Khalifa of his loyalty, and of the ability of his tribe to repel the enemy. He implored him not to impose the burden of an army upon them. He exaggerated the poverty of Metemma; he lamented the misfortunes of the times. Finally he begged forgiveness for making his protest.

The Khalifa was infuriated. Forgetting his usual self-control and the forms of public utterance, he broke out into a long and abusive harangue. He told the chief that he had long doubted his loyalty, that he despised his protestations, that he was worthy of a shameful death, that his tribe were a blot upon the face of the earth, and that he hoped Mahmud would improve their manners and those of their wives.

Abdalla-Wad-Saad crept from the presence, and returned in fury and disgust to Metemma. Having collected the head men of his tribe, he informed them of his reception and the Khalifa's intent. They did not need to be told that the quartering upon them of Mahmud's army meant the plunder of their goods, the ruin of their homes, and the rape of their women. It was resolved to revolt and join the Egyptian forces. As a result of the council the Jaalin chief wrote two letters. The first was addressed to the Sirdar, and reached him by messenger on the 24th of June. It declared the Jaalin submission to the Government, and begged for help, if possible in men, or, failing that, in arms; but ended by saying that, help or no help, the tribe was resolved to fight the Dervishes and hold Metemma to the death. The second letter—a mad and fatal letter—carried defiance to the Khalifa.

The Sirdar, who was at Merawi when the Jaalin messenger found him, lost no time. A large amount of ammunition and 1,100 Remington rifles were speedily collected and hurried on camels across the desert by the Korti-Metemma route, escorted by a strong detachment of the Camel Corps. The Khalifa did not receive his letter until the 27th of June. But he acted with even greater promptitude. Part of Mahmud's army had already started for the north. Mahmud and the rest followed on the 28th. On the 30th the advanced guard arrived before Metemma. The Jaalin prepared to resist desperately. Nearly the whole tribe had responded to the summons of their chief, and more than 2,500 men were collected behind the walls of the town. But in all this force there were only eighty serviceable rifles, and only fifteen rounds of ammunition for each. Abdalla expected that the Dervishes would make their heaviest attack on the south side of Metemma, and he therefore disposed his few riflemen along that front. The defence of the rest of the town had perforce to be entrusted to the valour of the spearmen.

On the morning of the 1st of July, Mahmud, with a force variously estimated at 10,000 or 12,000 men, began his assault. The first attack fell, as the chief had anticipated, on the southern face. It was repulsed with severe loss by the Jaalin riflemen. A second attack followed immediately. The enemy had meanwhile surrounded the whole town, and just as the Jaalin ammunition was exhausted, a strong force of the Dervishes penetrated the northern face of their defences, which was held only by spearmen. The whole of Mahmud's army poured in through the gap, and the garrison, after a stubborn resistance, were methodically exterminated. An inhuman butchery of the children and some of the women followed. Abdalla-Wad-Saad was among the killed.

A few of the Jaalin who had escaped from the general destruction fled towards Gakdul. Here they found the Camel Corps with their caravan of rifles and ammunition. Like another force that had advanced by this very road to carry succour to men in desperate distress, the relief had arrived too late. The remnants of the Jaalin were left in occupation of Gakdul Wells. The convoy and its escort returned to Korti.

But while the attention of the Khalifa was directed to these matters, a far more serious menace offered from another quarter. Unnoticed by the Dervishes, or, if noticed, unappreciated, the railway was stretching further and further into the desert. By the middle of July it had reached the 130th mile, and, as is related in the last chapter, work had to be suspended until Abu Hamed was in the hands of the Egyptian forces. The Nile was rising fast. Very soon steamers would be able to pass the Fourth Cataract. It should have been evident that the next movement in the advance of the 'Turks' impended. The Khalifa seems indeed to have understood that the rise of the river increased his peril, for throughout July he continued to send orders to the Emir in Berber—Yunes—that he should advance into the Monassir district, harry such villages as existed, and obstruct the frequent reconnaissances from Merawi. Yunes, however, preferred to do otherwise, and remained on the left bank opposite Berber until, at length, his master recalled him to Omdurman to explain his conduct. Meanwhile, determined with mathematical exactness by the rise of the Nile and progress of the railway, the moment of the Egyptian advance arrived.

At the end of July preparations were made, as secretly as possible, to despatch a flying column against Abu Hamed. The Dervish garrison, under Mohammed ez-Zein was not believed to exceed 600 men, but in order that there should be no doubt as to the result it was determined to employ a strong force.

A brigade of all arms was formed as follows:—

Commanding: Major-General Hunter

Cavalry		One troop
Artillery		No. 2 Field Battery[3]
Infantry	MACDONALD'S BRIGADE	3rd Egyptians
		IXth Soudanese
		Xth Soudanese
		XIth Soudanese

Major-General Sir Archibald Hunter, the officer to whom the operation was entrusted, was from many points of view the most imposing figure in the Egyptian army. He had served through the Nile Expedition of 1884–85, with some distinction, in the Royal Lancaster Regiment. In 1888 he joined the Khedive's service. Thenceforward his rise was rapid, even for an Egyptian officer, and in ten years he passed through all the grades from Captain to Major-General . His promotion was not, however, undeserved. Foremost in every action, twice wounded—once at the head of his brigade—always distinguished for valour and conduct, Hunter won the admiration of his comrades and superiors. During the River War he became, in spite of his hard severity, the darling of the Egyptian army. All the personal popularity which great success might have brought to the Sirdar focussed itself on his daring, good-humoured subordinate and it was to Hunter that the soldiers looked whenever there was fighting to be done. The force now placed under his command for the attack upon Abu Hamed amounted to about 3,600 men. Until that place was taken all other operations were delayed. The Sirdar awaited the issue at Merawi. The railway paused in mid-desert.

The necessity of continuing the construction of the line at the earliest moment and his own anxiety made Sir Herbert Kitchener very desirous of being connected with the Flying Column by field telegraph. He sent for Lieutenant Manifold and told him to make arrangements to lay the wire as the force advanced. This officer, whose

3 This battery consisted of six Krupp guns, two Maxims, one Gardner gun, and one Nordenfeldt—an effective medley.

enterprise and services in the management of the whole system of telegraphy during the war have never been questioned, as they have never been rewarded, was for once at a loss. He pointed out that there were no appliances for laying the wire, no spools to unwind it from, no saddles to carry it, and not even any transport animals. The Sirdar looked annoyed. After some reflection he said, 'Get some donkeys from the villagers. If they are given a free ration they will *like* to accompany the Flying Column with their donkeys.'

The next morning, when a sufficient number of villagers had been persuaded to see the matter in the proper light, Manifold ventured to ask about the saddles for carrying and the appliances for laying the wire. The Sirdar came slowly to the spot where the telegraph plant was collected. The coils of wire lay on the ground; the donkeys and their proud proprietors grouped themselves picturesquely around.

The General contemplated both for a long time sourly. Then he walked to the largest coil of wire, picked it up and approached the smallest donkey. He took the little animal's two hind legs in his left hand, and put them into the coil. He lifted the wire up until it passed around the donkey's back, like a horse-collar, only that it hung between the fore and hind legs. He caught hold of the loose end of

FIELD TELEGRAPH, 1897

the wire, and smacked the donkey with the other hand. The beast moved forward, tripping and stumbling over the wire which began, albeit jerkily, to unwind. Then he walked abruptly back to his house. By this method the Field Telegraph accompanied the Flying Column, and within a few days of the capture of Abu Hamed the wire was working between that place and Merawi.

The troops composing the 'Flying Column' concentrated at Kassingar, a small village a few miles above Merawi, on the right or Abu Hamed bank of the Nile. General Hunter began his march on the 29th of July. The total distance from Kassingar to Abu Hamed is 133 miles. The greatest secrecy had been observed in the preparation of the force, but it was known that as soon as the column actually started, the news would he carried to the enemy. Speed was therefore essential; for if the Dervish garrison in Abu Hamed were reinforced from Berber, the Flying Column might not be strong enough to take the village. On the other hand, the great heat and the certainty that the troops would have to fight an action at the end of the march, imposed opposite considerations on the commander. To avoid the sun, the greater part of the distance was covered at night. Yet the advantage thus gained was to some extent neutralised by the difficulty of marching over such broken ground in the darkness.

Throughout the whole length of the course of the Nile there is no more miserable wilderness than the Monassir Desert. The stream of the river is broken, and its channel obstructed by a great confusion of boulders, between and among which the water rushes in dangerous cataracts. The sandy waste approaches the very brim, and only a few palm-trees, or here and there a squalid mud hamlet, reveal the existence of life.

The line of advance lay along the river; but no road relieved the labour of the march. Sometimes trailing across a broad stretch of white sand, in which the soldiers sank to their ankles, and which filled their boots with a rasping grit; sometimes winding over a pass or through a gorge of sharp-cut rocks, which, even in the moonlight, felt hot with heat of the previous day always in a long, jerky, and interrupted procession of men and camels, often in single file—the Column toiled painfully like the serpent to whom it was said: 'On thy belly shalt thou crawl, and dust shalt thou eat.'

The Column started at 5.30 in the evening, and by a march of sixteen and a half miles reached Mushra-el-Obiad at about midnight.[4] Here a convenient watering-place, not commanded by the opposite bank, and the shade of eight or ten thorny bushes afforded the first suitable bivouac. At 3.30 p.m. on the 30th the march was continued eight and a half miles to a spot some little distance beyond Shebabit. The pace was slow, and the route stony and difficult. It was after dark when the halting-place was reached. Several of the men strayed from the column, wandered in the gloom, and reached the bivouac exhausted. General Hunter had proposed to push on the next day to Hosh-el-Geref, but the fatigues of his troops in the two night marches had already been severe, and as, after Abu Haraz, the track twisted away from the river so that there was no water for five miles, he resolved to halt for the day and rest. Hosh-el-Geref was therefore not reached until the 1st of August—a day later than had been expected; but the rest had proved of such benefit to the troops that the subsequent acceleration of progress fully compensated for the delay. The Column moved on again at midnight, and halted at daybreak at Salmi. In the small hours of the next morning the march was resumed. The road by the Nile was found too difficult for the Maxim guns, which were on wheels, and these had to make a detour of twenty-eight miles into the desert, while the infantry moved ten miles along the river. In order that the Maxims should not arrive alone at Dakfilli, General Hunter had marched thither with the IXth Soudanese at 11 p.m. on the previous day.

The rest of the Column followed a few hours later. On the 4th, by an eighteen-mile march through deep sand, El Kab was reached. A single shot was fired from the opposite bank of the river as the cavalry patrol entered the village; and there was no longer any doubt that the Dervishes knew of the advance of the Column. Both the troops and the transport were now moving admirably; nevertheless, their sufferings were severe.

The nights were consumed in movement. Without shade the soldiers could not sleep by day. All ranks wearied, and the men would frequently, during the night marches, sink down upon the ground in profound slumber, only to be sternly aroused and hurried on. But

4 Map 'The Nile from Merawi to Abu Hamed', page 241.

the pace of the advance continued to be swift. On the 5th, the force, by a fourteen-mile march, reached Khula. Here they were joined by Sheikh Abdel-Azim with 150 Ababda camel-men from Murat Wells. Up to this point three Egyptians had died and fifty-eight men had been left behind in depôts exhausted. A double ration of meat was issued to the whole force. The column moved on during the night, and arrived at Ginnifab at 8 a.m. on the morning of the 6th. Here startling news of the enemy was received. It was known that Mohammed ez-Zein was determined to fight, and a reliable report was now received that a large force was coining down from Berber to support the Abu Hamed garrison.

In spite of the long marches and the fatigues of the troops, General Hunter resolved to hurry on. He had already made up the day spent at Abu Haraz. He now decided to improve on the prescribed itinerary, accelerate his own arrival and anticipate that of the Dervish reinforcements. Accordingly the troops marched all through the night of the 6–7th with only a short halt of an hour and a half, so as to attack Abu Hamed at dawn. After covering sixteen miles of bad ground the 'Flying Column' reached Ginnifab, 131 miles from Kassingar and only two from the Dervish post, at 3.30 on the morning of the 7th of August.[5] A halt of two hours was allowed for

5 The following is the actual itinerary:

March of the 'Flying Column': Kassingar to Abu Hamed, (July 29th—August 7th, 1897)

(First March, 16½ miles: 5.30 p.m. July 29 to 3 a.m. July 30; =9½ hours; Rest till 3:30 P.M July 30, 1897;=12½ hours.)

(Second March, 8 miles: 3.30 p.m. July 30 to 9 p.m. July 30; = 5½ hours; Rest till 5 A.M. July 31, 1897; = 8 hours.)

(Third March, 9 miles: 5 A.M. July 31 to 10:30 A.M. July 31; = 5½ hours; Rest till 3:30 A.M. August 1, 1897; =17 hours.)

(Fourth March, 9½ miles: 3:30 A.M. August 1 to 9 A.M. August 1; = 5½ hours; Rest till midnight August 1, 1897; = 15 hours.)

(Fifth March, 11 miles: Midnight, August 1 to 7 A.M.; = 7 hours; Rest till 11 P.M. August 2, 1897; =16 hours.)

(Sixth March, 11 miles: 11 P.M August 2 to 5:30 A.M. August 3; = 6½ hours; Rest till midnight August 3, 1897; =18½ hours.)

(Seventh March, 18 miles: Midnight August 3 to 8 A.M. August 4; = 8 hours; Rest till 12:30 A.M. August 5, 1897; = 16½ hours.)

(Eighth March, 14 miles: 12:30 A.M. August 5 to 9 A.M. August 5; = 8½ hours; Rest till 7 P.M. August 5, 1897; = 10 hours.)

the troops to prepare themselves. Half the 3rd Egyptian battalion remained as escort to the transport and reserve ammunition, and then the force moved off in the darkness towards the enemy's position.

The village of Abu Hamed straggles along the bank of the Nile, and consists of a central mass of mud houses, intersected by a network of winding lanes and alleys, about 500 yards long by perhaps 100 yards wide. To the north and south are detached clusters of ruined huts, and to the south there rises a large, ragged pile of rocks. The ground slopes gradually up from the river, so that at a distance of 300 yards the village is surrounded on three sides by a low plateau. Upon this plateau stand three stone watch-towers, which were erected by General Gordon. The Dervish garrison were strongly posted in shelter trenches and loopholed houses along the eastern face of the village. The towers were held by their outposts.

Making a wide circuit to their left, and then swinging round to the right, so as to front facing the river, the brigade silently moved towards the enemy's position, and at a quarter past six occupied the plateau in a crescent-shaped formation; the IXth Soudanese on the right, opposite the north-east corner of the village; the battery, escorted by the remaining half-battalion of the 3rd Egyptians, next; then the XIth in the centre, and the Xth Soudanese on the left flank. As the troops approached the watch-towers the Dervish outposts fired and fell back, and the force continued to advance until the edge of the plateau was reached. From here the whole scene was visible. The day was just breaking, and the mist hung low and white over the steel-grey surface of the river. The outlines of the mud houses

---

(Ninth March, 18 miles: 7 P. M. August 5 to 8 A.M. August 6; = 13 hours; Rest till 5:30 P.M. August 6, 1897; = 9½ hours.)

(Tenth March, 18 miles: 5:30 P.M. August 6 to 6:30 A.M. August 7; =9½ hours; Intervals of halt; = 3½ hours.)

Total march time=78½ hours; Total time taken =126½ hours. From 5.30 p.m. July 29, 1897 to 6.30 a.m. August 7, 1897 = 205 hours, of which 78½ hours were spent in marching 133 miles, and 126 ½ hours in rest and camp duties. 205 hours = 8½¾ days, therefore 133 x 24 / 205 = 15.57 miles per diem. It is noticeable how much the marches improved after the troops had recovered from the fatigue of the unavoidably long march at starting. In the last 42 hours they marched 50 miles, and in the last 35 ½ hours they marched 36 miles, and then proceeded to the assault.

were sharply defined on this pale background. The Dervish riflemen could be seen lining the shelter trench that ran round the village. Their cavalry, perhaps a hundred strong, were falling in hurriedly on the sandy ground to the south near the ragged rocks. The curve of the hills, crowned with the dark line of the troops, completed and framed the picture. Within this small amphitheatre one of the minor dramas of war was now to be enacted.

At half past six the battery came into action, and after a few shells had been fired at the loopholed houses in the left centre of the position, a general advance was ordered. In very excellent order the three Soudanese battalions, with General Hunter, Major MacDonald, and the other British officers on horseback behind their line, advanced slowly down the hill, opening a destructive fire on the entrenchment. The distance was scarcely three hundred yards; but the crescent formation of the attack made the lines of advance converge, and before half the distance was covered the Xth were compelled to halt, lest the IXth Soudanese on the right flank should fire into them. The Dervishes remained silent until the troops were within 100 yards, when they discharged two tremendous volleys, which were chiefly effective upon the halted battalion. Major Sidney, Lieutenant Fitzclarence, and a dozen men were shot dead. More than fifty men were wounded. All the Soudanese thereupon with a loud shout rushed upon the entrenchment, stormed it, and hunted the Dervishes into the houses. In the street-fighting which followed, the numbers of the troops prevailed. The advance scarcely paused until the river bank was reached, and by 7.30 Abu Hamed was in the possession of the Egyptian forces. One single house, however, continued to hold out desperately.

A Baggara Dervish, whose name is not recorded had advised that each house should be separately held as a citadel, declaring that, if this were done, although the troops might enter the village, they could not take it. Mohammed ez-Zein thought differently, but the unknown Arab resolved to make the experiment alone. He had fortified and loopholed his own dwelling, and, even when he saw that all resistance was at an end, refused to surrender. He was well supplied with Martini-Henry and revolver ammunition, and when the troops endeavoured to force their way into the house, he succeed-

IN ABU HAMED

ed single-handed in killing four soldiers and wounding others. At length, after this stubborn man had held his foes at bay—for none wished to lose their lives in so profitless a quarrel—*for seven hours*, two field-guns were brought up. The house was then smashed to pieces by repeated shells at close range, and the intrepid defender perished amid the ruins. Had the rest of the garrison followed his advice and emulated his behaviour, the attacking force would have suffered terrible loss, and even, perhaps, defeat. But men of this mettle have already become scarce in the world.

The Dervish horsemen, who had remained spectators near the southern crag during the attack, fled towards Berber as soon as they saw the attack successful. Scarcely any of the infantry escaped. But in any case the column, who had only one troop of cavalry, and were wearied by their marches, would have been unable to pursue. The Dervish Emir, Mohammed ez-Zein, was among the prisoners, having surrendered to an Egyptian officer on a promise that his life should be spared. Hurried before General Hunter, he proved to be an interesting and intelligent man. He was a devout believer in Mahdism, and justified all the actions of the Khalifa as being those of the Lord's anointed. He informed the General that Abu Hamed would soon be retaken, and proclaimed his belief in the ultimate triumph of the Dervish cause. From his examination it transpired that the enemy's force in Abu Hamed had consisted before the action of 400 real Dervishes, of whom 120 were horsemen. Of these 250 were killed, 50 became prisoners, and the remnant bore the tale of disaster to the south. One small brass gun was captured. Three hundred local tribesmen, who were watching from the other side of the river, carried out their intention of joining the winning side and made their submission after the action. The losses of the troops were as follows:—

British Officers killed (2)
Major H. M. Sidney
Lieutenant E. Fitzclarence[6]
Native Ranks

	Killed	Wounded
3rd Egyptians	—	3
IXth Soudanese	5	19
Xth Soudanese	1	5
Transport	1	—
Total	21	61

The British officers were buried with their men in a *khor* near the village, and the spot is now marked by two large marble crosses. The months have grown years since the grey morning when the Khalifa's riflemen fought in the streets of Abu Hamed. The railway runs near the plateau where the battery opened on the village. The English world has forgotten the event. But the Arabs still shun the solitary desert khor, and whisper how that, when the nights are dark, the ghosts of the black soldiers march in a ceaseless 'sentry-go' beside the graves of the officers who led them straight, and challenge all who may approach. For more than a year, so prevalent was the belief, it was impossible to persuade servants to live in the adjacent houses. The superior philosophy of a sceptical age may enable us to smile at barbarous superstition; nevertheless, the tale is worth recording.

The news of the capture of Abu Hamed was carried swiftly by camel and wire to all whom it might concern. The Sirdar, anticipating the result, had already ordered the gunboats to commence the passage of the Fourth Cataract. The camp at Rail-head, 130 miles away from the river—or the world—sprang to life after an unaccus-

6 Lieut. E. Fitzclarence, Dorset Regiment and Egyptian army.

tomed rest, and the line began again to grow rapidly. The Dervishes who were hurrying from Berber were only twenty miles from Abu Hamed when they met the fugitives. They immediately turned back, and retired to the foot of the Fifth Cataract, whence after a few days' halt they continued their retreat. Their proximity to the captured village shows how little time the column had to spare, and that General Hunter was wise to press his marches. The Emir who commanded at Berber heard of the loss of the outpost on the 9th. He sent the messenger on to Metemma. Mahmud replied on the 11th that he was starting at once with his whole army to reinforce Berber. Apparently, however, he did not dare to move without the Khalifa's permission; for his letters, as late as the 20th, show that he had not broken his camp, and was still asking the Emir for information as to the doings of the 'Turks.' Of a truth there was plenty to tell.

On the 4th of August the gunboats *El Teb* and *Tamai* approached the Fourth Cataract to ascend to the Abu Hamed-Berber reach of the river. Major David was in charge of the operation. Lieutenants Hood[7] and Beatty (Royal Navy) commanded the vessels. Two hundred men of the 7th Egyptians were towed in barges to assist in hauling the steamers in the difficult places. The current was, however, too strong, and it was found necessary to leave three barges containing 160 soldiers at the foot of the rapids. Nevertheless, as the cataract was not considered a very formidable barrier, Major David determined to make the attempt. Early on the 5th, therefore, the *Tamai* tried the ascent. About 300 local Shaifffiria tribesmen had been collected, and their efforts were directed—or, as the result proved, misdirected—by those few of the Egyptian soldiers who had not been left behind. The steamer, with her engines working at full speed, succeeded in mounting half the distance. But the rush of water was then so great that her bows were swept round, and, after a narrow escape of capsizing, she was carried swiftly down the stream.

The officers thought that this failure was due to the accidental fouling of a rope at a critical moment, and to the fact that there were not enough local tribesmen pulling at the hawsers. Four hundred more Shaiggia were therefore collected from the neighbouring

7 Lieut. Hon. A. Hood, R.N.

villages, and in the afternoon the *Teb* attempted the passage. Her fortunes were far worse than those of the *Tamai.* Owing to the lack of co-operation and discipline among the local tribesmen, their utter ignorance of what was required of them, and the want of proper supervision, the hauling power was again too weak. Again the bows of the steamer were swept round, and as the hawsers held, a great rush of water poured over the bulwarks. In ten seconds the *Teb* heeled over and turned bottom upwards. The hawsers parted under this new strain, and she was swept down stream with only her keel showing. Lieutenant Beatty and most of the crew were thrown, or glad to jump, into the foaming water of the cataract, and, being carried down the river, were picked up below the rapids by the *Tamai,* which was luckily under steam. Their escape was extraordinary, for of the score who were flung into the water only one Egyptian was drowned. Two other men were, however, missing, and their fate seemed certain. The capsized steamer, swirled along by the current, was jammed about a mile below the cataract between two rocks, where she became a total wreck. Anxious to see if there was any chance of raising her, the officers proceeded in the *Tamai* to the scene. The bottom of the vessel was just visible above the surface. It was evident to all that her salvage would be a work of months. The officers were about to leave the wreck, when suddenly a knocking was heard within the hull. Tools were brought. A plate was removed, and there emerged, safe and sound from the hold in which they had been thus terribly imprisoned, the second engineer and a stoker. When the rapidity with which the steamer turned upside down, with the engines working, the fires burning, and the boilers full—the darkness, with all the floors become ceilings—the violent inrush of water—the wild career down the stream—are remembered, it will be conceded that the experience of these men was sufficiently remarkable.

Search was now made for another passage. This was found on the 6th nearer the right bank of the river. On the 8th the *Metemma* arrived with 300 more men of the 7th Egyptians. Three days were spent in preparations and to allow the Nile to rise a little more. On the 13th, elaborate precautions being observed, the *Metemma* passed the cataract safely, and was tied up to the bank on the higher reach. The *Tamai* followed the next day. On the 19th and 20th the

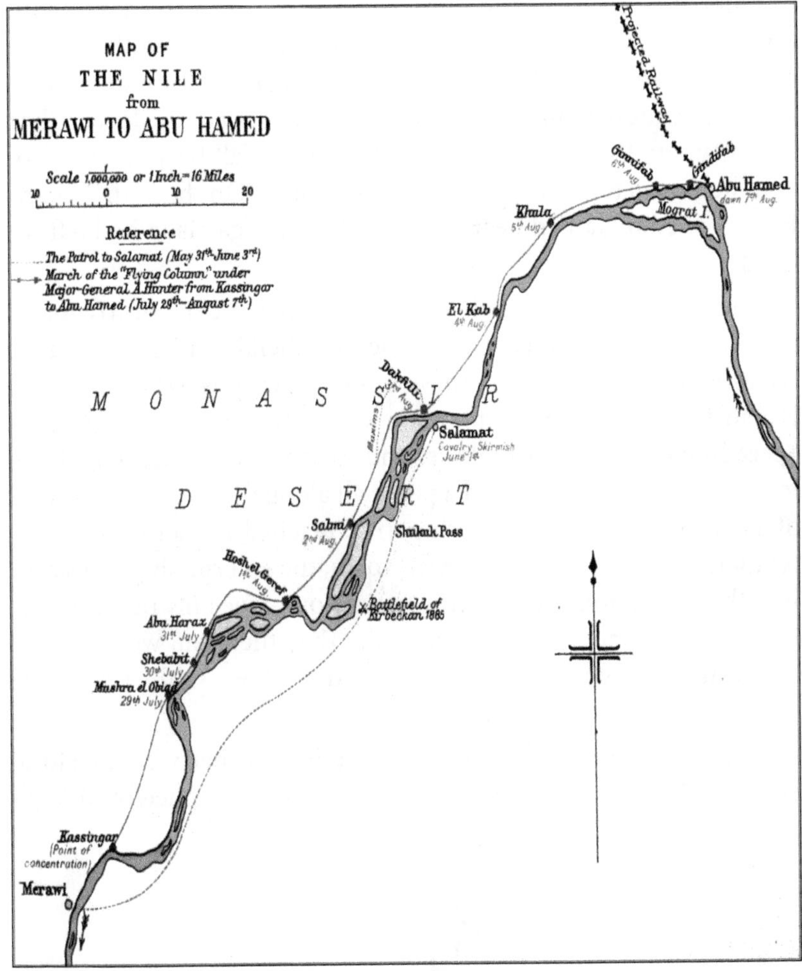
MAP OF
THE NILE
from
MERAWI TO ABU HAMED
Scale 1/1,000,000 or 1 Inch = 16 Miles
10 0 10 20
Reference
The Patrol to Salamat (May 31th–June 3rd)
March of the "Flying Column" under Major-General A. Hunter from Kassingar to Abu Hamed (July 29th–August 7th)
Projected Railway
Abu Hamed
dawn 7th Aug.
Mograt I.
Khula
5th Aug.
El Kab
4th Aug.
M O N A S S I R
D E S E R T
Salamat
Cavalry Skirmish June 1st
Salmi
2nd Aug.
Shukuk Pass
Hosh el Geref
1st Aug.
Battlefield of Kirbeckan 1885
Abu Harax
31st July
Shebabit
30th July
Mashra el Obiad
29th July
Kassingar
(Point of concentration)
Merawi

new gunboats *Fateh, Naser*, and *Zafir*, the most powerful vessels on the river, accomplished the passage. Meanwhile the *Metemma* and *Tamai* had already proceeded up stream. On the 23rd the unarmed steamer *Dal* made the ascent, and by the 29th the whole flotilla reached Abu Hamed safely.

After the arrival of the gunboats events began to move at the double. The sudden dart upon Abu Hamed had caused the utmost consternation among the Dervishes. Finding that Mahmud was not going to reinforce him, and fearing the treachery of the local tribes, Zeki Osman, the Emir in Berber, decided to fall back, and on the 24th he evacuated Berber and marched south. On the 27th General Hunter at Abu Hamed heard that the Dervish garrison had left the town.

The next day he despatched Abdel-Azim, the chief of Irregulars, and Ahmed Bey Khalifa, another friendly Sheikh, with forty Ababda tribesmen, to reconnoitre. These bold fellows pushed on recklessly and found the inhabitants everywhere terrified or acquiescent. Spreading extraordinary tales of the strength of the army that was following them, they created a panic all along the river, and, in spite of a sharp fight with a Dervish patrol, reached Berber on the 31st. As there was no armed force in the town, the enterprising allies rode into the streets and occupied the grain store—the only public building—in the name of the Government. They then sent word back to Abu Hamed of what they had done, and sat down in the town, thus audaciously captured, to await developments.

The astonishing news of the fall of Berber reached General Hunter on the 2nd of September. He immediately telegraphed to Merawi.

A DERVISH MARE

Sir Herbert Kitchener was confronted with a momentous question: should Berber be occupied or not? It may at first seem that there could be little doubt about the matter. The objective of the expedition was Omdurman. The occupation of Berber by an Egyptian garrison would settle at once the difficulties near Suakin. The town was believed to be on the clear waterway to the Dervish capital. The moral effect of its capture upon the riverain tribes and throughout the Soudan would be enormous. Berber was in fact the most important strategic point on the whole line of advance. This great prize and advantage was now to be had for the asking.

The opposite considerations were, however, tremendous. Abu Hamed marked a definite stage in the advance. As long as Merawi and the other posts in Dongola were strongly held, the line from Abu Hamed to Debba was capable of easy defence. Abu Hamed could soon be made impregnable to Dervish attack. The forces in Dongola could be quickly concentrated on any threatened point. At this moment in the campaign it was possible to stop and wait with perfect safety. In the meantime the Khalifa would steadily weaken and the railway might steadily grow. When the line reached the angle of the river, it would be time to continue the systematic and cautious advance. Until then prudence and reason counselled delay. To occupy Berber was to risk much. Mahmud with a large and victorious army lay at Metemma. Osman Digna with 2,000 men held Adarama almost within striking distance. The railway still lagged in the desert. The Dongola garrisons must be weakened to provide a force for Berber. The Dervishes had the advantage of occupying the interior of the angle which the Nile forms at Abu Hamed. The troops in Berber would have to draw their supplies by a long and slender line of camel communication, winding along all the way from Merawi, and exposed, as a glance at the map will show, throughout its whole length to attack. More than all this: to advance to Berber must inevitably force the development of the whole war. The force in the town would certainly have its communications threatened, would probably have to fight for its very existence. The occupation of Berber would involve sooner or later a general action; not a fight like Firket, Hafir, or Abu Hamed, with the advantage of numbers on the side of the Egyptian troops, but an even battle. For such a struggle British troops were necessary. At . this time it seemed most unlikely that they would be granted. But if Berber were occupied, the war, until the arrival of British troops, would cease to be so largely a matter of calculation, and must pass almost entirely into the sphere of chance. The whole situation was premature and unforeseen. The Sirdar had already won success. To halt was to halt in safety; to go on was to go on at hazard. Most of the officers who had served long in the Egyptian army understood the question. They awaited the decision in suspense.

The Sirdar and the Consul-General unhesitatingly faced the responsibility together. On the 3rd of September General Hunter received orders to occupy Berber. He started at once with 350 men of the IXth Soudanese on board the gunboats *Tamai, Zafir, Naser,* and *Fateh.* Shortly after daybreak on the 5th the Egyptian flag was hoisted over the town. Having disembarked the infantry detachment, the flotilla steamed south to try to harass the retreating Emir. They succeeded; for on the next day they caught him, moving along the bank in considerable disorder, and, opening a heavy fire, soon drove the mixed crowd of fugitives, horse and foot, away from the river into the desert. The gunboats then returned to Berber, towing a dozen captured grain-boats. Meanwhile the Sirdar had started for the front himself. Biding swiftly with a small escort across the desert from Merawi, he crossed the Nile at the Baggara Cataract and reached Berber on the 10th of September. Having inspected the immediate arrangements for defence, he withdrew to Abu Hamed, and there busily prepared to meet the developments which he well knew might follow at once, and must follow in the course of a few months.

CHAPTER XI
BERBER[1]

Berber—The Khalifa's plans—Gunboat reconnaissance of Metemma—An uneven combat—Mahmud's army—Osman Digna moves to Shendi—Flying column to Adarama—The beginning of the Atbara entrenchment—Gunboat patrolling—Kassala—Its retrocession—The Khalifa threatens to advance—Critical situation—Concentration towards Berber—The British Brigade—General Gatacre—Railway work—Disposition of the Egyptian forces January 15, 1898—Field training—Bad boots and worse bullets—The Khalifa's difficulties—Break-up of the Kerreri camp—An unexpected development—Forward to the Atbara.

The town of Berber stands at a little distance from the Nile, on the right bank of a channel which is full only when the river is in flood. Between this occasional stream and the regular waterway there runs a long strip of rich alluvial soil, covered during the greater part of the year with the abundant crops which result from its annual submersion and the thick coating of Nile mud which it then receives. The situation of Berber is fixed by this fertile tract, and the houses stretch for more than seven miles along it and the channel by which it is caused. The town, as is usual on the Nile, is comparatively narrow, and in all its length it is only at one point broader than three-quarters of a mile. Two wide streets run longitudinally north and south from end to end, and from these many narrow twisting alleys lead to the desert or the river. The Berber of Egyptian days lies in ruins at the southern end of the main roads. The new town built by the Dervishes stands at the north. Both are foul and unhealthy; and if Old Berber is the more dilapidated, New Berber seemed to the British officers who visited it to be in a more active state of decay. The architectural style of both was similar. The

1 Map, 'The Nile from Abu Hamed to Shabluka,' page 265.

houses were constructed by a simple method. A hole was dug in the ground. The excavated mud formed the walls of the building. The roof consisted of palm-leaves and thorn-bushes. The hole became a convenient cesspool. Such was Berber, and this 'emporium of Soudan trade,' as it has been called by enthusiasts, contained at the time of its recapture by the Egyptian forces a miserable population of 5,000 males and 7,000 females, as destitute of property as their dwellings were of elegance.

The Egyptian, garrison of Berber at first consisted only of the 350 men of the IXth Soudanese, and two companies of the Camel Corps, who arrived on the 16th of September, having marched across the desert from Merawi. But the proximity of Osman Digna at Adarama made it necessary to speedily strengthen the force.

During the latter part of September MacDonald's brigade, with the exception of half the 3rd Egyptians, was moved south from Abu Hamed, and by the end of the month the infantry in Berber were swelled to three and a half battalions. This was further increased on the 11th of October by the arrival of the XIIIth Soudanese and the remaining half of the 3rd Egyptians, and thereafter the place was held by five battalions (3rd, IXth, Xth, XIth, XIIIth), No. 2 Field Battery, and two companies of the Camel Corps. As all the Dervishes on the right bank of the Nile had fled to the south of the Atbara, it was found possible to establish a small advanced post of Camel Corps and friendly Arabs in the village of Dakhila,[2] at the confluence of the rivers. From this humble beginning the Atbara fort with its great entrenchment was soon to develop.

The effect of the occupation of Berber upon the tribes around Suakin was decisive, and the whole country between these towns became at once tranquil and loyal. Osman Digna's influence was destroyed. The friendly villages were no longer raided. The governor of the town became in reality, as well as in name, the governor of the Red Sea littoral. The route from Suakin to Berber was opened; and a Camel Corps patrol, several small caravans of traders, and a party of war correspondents—who might boast that they were the first Europeans to make the journey for thirteen years—passed safely along it.

2 Dakhila is marked on the map as Atbara Fort.

It is now necessary to look to the enemy. Had the Khalifa allowed the Emir Mahmud to march north immediately after the destruction of the Dervish outpost in Abu Hamed, the course of the operations would have been very different. Mahmud would certainly have defended Berber with his whole army. The advance of the Expeditionary Force must have been delayed until the desert railway reached the river, and probably for another year. But, as the last chapter has described, the sudden seizure of Abu Hamed, the defection of the riverain tribes, and the appearance of the gunboats above the Fourth Cataract persuaded Abdullahi that the climax of the war approached, and that he was about to be attacked in his capital. He accordingly devoted himself to his preparations for defence, and forbade his lieutenant to advance north of Metemma or attempt any offensive operations.

In consequence Berber fell, and its fall convinced the Khalifa that his belief was well founded. He worked with redoubled energy. An elaborate system of forts armed with artillery was constructed outside the great wall of Omdurman along the river-bank. The concentration of Arab and black soldiery from Gedaref, Kordofan, and Darfur continued. Large quantities of grain, of camels and other supplies, were requisitioned from the people of the Ghezira[3] and stored or stabled in the city. The discontent to which this arbitrary taxation gave rise was cured by a more arbitrary remedy. As many of the doubtful and embittered tribesmen as could be caught were collected in Omdurman, where they were compelled to drill regularly, and found it prudent to protest their loyalty. The strength and tenacity of the ruler were surprisingly displayed. The Khalifa Sherif, who had been suspected of sympathising with the Jaalin, was made a prisoner at large. The direct penalties attended the appearance of sedition. A close cordon around the city, and especially towards the north, prevented much information from reaching the Egyptian troops; and though small revolts broke out in Kordofan in consequence of the withdrawal of Mahmud's army, the Dervish Empire .as a whole remained submissive, and the Khalifa was able to muster all its remaining force to meet the expected onslaught of his enemies.

3 The country lying between the Blue and White Niles. *Ghezira* (Arabic) = island.

During the first week in October the Sirdar decided to send the gunboats—which now plied, though with some difficulty, up and down the Fifth Cataract—to reconnoitre Metemma and discover the actual strength and position of Mahmud's army. On the 14th the *Zafir*, *Fateh*, and *Naser* steamed south from Berber, under Commander Keppel,[4] each carrying, besides their ordinary native crews, fifty men of the IXth Soudanese and two British sergeants of Marine Artillery. Shortly after daybreak on the 16th the flotilla approached the enemy's position. So silently had they moved that a small Dervish outpost a few miles to the north of Shendi was surprised still sleeping, and the negligent guards, aroused by a splutter of firing from the Maxim guns, awoke to find three terrible machines close upon them.

The gunboats pursued their way, and, disdaining a few shots which were fired from the ruins of Shendi, arrived, at about seven o' clock, within range of Metemma. The town itself stood more than a thousand yards from the Nile, but six substantial mud forts armed with artillery, lined and defended the riverside. Creeping leisurely forward along the east bank, remote from the Dervish works, the flotilla came into action at a range of 4,000 yards. The fire was at first concentrated on the two northern forts, and the shells, striking the mud walls in rapid succession or bursting in the interior, soon enveloped them in dust and smoke.

The Dervishes immediately replied, but the inferiority of their skill and weapons was marked, and, although their projectiles reached the flotilla, very few took effect. One shell, however, crashed through the deck of the *Zafir*, mortally wounding a Soudanese soldier, and two struck the *Fateh*. After the long-range bombardment had continued for about an hour the gunboats moved forward opposite to the enemy's position, and poured a heavy and continuous fire of shrapnel and double shell into all the forts, gradually subduing their resistance. The fugitives from the batteries, and small parties of Baggara horse who galloped about on the open plain between the works and the town, afforded good targets to the Maxims, and many were licked up even at extreme ranges. No sooner had the gunboats passed the forts than the Dervish fire ceased entirely,

4 Commander Colin Keppel. D.S.O., R N.

and it was discovered that their embrasures only commanded the northern approach. As the guns could not be pointed to the southward, the flotilla need fear nothing from any fort that had been left behind. The officers were congratulating themselves on the folly of their foes, when danger threatened from another quarter. The boats had hugged the eastern bank as closely as possible during their duel with the forts. They were scarcely a hundred yards from the shore, when suddenly a sharp fire of musketry was opened from twenty or thirty Dervish riflemen concealed in the mimosa scrub. The bullets pattered all over the decks, but while many recorded narrow escapes no one was actually hit, and the Maxim guns, revolving quickly on their pivots, took a bloody vengeance for the surprise. The flotilla then steamed slowly past the town, and, having thoroughly reconnoitred it, turned about and ran down stream, again exchanging shells with the Dervish artillery. All firing ceased at half-past two; but six sailing-boats containing grain were captured on the return voyage, and with these the gunboats retired in triumph to a small island six miles north of Metemma, where they remained for the night.

It being now known that bombarding the Dervishes was no less enjoyable than exciting, it was determined to spend another day with them; and at four o' clock the next morning the flotilla again steamed southward, so as to be in position opposite Metemma before daylight. Fire was opened on both sides with the dawn, and it was at once evident that the Dervishes had not been idle during the night. It appeared that on the previous day Mahmud had expected a land attack from the direction of Gakdul, and had placed part of his artillery and nearly all his army in position to resist it. But as soon as he was convinced that the gunboats were unsupported he moved several of the landward guns into the river forts, and even built two new works, so that on the 17th the Dervishes brought into action eleven guns, firing from eight small round forts. The gunboats, however, contented themselves with keeping at a range at which their superior weapons enabled them to strike without being struck, and so, while inflicting heavy loss on their enemies, sustained no injury themselves. After four hours' methodical and remorseless bombardment Captain Keppel considered the reconnaissance complete, and gave the order to retire down stream. The

Dervish gunners, elated in spite of their losses by the spectacle of the retreating vessels, redoubled their fire, and continued hurling shell after shell in defiance down the river until their adversaries were far beyond their range. As the gunboats floated northward their officers, looking back towards Metemma, saw an even stranger scene than the impotent but exulting forts. During the morning a few flags and figures had been distinguished moving about the low range of sandhills near the town; and as soon as the retirement of the flotilla began, the whole of the Dervish army, at least 10,000 men, both horse and foot, and formed in an array more than a mile in length, marched triumphantly into view, singing, shouting, and waving their banners amid a great cloud of dust. It was their only victory.

The loss on the gunboats was limited to the single Soudanese soldier, who died of his wounds, and a few trifling repairs. The Arab slaughter is variously estimated, one account rating it at 1,000 men. But half that number would probably be no exaggeration. The gunboats fired in the two days' bombardment 650 shells and several thousand rounds of Maxim-gun ammunition. They then returned to Berber, reporting fully on the enemy's position and army.[5]

As soon as Berber had been strongly occupied by the Egyptian troops, Osman Digna realised that his position at Adarama was not only useless but very dangerous. The force at his disposal was small. He reflected that if the garrison near Berber was within striking distance of Adarama, Adarama was also within the reach of the garrison. And while he knew that the entrenched camp of the Egyptians was too strong for him to attack, he felt no assurance that his antagonists would be equally unable to profit by the proximity. Besides if, as the Khalifa believed, 'the Turk' were about to make their final advance to Omdurman, he might be very easily cut off and prevented from rejoining his master.

Mahmud had long been imperiously summoning him to join the forces at Metemma; and although he hated the Kordofan general, and resented his superior authority, the wary and cunning Osman

5 I have followed in this episode the account of the then correspondent of the *Morning Post,* which is the most reliable and vivid record that has been preserved of the reconnaissance.

decided that in this case it would be convenient to obey and make a virtue of necessity. Accordingly about the same time that the gunboats were making their first reconnaissance and bombardment of Metemma, he withdrew with his two thousand Hadendoa from Adarama, moved along the left bank of the Atbara until the tongue of desert between the rivers became sufficiently narrow for it to be crossed in a day, and so made his way by easy stages to Shendi.

When the Sirdar heard of the evacuation of Adarama he immediately determined to assure himself of the fact, to reconnoitre the unmapped country in that region, and to destroy any property that Osman might have left behind him. On the 23rd of October therefore a living column started from Berber under the command of General Hunter, and formed as follows:—XIth Soudanese (Major Jackson[6]), two guns, one company of the Camel Corps, and Abdel-Azim and 150 irregulars.

Lightly equipped, and carrying the supplies on a train of 500 camels, the small force moved rapidly along the Nile and reached the post at the confluence on the 24th. On the next day the column turned south-east along the Atbara river, and marching *viâ* Hudi, Umdabia, El Hilgi, Gemaiza, and Abruk, arrived at Adarama on the 29th, after a journey of eighty-four miles. The report that Osman Digna had returned to the Nile proved to be correct. His former headquarters were deserted, and although a patrol of sixty Camel Corps and the Arab irregulars scouted for forty miles further up the river, not a single Dervish was to be seen. Having thus collected a great deal of negative information, and delaying only to burn Adarama to the ground, the column returned to Berber. A rough sketch of the country covered by the reconnaissance was made by one of the officers. As the only instrument used was the cavalry sketching-case, and as the distances were judged or paced, this chart was afterwards found very inaccurate. But there seemed no necessity to make a more elaborate sketch, for the returning soldiers little thought, as they marched back through Nakheila, Mutrus, Umdabia, and Hudi, of the significance these places would acquire, or that within six months they would camp again by the banks of the Atbara on a much more serious expedition.

---

6 Major H. W. Jackson, Gordon Highlanders and Egyptian army.

It was now November. The Nile was falling fast, and an impassable rapid began to appear at Urn Tiur, four miles north of the confluence. The Sirdar had a few days in which to make up his mind whether he would keep his gunboats on the upper or lower reach. As in the latter case their patrolling limits would have been restricted, and they would no longer have been able to watch the army at Metemma, he determined to leave them on the enemy's side of the obstruction. This involved the formation of a depôt at Dakhila, where simple repairs could be executed and wood and other necessities stored. To guard this little dockyard half the 3rd Egyptian battalion was moved from Berber and posted in a small entrenchment. The other half-battalion followed in a few weeks. The post at the confluence was gradually growing into the great camp of a few months later.

A regular system of gunboat patrolling was established on the upper reach, and on the 1st of November the *Zafir*, *Naser*, and *Metemma,* under Commander Keppel, again steamed south to reconnoitre Mahmud's position. The next day they were joined by the *Fateh*, and on the 3rd the three larger boats ran the gauntlet of the forts. A brisk artillery duel ensued, but the Dervish aim was, as usual, erratic, and the vessels received no injury. It was observed that the position of the Dervish force was unchanged, but that three new forts had been constructed to the south of the town. The gunboats continued on their way and proceeded as far as Wad Habeshi. The Arab cavalry kept pace with them along the bank, ready to prevent any landing. Having seen all there was to be seen, the flotilla returned and again passed the batteries at Metemma. But this time they were not unscathed, and a shell struck the *Fateh*, slightly wounding three men.

No other incident enlivened the monotony of November. The Khalifa continued his defensive preparations. Mahmud remained motionless at Metemma; and although he repeatedly begged to be allowed to advance against the force near Berber he was steadily refused, and had to content himself with sending raiding parties along the left bank of the Nile, and collecting large stores of grain from all the villages within his reach. Meanwhile the railway was stretching further and further to the south, and the great strain which the sudden occupation of Berber had thrown upon the transport was to some extent relieved. The tranquillity which had followed the advance to Berber was as opportune as it was unexpected. The Sirdar, delighted that no evil consequences had followed his daring move, and finding that he was neither attacked nor harassed in any way, journeyed to Kassala to arrange the details of its retrocession.

The convenient situation of Kassala—almost equally distant from Omdurman, Berber, Suakin, Massowa, and Bosaires—and the fertility of the surrounding region raise it to the dignity of the most important place in the Eastern Soudan.[7] The soil is rich; the climate not unhealthy. A cool night breeze relieves the heat of the day, and the presence of abundant water at the depth of a few feet below the surface supplies the deficiency of a river. In the year 1883 the population is said to have numbered more than 60,000. The Egyptians considered the town of sufficient value to require a garrison of 3,900 soldiers. A cotton mill adequately fitted with machinery and a factory chimney gave promise of the future development of manufacture. A regular revenue attested the existence of trade. But disasters fell in heavy succession on the Eastern Soudan and blighted the prosperity of its mud metropolis. In 1885, after a long siege and a stubborn resistance, Kassala was taken by the Dervishes. The garrison were massacred, enslaved, or incorporated in the Mahdi's army. The town was plundered and the trade destroyed. For nearly ten years an Arab force occupied the ruins and a camp outside them. Kassala became a frontier post of the Dervish Empire. Its population perished or fled to the Italian territory.

This situation might have remained unaltered until after the battle of Omdurman if the Dervishes had been content with the possession of Kassala. But in 1893 the Emir in command of the garrison, being anxious to distinguish himself, disobeyed the Khalifa's instructions to remain on the defensive and attacked the Europeans at Agordat. The Arab force of about 8,000 men were confronted by 2,300 Italian troops, protected by entrenchments, under Colonel Arimondi. After a fierce but hopeless attack the Dervishes were repulsed with a loss of 3,000 men, among whom was their rash leader. The engagement was, however, as disastrous to Italy as to the Khalifa. The fatal African policy of Signor Crispi received a decided im-

7 Map, 'The Soudan,' page xiv.

petus, and in the next year, agreeably with their aspirations in Abyssinia, the Italians under General Baratieri advanced from Agordat and captured Kassala. The occupation was provisionally recognised by Egypt without prejudice to her sovereign rights, and 900 Italian regulars and irregulars established themselves in a well-built fort. The severe defeat at Adowa in 1896, the disgrace of Baratieri, the destruction of his army, and the fall of the Crispi Cabinet, rudely dispelled the African ambitions of Italy.

Kassala became an encumbrance. Nor was that all. The Dervishes, encouraged by the victory of the Abyssinians, invested the fort, and the garrison were compelled to fight hard to hold what their countrymen were anxious to abandon. Under these circumstances the Italian Government offered, at a convenient opportunity, to retrocede Kassala to Egypt. The offer was accepted, and an arrangement made. The advance of the Khedivial forces into the Dongola province relieved, as has been described, the pressure of the Dervish attacks. The Arabs occupied various small posts along the Atbara and in the neighbourhood of the town, and contented themselves with raiding. The Italians remained entirely on the defensive, waiting patiently for the moment when the fort could be handed over to the Egyptian troops.

The Sirdar had no difficulty in coming to a satisfactory arrangement with General Caneva, the Italian commander. The fort was to be occupied by an Egyptian force, the stores and armament to be purchased at a valuation, and a force of Italian Arab irregulars to be transferred to the Egyptian service. Sir H. Kitchener then returned to the Nile, where the situation had suddenly become acute. During November Colonel Parsons, the 16th Egyptian battalion and a few native gunners marched from Suakin, and on the 20th of December arrived at Kassala. The Italian irregulars—henceforth to be known as the Arab battalion—were at once despatched to the attack of the small Dervish posts at El Fasher and Asubri, and on the next day these places were surprised and taken with scarcely any loss. The Italian officers, although a little disgusted at the turn of events, treated the Egyptian representatives with the most perfect courtesy, and the formal transference of Kassala fort was arranged to take place on Christmas Day.

An imposing ceremonial was observed, and the scene itself was strange. The fort was oblong in an, with mud ramparts and parapets pierced for musketry. Tents and stores filled the enclosure. In the middle stood the cotton factory. Its machinery had long since been destroyed, but the substantial building formed the central keep of the fort. The tall chimney had become a convenient look-out post. The lightning-conductor acted as a flagstaff. The ruins of the old town of Kassala lay brown and confused on the plain to the southward, and behind all rose the dark rugged spurs of the Abyssinian mountains. The flags of Egypt and of Italy were hoisted. The troops of both countries, drawn up in line, exchanged military compliments. Then the Egyptian guard marched across the drawbridge into the fort and relieved the Italian soldiers. The brass band of the 16th battalion played appropriate airs. The Italian flag was lowered, and with a salute of twenty-one guns the retrocession of Kassala was complete.

Here, then, for a year we leave Colonel Parsons and his small force to swelter in the mud fort, to carry on a partisan warfare with the Dervish raiders, to look longingly towards Gedaref, and to nurse the hope that when Omdurman has fallen their opportunity will come. The reader, like the Sirdar, must return in a hurry to the Upper Nile.

Towards the end of November the Khalifa had begun to realise that the Turks did not mean to advance any further till the next flood of the river. He perceived that the troops remained near Berber, and that the railway was only a little way south of Abu Hamed. The blow still impended, but it was delayed. As soon as he had come to this conclusion, he no longer turned a deaf ear to Mahmud's solicitations. He knew that the falling Nile would restrict the movements of the gunboats. He knew that there were only 2,000 men in Berber —a mere handful. He did not realise the tremendous power of rapid concentration which the railway had given his enemies; and he began to think of offensive operations. But Mahmud should not go alone. The whole strength of the Dervish army should be exerted to drive back the invaders. All the troops in Omdurman were ordered north. A great camp was again formed near Kerreri. Thousands of camels were collected, and once more every preparation was made for a general advance. At the beginning of December he sent his own secretary to Mahmud to explain the plan, and to assure him of early reinforcements and supplies. Lastly, Abdullahi preached a new Jehad, and it is remarkable that, while all former exhortations had been directed against 'the infidel' —*i.e.* those who did not believe in the Mahdi—his letters and sermons on this occasion summoned the tribes to destroy, not the Egyptians, but the Christians. The Khalifa had no doubts as to who inspired the movement which threatened him. There were at this time scarcely 150 Europeans in the Soudan; but they had made their presence felt.

The Sirdar was returning from Kassala when the rumours of an intended Dervish advance began to grow. Every scrap of information was assiduously collected by the Intelligence Department, but it was not until the 18th of December, just as he reached Wady Halfa, that the General received apparently certain news that the Khalifa, Mahmud, all the Emirs, and the whole army were about to march north. There can be no doubt that even this tardy movement of the enemy seriously threatened the success of the operations. If the Dervishes moved swiftly, it looked as if a very critical engagement would have to be fought to avoid a damaging retreat. Sir H. Kitchener's reply to the Khalifa's open intent was to order a general concentration of the available Egyptian army towards Berber, to telegraph to Lord Cromer asking for a British brigade, and to close the Suakin-Berber route.

The gunboat depôt at the confluence, with half-battalion escort, was now in an extremely exposed position. The gunboats could not steam north, for the cataract four miles below the confluence was already impassable. Since they must remain on the enemy's side, so must their depôt: and the depôt must be held by a much stronger force. Although the Sirdar felt too weak to maintain himself even on the defensive without reinforcements, he was now compelled to push still further south. On the 22nd of December Lewis's brigade of four battalions and a battery was hurried along the Nile to its junction with the Atbara, and began busily entrenching itself in the angle formed by the rivers. The Atbara fort sprang into existence.

Meanwhile the concentration was proceeding. All the troops in Dongola, with the exception of scanty garrisons in Merawi, Korti, and Debba, were massed at Berber. The infantry and guns, dropping down the river in boats, entrained at Kerma, were carried back to Halfa, then hustled across the invaluable Desert Railway, past Abu Hamed, and finally deposited at Rail-head, which then (January 1) stood at Dakhesh. The whole journey by rail from Merawi to Dakhesh occupied four days, whereas General Hunter with his flying column had taken eight—a fact which proves that, under certain circumstances which Euclid could not have foreseen, two sides of a triangle are together shorter than the third side. The Egyptian cavalry at Merawi received their orders on the 25th of December, and the British officers hurried from their Christmas dinners to prepare for their long march across the bend of the Nile to Berber. Of the eight squadrons, three were pushed on to join Lewis's force at the position which will hereinafter be called 'the Atbara encampment,' or more familiarly 'the Atbara'; three swelled the gathering forces at Berber; and two remained for the present in the Dongola province, looking anxiously out towards Gakdul Wells and Metemma.

The War Office, who had been nervous about the situation in the Soudan since the hasty occupation of Berber, and who had a very lively recollection of the events of 1884 and 1885, lost no time in the despatch of British troops: and the speed with which a force, so suddenly called for, was concentrated, shows the capacity for energy which may on occasions be developed even by our disjointed military organisation. The 1st battalions of the Royal Warwickshire Regiment, of the Lincoln Regiment, and of the Cameron Highlanders were formed into a brigade and moved from Cairo into the Soudan. The 1st battalion of the Seaforth Highlanders was brought from Malta to Egypt, and held in immediate readiness to reinforce the troops at the front. Other battalions were sent to take the places of those moved south, so that the Army of Occupation was not diminished.

The officer selected for the command of the British brigade was a man of high character and ability. General Gatacre[8] had already led a brigade in the Chitral expedition, and, serving under Sir Robert Low and Sir Bindon Blood, had gained so good a reputation that after the storming of the Malakand Pass and the subsequent action

8 Major-General W. F. Gatacre, C.B.

in the plain of Khar it was thought desirable to transpose his brigade with that of General Kinloch, and send Gatacre forward to Chitral. From the mountains of the North-West Frontier the General was ordered to Bombay, and in a stubborn struggle with the bubonic plague, which was then at its height, he turned his attention from camps of war to camps of segregation. He left India, leaving behind him golden opinions, just before the outbreak of the great Frontier rising, and was appointed to a brigade at Aldershot. Thence we now find him hurried to the Soudan—a spare, middle-sized man, of great physical strength and energy, of marked capacity and unquestioned courage, but disturbed by a restless irritation, to which even the most inordinate activity afforded little relief, and which often left him the exhausted victim of his own vitality.

General Gatacre's Staff officer, Major Snow,[9] was a soldier of varied experience in war, having previously served on the Indian Frontier, at the Cape, and in the Soudan. Like many private people he had nursed in his heart the long quarrel with the Dervish power since the days of '84. As a subaltern he marched with the Desert Column of the Gordon Relief Expedition. Someone in England had given him a pint of champagne to drink in Khartoum. Strapped in his wallets the bottle had passed safely through the actions of Abu Klea and Abu Kru, had waited at Metemma, and returned unopened to England with the disappointed troops. The subaltern put it carefully away. An interval of twelve years followed, and there were times when it seemed very unlikely that the wine would ever be drunk in the ruined town. But at last, in the inevitable continuity of British policy, the hour approached. The subaltern, become a major, was again ordered to the Soudan, and with him, protected by a stout leather case, came the patient bottle. Its suspense was nearly at an end.

The concentration on Berber strained the carrying powers of the Desert Railway to the full. The terminus at Halfa was the scene of frantic and unceasing effort. The whole weight of the war fell upon the Railway Staff, and many minor worries were added to their great responsibilities. Mournful-looking officials of varied or doubtful nationality argue daily with the Traffic Manager—one of

9 Major T. D. O. Snow, *p.s.c*, Royal Inniskillen Fusiliers.

the subalterns—demanding transport and backing their demands with 'urgent,' 'very urgent,' and 'most important' (all written in red ink) telegrams from their superiors at the front. A motley crowd of would-be passengers —merchants (Greek and native), camel-men, officers' servants, syces with their masters' horses, all the ragtag and bobtail of an army—clamour for railway transport. The Traffic Manager states the utmost he can do. All look alarmed, miserable, or angry, according as their station in life entitles them. The trucks are loaded till the springs are in danger of breaking. The officers toil till far into the night. The trains depart on their long journey amid general disappointment and vexation.

Presently the rumours of a Dervish advance grow into certainty. The British brigade is hurried to the front: the Merawi garrison hurled into Berber: the Egyptian Horse Artillery Battery despatched from Halfa to Rail-head. The Merawi garrison, consisting of four Egyptian and Soudanese battalions, appears at Kerma, and is hustled 450 miles round the great loop *viâ* Halfa and Abu Hamed. One by one the half-battalions of the British brigade arrive at Halfa from Cairo and beyond. Swiftly they are bundled into trains and hurried south. Then follow departmental officers with stores and peculiar supplies; medical officers armed to the teeth, and guarding weird-looking packages—stretchers, cacolets, and such like; Staff officers full of importance and resplendent with red tabs on their collars; parsons with revolvers; and war correspondents equipped with ice machines, type-writers, cameras, and even cinematographs. All are bundled off south.[10]

By the end of January the concentration was complete, and a powerful force lay encamped along the river from Abu Hamed to the Atbara. The general distribution was as follows:

Abu Hamed	5th Egyptians (half-battalion)
Dakhesh (Rail-head)	1 Squadron Lincolns Warwicks Camerons No. 1 Battery

10 It is a pity that these varied stores did not include the Rontgen rays apparatus. This neglectful omission was afterwards to cause much need less suffering to the officers and men who sustained gunshot wounds at the battle of the Atbara—EDITOR.

ON GUARD

Neddi	1st and 8th Egyptians
Geneinetti	2nd Egyptians
Berber (Headquarters)	3 squadrons 2 companies Camel Corps IXth,Xth, XIth,XIIth, XIIth, XIVth Soudanese Nos. 4 and 5 Batteries
Dakhila (Atbara Fort)	3 Squadrons 3rd, 4th, 7th & 15th Egyptians No. 2 Battery

General Gatacre had no sooner collected the three battalions of his brigade than he began a most severe and rigorous training. The camp of the British was formed at Gruheish, a placeless name printed on the map a few miles south of Rail-head. The new Brigadier insisted, in spite of the distance at which the enemy then were, on the utmost precautions of war being observed. Officers and men were compelled to sleep in their boots, and the rest of the troops was disturbed by frequent night-alarms. Regular route-marching twice a week and much field-firing busily occupied the brigade, while every conceivable formation to resist a Dervish attack was assiduously practised. The excessive enthusiasm of the General may have provoked some dissatisfaction among the soldiers; but it is impossible to deny that, while discipline and health were successfully maintained, the general efficiency was greatly increased. On the 13th of February the brigade moved into a new camp at Abu Dis, a few miles further south, where they enjoyed a greater immunity from sandstorms, and here they made preparations for a prolonged stay.

The British soldiers enjoyed two occupations in their spare time which must not escape the chronicler or the public. Their equipment was in many respects excellent. Their boots and their bullets were, however, useless. The former, manufactured by the worst though by no means the cheapest process, were soon completely worn out. It was found that the soles dropped to pieces after a fortnight's hard marching. The material of which they were made resembled brown paper rather than leather. The simplicity of the War Office and the knavery of the contractors had combined to produce the most expensive and least durable boot in the Soudan. And the astonished Egyptian saw the British infantry tying the soles of their boots to their feet with string, with strips of hide, and even with pieces of linen.

The case of the bullets was even more serious. The British brigade had been sent to the Soudan armed with the nickel-cased Lee-Metford bullets (Mark II.). As these bullets do not kill an enemy, General Gatacre considered it desirable to have them altered to meet that requirement; and during the month at Gruheish a million rounds of ammunition were converted into improvised Dum-Dum bullets by filing off the tips, so as to expose the heavy core within the outer case. These missiles were afterwards used at the Atbara, and the results were found satisfactory as far as killing power was concerned. But two serious disadvantages must be recorded. The roughly cut bullets destroyed much of the accuracy of flight. The fact that their filed tips were uneven caused them to jam when used in the magazine of the rifle. It was therefore necessary to have unconverted bullets to fire when the magazine action was used, and converted bullets when the single action was desired. By this arrangement, which was undoubtedly the best that the General could devise, the British troops were so equipped that at single action at the longer ranges they might fire converted bullets, which were unlikely to hit, and at the critical moment, when magazine action was necessary, they might fire unconverted bullets, which were unlikely to kill.[11]

11 The Author is hardly exaggerating. Moreover, it was not discovered that

There was at this time in India a large supply of the Dum-Dum bullet—a bullet which in the Frontier war had had an exhaustive practical test, and had been found to be in every respect satisfactory. Its advantages were not denied, but it was felt that the dignity of Hythe could not support the general adoption of an Indian invention. The British brigade was therefore sent to face the enemy armed with the obsolete bullet, pending the 'invention' by the musketry experts at home of some missile which should produce the results of the Dum-Dum bullet without resembling it too closely. The parties guilty of this crime have not yet been brought to justice.

While the concentration of the troops was being effected the Dervishes made no forward movement. Their army was collected at Kerreri; supplies were plentiful; all preparations had been made. Yet they tarried. The burning question of the command had arisen. A dispute that was never settled ensued. When the whole army was regularly assembled, the Khalifa announced publicly that he would lead the faithful in person; but at the same time he arranged privately that many Emirs and notables should beg him not to expose his sacred person. After proper solicitation therefore he yielded to their appeals. Then he looked around for a subordinate. The Khalifa Ali-Wad-Helu presented himself. In the Soudan every advantage and honour accrues to the possessor of an army, and the rival chief saw a chance of regaining his lost power. This consideration was not, however, lost upon Abdullahi. He accepted the offer with apparent delight, but he professed himself unable to spare any rifles for the army which Ali-Wad-Helu aspired to lead. 'Alas!' he cried, 'there are none. But that will make no difference to so famous a warrior.' Ali-Wad-Helu , however, considered that it would make a great deal of difference, and declined the command. Osman Sheikh-ed-Din offered to lead the army, if he might arm the riverain tribes and use them as auxiliaries to swell his force. This roused the disapproval of

---

the filing of the tips of the bullets would prevent them from being used in the magazines, until nearly all the bullets had been altered. There was therefore no reserve of ammunition for the magazines, and each British soldier on the Atbara just had his magazine full, and that was all. The spectacle of a British brigade, sitting down within striking distance of the enemy, manufacturing their ammunition, with the sole's dropping off their boots, would make one laugh, if it were not so serious.—EDITOR.

Yakub. Such a policy, he declared, was fatal. The riverain tribes were traitors —dogs—worthy only of being destroyed. He enlarged upon the more refined methods, by which his policy might be carried out. The squabble continued, until at last the Khalifa, despairing of any agreement, decided merely to reinforce Mahmud, and accordingly ordered the Emir Yunes to march to Metemma with about 5,000 men. But it was then discovered that Mahmud hated Yunes, and would have none of him. At this the Khalifa broke up his camp, and the Dervish army marched back for the second time, in vexation and disgust, to the city.

It seemed to those who were acquainted with the Dervish movements that all offensive operations on their part had been definitely abandoned. Even in the Intelligence Department it was believed that the break-up of the Kerreri camp was the end of the Khalifa's determination to move north. There would be a hot and uneventful summer, and with the flood Nile the expedition would begin its final advance. The news which was received on the 15th of February came as a great and pleasant surprise. Mahmud was crossing the Nile and proposed to advance on Berber without reinforcements of any kind. The Sirdar, highly satisfied at this astounding piece of good fortune, immediately began to mass his force nearer the confluence. On the 21st the British at Abu Dis were instructed to hold themselves in readiness. The Seaforths began their journey from Cairo, and the various battalions of the Egyptian army pressed forward towards Berber and Atbara fort, On the 25th, Mahmud being reported as having crossed to the right bank, the general concentration was ordered.

The British brigade had just returned from a route-march of fourteen miles, when at 1.45 on that date the telegram was received instructing them to move to Dabeika, a village ten miles south of Berber, by forced marches. During the night the battalions left by train for Rail-head, which was by then at Shereik, some sixteen miles further south.

From here they started to march to the front. Owing to a clerical error in a war correspondent's telegram, the march that followed has excited more attention than it perhaps deserves. Marching steadily, and with a halt of one day at a camping ground seven miles north of Berber, the brigade reached Dabeika on the 3rd of March. The actual itinerary was as follows:—

Arrived at Shereik by train on the morning of the 26th February

26-27 February, marched to Bashtinab	13 miles
27-28 February, marched to Omsheyo	14 miles
28 February, marched to Abadia	22 miles
1 March, marched to El Hasa[12]	9 miles
2 March, (halt)	
3 March marched through Berber to Dabeika	13½ miles
	71½ miles

Average: about eleven miles a day.

The brigade remained encamped at Dabeika for eight days, disturbed by conflicting rumours, but delighted that the campaign was going to begin; and meanwhile all the forces at the disposal of the Sirdar were gradually drawing near the front.

12 A hamlet three miles north of Berber.

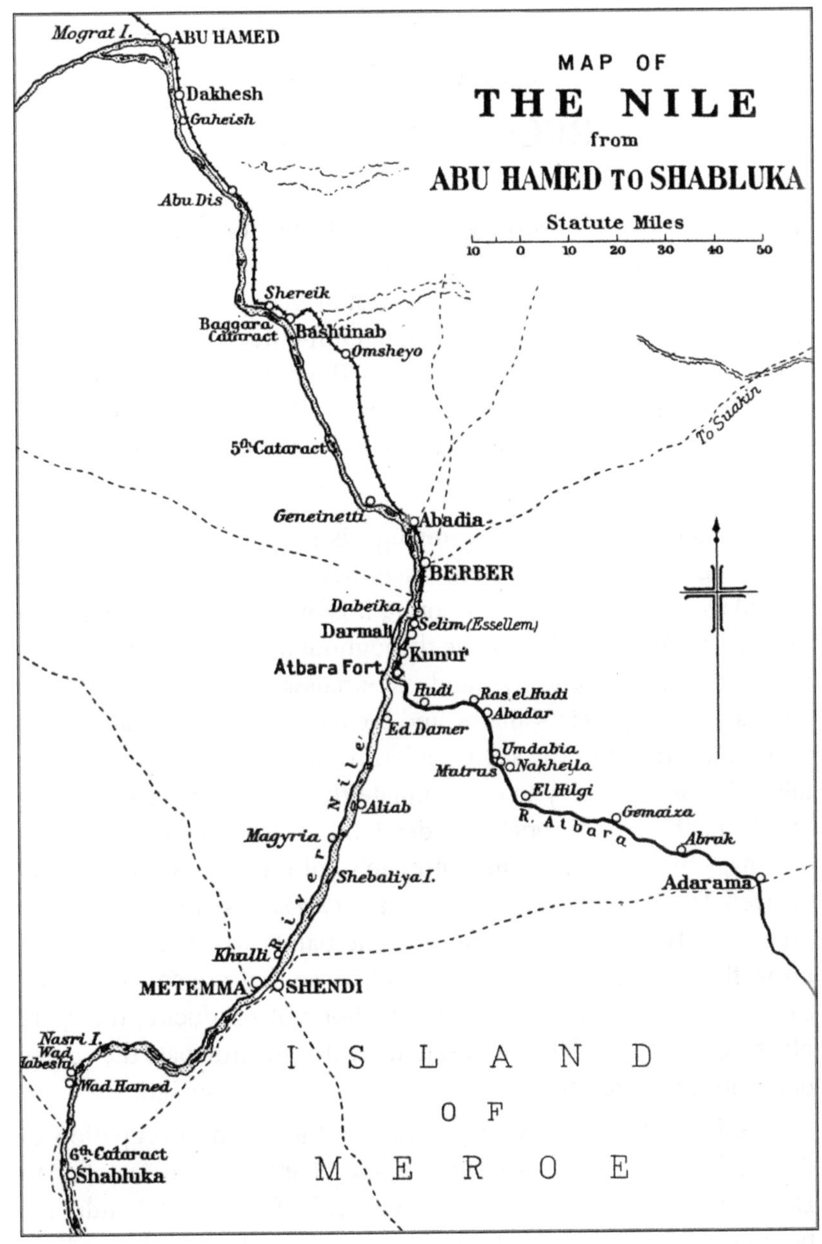
MAP OF
THE NILE
from
ABU HAMED TO SHABLUKA
Statute Miles
10 0 10 20 30 40 50
Mograt I.
ABU HAMED
Dakhesh
Gaheish
Abu Dis
Shereik
Baggara Cataract
Bashtinab
Omsheyo
5th Cataract
Geneinetti
Abadia
To Suakin
BERBER
Dabeika
Selim (Essellem)
Darmali
Kunur
Atbara Fort
Hudi
Ras el Hudi
Abadar
Ed Damer
Umdabia
Nakheila
Matrus
El Hilgi
R. Atbara
Gemaiza
Abrak
Adarama
River Nile
Aliab
Magyria
Shebaliya I.
Khalli
METEMMA
SHENDI
Nasri I.
Wad Habeshi
Wad Hamed
6th Cataract
Shabluka
ISLAND
OF
MEROE

CHAPTER XII
RECONNAISSANCE

A general view—The strategic aspect—Concentration at Kunur—March to Hudi—The Dervish march—Kas-el-Hudi—The Atbara scenery—The outpost affair of the 21st of March—Deserters—The camp at Kas- el-Hudi—Capture of Shendi—Reconnaissance of the 30th of March—Dervish prisoners—The moment approaches—The reconnaissance of the 5th of April—The Egyptian trooper—His officers—Advance to Abadar—The eve of battle.

Although the story of a campaign is made up of many details which cannot be omitted, since they are essential to the truth as well as the interest of the account, it is of paramount importance that the reader should preserve throughout a general idea. For otherwise the marches, forays, and reconnaissance will seem disconnected and purposeless affairs, and the battle simply a greater operation undertaken in the same haphazard fashion. To appreciate the tale it is less necessary to contemplate the wild scenes and stirring incidents, than to thoroughly understand the logical sequence of incidents, which all tend to and ultimately culminate in a decisive trial of strength. The difference between the two styles of narration is as great as between the appearance of the paints which are squeezed on to the palette of the artist, and of those that are spread on the canvas of a picture. In the ambitious hope of producing the more pleasing effect, I shall to some extent recall and anticipate the course of events and take a general view of the Atbara campaign.

The hazards which were courted by the daring occupation of Berber have been discussed in the last chapter. From October to December the situation was threatening. In December it suddenly became critical. Had the Emir Mahmud advanced with the Dervishes at Metemma even as late as the middle of January, he might possibly have recaptured Berber. If the great Omdurman army had taken the field, the possibility would have become a certainty. The young Kordofan general saw his opportunity, and begged to be allowed to seize it. But it was not until the Khalifa had sent his own army back into the city that, being very badly informed of the numbers and disposition of the Egyptian force, he allowed the Metemma Dervishes to move.[1]

Mahmud received permission to advance at the end of January. He eagerly obeyed the longed-for order. But the whole situation was now changed. The Egyptian army was concentrated; the British brigade had arrived; the railway had reached Geneinetti; the miserable hamlet of Dakhila, at the confluence, had grown from a small depôt to a fort, and from a fort to an entrenched camp, against which neither Dervish science nor strength could by any possibility prevail. Perhaps Mahmud did not realise the amazing power of movement that the railway had given his foes; perhaps he still believed, with the Khalifa, that Berber was held only by 2,000 Egyptians; or else—and this is the more probable—he was reckless of danger and strong in his own conceit. At any rate, during the second week in February he began to transport himself across the Nile, with the plain design of an advance north. With all the procrastination of an Arab he crawled leisurely forward towards the confluence of the rivers. At El Aliab some idea of the strength of the Atbara entrenchment seems to have dawned upon him. He paused undecided. A council was held. Mahmud was for a continued advance and for making a direct attack on the enemy's position.

Osman Digna urged a more prudent course. Many years of hard fighting against disciplined troops had taught the wily Hadendoa slaver the power of modern rifles, and much sound tactics besides. He pressed his case with jealous enthusiasm upon the commander he detested and despised. An insurmountable obstacle confronted them. Yet what could not be overcome might be avoided. The hardy Dervishes could endure privations which would destroy the soldiers of civilisation. Barren and inhospitable as was the desert, they might move round the army at the Atbara fort and so capture Berber after all. Once they were behind the Egyptians, these accursed ones were lost. The railway—that mysterious source of strength —could be

1 Map, 'The Campaign on the Atbara,' page 295.

cut. The host that drew its life along it must fight at a fearful disadvantage or perish miserably. Besides, he reminded Mahmud—not without reason—that they could count on help in Berber itself.

The agreement of the Emirs, called to the council, decided the Dervish leader. His confidence in himself was weakened, his hatred of Osman Digna increased. Nevertheless, following the older man's advice he left Aliab on the 18th of March, and struck north-east into the desert towards the village and ford of Hudi on the Atbara river. Thence by a long desert march he might reach the Nile and Berber. But while his information of the Sirdar's force and movements was uncertain, the British General was better served. What Mahmud failed to derive from spies and 'friendlies,' his adversary obtained by gunboats and cavalry. As soon, therefore, as Sir H. Kitchener learned that the Dervishes had left the Nile and were making a *détour* around his left flank, he marched up the Atbara river to Hudi. This offered Mahmud the alternative of attacking him in a strong position or of making a still longer *détour*. Having determined upon caution he chose the latter, and, deflecting his march still more to the east, reached the Atbara at Nakheila. But from this point the distance to Berber was far too great for him to cover. He could not carry enough water in his skins. The wells were few, and held against him. Further advance was impossible. So he waited and entrenched himself, sorely troubled, but uncertain what to do. Supplies were running short. His magazines at Shendi had been destroyed as soon as he had left the Nile. The Dervishes might exist, but they did not thrive, on the nuts of the *dôm*-palms. Soldiers began to desert. Osman Digna, although his advice had been followed, was at open enmity. His army dwindled.

And all this time his terrible antagonist watched him as a tiger gloats on a helpless and certain prey—silent, merciless, inexorable. Then the end came suddenly. As soon as the process of attrition was sufficiently far advanced to conveniently demoralise the Dervish host, without completely dissolving them, the Sirdar and his army moved. The victim, as if petrified, was powerless to fly. The tiger crept forward two measured strides—from Eas-el-Hudi to Abadar, from Abadar to Umdabia—crouched for a moment, and then bounded with irresistible fury upon its prey and tore it to pieces.

Such is a brief strategic account of the Atbara campaign; but the tale must be told in full.

On the 23rd of January the Khalifa, having learned of the arrival of British troops near Abu Hamed, and baffled by the disputes about the command of his army, ordered Kerreri camp to be broken up, and permitted his forces to return within the city, which he continued to fortify. A few days later he authorised Mahmud to advance against Berber. I shall not try to guess his reason for such policy, if reason there was. What he had not dared with 60,000 men he now attempted with 20,000. The course of action which had for three months offered a good hope of success he resolved to pursue only when it led to ruin. He forbade the advance while it was advisable. When it had already become mad and fatal he commanded it. And this was a man whose reputation for intelligence and military skill had been bloodily demonstrated! Explanation there is none, save such as may lie in a Latin proverb which is too hackneyed to quote.

The gunboats ceaselessly patrolled the river, and exchanged shots with the Dervish forts. Throughout January nothing of note had happened. The reports of spies showed the Khalifa to be at Kerreri or in Omdurman. Ahmed Fedil held the Shabluka Gorge. Osman Digna was at Shendi, and his presence was attested by the construction of two new forts on that side of the river. But beyond this the Dervishes had remained passive. On the 12th of February, however, it was noticed that their small outpost at Khulli had been withdrawn. This event seemed to point to a renewal of activity. It was fell that some important movement impended. But it was not until the 15th that its nature was apparent, and the gunboats were able to report definitely that Mahmud was crossing to the east bank of the Nile. The flotilla exerted itself to harass the Dervishes and impede the transportation; but although several sailing-boats and other river craft were captured, Mahmud succeeded in moving his whole army to Shendi by the 28th of February. His own headquarters were established at Hosh-ben-Naga, a little village about five miles further south. A delay of more than a fortnight followed, during which the gunboats exercised the utmost vigilance. The Suakin-Berber road was again closed for caravans, and the Sirdar himself proceeded to Berber. On the 11th of March the remnants of the Jaalin tribe, having collected at Gakdul, re-occupied the now abandoned Metemma, to find its streets and houses choked with the decaying bodies of their relations. On the 13th the Egyptian look-out station, which had been established on Shebaliya island, was attacked by the Dervishes, and in the skirmish that ensued Major Sitwell[2] was wounded. On the same day the enemy were reported moving northwards to Aliab, and it became evident that Mahmud had begun his advance.

He started from Shendi with a force which has been estimated at 19,000 souls, but which included many women and children, and may have actually numbered 12,000 fighting men, each and all supplied with a month's rations and about 90 rounds of ammunition. The Sirdar immediately ordered the Anglo-Egyptian army, with the exception of the cavalry and Lewis's Egyptian brigade—which with three squadrons held the fort at the confluence—to concentrate at Kunur. Broadwood, with the remaining five squadrons, marched thither on the 16th; and the whole cavalry force, with the Camel Corps in support, on the three subsequent days reconnoitred twenty miles up the Nile and the Atbara.

Meanwhile the concentration at Kunur was proceeding apace. On the 14th the inhabitants of Berber were startled by the departure of both the Soudanese brigades which had been holding the town, and by the publication of the following order:—

His Excellency the Sirdar desires, and strongly recommends, that all merchants in Berber should remove themselves and their belongings to Geneinetti as soon as possible. He can guarantee no military protection

March 14*th*, 1898

By Order

As Geneinetti was twenty miles away, and hardly any transport was procurable, the 'merchants' —that is to say, the Greek traders—for the most part determined to stay where they were, and risk their lives with their property. To those who remained Remington rifles were served out, and they began to make feeble preparations for defence. The two Soudanese brigades, formed into a division under command of Major-General Hunter, with the artillery reached

2 Major W. H. Sitwell, *p.s.c*, Northumberland Fusiliers and Egyptian army.

Kunur on the night of the 15th. The British brigade—the Lincolns, the Warwicks, and the Camerons—marched thither from Dabeika. The Seaforth Highlanders, who on the 13th were still at Wady Halfa, were swiftly railed across the desert to Geneinetti. Thence the first half-battalion were brought to Kunur in steamers. The second wing—since the need was urgent and the steamers few—was jolted across the desert from Rail-head on camels, an experience for which neither their training nor their clothes had prepared them. By the 16th the whole force was concentrated at Kunur, and on the following day they were reviewed by the Sirdar. With the exception of the British brigade, whose boots of inferior quality were much worn, and whose converted cartridges would not fit their magazines, the army was in every respect efficient and well equipped. The first three days at Kunur were days of eager expectation. Rumour was king. The Dervish army had crossed the Atbara at Hudi, and was within ten miles of the camp. Mahmud was already making a flank march through the desert to Berber. A battle was imminent. A collision must take place in a few hours. Officers with field-glasses scanned the sandy horizon for the first signs of the enemy. But the skyline remained unbroken, except by the wheeling dust devils, and gradually the excitement abated, and the British brigade began to regret all the useful articles they had scrupulously left behind them at Dabeika, when they marched in a hurry and the lightest possible order to Kunur.

AT KUNUR—THE ONLY SHIRT

On the 19th of March the gunboats reported that the Dervishes were leaving the Nile, and Mahmud's flanking movement became apparent. The next day the whole force at Kunur marched across the desert angle between the rivers to Hudi. The appearance of the army would have been formidable. The cavalry, the Camel Corps, and the Horse Artillery covered the front and right flank; the infantry, with the British on the right, moved in line of brigade masses; the transport followed. All was, however, shrouded in a fearful dust-storm. The distance, ten miles, was accomplished in five hours, and the army reached Hudi in time to construct a strong *zeriba* before the night. Here they were joined from Atbara Fort by Lewis's brigade of Egyptians—with the exception of the 15th battalion, which was left as garrison—and the troops at the Sirdar's disposal were thus raised to nearly 14,000 men of all arms. This force was organised as follows:

Commander-in-Chief: The Sirdar

British Brigade: Major-General Gatacre

1st Battalion Royal Warwickshire Regiment (6 Companies)

1st Battalion Lincolnshire Regiment

1st Battalion Seaforth Highlanders

1st Battalion Cameron Highlanders

Egyptian Infantry Division: Major-General Hunter

1st Brigade	*2nd Brigade*	*3rd Brigade*
Lieut.-Col. Maxwell	Lieut. -Col. MacDonald	Lieut. -Col. Lewis
8th Egyptians	2nd Egyptians	3rd Egyptians
XIIth Soudanese	IX Soudanese	4th Egyptians
XIIIth Soudanese	Xth Soudanese	7th Egyptians
XIV Soudanese	XI Soudanese	

Cavalry: Lieut.-Col. Broadwood

8 Squadrons

2 Maxim guns

Camel Corps: Major Tudway[3]

6 Companies

3 Captain (temporary Major) R. J. Tudway, Essex Regiment and Egyptian army.

Artillery: LIEUT.-COL. LONG[4]

Detachment, No. 16 Company, E Division R.A., with 6 five-inch B.L howitzers
Egyptian Horse Battery (6 guns)
Nos. 1, 2. and 3 Field Batteries Egyptian Army (18 guns)
British Maxim Battery (4 guns)
Rocket Detachment (2 sections)

Mahmud had early intelligence of the movement of the Anglo-Egyptian army. His original intention had been to march to Hudi. But he now learned that at Hudi he would have to fight the Sirdar's main force. Not feeling strong enough to attack them, he determined to march to Nakheila. The mobility of the Arabs was now as conspicuous as their dilatory nature had formerly been. The whole Dervish army—horse, foot, and artillery, men, women, children, and animals—actually traversed in a single day the forty miles of waterless desert which lie between Aliab and Nakheila, at which latter place they arrived on the night of the 20th. The Sirdar's next object was to keep the enemy so far up the Atbara that they could not possibly strike at Berber or Rail-head. Accordingly at dawn on the 21st the whole force was ordered to march to Bas-el-Hudi, five miles nearer the Dervishes' supposed halting-place. The *détour* which the Arabs would have to make to march round the troops was nearly doubled by this movement. The utter impossibility of their flank march with a stronger enemy on the radius of the circle was now apparent.

The movement of the Anglo-Egyptian force was screened by seven squadrons of cavalry and the Horse Artillery, and Colonel Broadwood was further instructed to reconnoitre along the river and endeavour to locate the enemy. The country on either bank of the Atbara is covered with dense scrub, impassable for civilised troops. From these belts, which average a quarter of a mile in depth, the *dôm*-palms rise in great numbers. All the bush is leafy, and looks very pretty and green contrast to the sombre vegetation of the Nile. Between the trees flew green parrots and many other bright birds. The river itself above Eas-el-Hudi is, during March and April, only a dry bed of hot white sand about 400 yards broad, but dotted with deep and beautifully clear pools, in which peculiarly brilliant fish

4 Lieutenant-Colonel C. J. Long, Royal Artillery and Egyptian army.

THE MULE

and crocodiles, deprived of their stream, are crowded together. The atmosphere is more damp than by the Nile, and produces, in the terrible heat of the summer, profuse and exhausting perspiration. The natives dislike the water of the Atbara, and declare that it does not quench the thirst like that of the great river. It has, indeed, a slightly bitter taste, which is a strong contrast to the sweet waters of the Nile. Nevertheless the British soldiers, with characteristic contrariness, declared their preference for it. The belt of bushes by the river was formerly the abode of the Bisharin Arabs, whose deserted villages now alone display their former numbers. This tribe, which at one time numbered nearly ninety thousand souls, was famous for its breed of swift riding-camels; but pestilence, famine, war, and oppression have practically destroyed the breed and reduced the tribe to scarcely ten thousand. Like the surviving Jaalin, this small remnant were not unnaturally the implacable enemies of the Dervish power. Their hatred was animated by the fact that large numbers of their women had become the prisoners and—worse than the prisoners—the concubines of the Khalifa's soldiery. Their chief, the Sheikh Ahmed, a tall, handsome Arab, accompanied all the reconnaissances and gave valuable information. His whole soul was surrendered to the desire for vengeance, and since, as a fighting man, he won the respect of the British officers, his reputation need not be further examined. Outside the bush the ground undulated gently, but the surface was either stony and uneven, or else cracked and fissured by the annual overflow. Both these conditions made it hard for cavalry and still more for artillery to move freely: and the difficulties were complicated by frequent holes and small *khors* full of long grass.

Amid such scenes the squadrons moved cautiously forward. By 10.30, having made the ground good for fifteen miles from Hudi, Colonel Broadwood halted his force at Abadar, an old fort, and sent one squadron under Captain Le Gallais seven miles further. At two o'clock this squadron returned, having met a few of the enemy scouts, but no formed bodies. While the force watered by turns at the river Captain Baring's[5] squadron was extended in a line of outposts about a mile and a quarter to the south-east. But the reconnoitring squadron had been followed homeward by several hundred Dervish horsemen. Creeping along through the dense bush by the bank and evading the vedettes, these suddenly fell on the picket line and drove in all the outposts. Captain Baring, indeed, had scarcely time to mount, and owed his life to his skill in the use of the revolver.

A TIMELY SHOT

5 Captain Hon. E. Baring, 10th Hussars and Egyptian army.

The Arabs pressed on impetuously at the heels of the outposts, and a sharp hand-to-hand fight began. But the other squadrons, duly alarmed by the firing, now came galloping up , and the Dervishes found themselves in a moment confronted by a powerful force, and thereat fled back into the bush incontinently.

Colonel Broadwood then ordered Captain Persse,[6] with his squadron, to clear the scrub. That officer dismounted his men and they pushed in among the bushes, opening fire with their carbines. But the Dervishes proved to be in much greater strength than had been estimated, and, firing from their horses with skill and frequency, began to inflict loss. The firing grew louder and more sustained, and not wishing to lose men Broadwood sent his galloper, Lord Tullibardine,[7] to tell Persse to withdraw. As soon as the squadron was clear of the bush the Horse Artillery battery came into action and shelled it.

This obliged the Dervishes to retire, and as they did so the squadrons advanced for six miles along the edge, keeping pace with them. In this manner the whole of the cavalry reached Umdabia, whence the fires of a large hostile force were visible. Then as the hour was late they returned towards the camp. On reaching the scene of the skirmish the losses were found to be more severe than had been believed. Eight troopers were killed and seven wounded, most of them in the attempt to clear the bush by dismounted fire. Thirteen horses were also lost, as, having rid themselves of their riders on the broken ground, they galloped off after the Arab mares on which the Dervishes were mostly mounted. The wounded delayed the homeward march, and it was not until nearly midnight that the cavalry reached the camp at Eas-el-Hudi. The enemy left ten killed on the ground and bore their wounded off to their *zeriba*.

The news of an attack on Adarama was received on this same afternoon. It appeared that the Arabs had been repulsed by the Abyssinian irregulars raised by Colonel Parsons. Glowing details were forthcoming, but I do not propose to recount the Homeric struggles of the 'friendlies.' Little in them is worthy of remembrance; much seeks oblivion.

6 Captain W. H. Persse, 2nd Dragoon Guards and Egyptian army.
7 Lieut. J. G., Marquis of Tullibardine, Royal Horse Guards.

With the first light of the next morning one squadron was sent out to bury the dead, which after the skirmish had been left on the ground, and also to patrol the country towards the Dervish position. Major Collinson, with the XIIth Soudanese battalion, acted in support. The corpses of the fallen troopers were found stripped of their boots and bandoliers, but not mutilated in any way. Their first duty performed, the squadron pushed on along the river and confronted by a large force of mounted Arabs. . In the face of these superior numbers the cavalry at once fell back on the supporting infantry. The Dervishes following came within range, and were saluted with volleys at 900 yards, which are said to have inflicted some loss. The noise of the firing was heard in the camp at Eas-el-Hudi, and in the belief that the Dervishes were advancing to the attack, the Sirdar and his whole army sallied out into the desert to meet them. The wish may have been the parent of the thought, for Mahmud had no intention of assuming the offensive. After waiting in the desert for two hours the force returned to camp, followed after a while by Collinson's battalion, and last of all by the cavalry.

During the day several deserters from the enemy surrendered themselves, approaching the camp with caution and humility, holding up their weaponless hands and tearing the motley patches from off their *jibbas*, in token that their vows to slay the infidel were abandoned and that they were Dervishes no longer. They were mostly of the lowest rank. All were ravenously hungry. Indeed, they had to be protected from the fury of their appetites, and only a small allowance of biscuit was at first given to them. All brought tales of hardship and suffering, and, in the hopes of conciliating their captors, painted the condition of Mahmud's army in the darkest hues. The black riflemen, they said, were aggrieved because the Baggara had the larger allowance of grain. Osman Digna was still at variance with Mahmud. As for them, they had received nothing but the nuts of the *dôm*-palm, an exclusive diet of which had produced internal disorders. Their appearance attested the truth of their words. The process of attrition was working on the Arab host.

For more than a week the Anglo-Egyptian force remained halted at Eas-el-Hudi, waiting for the privations to demoralise Mahmud's army or to exasperate him into making an attack. Every morning

A DUST DEVIL

the cavalry rode out towards the enemy's camp. All day long they skirmished with or watched the Baggara horse, and at night they returned wearily to camp. Each morning the army awoke full of the hopes of battle, waited during the long hours, and finally retired to sleep in deep disgust and profound peace. The continual arrival of deserters was their chief interest.

Sometimes a few common spearmen, driven by hunger to leave their leaders, were brought in. Once there came a subordinate Emir, mounted on a camel and looking a very guilty wretch. And while the army halted, the camp began to assume a more homely appearance. The *zeriba* grew stronger and thicker; the *glacis* wider; the field kitchens more elaborate; the pools of the Atbara more dirty. Half a mile behind the troops another encampment sprang up. Here a score of brave and daring Greek traders opened a bazaar, and a scanty supply of tinned meats and tobacco was offered to all customers, at prices which, though high, were not disproportioned to the risk of business. Behind this bivouac a ragged crew of 'friendlies' —the jackals of an army—lurked in the bushes, ready, were the chance to arise, to turn a defeat into a rout or a victory into a massacre. Last of all was the abode of the wives and other women of the black soldiers. Without fear, if not without reproach, these hardy and brazen creatures hung upon the tail of the brigades, their only baggage a few earthenware pots, some scanty rags, and a litter of ebony babies. Over all the sun beat down in merciless persistence, till all white men quivered with weary suffering when in the open air, and even under the grass huts or improvised tents the temperature always registered 115° during the hottest hours of the day The nights were, however, cool and pleasant.

But although the main part of the force found the days long and tedious, the time which the army spent at Eas-el-Hudi was by no means uneventful. The work of the squadrons was hard, and ceased only with the night. The continual patrolling told severely on men and horses; and the fact that the Dervishes were far stronger in the mounted arm than the Sirdar's army required the utmost vigilance of the cavalry commander. Employment was also found for the gunboats.

When Mahmud had left the Nile he had established a sort of depôt at Shendi, in which the wives of the Emirs and the surplus stores had been deposited. This treasure house was protected only by a slender garrison of 700 riflemen and 25 horsemen. On ordinary military grounds, and also since the event might infuriate the Arabs, it was decided to capture this place and disperse its defenders. Accordingly on the afternoon of the 24th the 3rd Egyptian battalion from Lewis's brigade marched from Eas-el-Hudi to Atbara fort and relieved the loth Egyptians then in garrison, and a small force under Commander Keppel—consisting of the 15th Egyptians under Major Hickman,[8] of two field-guns of Peake's battery, and 150 Jaalin Irregulars—was embarked on, or in boats towed by, the three gunboats *Zafir*, *Naser*, and *Fateh*, and started the same night for Shendi. It had been proposed to arrive at daylight on the 26th; but the *Zafir*, dogged by persistent evil luck, ran on a sandbank, and as it took several hours to float her the enterprise was postponed until the following day. At dawn on the 27th the flotilla appeared off Shendi. The Dervishes had been apprised of its approach and prepared to

8 Major T. E. Hickman, D.S.O.. Worcester Regiment and Egyptian army. This officer commanded the troops of the force when disembarked.

oner resistance. But the force against them was overwhelming. Under cover of the gunboats the infantry and guns were landed. The artillery then came into action, but after they had discharged two shells, the Arabs fled, firing their rifles with little effect. Shendi was occupied by the Egyptians. The pursuit was left to the Jaalin, and in it they are said to have killed 160 men—a revenge which must have been doubly sweet since it was consummated so near to the scene of the destruction of their tribe, and was also attended by scarcely any danger. Loot of all kinds fell to the victors, and the gunboats were soon laden with a miscellaneous spoil. The wives of the important Emirs made their escape to Omdurman, but upwards of 650 women and children of the inferior ranks were taken prisoners and transported to the Atbara, where in due course they contracted new family ties with the Soudanese soldiery and, as far as can be ascertained, lived happily ever afterwards. There were no casualties among the troops, but the Jaalin lost a few men in their pursuit. The force then returned to the Atbara.

Meanwhile at Eas-el-Hudi the cavalry continued their patrolling and reconnaissance. Every day they felt themselves in contact with a superior force of Dervishes, although only the smallest outpost affairs took place. The position of the hostile camp had been approximately located on the 21st; but as the tales of the deserters showed that the demoralisation of the Dervishes was proceeding, and it was evident that the moment for offensive action approached, a reconnaissance in force was ordered on the 30th to obtain precise and detailed information.

On the afternoon of the 29th, the XIIth and XIIIth Soudanese battalions, with two squadrons and four Maxim guns, marched to Abadar and halted there during the night. At 4 a.m. on the 30th General Hunter, with six squadrons, two companies of the Camel Corps, the Horse battery, and a battery of howitzers, left Eas-el-Hudi and joined the force at Abadar. Thence Colonel Broadwood, with all the cavalry, the Maxim guns, and Horse Artillery, started at once for Nakheila. General Hunter accompanied the cavalry reconnaissance. The supporting force moved two miles to the south of Abadar and occupied a strong defensive position, in which they were not molested, during the day. In the afternoon, indeed, a troop of Der-

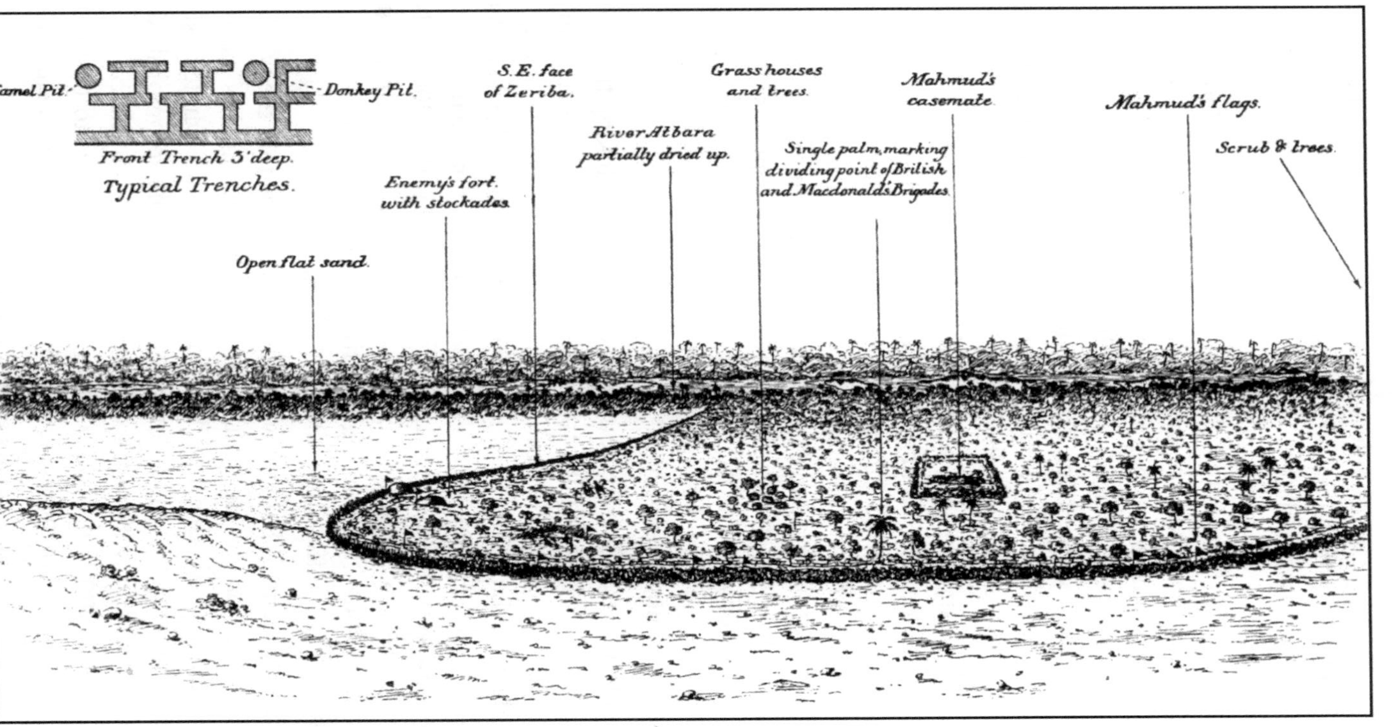

VIEW SKETCH OF THE DERVISH "DÊM" ON THE ATBARA, APRIL 1898

vish horsemen appeared a mile to the southward and were dispersed by two shells from the howitzers. The cavalry were meanwhile trotting rapidly across the desert. One of the deserters was compelled to act as guide, and did not appear to enjoy his prominent position at the head of the force. After going south-east for about four miles the Dervish outposts were encountered. These at once fell back, and the squadrons pushed on behind them for nearly twelve miles. At length the wretched guide began to evince a most lively excitement. He pointed towards the river. From among the bushes there arose a high clump of palms. The cavalry turned half right and rode in the direction of the trees at a walk.

A single squadron was sent on to reconnoitre, and reported 1,000 infantry and 400 cavalry in the scrub. Major Mahon then rode still closer and reported infantry in trenches, palisades, and other defences. The reconnaissance halted at a distance of about 1,200 yards from the position and examined it carefully. But the result was indefinite, and it was evident that a nearer view was necessary. The artillery and the Maxims were brought into action at 1,000 yards, and began to fire into the entrenchments in the hope of inducing the enemy to show themselves.

The Dervishes, however, vouchsafed no reply. Thinking that the position might be weakly held, and determined to obtain clear information at all costs, General Hunter, Colonel Broadwood, Captain Haig,[9] and Lord Tullibardine then rode directly towards it. As they advanced they perceived a long *zeriba* in front of the trenches. The ground sloped gently down on all sides until within 200 yards of the defences, when it rose rather suddenly to a large, low, flat knoll, which constituted the right of the position. The officers rode steadily forward until within 300 yards of the *zeriba*.

Suddenly General Hunter, who was leading, saw that the whole interior space was crowded with men, and the adventurous patrol immediately retired. They had, however, examined the whole position, and the object of the reconnaissance was thus accomplished. It appears that the Dervishes expected an attack from the cavalry, and that Mahmud had issued orders that no shot was to be fired until the troops were 'near enough for their faces to be seen.' This

9 Captain D. Haig, 7th Hussars and Egyptian army.

AFTER THE RECONNAISSANCE

explains how it was that the officers making this perilous reconnaissance were not all killed, as they would assuredly have been, had they been opposed to any other foe but the Dervishes. Their end attained, the cavalry returned. The Dervish horse hung on the flanks and rear of the force for ten miles, but did not attack, and contented themselves with cursing their enemies and brandishing their spears. The whole force, including Maxwell's two battalions, returned that night to the main camp at Ras-el-Hudi.

The two succeeding days were occupied only by the usual patrolling, but on the 2nd of April a reconnaissance of two squadrons and fifty Camel Corps was sent along the left bank of the Atbara to see what the Arab camp looked like from that side. On the way the cavalry fell in with a party of eight Dervish foot soldiers and took them all prisoners.

They were returning from Ed Darner with forage, and told their captors a pitiful tale. Out of thirty-one men, sent out on this foray from the Dervish *zeriba*, these eight alone survived. The others had fallen into the hands of the 'friendlies,' and had of course been killed. The Jaalin had suffered severely in the past from the Dervishes, but they were lucky in having a civilised army to help them settle their tribal feuds. Of their good fortune they took a bloody advantage. After this incident the squadrons pursued their way towards Nakheila. But the bush on this side of the river was so dense and impenetrable for all civilised troops that it was evident the position must be attacked from the eastern side or not at all.

The event of the next day is best chronicled in the laconic words of an officer's diary:—

'*March* 3.—The enemy to-day captured on the left bank two camels and a friendly. What a jolly afternoon he will have! '

It was the last day the army spent at Bas-el-Hudi. The period of waiting was over. The enemy's position had been duly reconnoitred. His strength was believed to be sufficiently impaired for a successful attack to be made. The camp at Hudi was becoming very insanitary. Moreover the situation, satisfactory though it was, was not one which the commander could view without anxiety. All the time that the army was operating on the Atbara it drew its supplies from the fort at the confluence. Between this and the camp, convoys, protected only by a handful of Camel Corps, passed once in every four days. Only the idiotic apathy of the Dervishes allowed the communications to remain uninterrupted. Mahmud was strong in cavalry. It will be evident to anyone who looks at the map how easily a force might have moved along the left bank to attack the convoys. Such tactics would have occurred to most savage tribes. But in their last campaigns the Dervishes thought only of battles, and disregarded all smaller enterprises. Had they assailed the communications, the Sirdar might have been forced to build a chain of forts and to guard his convoys with strong infantry escorts. The fighting force would have been weakened; the troops have been wearied; and the result must have been delayed. The Dervishes had as yet attempted nothing. But there was no reason why they should not at any moment become enterprising. It was time to make an end. On the 4th of April the whole force moved to Abadar, and established themselves in a new camp five miles nearer the enemy. The tiger was tired of watching; he had taken his first stride towards his prey.

Although the information as to the enemy's strength and position was accurate and complete, the Sirdar decided to order a final reconnaissance on the 5th of April. The various Brigadiers were permitted to accompany the cavalry and examine the ground over which they would move to the assault. Colonel Maxwell was, however, the only one to avail himself of the opportunity. Colonel Long, Chief of Artillery, looking for positions for his guns, and General Hunter, looking for adventures, also rode with the cavalry, but the entire conduct of the reconnaissance was in the hands of Colonel Broadwood. The force at his disposal consisted of eight squadrons, the Horse Artillery battery, and four Maxim guns. The reconnaissance was not this time supported by an infantry brigade.

At four o' clock the cavalry started, and the first light of morning found them already on their way across the desert. Broad wood cut off the sharp angle which the Atbara forms at Umdabia, and, avoiding the thick bush, soon approached the Dervish camp. Not a sign of the enemy was seen during the march, nor was it until the squadrons were within a mile of the *zeriba* that a single picket, retiring slowly towards the river, attested their presence. The bush by the Atbara appeared deserted. The camp gave no sign of life; an ominous silence prevailed. The squadrons moved forward at a walk, keeping about 1,200 yards away from the *zeriba* and almost parallel to it.[10]

Presently, as they did so, a large force of cavalry became visible in front. It was difficult to estimate their strength, but they appeared to be superior in numbers to the reconnaissance. The Dervish horsemen continued to retire towards the south-east, always reaching round the Egyptian left flank. Their position prevented the squadrons from moving on the *zeriba* without exposing their rear. In consequence of this Colonel Broad wood decided either to disperse them or to compel them to retire along the river, into the bush or back to the camp, before attempting to examine the main position. The possibility of a cavalry action was very welcome to all the British officers.

But while the Egyptian force advanced, and as soon as they were opposite the southern end of the *zeriba*, another considerable body of Dervish horse issued from the northern side and threatened the line of retreat. At the same time the camp began to swarm with men, and crowds of tiny figures were observed clambering on to the entrenchments and gun emplacements, eagerly watching the development of the fight. The cavalry had by this time approached to within 1,000 yards of the *zeriba*, and the Arab artillery began to fire occasional round shot and clumsily fused shells. The direction of the gunners was good, but as they shot high the projectiles roared over the moving squadrons, and either buried themselves in the de-

10 Plan, 'The Reconnaissance of April 5, 1898,' page 291.

sert beyond or burst without doing any harm; and meanwhile the position of the guns was carefully noted.

The scene at this moment was picturesque, although it was not without its serious aspect. The Egyptian cavalry—in solid, ordered masses, but looking a very small force—moved steadily forward over the smooth plain, whose surface was broken only by occasional bushes. All along their right ran the belt of palm-trees and dense scrub by the river, and among the dark green foliage the thin line of the *zeriba* showed brown and irregular, rimmed and spotted by little white figures, and surmounted by a great array of flags of many colours. Behind the thorn fence a confusion of straw huts was visible, clustering among the trees and filling the interior of the *dêm* with a blur of yellow. Every now and then a great puff of smoke marked the firing of a field-gun. In front, in a wide crescent to the south and south-east, the Dervish cavalry gradually retired; some in large masses, others galloping about singly, but always moving and always reaching out round the Egyptian left. And behind between the squadrons and the camp, other strong bodies showed at the edge of the scrub, and, slowly advancing, stretched into the desert. It was as if two giant arms were enveloping the little force to crush and squeeze its life out.

Colonel Broadwood now brought his guns into action, and began shelling the cavalry in his front. The artillery displayed the marvellous accuracy of their arm and, although firing 'snap-shots,' inflicted considerable loss. The squadrons halted when the battery opened fire, and the officers watched the practice with fascinated interest. 'Aim at that cluster with the white flag, near the solitary palm—1,800 yards.' A pause while the layer cranes along his gun and turns the elevating wheel. Then all the gunners stand back and away—stiff and rigid. 'Fire!' The loud explosion makes the horses of the attendant squadrons start and toss their heads. All the field-glasses are directed to the distant group of Arabs. Suddenly the projectile arrives in their midst: a puff of smoke and great confusion. The group breaks into fragments, like the shell that broke it. The horsemen scatter and gallop away. Yet some remain. Two or three brown spots—the stricken horses—are lying on the ground. One kicks and twists; the others are still. Another pause. Then a

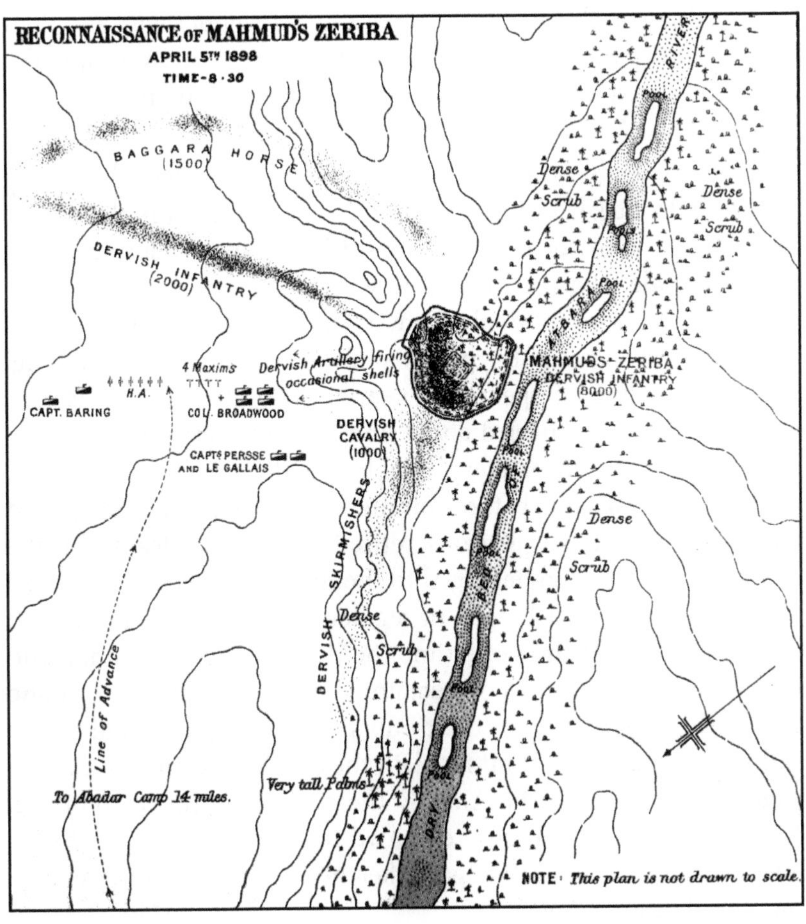
RECONNAISSANCE OF MAHMUD'S ZERIBA
APRIL 5TH 1898
TIME-8·30
BAGGARA HORSE
(1500)
DERVISH INFANTRY
(2000)
4 Maxims
Dervish Artillery firing
occasional shells
H.A.
CAPT. BARING
COL. BROADWOOD
DERVISH
CAVALRY
(1000)
CAPTS PERSSE
AND LE GALLAIS
MAHMUD'S ZERIBA
DERVISH INFANTRY
(8000)
Dense
Scrub
Dense
Scrub
Dense
Scrub
Dense
Scrub
DERVISH SKIRMISHERS
DRY BED OF ATBARA RIVER
Pool
Line of Advance
To Abadar Camp 14 miles.
Very tall Palms
NOTE: This plan is not drawn to scale.

few Arabs gallop back, hurriedly dismount, and pull smaller figures, limp and shapeless, from underneath and among the dead and dying steeds: and so away again, corpses and wounded thrown across their saddles.

Less imposing, but not less formidable, the Maxim guns had also come into action. A dozen Dervishes are standing on a sandy knoll. All in a moment the dust begins to jump in front of them, and then the clump of horsemen melts into a jumble on the ground, and a couple of scared survivors scurry to cover. Yet even then a few brave men come back to help their fallen comrades.

Their movements accelerated by the fire, the Dervish cavalry to the south began to retire more rapidly. The guns limbered up, and the Egyptian squadrons followed with caution, suspicious of an ambuscade. Nor was their care without reason, for as they advanced there arose suddenly from a shallow *khor* about 300 yards away, and between the Egyptians and the retreating Arabs, a long, well-ordered line of spearmen nearly 2,000 strong. The Maxim guns immediately wheeled about and began to fire, stuttering out death-sentences. The artillery, unable to risk such close proximity, trotted back 200 yards before coming into action, and then opened with case-shot. The squadrons retired at a walk. Meanwhile the Dervish infantry, who belonged to the flag of Ali Senusi, advanced swiftly and steadily, arranged in regular companies, each preceded by a white flag. At the same time the defenders of the camp, who up to this period had been spectators, opened a sharp and galling fire on the Egyptian right, their bullets flicking up the sand with a significant *phut!* Far out in the plain the enveloping arms of cavalry were closing for the grip. Already the circle was almost complete, and only a narrow opening remained towards the north-east. The enemy's position had been again sketched and the approaches reconnoitred. It was time to go.

At nine o' clock Colonel Broadwood ordered the retirement to begin. The Maxims and artillery were in the centre, supported by Colonel Broadwood and three squadrons. Captain Baring with three squadrons watched the left flank, now in retirement become the right. Captains Le Gallais and Persse guarded the river flank. Very slowly the troops crept back. Under cover of the Maxims the artillery would retire perhaps 200 yards, and then come into action rear. Protected by the shells, the machine guns might trot back to a new position.[11] The cavalry retired alternate wings in the same measured fashion. But the enemy pressed on impetuously, and their horsemen, soon completely enveloping the desert flank of the Egyptians, began to threaten a charge. To meet this, Colonel Broadwood sent one of his squadrons from the centre to join those under Captain Baring, so that at about a quarter to ten the reconnoitring force was formed with four squadrons towards the desert—two with the guns, and two towards the river.

The weakness of the river flank of the troops encouraged the Dervish horse lurking in the scrub to make a bold attempt to capture the guns. The movement was shrewd and daring, but the cavalry commander met it with admirable skill. The springing-up of dust-clouds hardly 300 yards away was his only warning. He immediately took command of the two squadrons under Persse and Le Gallais, and ordered them to 'right about wheel' and charge. Headed by Broadwood himself, and with their British officers several horse lengths in front, the Egyptians broke into a gallop and encountered the Baggara line, which numbered not less than 400 men, but was in loose order, with firmness.

They struck them obliquely and perhaps a third of the way down their line, and, breaking through, routed them utterly. Colonel Broadwood, sword in hand, rode at the Emir; but the latter declined the proffered combat, only to fall ignominiously by the revolver of a trumpeter. Lord Tullibardine, the Colonel's galloper, lost control of his horse, which bolted, but fortunately carried him through the Dervishes in safety and back towards the guns. The Sheikh of the Bisharin, who rode with the Staff, cut his antagonist from the shoulder to the middle of the body—a stroke impelled alike by physical strength and vengeful fury.

While this dashing operation was carried out on the river flank the Dervish cavalry, following up the retirement, also delivered an attack towards the guns. Thereupon Captain Baring with two squadrons galloped from the desert flank across the front of the artillery, and, riding through the advancing enemy, repulsed them with loss.

11 Plan, 'The Reconnaissance of April 5, 1898,' page 291.

The charge was good and effective, but the shock and confusion broke both squadrons, and, although successful, they came through the Dervishes and back on to the river flank in some disorder. Persse and Le Gallais, who had just rallied, at once dismounted their men and opened carbine fire on the retreating Dervishes. Their action not only checked the enemy, but prevented, by getting the troopers off their horses, any chance of their being involved in the disorder of the squadrons who had just charged. Captain Baring immediately rallied and re-formed behind them. In both these charges the improved behaviour of the *fellahin* soldiers was no less remarkable than the enterprise and decision of the British officers. Although their horsemen were thus sharply checked, the Dervish infantry continued in spite of losses to advance rapidly, and for a few minutes a hot musketry fire was exchanged by the Arab riflemen and the two dismounted squadrons. Captain Persse was severely wounded, and several other casualties occurred. But the whole force was drawing away from the enemy, and by eleven o' clock it had passed through the gap to the north-east and had shaken off all pursuit. The casualties in the operation were fortunately small. One British officer was wounded; six Egyptian troopers were killed, ten wounded; and about thirty horses were lost or disabled. That the loss was no greater was due solely to the skill and experience of the cavalry leader. Although the squadrons returned without being further molested, the thirteen-mile march across the desert was a painful experience to the wounded. The camp was reached at one o' clock.

Meanwhile the sound of the firing, and particularly of the Maxim guns, had been distinctly heard in the British camp, and considerable excitement prevailed. It was rumoured that the reconnaissance had drawn the enemy from their *zeriba,* and that a general attack was imminent. The belief was encouraged when the Sirdar ordered both Soudanese brigades to stand to arms, and later on when the British brigade was warned to hold themselves in readiness to assist the cavalry in their retirement if necessary. It was, therefore, with considerable disappointment that the battalions saw the cavalry coming back with no enemy at their heels. Yet a reflection on the distance—fourteen miles—which intervened between the hostile camps should have satisfied the soldiers that no attack by day was possible for either side, unless preceded by a night march.

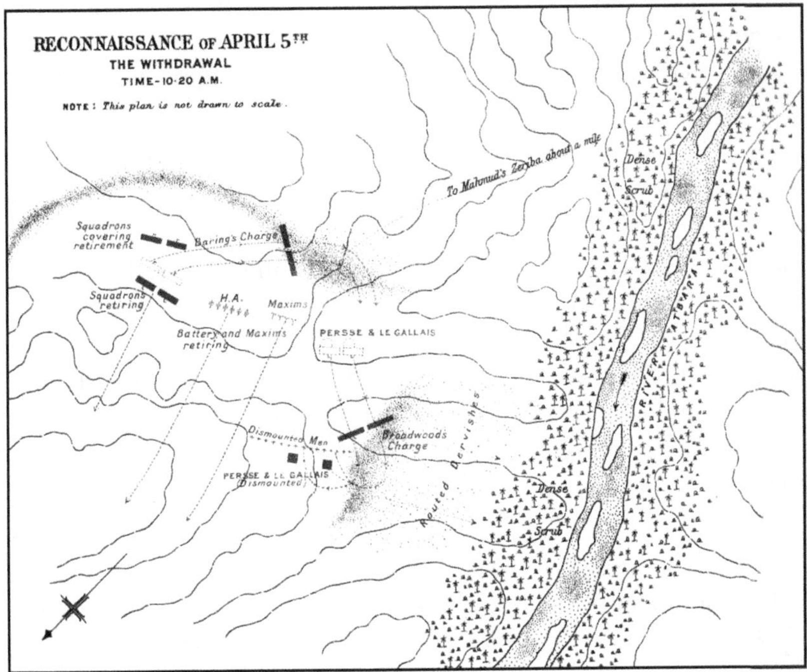

The bodies of the dead Egyptians fell into the hands of the enemy, and after the capture of the *zeriba* a few days later their heads were discovered nailed to a palm-tree. One unfortunate trooper was taken prisoner. Being unhorsed, he was about to be despatched, when a Sheikh rode up and saved him. Thereupon the Arabs rushed upon him and bore him off alive. But their clemency was explained when his remains were afterwards found, shockingly mutilated, in the bed of the river. The Dervish loss in the affair was believed to amount to 200, for which the Maxim guns, which together discharged more than 4,000 rounds, were undoubtedly responsible.

I have described the reconnaissance of the 5th of April at length because the campaigns on the Nile afford few instances of minor tactics. The nice and delicate operation of withdrawing a small force from the jaws of an active and powerful enemy is one with which military officers on the Indian Frontier have become familiar. But this is the only occasion of a rearguard action in Sir H. Kitchener's campaigns. It is therefore the more creditable that it should have been so ably conducted. Of course, as usual, the shooting of the Dervishes was contemptible; and it is easy to imagine that if—as would have happened on the Frontier—three or four of the British officers had been killed or badly wounded, the squadrons would not have been so skilfully handled, and in such operations the consequences of mistakes are always serious.

But the great reason for which this reconnaissance and retirement are remarkable is apparent when the affair of the 1st of May, or the incident near Teroi Wells two years before, are remembered. The extraordinary contrast which the behaviour of the Egyptian troopers on these two occasions presents, is indisputable evidence of the wonderful work of the British officers. I shall embrace the opportunity of appreciating their achievement, which in the story of the Nile campaigns ranks second only to the triumph of the railway subalterns.

Throughout the war the Egyptian infantry brigades were carefully kept out of all trying situations. The brunt of the fighting invariably fell upon the Soudanese. Only at the action of Firket, where the Dervishes were outnumbered by six to one, and the chances of a reverse were small, were the *fellahin* troops made to share the dangers equally with the black regiments. But the Egyptian squadrons could not be nursed in this fashion.

With the exception of the last campaign, when they were supported by the 21st Lancers, the whole of the cavalry duties fell upon them. All patrolling and reconnaissance, all cavalry operations on the field of battle, all the pursuits, were carried out by the Egyptian troopers. On some occasions they exposed the military incapacity of their race; once at least they behaved badly; but they many times discharged their perilous and difficult duties in an honourable manner, and towards the end of the war they were distrusted neither by their Soudanese comrades nor by the British cavalry, with whom they had the honour to serve.

The great work of forming an army of Egyptians for the defence of Egypt, which will for ever stand as a plain proof of the intrinsic merits of British military officers, finds its most perfect example in the case of the cavalry. The squadrons were many times tried, and they were not found wanting.

The Egyptian cavalry consists of ten squadrons, each commanded by an officer of the local rank of major. During the war six of these officers were British, and to their efforts the admirable result must be entirely attributed. The squadron officers are absolutely responsible for all the arrangements within their command. The training, the discipline, the pay of the soldiers, the forage, the shoeing and management of the horses, are left to their discretion, and they exercise wider powers than the colonel of an English regiment. The whole ten squadrons are under the command of a Brigadier, who maintains a general supervision, but does not interfere with the interior economy. They are occasionally formed into two regiments and drilled in brigade, and were actually so used at the battle of Omdurman.

The recruits are-obtained by conscription, and drawn entirely from the amiable and pacific inhabitants of the Delta. The cavalry pick the best from the annual batch of conscripts, but in race and qualities the troopers are no way different from the *fellahin* infantry.[12] The inoffensive peasants have no love for scenes of war; they are devoid of fighting instincts. Although under their British officers they are well fed, regularly paid and fairly treated, they long for the happy day when they will return in peace to their village homes. In the meanwhile they try their best to perform an uncongenial task, and are therefore worthy of much respect. But neither praise nor pay, promotion nor medals, will induce them to prolong the period, and scarcely any re-engage after completing their six years' compulsory service. As soldiers they lack both vices and virtues. Their limbs, though of great strength, are clumsy and unfitted for quick and active movements. Their seat on a horse is firm, but their heavy hands soon spoil the animal's mouth, and in all other respects they are bad horsemen. They treat their horses with kindness, but, like all natives, they are thoughtless; and were it not for the vigilance of their officers, their steeds would often go thirsty and unfed. On parade their appearance is scarcely smart, for they cannot be

12 Upon Colonel Broadwood's recommendation three black squadrons are now being raised. The arguments against the scheme have always been: (1) the black will be unrestrainable on a horse; (2) he will not look after his horse properly. The answer is: (1) a keen hunter that wants steadying is a better mount than an unwilling one that wants driving; (2) why not?—EDITOR.

made to understand the importance of lacing up their boots and such like minor matters of tidiness. Their uniforms, their saddlery, and their arms, however, claim their ceaseless care; for in their poor homes they have never seen such valuable things, and they regard them with awe and wonder. They are obedient, quiet, and docile, and their only serious troubles arise from smoking opium, which is strictly forbidden, or through some dusky beauty.

To such simple souls the white officer—rich, strange, sharp-spoken, just, and always apparently fearless seemed a splendid demigod—a being of superior knowledge and resource. Whatever the dangers he would help them out. Certainly he would never desert them. The only chance of safety was to stay by him. And when this wild and wonderful creature showed that he was studying them and was learning their peculiarities their confidence increased. He, for his part, began to find out much. He learned that a squadron of a hundred good and twenty bad men was a poorer weapon in action than a squadron of only eighty reliable men. He learned which were the soldiers to leave in camp when there was going to be a fight, and what he could ask of those he took to the field. He gauged the capacity of his squadron. Besides, he understood the great secret of command.

There is one spirit which animates all the dealings of the British officer with the native soldier. It is not seen only in Egypt; it exists wherever Britain raises mercenary troops. The officer's military honour is the honour of his men. In many countries where the Empire has varying shades of responsibility and power, the natives are formed into regiments and squadrons. Some are cowardly and debased; others reckless and excitable. But whatever they are, or wherever they are, the officer who leads them believes in them and swears by them. The British officer of a native corps is never known—on duty or off duty, officially or in private, before or after dinner, by word or implication—to speak disparagingly of his own men. The captain who commands a squadron of Bengal Lancers boasts proudly of his stately Sikh *sowars*, and does not hesitate to declare that they are better all round than British cavalry—which is, of course, absurd. The officer of Guides prefers the long-limbed, hawk-eyed Afridi. The Gurkha subaltern's eyes glisten as he tells of

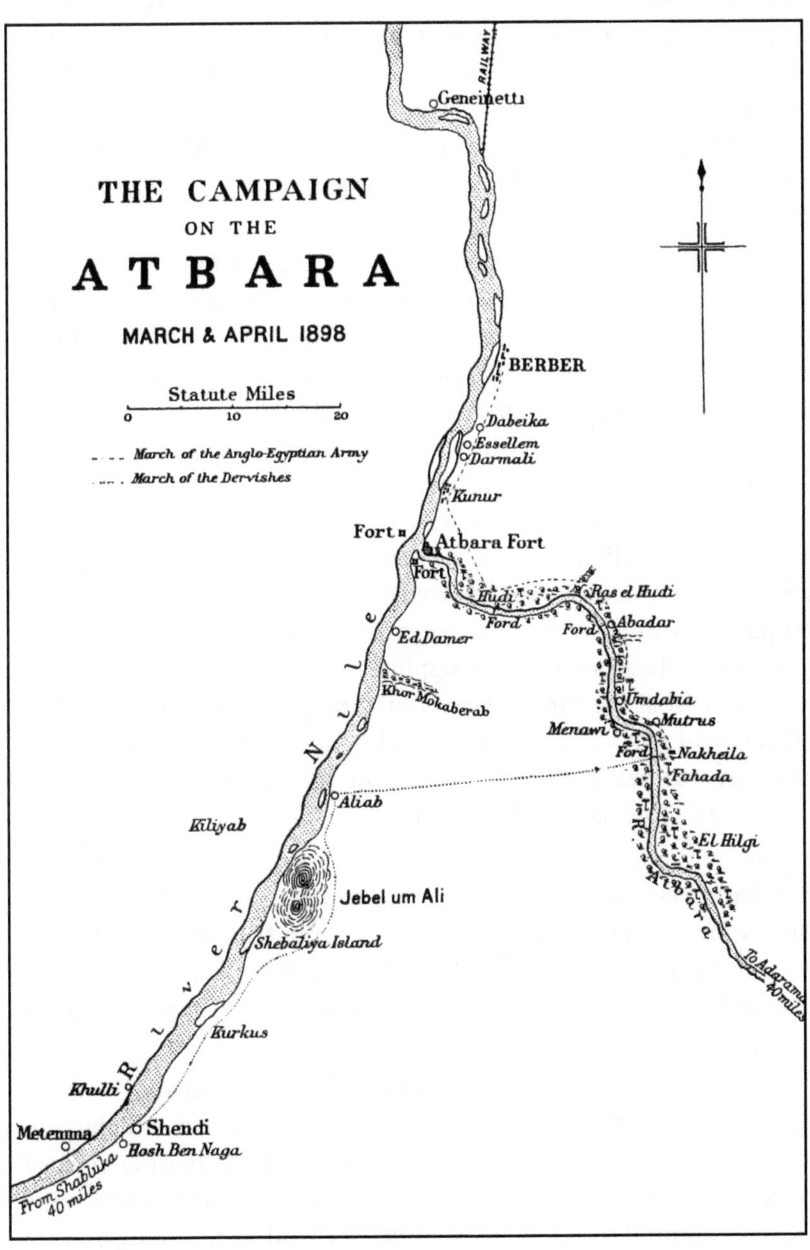
THE CAMPAIGN
ON THE
ATBARA
MARCH & APRIL 1898
Statute Miles
0
10
20
March of the Anglo-Egyptian Army
March of the Dervishes
RAILWAY
Geneinetti
BERBER
Dabeika
Essellem
Darmali
Kunur
Fort
Atbara Fort
Fort
Hudi
Ras el Hudi
Ford
Ford
Abadar
Ed Damer
Khor Mokaberab
Umdabia
Mutrus
Menawi
Ford
Nakheila
Fahada
Aliab
Kiliyab
El Hilgi
River Nile
Atbara
Jebel um Ali
Shebaliya Island
To Adarama 40 miles
Kurkus
Khulli
Metemma
Shendi
Hosh Ben Naga
From Shabluka 40 miles

the dark little devils whom he believes would follow wherever he would dare to go. There is no exception. Hardly any race in India is despised, for fighting purposes, so much as the Madrassi. Yet let the reader talk to an officer of the 'Queen's Own Sappers and Miners,' and he will learn all about 'Tofrek' and how the Madrassi company stood firm, though half were killed and finer soldiers ran. Here, then, is the explanation of all that has been achieved in the Egyptian cavalry.

Gradually the timid recruit began to perceive that the splendid stranger was actually proud of him although he was poor and despised. Gradually the trooper learned that the officer who led him—and they used sometimes to have a very long lead—would never allow him to be insulted or abused by anybody, even though he deserved it richly. In time, since all men improve under a generous treatment, he rose to the idea and learned to follow. Now, trained and encouraged by three years of successful war, the peasant was developing a military spirit. Initiative he did not possess, high resolve he did not know, but he would ride out boldly into the desert on patrol, would fire steadily when dismounted, would charge—if not with dash, at least with discipline. He had learned to drill, and no matter what the danger, he would, though fearful, obey the white officer. And when I met the officers, I no longer wondered. The certainty of war had attracted the best; the field of selection had been large; the choice has justified itself.

I hasten to return to the course of the narrative. Mahmud's position had been thoroughly reconnoitred. The details of his defences were known; his strength was estimated from trustworthy information. It was evident from the frequent desertions that his army was disheartened, and from his inactivity that he was scarcely hopeful of success.

The moment for destroying him had arrived. At daybreak on the morning of the 6th the whole army broke camp at Abadar and marched to the deserted village of Umdabia, where they bivouacked close by a convenient pool of the Atbara and seven miles nearer the Dervish camp. Detachments were left behind at the old *zeriba* to guard surplus stores, and it was also occupied by a force of Jaalin friendlies who moved southwards from Bas-el-Hudi.

The village had formerly been the scene of a salt industry, and several of the ruined houses were of substantial appearance and construction. Around these the new camp was formed. A very strong *zeriba* of thorn bushes was built, and all the scrub, which here runs far out into the desert, was cleared to make a *glacis* of 400 yards on every side of the perimeter. The 15th Egyptian battalion—moved up from Atbara fort—was established as the garrison to hold the camp when the force marched out to fight: a division of labour less agreeable to the British officers than to their men. After the camp had been formed several of the Brigadiers with their Staffs and a small cavalry escort rode out to examine the line of advance towards the Dervish camp—now only one march distant. They proceeded four miles, and returned without seeing a sign of the enemy. Extreme precautions were observed all night against attack, and a proportion of the force was kept actually under arms; but the dark hours passed quietly.

Thursday was occupied by everyone in final preparations. The British brigade mended their boots, the condition of which had now become disgraceful. General Gatacre explained to the regiments the whole formation of attack, and the Cameron Highlanders learned what duty was reserved for them. The Soudanese celebrated the approaching event with barbaric songs and the beatings of drums. Officers wrote letters home. The Sirdar muzzled the correspondents, and allowed no telegrams to pass. All the camp throbbed with suppressed excitement. Only the Egyptian soldiers were unaffected, and patiently awaited the utmost stroke of fortune.

Thus passed a day of strange elation, when the civilised soldiers felt that a wonderful experience awaited them—an experience by which some at least would never be able to profit.

CHAPTER XIII
THE BATTLE OF THE ATBARA
APRIL 8, 1898

The beginning of the march—Night marches—A halt—Nearing the *zeriba*—Waiting for dawn—Sunrise—Mahmud's dêm—The bombardment—The cavalry—The formation for attack—The plan—The general advance—The passage of the zeriba—The storm of the trenches—The capture of the enclosure—The bed of the river—The pursuit—The Sirdar—On the ridge—The wounded—The funerals—Description of the zeriba—The Dervish prisoners—Mahmud—The return to Umdabia—The casualties.

In the evening of Thursday, the 7th of April, the army at Umdabia paraded for the attack on Mahmud's *zeriba* [1] The camp lay in the scrub which grows by the banks of the Atbara, as by those of the Nile, and in order to profit by the open, level ground the four infantry brigades moved by parallel routes into the desert, and then formed facing south-east in column of brigade squares, the British brigade leading. The mounted forces, with four batteries of artillery, waited in camp until 2 a.m. the next morning, and did not break their march. The distance from the river-bank to the open was perhaps a mile and a half, and the whole force had cleared the scrub by six o' clock. The sun was setting, and the red glow, brightening the sandy hillocks, made the western horizon indefinite, so that it was hard to tell where the desert ended and the sky began. A few gazelle, intercepted on their way to the water by the unexpected movement of troops, trotted slowly away in the distance—white spots on the rosy brown of the sand—and on the great plain twelve thousand infantry, conscious of their strength and eager to encounter the enemy, were beautifully arranged in four solid masses. Then the march

1 Map, 'The Night March,' page 301.

began. The actual distance from the camp to the Dervish position was scarcely seven miles, but the circle necessary to avoid the bushes and the gradual bends of the river added perhaps another five to the length of the road. The pace of the advance was slow, and the troops had not gone far when the sun sank and, with hardly an interval of twilight, darkness enveloped everything. In the stillness of the night the brigades moved steadily forward, and only the regular scrunching of the hard sand betrayed the advance of whelming force upon their enemies.

No operation of war is more critical than a night march. Over and over again in every country frightful disaster has overtaken the rash or daring force that has attempted it. In the gloom the shape and aspect of the ground is altered. Places, well known by daylight, appear strange and unrecognisable. The smallest obstacle obstructs the column, which can only crawl sluggishly forward with continual checks and halts. The effect of the gloom upon the nerves of the soldiers is not less than on the features of the country. Each tries to walk quietly, and hence all are listening for the slightest sound. Every eye seeks to pierce the darkness. Every sense in the body is raised to a pitch of expectancy. In such hours doubts and fears come unbidden to the brain, and the marching men wonder anxiously whether all will be well with the army, and whether they themselves will survive the event. And suddenly out of the black silence there burst the jagged glare of rifles and the crash of a volley, followed by the yell of an attacking foe, the steadiest troops may be thrown into confusion, and a panic, once a-foot, stops only with the destruction or dispersal of the whole force. Nevertheless, so paramount is the necessity of attacking at dawn, with all the day to finish the fight, that in spite of the recorded disasters and the known dangers, the night-march is a frequent operation.

The Sirdar had neglected no precaution which thought and experience could suggest. The line of advance had been carefully reconnoitred. The information as to the enemy was exact. Mahmud kept to his defences. The Expeditionary Force had been moved to within easy striking distance of the *zeriba*. Many of the officers were familiar with the intervening ground. An officer of special knowledge and, judging from his success, of special talents, with trusty native guides, maintained the true direction. Near the camp at Umdabia, where the scrub might have impeded the advance, a path a hundred feet wide had been cut by fatigue parties. Careful patrolling prevented surprise. The nature of the country assisted the care of the General; for the open desert enabled the troops to march on a comparatively broad front, and to make effective use of their rifles if attacked.

For more than two hours the force advanced, moving across smooth swells of sand broken by rocks and with occasional small bushes. Several shallow *khors* traversed the road, and these rocky ditches, filled with a strange, sweet-scented grass, delayed the brigades until the pace was hardly two miles an hour. The smell of the grass was noticed by the alert senses of many, and will for ever refresh in their minds the strong impression of the night. The breeze which had sprung up at sundown gradually freshened and raised clouds of fine sand, which deepened the darkness with a whiter mist.

At nine o' clock the army halted in a previously selected space, near the deserted village of Mutrus and about two miles from the river. Nearly half the distance to Mahmud's *zeriba* was accomplished. Barely four miles in the direct line divided the combatants. It was not desirable to arrive before the dawn. The soldiers, still formed in their squares, lay down upon the ground. Meat and biscuits were served out to the men. The transport animals went by relays to the pools of the Atbara bed to drink and to replenish the *fantasses.*[2] All water-bottles were refilled. Pickets were thrown out to cover the business. Then, after sufficient sentries had been posted, the army slept, still in its array. The expectations of the morning, no less than the coldness of the night and the driving sand, disturbed the slumbers of the troops, and all were restless. Just before midnight a vicious mule kicked a Highlander. The man, thus painfully awakened, yelled. Half the brigade stood to arms, the soldiers falling swiftly into their places and gazing with fierce, eager eyes into the darkness. The grating buzz of armed men suddenly alarmed and forming in their ranks—a sound once heard, never to be forgotten—aroused the rest of the square. No sooner had silence been restored than it was time to move on again.

2 Portable iron water-tanks.—EDITOR.

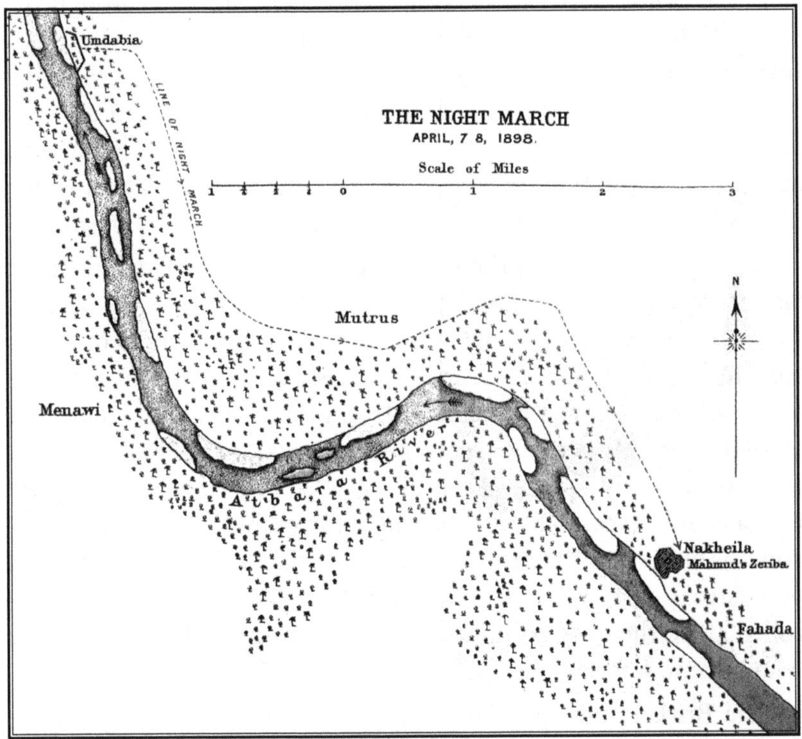

During the halt the moon had risen, and when at one o' clock the advance was resumed, the white beams revealed a wider prospect and, glinting on the fixed bayonets, crowned the squares with a sinister glitter. For three hours the army toiled onwards at the same slow and interrupted crawl. Strict silence was now enforced, and all smoking was forbidden. The cavalry, the Camel Corps, and the five batteries had overtaken the infantry, so that the whole attacking force was concentrated. Meanwhile the Dervishes slept.

At three o' clock the glare of fires became visible to the south, and the soldiers learned with satisfaction that their enemy awaited them at no great distance. Thus arrived before the Dervish position, the squares, with the exception of the reserve brigade, were unlocked, and the whole force assumed formation of attack. The British, who were on the extreme left, turned back their left battalion, the Warwickshire Regiment, to guard the flank, and the brigade thus formed a horizontal **L** three battalions on the longer and one on the shorter side. The whole force now advanced in one long line through the scattered bush and scrub. The direction of the march had been admirably kept by Captain Fitton, the officer entrusted with this vital matter, and the army, unknown to itself, had shouldered so as to accurately face the north front of the Dervish position. Presently the scrub ended, and the brigades emerged on to a large plateau which overlooked Mahmud's *zeriba* from a distance of about 900 yards.

It was still dark, and the haze that shrouded the Dervish camp was broken only by the glare of the watch-fires. The silence was profound. It seemed impossible to believe that more than 25,000 men were ready to join battle at scarcely the distance of half a mile. Yet the advance had not been unperceived, and the Arabs knew that their terrible antagonists crouched on the ridge waiting for the morning. For a while the suspense was prolonged. At last, after what seemed to many an interminable period, the uniform blackness of the horizon was broken by the first glimmer of the dawn. Gradually the light grew stronger until, as a theatre curtain is pulled up, the darkness rolled away, the vague outlines in the haze became definite, and the whole scene was revealed.[3]

The British and Egyptian army lay along the low ridge in the form of a great bow—the British brigade on the left, MacDonald in the centre, Maxwell curving forward on the right. The whole crest of the swell of ground was crowned with a bristle of bayonets and the tiny figures of thousands of men sitting or lying down and gazing curiously before them. The *khaki*-clad British were but a paler and yellower confusion on the sand, but the dark jerseys of the Egyptian and Soudanese brigades displayed their formidable array. Behind them, in a solid square, was the transport, guarded by Lewis's brigade. The leading squadrons of the cavalry were forming leisurely towards the left flank. The four batteries and a rocket detachment, moving between the infantry, ranged themselves on two convenient positions about a hundred yards in front of the line of battalions. All was ready. Yet everything was very quiet, and in the stillness of the dawn it almost seemed that Nature held her breath.

Half a mile away, at the foot of the ridge, a long irregular black line of thorn bushes enclosed the Dervish defences. Behind this *ze-*

3 Map, 'Atbara: the Artillery Preparation,' page 305.

riba low palisades and entrenchments bent back to the scrub by the river. Odd shapeless mounds indicated the positions of the gun-emplacements, and various casemates could be seen in the middle of the enclosure. Without, the bushes had been cleared away and the smooth sand stretched in a gentle slope to where the army waited. Within were crowds of little straw huts and scattered bushes, growing thicker to the southward. From among this rose the palm-trees, between whose stems the dry bed of the Atbara was exposed, and a single pool of water gleamed in the early sunlight. Such was Mahmud's famous *zeriba*, which for more than a month had been the predominant thought in the minds of the troops. It was scarcely imposing, and at first the soldiers thought it deserted. Only a dozen stray horsemen sat silently on their horses outside the entrenchment, watching their enemies, and inside a few dirty-white figures appeared and disappeared behind the parapets. Yet, insignificant as the *zeriba* looked, the smoke of many fires cooking the morning meal—never to be eaten—showed that it was occupied by men; and gay banners of varied colour and device, flaunting along the entrenchments or within the enclosure, declared that some at least were prepared to die in its defence.

The hush of the hour and the suspense of the army was broken by the bang of a gun. Everyone on the ridge jumped up and looked towards the sound. A battery of Krupps a little to the right of the Cameron Highlanders had opened fire. A great cloud of smoke shot swiftly to the front, and then thinned and drifted back to the northward. Over the centre of the *zeriba* a pale yellow flash and a round white puff showed the bursting shell. Underneath it the dust, beaten by the bullets, sprang into the air. The *wop!* of the distant explosion came back, like the echo of the report. Another gun further to the right was fired. Another shell burst over the straw huts among the palm-trees. The two Maxim-Nordenfeldt batteries had come into action. The officers looked at their watches. It was a quarter-past six. The bombardment had begun.

Explosion followed explosion in quick succession until all four batteries were busily engaged. The cannonade grew loud and continuous. The rocket detachment began to fire, and the strange projectiles hissed and screamed as they left the troughs and jerked erratically towards the *zeriba*. In the air above the enclosure shell after shell flashed into existence, smote the ground with its leaden shower, and dispersed—a mere film—into the haze and smoke which still hung over the Dervish encampment. At the very first shot all the dirty-white figures disappeared, bobbing down into their pits and shelters; but a few solitary horsemen remained motionless for a while in the middle of the enclosure, watching the effect of the fire, as if it had no concern with them. The British infantry stood up on tip-toe to look at the wonderful spectacle of actual war, and at first every shell was eagerly scrutinised and its probable effect discussed. But the busy gunners multiplied the projectiles, until so many were alive in the air at once that all criticism was prevented. Gradually even the strange sight became monotonous. The officers shut up their glasses. The men began to sit down again. Many of them actually went to sleep. The rest were soon tired of the amazing scene, the like of which they had never looked on before, and awaited impatiently further developments and 'some new thing.'

After the bombardment had lasted about ten minutes a great cloud of dust sprang up in the *zeriba*, and hundreds of horsemen were seen scrambling into their saddles and galloping through a gap in the rear face out into the open sand to the right. To meet the possibility of an attempt to turn the left flank of the attack, the eight squadrons of cavalry and two Maxim guns jingled and clattered off in the direction of the danger. The dust, which the swift passage of so many horsemen raised, shut the scene from the eyes of the infantry, but continual dust-clouds above the scrub to the left and the *tat-tat-tat-tat* of the Maxims seemed to indicate a cavalry fight. The Baggara horse, however, declined an unequal combat, and made no serious attempt to interfere with the attack. Twice they showed some sort of front, and the squadrons thought they might find opportunity to charge; but a few rounds from the Maxims effectually checked the enemy, and inflicted on each occasion the loss of about twenty killed and wounded. With the exception of one squadron detached on the right, the Egyptian cavalry force, however, remained on the left flank, and shielded the operations of the assaulting infantry.

Meanwhile the bombardment—no longer watched with curiosity—continued with accuracy and precision. The batteries searched

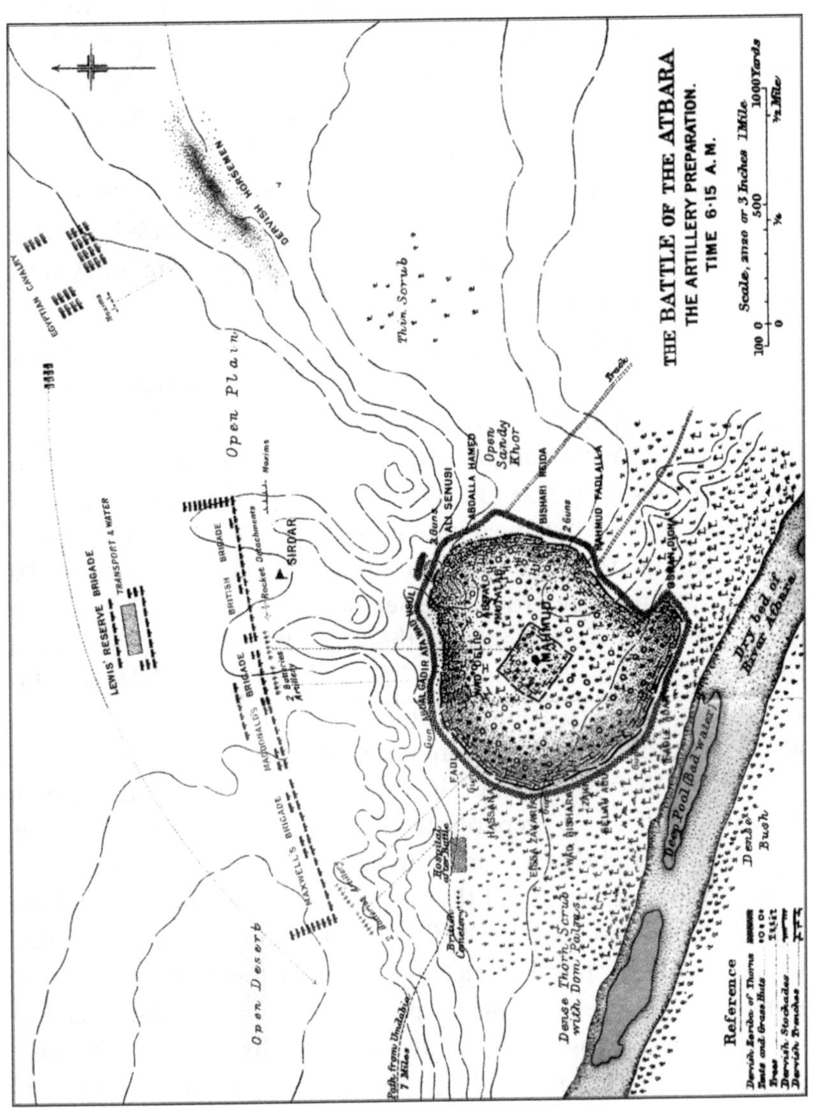
THE BATTLE OF THE ATBARA
THE ARTILLERY PREPARATION.
TIME 6·15 A.M.
Scale, 1in20 or 3 Inches 1Mile
100 0 500 1000 Yards
0 ¼ ½ Mile
Reference
Dervish Zeriba of Thorns
Tents and Grass Huts
Trees
Dervish Stockades
Dervish Trenches
Dry bed of River Atbara
Deep Pool (Bad Water)
Dense Bush
Dense Thorn Scrub with Dom Palms
Open Desert
Open Plain
Thin Scrub
Open Sandy Khor
DERVISH HORSEMEN
EGYPTIAN CAVALRY
Maxims
LEWIS' RESERVE BRIGADE
TRANSPORT & WATER
BRITISH BRIGADE
Rocket Detachments
SIRDAR
MACDONALD'S BRIGADE
2 Batteries Artillery
MAXWELL'S BRIGADE
Hospital
British Cemetery
Path from Umdabia 7 Miles
Track
MAHMUD
ALI SENUSI
ABDALLA HAMED
BISHARI REIDA
26 Guns
OSMAN DIGNA
HASSAN
WAD BISHARA
FADL

the interior of the *zeriba*, thrashing out one section after another, and working the whole ground regularly from front to rear. The *zeriba* and palisades were knocked about in many places, and at a quarter to seven a cluster of straw huts caught fire and began to burn briskly. At the same time a spluttering musketry was opened for a moment from the centre of the Dervish line and directed apparently at the batteries. A single gunner was wounded. For the rest, the Arabs bore their terrible ordeal in absolute silence.

During the artillery preparation the force had been drawn up, three infantry brigades in line with the left flank refused, and the fourth brigade in reserve. At a quarter-past seven the infantry were ordered to form in column for assault.[4]

Maxwell and MacDonald, on the right and centre, assumed a formation with two battalions deployed, three companies in line and three in support, covering a central assaulting column of two battalions in double companies, with the right flank well protected. The British array was much deeper. The Camerons crossed over from the right and deployed into line. The Lincoln Regiment moved to the right, and formed in column of companies in rear of the 1st Company of the Camerons. The Seaforths formed similarly in rear of the centre. Two companies of the Royal Warwickshire Regiment formed behind the 8th Company of the Camerons, and the remaining four[5] followed in column of route (i.e. fours deep) in order to be able to show an immediate front to the left flank should it be threatened by the Dervish cavalry. The British Maxim battery drew up on the extreme left and prepared to conform to the general advance. Thus the British brigade was formed into columns nine companies deep, whereas the depth of the centre brigade was but six, and the right brigade—exclusive of its flank column only three companies. General Gatacre, besides selecting a deeper formation, had made more elaborate preparations for passing the *zeriba*; and the Cameron Highlanders, covering the advance of the British columns, were provided with thick raw-hide gloves and bill-hooks in order to pull it to pieces, blankets and sacks to throw on the top of the thorns,

4 Map, 'Atbara: Formation for Assault,' page 307.

5 It will be remembered that two companies of the Royal Warwickshire Regiment were in garrison at Merawi, and hence the battalion had but six companies in action at the Atbara.—EDITOR.

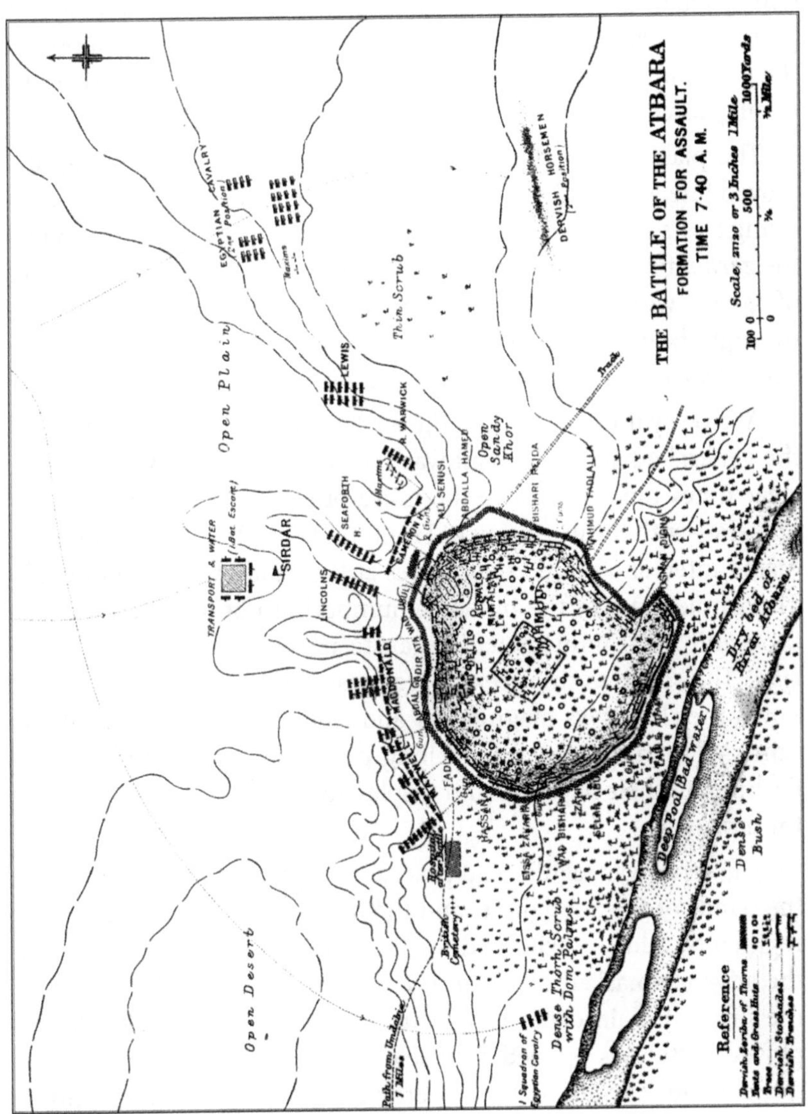
THE BATTLE OF THE ATBARA
FORMATION FOR ASSAULT.
TIME 7·40 A.M.
Open Plain
Open Desert
Thin Scrub
Open Sandy Khor
Dense Thorn Scrub with Dom Palms
Dense Bush
Dry bed of River Atbara
Deep Pool (Bad water)
EGYPTIAN CAVALRY
DERVISH HORSEMEN
TRANSPORT & WATER
SIRDAR
LINCOLNS
SEAFORTH
CAMERON
MACDONALD
MAXWELL
LEWIS
WARWICK
MAHMUD
ALI SENUSI
ABDALLA HAMED
BISHARI REIDA
British Cavalry
Path from Umdabia 7 Miles
1 Squadron of Egyptian Cavalry
Track
Reference

and two improvised scaling-ladders to each company. An interval of 200 yards was left between the British brigade and. MacDonald's Soudanese, to enable the Lincolnshire Regiment to deploy as ordered. One battalion of Lewis's brigade in reserve formed square around the transport and water. The other two battalions supported the extreme left flank, which was also secured by the display of the cavalry force.

The plan of the attack for the army was simple. The long, deployed line was to advance steadily against the entrenchments, subduing by its continual fire that of the enemy. They were then to tear the *zeriba* to pieces. Covered by their musketry, the dense columns of assault which had followed the line were to enter the defences through the gaps, deploy to the right, and march through the enclosure, clearing it with the bayonet and by fire.

At twenty minutes to eight the Sirdar ordered his bugles to sound the general advance. The call was repeated by all the brigades. The clear notes rang out above the noise of the artillery. The superior officers—with the exception of Hunter, Maxwell, and MacDonald—dismounted and placed themselves at the head of their commands. The whole mass of the infantry, numbering not less than thirteen thousand men, immediately began to move forward upon the *zeriba*. The scene as this great force crested the ridge and advanced down the slope was magnificent and tremendous. Large solid columns of men, preceded by a long double line, with the sunlight flashing on their bayonets and displaying their ensigns, marched to the assault.

The array was regular and precise. The pipes of the Highlanders, the bands of the Soudanese, and the drums and fifes of the English regiments, added a wild and thrilling accompaniment. As soon as the advance masked the batteries, the guns were run forward with the firing line, in order to effectually support the attack. The deployed battalions opened a ceaseless and crushing fire on the entrenchment. The fire of the Cameron Highlanders was distinguishable by the regular precision of the section volleys, no less than by the sharp rattling report of the Lee-Metford rifle. The necessity of firing delayed the advance of the attacking columns, and the pace did not exceed a slow march.

The Dervishes remained silent until the troops were within 300 yards. Then the smoke-puffs spurted out all along the stockades, and a sharp fusillade began, gradually and continually growing in intensity until the assaulting troops were exposed to a furious and effective fire. The right of the attack curved forward, and hence the whole line faced the Dervish position obliquely. The right and centre gained ground to the left, and the lines of advance of the different brigades slowly converged. The pressure of Maxwell's brigade pushed MacDonald towards the British, and the XIth Soudanese, who were the left battalion of the centre brigade, closed in upon the British right until they absorbed the 200 yards of interval which had been left for the deployment.

Along the centre of the line of advance of the British brigade ran a dry *khor,* a gentle **V**-shaped re-ëntrant, to the lowest line of which the ground sloped on either side. As the XIth drew nearer, the Lincoln Regiment edged away towards the Seaforth Highlanders, and so sidled towards the khor. The Seaforth Highlanders on the opposite slope also inclined in towards the bottom, so that these two battalion columns flowed down the water-course together, like streams which run into a common gutter.

The Royal Warwickshire Regiment, to guard against the Dervish cavalry, formed to the left, and, delayed by this, became practically a reserve. The slow advance of the firing line, and the impatience of those in rear, closed the columns to quarter-column distance; and thus, even before the enemy's fire had begun to take effect, the nice and well-considered plan of assault was deranged, and the British brigade was wedged into one great mass which drove steadily onward along the *khor.*

From 250 yards up to the position the troops began to suffer loss. The whole entrenchment was rimmed with flame and smoke, amid which the active figures of the Dervish riflemen were momentarily visible, and behind the filmy curtain solid masses of swordsmen and spearmen appeared. The fortunate interposition of a small knoll in some degree protected the advance of the Lincoln Regiment, but in both Highland battalions soldiers began to drop. The whole air was full of a strange chirping whistle . The hard pebbly sand was everywhere dashed up into dust-spurts. Numerous explosive bullets, fired by the Arabs, made queer startling reports. The roar of the rifles drowned even the noise of the artillery. All the deployed battalions began to suffer. But they and the assaulting columns, regardless of the fire, bore down on the *zeriba* in all the majesty of war—a mighty avalanche of men, stern, unflinching, utterly irresistible.

Two hundred yards from the entrenchment and one hundred and fifty from the thorn bushes the Cameron Highlanders abandoned their section volleys, and independent firing broke out, running along the line from end to end. Shooting continually, but without any hurry or confusion, the British and Soudanese battalions continued their slow, remorseless advance; and it was evident that, in spite of the fierce fire of the defence, which was now causing many casualties, the assault would be successful. When only a hundred yards intervened, both Soudanese brigades charged the *zeriba* with a wild and furious shout. But the British infantry, heedless of their losses, steadfastly adhered to the original orders, and marched slowly and in disdainful silence up to the thorn fence.[6]

Here the whole assault halted. The Cameron Highlanders had been ordered to tear the *zeriba* to pieces, and, although exposed to a heavy fire at fifty yards' range from the entrenchment, they began to deliberately drag the thorn bushes round the flanks of the column so as to open a gap. General Gatacre, who had marched in the centre of that regiment, his position indicated by a large Union Jack, himself laid hands upon the thorn bushes. His Staff assisted him in task which, however honourable, might with propriety have been left to others. But the *zeriba* proved a weak defence, and the pressure of the mass rolling along the *khor* was so great that before the path was clear the whole brigade—Seaforths, Lincolns, and finally Warwicks—crashed through and, deploying as best they could, advanced at once on the stockades and entrenchments behind. The more impulsive men of the Cameron Highlanders, carried away by the vigour of the attack, trampled through the thorns with the heads of the columns, and were the first to plunge their bayonets into the bodies of the foe.

The others—unmoved alike by the danger, the din, and the enthusiasm continued calmly and methodically to pull the *zeriba* to

6 Map, 'Atbara: the Assault,' page 311.

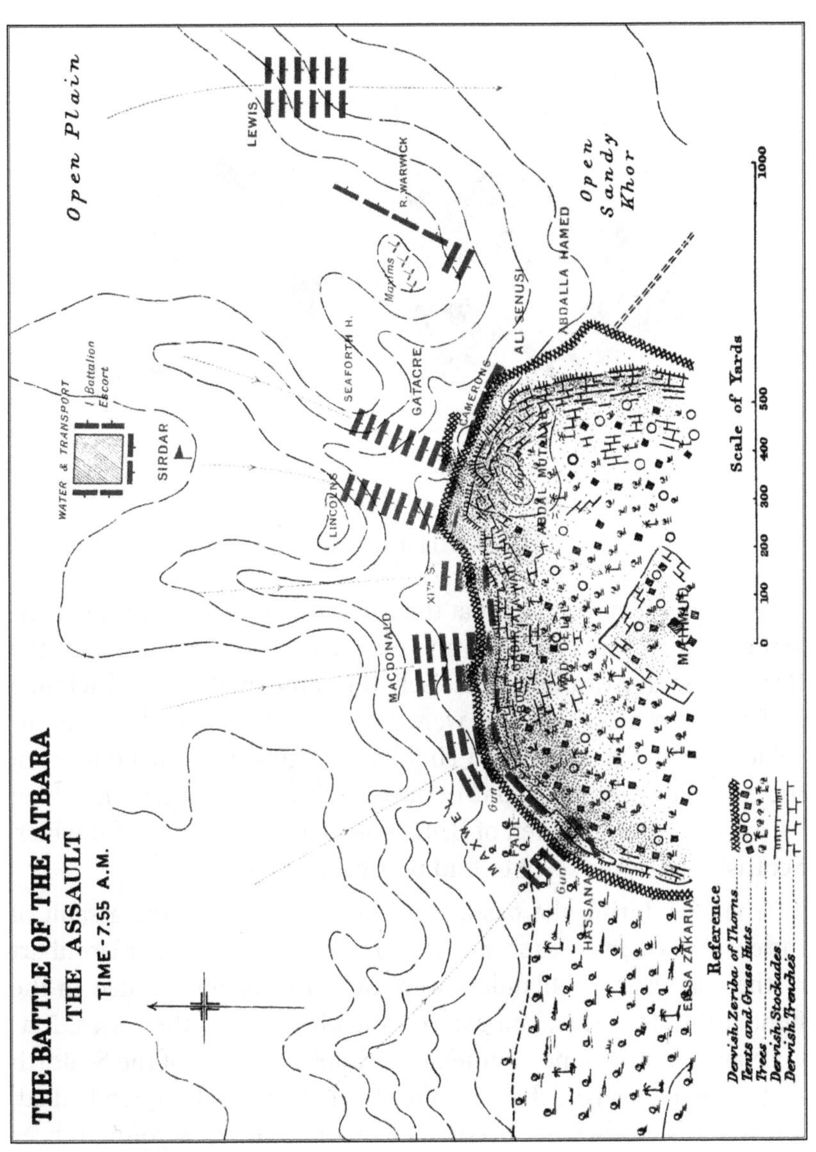
THE BATTLE OF THE ATBARA
THE ASSAULT
TIME - 7.55 A.M.
Open Plain
Open Sandy Khor
WATER & TRANSPORT
1 Battalion Escort
SIRDAR
LEWIS
R. WARWICK
Maxims
SEAFORTH H.
GATACRE
CAMERONS
LINCOLNS
XIth S.
MACDONALD
MAXWELL
Gun
ALI SENUSI
ABDALLA HAMED
ABDAL MUTALIB
WAD DE LIL
MAHMUD
HASSANAB
EISSA ZAKARIA
Scale of Yards
0 100 200 300 400 500 1000
Reference
Dervish Zeriba of Thorns
Tents and Grass Huts
Trees
Dervish Stockades
Dervish Trenches

THROUGH THE ZERIBA

pieces and widen the gap, that the rear companies might more conveniently pass through. Now, and during the measured advance, the British infantry displayed precisely the same qualities of discipline and firmness for which they were renowned throughout the Peninsular War; and the Cameron Highlanders, to whom the honours of the day belong, achieved one of those sublime feats of arms of which we are convinced all men of British birth are capable, but for which Scottish regiments seem to find particular opportunities.

The loss during the passage of the *zeriba* and in the assault of the entrenchments was severe. Captain Findlay and Major Urquhart of the Cameron Highlanders were both mortally wounded in the fight at the stockades, and expired still cheering on their men. Major Napier of the same regiment and Captain Baillie of the Seaforth Highlanders received the wounds, of which they subsequently died, a few yards further on. Second-Lieutenant Gore,[7] a young officer fresh from Sandhurst, was shot dead between the thorn fence and the stockade. Other officers in the Lincoln and the Warwickshire

7 For full designations of these officers, see casualty list, page xx.

regiments sustained severe wounds. Many soldiers were killed and wounded in the narrow space. These losses were general throughout the assaulting brigades. In the five minutes which were occupied in the passage of the obstruction about four hundred casualties occurred. The attack continued.

All along the front the brigades had struck the *zeriba*, had burst through it, and had fallen upon the stockades and entrenchments. It was as if a wave had broken on a child's castle in the sand, toppling over the weak walls, pouring in from every side, and sweeping the whole place clear and level; and the Arab musketry was as little able to stop the advance as the pebbles which a child might throw at rising waters.

At all points the troops broke into the enclosure. Behind the stockade there ran a treble trench. The whole interior was honeycombed with pits and holes. From these there now sprang thousands of Dervishes, desperately endeavouring to show a front to the attack. But the superior discipline, numbers, and weapons of the troops bore down all resistance. The British brigade had struck the extremity of the north front of the *zeriba*, and thus took the whole of the eastern face in enfilade, sweeping it with their terrible musketry from end to end, and strewing the ground with corpses. Although, owing to the lines of advance having converged, there was not room for more than half the force to deploy, the brigades pushed on. The conduct of the attack passed to the company commanders. All these officers kept their heads, and brought their companies up into the general line as the front gradually widened and gaps appeared. So the whole force—companies, battalions, even brigades—mixed up together and formed in one dense, ragged, but triumphant line, -marched on unchecked towards the river bed, driving their enemies in hopeless confusion before them.

Yet, although the Dervishes were unable to make head against the attack, they disdained to run. Many hundreds held their ground, firing their rifles valiantly till the end. Others charged with spear and sword. The greater part retired in skirmishing order, jumping over the numerous pits, walking across the open spaces, and repeatedly turning round to shoot. The XIth Soudanese encountered the most severe resistance after the defences were penetrated. As their three deployed companies pressed on through the enclosure, they were confronted by a small inner *zeriba* stubbornly defended by the Emir Mahmud's personal bodyguard. These devoted men poured a sudden volley into the centre company at close range, and so deadly was the effect that nearly all the company were shot, falling to the ground still in their ranks, so that a British officer passing at a little distance was provoked to inquire 'what they were doing lying down.' Notwithstanding this severe check the regiment, gallantly led by their beloved Colonel and supported by the Xth Soudanese, rushed this last defence and slew its last defenders. Mahmud was himself captured. Having duly inspected his defences and made his dispositions, he had sheltered in a specially constructed casemate. Thence he was now ignominiously dragged, and, on his being recognised, the intervention of a British officer alone saved him from the fury of the excited Soudanese.

During the advance through the enclosure the firing of the black troops was of the wildest and most reckless description, and although their pluck was undeniable their discipline contrasted unfavourably with the steadiness of the British infantry. The broken nature of the ground and the confusion of the assault led to a good many casualties from our own fire.[8]

Still the advance continued, and it seemed to those who took part in it more like a horrible nightmare than a waking reality. Captains and subalterns collected whatever men they could, heedless of corps or nationality, and strove to control and direct their fire. *Jibba*-clad figures sprang out of the ground, fired or charged, and were destroyed at every step. And onwards over their bodies—over pits choked with dead and dying, among heaps of mangled camels and donkeys, among decapitated or eviscerated trunks, the ghastly results of the shell fire; women and little children killed by the bombardment or praying in wild terror for mercy; blacks chained in their trenches, slaughtered in their chains—always onwards marched the conquerors, with bayonets running blood; clothes, hands, and faces all besmeared; the foul stench of a month's accumulated filth in their nostrils, and the savage whistle of random bullets in their ears.

---

8 The shooting was generally very free, and no unit can be either entirely exonerated or severely blamed.—EDITOR.

AT THE END OF THE BATTLE

But at about twenty minutes past eight the whole force, with the Seaforth Highlanders well forward on the left, arrived at the bank of the Atbara, having marched completely through the position, and shot or bayoneted all in their path. Hundreds of Dervishes were still visible retiring across the dry bed of the river, and making for the scrub on the opposite bank. The leading companies of the Seaforth Highlanders and Lincolns, with such odd parties of Camerons as had been carried on with the attack, opened a murderous fire on these fugitives. Since they would not run, their loss was heavy, and it was a strange sight—the last vivid impression of the day—-to watch them struggling through the deep sand, with the dust knocked up into clouds by the bullets which struck all round them. Very few escaped, and the bodies of the killed lay thickly dotting the river-bed with heaps of dirty- white. Then at 8.25 the 'Cease fire' sounded, and the battle of the Atbara ended.

Forthwith the battalions began to re-form, and in every company the roll was called. There were many surprises, and men thought to have fallen, dead or wounded, reappeared—grinning and ensanguined—in their places. Yet the losses had been severe. In the assault—a period not exceeding half an hour—eighteen British and sixteen native officers and 525 men had been killed or wounded, the greater part during the passage of the *zeriba*. While the regiments were reforming the Sirdar rode along the line, and the British brigades, raising their helmets on the dark smeared bayonets, cheered him in all the loud enthusiasm of successful war. For almost the only moment in the course of this story he evinced emotion. 'He was,' said an officer who watched him closely, 'quite human for a quarter of an hour.' And indeed, if anything could break this stern man's reserve, it should have been the cheers of the soldiers who had stormed the Atbara *zeriba*; for this was the most memorable day in all his life that had yet run out. Within the space of two hours not only were Mahmud and his army—the scourge of Kordofan and Darfur, the victors of Metemma, the destroyers of the Jaalin—practically annihilated, but there was now no possibility of his being superseded in the command of the expedition to Khartoum.

The actual pursuit was abortive. Colonel Lewis with his two battalions followed a line of advance which led south of the *zeriba*, and just before reaching the river-bank found and fired upon a few Dervishes retreating through the scrub. All the cavalry and the Camel Corps crossed the Atbara and plunged into the bush on the further side. But so dense and tangled was the country that after three miles of peril and perplexity they abandoned the attempt, and the routed Arabs fled unmolested.

The Baggara horse had ridden off during the action, headed by the prudent Osman Digna—whose position in the *zeriba*[9] was conveniently suited to such a manoeuvre—and under that careful leadership suffered little loss. The rest of the army was, however, destroyed or dispersed. The fugitives fled up the Atbara river, leaving many wounded to die in the scrub, all along their line of retreat. A strong patrol of friendly Arabs under Major Benson,[10] moving west from Kassala, struck in upon their flank and harried them incessantly, killing 350 men, including several Emirs, and making 580 prisoners. Of the powerful force of 12,000 fighting men which Mahmud had gathered at Metemma, scarcely 4,000 reached Ge-

9 See map, 'Atbara: Formation for Assault,' page 307.

10 Major G. E. Benson, R.A.

daref in safety. These survivors were added to the army of Ahmed Fedil, and thus prevented from spreading their evil tidings among the populace at Omdurman. Osman Digna, Wad Bishara, and other important Emirs whose devotion and discretion were undoubted, alone returned to the capital.

As soon as the troops were re-formed, the *zeriba* was evacuated and the army drew up in line along the neighbouring ridge. It was then only nine o' clock, and the air was still cool and fresh. The soldiers lit fires, made some tea, and ate their rations of biscuits and meat. Then they lay down and waited for evening. Gradually, as the hours passed, the sun became powerful. There was no shade. Only a few thin, leafless bushes rose from the sand. The hours dragged wearily away. The day was peculiarly hot, even for the country and season. The sandy ridge beat back the rays till the air above was like the breath of a furnace and the pebbly ground burned. The British troops suffered acutely. The fierce sun absorbed even the gratitude which all men, freed from the immediate presence of death, feel towards some vaguely defined Providence. The ridge was like a kitchen range. The water in the *fantasses* and bottles was hot and scarce. The pool of the Atbara was foul and tainted. The water, a thick, muddy-coloured liquid, exuded a vile smell. A little pure water was obtained by digging holes in the river bed and letting them gradually till. But for the most part the soldiers drank the filth. As the day drew on the troubles of the British were aggravated. The hardy negroes cared nothing for the sun, and slept phlegmatically. Some of the Highlanders took off their kilts and spreading those invaluable garments on the bushes made little patches of shade under which they existed until the evening. But even this desperate remedy was denied to the English regiments.

The condition of the wounded was painful in the extreme. They were placed beneath such shade as was available, and every effort was made to attend to their wants. But the Sirdar had reduced the Medical Staff to insignificant proportions. Seven doctors were available for the whole of the British brigade. The Soudanese and Egyptians were equally stinted. Only the simplest appliances were at hand. Instead of the comfortable Indian doolies, with their ample hoods and white curtains, the ordinary stretcher was provided even for the most serious cases. In spite of the devoted efforts of the few medical officers who had been allowed to accompany the force, the wounded officers and soldiers endured the greatest miseries, and it is certain that several died of their wounds who might under happier circumstances have been saved. It must be remembered with regard to the Atbara that, although the victory had been decisive, it was followed by a retreat; and instead of the Field Hospitals coming up after the action, the troops had to march back to Umdabia. Hence the wounded were in the position of the wounded of a defeated army, and suffered accordingly. It was impossible to avoid this. Misery is inseparable from war. The care of the wounded is, after all, a minor matter. After a great European battle they would lie rotting in holes and corners for perhaps three days. The business of the General is to defeat the enemy. Nevertheless, when all has been fairly stated, it is evident that, if more attention had been paid to the subject, arrangements might have been made which would have increased the popularity of the commander and diminished the sufferings of the troops.

At three o' clock the soldiers who were stewing on the ridge received—almost with feelings of relief—the order to attend the funerals of the dead. The digging of the graves was a long and tedious business, for the men were weary, and the sand was hard and stony. But at length a shallow trench, scarcely twelve inches deep, was scraped, and in this the bodies were laid. Surrounded by the comrades who had shared their perils, the remains of those who had 'paid a soldier's debt' were reverently interred. The clergymen of the various denominations read the last words of hope and consolation. The pipes wailed 'Lochaber-no-more.' The parting volleys crashed in the air, and then the row of figures, each shrouded in a blanket, were hidden by the hot sand on which they had met their fates, in which they must for ever lie. Then everyone marched away and left the lonely grave in the African bush to the silence of the desert and the oblivion of the past; and so turned busily to their own affairs and the strong enthusiasms of life.

Such is the melancholy end of brave men who fall in war. The living .divide the triumph. The dead—without whom perchance it would hardly have been won—have but a dull occupation. Yet theirs

THE LAMENT

is no worse than the common fate of man; for, I suppose, when we are ourselves overtaken by death, the surroundings of home and friends will not make much appreciable difference. To struggle and choke in the hushed and darkened room of a London house, while, without, the great metropolis is planning and contriving—while the special editions report the progress of the latest European crisis, and all the world is full of the business of the morrow—will not seem less unsatisfactory than, when thrilled with fierce yet generous emotions, to die in the sunshine and be spaded under before the night.

During the afternoon many officers visited the *zeriba* and examined the hideous sights it contained. The *dêm* or enclosure was about 1,000 yards long by 800 deep. All around the outside, except at the two gaps by which the Dervishes had fled, ran the thorn fence. On the side of the river it was very strong, and made a formidable stockade. Towards the desert, whence the troops had attacked, it was weak and badly made. Some have therefore concluded that Mahmud expected to be attacked from the direction of the river, and was surprised by the arrival of the troops on the opposite side. It seems more probable, however, that the Arabs found the labour of drawing the bushes into the bare desert too arduous for their lazy dispositions, and so did not finish the work. It was a dangerous neglect. Behind the *zeriba,* at about sixty yards' distance, was a line of trenches, sometimes double, sometimes treble. The counterscarp of the first trench was revetted with *dôm*-palm logs, which stuck up above the ground in lengths varying from two to five feet, and made the so-called stockade. The trenches were about four feet deep. From the rear trenches, and at right angles to them, smaller ones, about eight yards long, ran back at intervals of about ten yards. These were apparently used as places of storage, for littered about within them were bags of grain, meal, and *dôm* -palm nuts, occasionally meat, cooking-pots, picks, shovels, and such like. The ten gun-emplacements were dotted about the interior. Most of the guns, brass rifled seven-pounders, appeared to have been fired once or twice before they were taken.

They had no time for more. In the centre of the position was a small enclosure—a sort of citadel—made of logs about ten feet high and loop-holed. Here was where Mahmud had sheltered during the bombardment, and where the XIth Soudanese had suffered such severe loss in the assault. The whole inside of the *zeriba* was one mass of pits, in all of which were animals tied leg to leg and thrown. Thousands of these had been killed by the artillery. The dead were ripped in pieces by the splinters of the shells. The living lay gasping beneath the dead. The fallen Arabs lay thickest on the front assaulted by the British brigade. All the trenches were filled with dead riflemen, each with his weapon and a pile of eighty to a hundred cartridges beside him. They were chiefly armed with Remingtons, but many had elephant-guns or Tower muskets, and a few Swiss repeating Vetterli rifles of the ' 86 pattern were noticed.

The front of the *zeriba* had sustained the assault. But the defenders of the right face had not escaped. As soon as the British had entered the enclosure they swept all the trenches of the right face

AFTER THE ATBARA

with their terrible musketry, and the corpses were huddled together as thickly there, as in the actual path of the assault. All through the position the spearmen were scattered about as they had fallen. In many of the pits dead men were mixed indiscriminately with the slaughtered animals—a shocking jumble. At the further edge of the enclosure the crowding of the bodies marked where the last vain effort had been made. Beyond, in the sands of the river-bed, lay the fugitives who had failed to reach the bushes. It was a dreadful carnage. More than 2,600 corpses were counted in the *zeriba* and its vicinity. The assessors did not go across the Atbara; but the scrub must have been full of wounded who had crawled there to die. The smell of the enclosure was appalling. For a fortnight Mahmud, fearing desertion-, had forbidden his soldiers to leave the *zeriba* by night. Donkeys and mules left unburied, and in an advanced state of putrefaction, intensified the stench. The blazing sun beating down on the corpses increased its volume. The raw odour of new blood added a final horror. The wandering officer soon sickened and fled back to the burning ridge. Only the Soudanese continued to despoil the slain, and collected a great number of swords, spears, and other trophies of victory.

I rejoice to record the fact that, before the night march against the *zeriba*. Sir H. Kitchener issued distinct orders that quarter was to be given to all who asked for it, and that the wounded Dervishes were not to be despatched unless they were dangerous. This was carefully impressed upon the troops, and the Arabic word for quarter, *Aman!* was explained to the British brigade. Of course, in the actual assault very few were spared. Even in European war indiscriminate bayoneting often follows the storm of an entrenchment. Men do not come across the open and let themselves be shot at for nothing. The black soldiers were beyond regular control, and scattered shots were heard throughout the morning as odd Dervishes were discovered. But the private and unofficial testimony of many impartial persons convinces me that nearly all the Arabs fought to the death; that hardly any unresisting men were killed; that such few were killed in error or by the Soudanese without the knowledge and in spite of the efforts, of the British officers. In any case, the formal orders issued completely vindicate the General.

In obedience to these humane orders, several hundred prisoners were taken. They were mostly negroes—for the Arabs refused to surrender, and fought to the last or tried to escape. The captive blacks, who fight with equal willingness on either side, were content to be enlisted in the Soudanese regiments; so that many of those who served the Khalifa on the Atbara helped to destroy him at Omdurman. The most notable prisoner was the Emir Mahmud—a tall, strong Arab, about thirty years old. Immediately after his capture he was dragged before the Sirdar. 'Why,' inquired the General, 'have you come into my country to burn and kill?' 'I have to obey my orders, and so have you,' retorted the captive sullenly, yet not without a certain dignity. To other questions he returned curt or evasive answers, and volunteered the opinion that all this slaughter would be avenged at Omdurman. He was removed in custody—a fine specimen of proud brutality, worthy perhaps of some better fate than to linger indefinitely in the gaol at Wady Halfa.

With the cool of the evening the army left its bed of torment on the ridge and returned to Umdabia. The homeward march was a severe trial; the troops were exhausted; the ground was broken; the guides, less careful or less fortunate than on the previous night, lost their way. The columns were encumbered with wounded, most of whom were already in a high state of fever, and whose sufferings were painful to witness. It was not until after midnight that the camp was reached. The infantry had been continuously under arms—marching, fighting, or sweltering in the sun—for thirty hours. The majority had hardly closed their eyes for two days.

Officers and soldiers—British, Soudanese, and Egyptian—struggled into their bivouacs, and fell asleep, very weary but victorious.

The full list of casualties on the Atbara was as follows:—

British Officers Killed or Died of Wounds (5)

Major R. E. L. Napier, Cameron Highlanders
Major B. C. Urquhart, Cameron Highlanders
Captain C. Findlay, Cameron Highlanders
Captain A. C. D. Baillie, Seaforth Highlanders
Second Lieut. P. Gore, Seaforth Highlanders

British Officers Wounded (8)

Lieut. M. Green, Royal Warwickshire
Colonel T. E. Verner, Lincolnshire
Lieut. H. E. R. Boxer, Lincolnshire
Lieut. C. J. Rennie, Lincolnshire
Colonel R. H. Murray, C.B., Seaforth Highlanders
Captain N. C. Maclachlan, Seaforth Highlanders
Lieut. R. S. Vandeleur, Seaforth Highlanders
Lieut. N. A. Thomson, Seaforth Highlanders

BRITISH BRIGADE

	Killed		Wounded		Total number of casualties
	Officers	Rank and file	Officers	Rank and file	
1st Battalion Royal Warwickshire Regiment	1	2	1	11	14
1st Battalion Lincolnshire Regiment	—	1	3	13	17
1st Battalion Seaforth Highlanders	1	5	5	22	33
1st Battalion Cameron Highlanders	2	13	1	44	60
Army Service Corps	—	—	—	1	1
Total	3	21	10	91	125

EGYPTIAN ARMY

British Officers Wounded (5)

CAPTAIN W. H. PERSSE, 2nd Dragoon Guards and Egyptian Army
CAPTAIN HON. C. E. WALSH, Rifle Brigade and Egyptian Army
MAJOR A. K. HARLEY, D.S.O., Indian Staff Corps and Egyptian Army
MAJOR H. P. SHEKELTON, *p.s.c,* South Lancashire Regiment & Egyptian Army
CAPTAIN W. F. WALTER, *p.s.c,* Lancashire Fusiliers and Egyptian Army

British N.C Officers Wounded (2)

Native Ranks

		Killed	Wounded
Cavalry		6	12
Camel Corps		—	2
Artillery		3	15
Infantry Brigades:—			
MAXWELL'S	8th Egyptians	1	—
	XIIth Soudanese	4	40
	XIIIth Soudanese	6	52
	XIVth Soudanese	6	61
MACDONALD'S	2nd Egyptians	—	5
	IXth Soudanese	7	61
	Xth Soudanese	6	37
	XIth Soudanese	17	17
LEWIS'S	3rd Egyptians	—	5
	4th Egyptians	—	—
	7th Egyptians	—	3
Total		56	371

General Total all ranks (British and Egyptian) 19 British officers and 552 men.

The ammunition expenditure was as follows

Artillery:

Case Shot	30
Common Shell	270

Double Shell	143
Shrapnel Shell	690
Rocket Detachment	
Rockets	13
Maxim Guns	4,800 Rounds
Cavalry (Carbine)	4,000 Rounds
Infantry:	
British Brigade (Lee-Metford)	56.000 Rounds
Maxwell's Brigade (Martini-Henry)	101,000 Rounds
MacDonald's Brigade (Martini-Henry)	75,000 Rounds

The field states on the 8th April were as follows:

British Brigade	101 Officers and 3,357 men
Egyptian Army	83 British Officers and 10,202 men

The Dervish loss was officially estimated at 40 Emirs and 3,000 Dervishes killed. No statistics as to their wounded are forthcoming.

CHAPTER XIV
IN SUMMER QUARTERS

Summer quarters—'Ferntit'—The British camp—The day's work—Greek traders—'The Atbara Derby'—Footprints of conquest—Monotony—The strategy of the Atbara campaign—The tactics—The British formation—General Gatacre's mistake—The artillery preparation—The palm of honour—An insane dispute—The Sirdar's summer.

Although this chapter is among the shortest in the book, the period it describes seemed to the troops tediously prolonged. As the battle of the Atbara had been decisive, the whole Expeditionary Force went into summer quarters. The Egyptian army was distributed into three principal garrisons—four battalions at Atbara camp, six battalions and the cavalry in Berber, three battalions at Abadia. The artillery and transport were proportionately divided. The British brigade encamped with two battalions at Darmali and two at the village of Selim, about a mile and a half distant.

I have invited several officers who spent the summer at these various resorts, to give me some account of their doings and of the life of the troops. But the most imaginative are unable to write more than a few pages on the dull months which dragged wearily away. The Soudanese and Egyptian soldiers were accustomed to the heat and impervious to the flies. Monotony had no terrors for them; they were content to exist. Only two troubles, with both of which we may sympathise, assailed their happiness. The first was the continued separation from their wives, very few of whom had managed to make their way to the front; the second was the prevalence of 'Ferntit,' an odious disease which chiefly attacked the troops holding Berber.

The African continent is rich in mystery and horror. To the ills that flesh is heir to, it has contributed some of the most peculiar and disgusting maladies known to science. 'Ferntit' is a common instance. Those who have travelled in the Equatorial regions will find no difficulty in recalling others still more strange and loathsome. 'Ferntit,' or guinea-worm, is, however, sufficiently unpleasant. A small worm enters the foot or leg of the incautious bather; after some time the foot swells and becomes acutely painful. The swelling is carefully opened and the worm emerges, no longer small. A long and delicate treatment is now necessary. Gradually, and bit by bit, the parasite must be extracted from the body of his victim. The greatest care must be exercised not to break the worm, for if this unwittingly be done, he multiplies himself. What is extracted is wound round a small twig. Every day a little progress—perhaps a quarter of an inch—is made. But since the worm often attains a length of four feet the recovery is slow and tedious. With a single worm there is little danger; but when twenty or more are present the prognosis is bad.

The Soudanese troops who were stationed at Berber suffered acutely from this disease, which appeared endemic in the town, and in one of the battalions as many as thirty per cent, of the soldiers were at one time affected. The British brigade at Darmali, however, escaped entirely, though whether this was due to the precautions they observed or to the local conditions it is impossible to say. Nevertheless, the summer was a weary season.

DARMALI

The villages of Selim and Darmali stand close to the banks of the Nile. But the desert here approaches the river, and the belt of scrub is narrow and thin. The scraggy, miserable *dôm*-palms, sombre in colour and ungraceful in shape, afford the only shade. Every morning the sun rose above the desert, climbed higher in the cloudless sky, blazed with a fierce and merciless persistence, crossed the river, and disappeared behind the bushes on the opposite bank. At times high hot winds whirled the dust and sand into clouds and brought annoyance instead of relief to the waiting soldiers. More usually a deadly calm enabled the full intensity of the heat to be appreciated. The average temperature by day was 109° in the shade; the maximum often exceeded 120°.

The huts of the villages were thoroughly cleaned; the floors raised by at least a foot of fresh Nile mud; and the walls in many cases levelled to permit the free passage of air. The troops were thus fairly well housed. The rations with which they were supplied were also of excellent quality. The enforced abstinence from beer was compensated by a free issue twice a week of rum, bacon, and jam. To occupy their time and to make them handy the men were made to do their own cooking, and by degrees they grew into cunning campaigners, intent on making themselves comfortable, and acquainted with every trick and makeshift by which that result could be obtained. The effects of the bad water which had been generally drunk during the few days preceding the battle of the Atbara produced a number of cases of typhoid, euphemistically termed 'enteric fever.' But after this period was passed, the health of the brigade was uniformly good. Still the days dragged.

Every morning, before the sun began to blister, the bugles sounded for parade. For an hour, or perhaps an hour and a half, the troops were exercised and drilled; then the rest of the day was at their disposal. The officers, taking guns or rifles, would stroll out into the scrub in search of sand grouse or gazelle; several devoted themselves to fishing. Their example was largely imitated by their men, and a considerable number of Nile fish—weird-looking creatures with long gelatinous appendages hanging from their jaws and gills, and red and blue flushes on their fins—were captured and considered a great delicacy. During the heat of the day everyone remained silent and motionless. Those who were lucky slept. All books and newspapers were eagerly read. The incoming mail punctuated the weeks with a single dot of excitement. The gifts of magazines and newspapers, which thoughtful and patriotic people at home sent to their soldiers in the desert, were warmly welcomed. Thus in some fashion the hours passed. In the cool of the evening, the camp began to stir again. Cricket indeed proved a failure; but the footballs were always in demand, and the wilds of Africa witnessed the sports of civilisation.

The necessities of life were well supplied by the State, but the demand for all kinds of comforts and conveniences soon drew a supply through the medium of the Greek trader. A regular colony of these enterprising creatures arrived. With astonishing adaptability they built a village and opened shops. They proved themselves invaluable, catering with business instinct for every want, and during the whole summer their stores supplied all conceivable commodities—from fishing-tackle to tinned asparagus.

The greatest, almost the only, pleasure of the soldiers was to bathe in the river. But since they carried this to excess, it was soon found necessary to regulate the indulgence. The officers threw themselves with energy into the business of amusing themselves and their men. Smoking concerts took place at frequent intervals. Athletic sports and gymkhanas were held every fortnight. On one occasion a regular race meeting was organised. The officers of the troops in Berber and at the Atbara hurried down the line to attend or compete. A rude stand was erected. An enclosure, rigidly select, was formed.

THE ATBARA DERBY

The fields were large and the sport good. Several exciting struggles aroused the enthusiasm of the spectators. The hurdle race was won by Lieutenant McNeill[1] of the Seaforth Highlanders; but his modesty excludes a picture of the finish, and the reader will be satisfied with a representation of 'The Atbara Derby'—'The Blue Ribbon of the Desert'—which was won by an officer of the 21st Lancers, on duty with the Transport.

The camp at Darmali exists no longer. The renovated mud huts are deserted or have become again the homes of the Arabs. The bazaar of the Greek traders is empty and silent. It is unlikely that the civilised traveller will visit for pleasure or profit the arid, sandy hamlet by the banks of the Nile. Yet, should such a wanderer chance to pause on his way, he would find the temporary resting-place of a British legion marked here—as on the African *veldt* or the Indian Frontier—by a racecourse, a polo-ground, and a cemetery.

Enlivened only by small incidents, the weeks passed uneventfully. All officers who could obtain leave hurried for a month to Cairo or a fortnight to London. But those who stayed behind in the camps by the Nile have no pleasant memories of the summer. The hot days tried the tempers and depressed the spirits of the soldiers. All the correspondents had gone home, and the public eye was averted from the scenes in the Soudan. All the songs had been sung at the concerts, and all the jokes made so often that they ceased to amuse. The game soon left the neighbourhood in search of less-frequented scrub. Even the Nile fish no longer delighted the angler or the epicure. Only the nights were cool and fresh; and the soldiers, leaving the huts which the heat of the day made hot as ovens, would lie on the sand underneath the bright stars and wonder when the war was going to begin again.

Of course, the one unfailing subject of discussion during the summer was the battle of the Atbara. Its incidents were re-told and its tactics examined from every conceivable point of view. It will not, therefore, be inappropriate if I take this opportunity of considering some of the questions which have been raised.

The strategy of the Atbara campaign was undoubtedly correct. There are some who say that the Sirdar's position at Eas-el-Hudi

1 Lieut. A. J. McNeill. Seaforth Highlanders.

compelled Mahmud to attack or retire, and that there was therefore no necessity for an offensive action. It is unlikely that he could have returned to the Nile by the way he came, for he might have been headed off by the army moving along the east bank, supported by its gunboats. It was impossible for him to strike at Berber without exposing his left flank. A third course, however, was open. He might have retired up the Atbara river, and threatened or even attacked Kassala. It will be contended that he had no supplies. But the want of supplies has very little influence on Dervish movements. A few handfuls of grain and the nuts of the *dôm*-palm enable the hardy Arab, as long as there is sufficient water, to march for a week through regions in which civilised troops could not operate without enormous preparations. But the great consideration was prestige. The long line of communications was safe while the army at its head was feared. All the inhabitants along the stretch of the Nile from Berber to Abu Hamed doubted and wavered. They feared the Khalifa: they hated the Government. The destruction of Mahmud's army decided them. Henceforward they recognised that a new order of things had been established. Their altered demeanour when the troops returned victorious, with the Dervish General prisoner and the spoils and trophies of war displayed on all sides, was noticed by officers of every rank. It has been the custom to regard the re-conquest of the Soudan as a work of deliverance. Pathetic pictures of the unspeakable joy of the Arab, freed from the accursed yoke of the Khalifa, have been drawn with skill and elaboration. The idea is accepted in England. But the Sirdar, although preserving such pleasing legends for domestic circulation, was far too shrewd a soldier to allow them to influence his military calculations.

The tactics of the battle afford a wider field for controversy. Of course, after the *zeriba* had been taken, and when its strength and structure were familiar to everyone, there were many wise plans evolved by which it might have been captured with less loss. That is the invariable rule. The tactics of Napoleon's greatest victories have been shown over and over again to have been utterly foolish and puerile by the military critics. The composition of the Anglo-Egyptian army was such that few liberties could be taken with fire-discipline. It was essential that all units—particularly the Soudanese—should have a clear field of fire to their right and left fronts. This excluded all idea of a simultaneous attack from different angles, and therefore the General had very little choice in the plan of attack.

The formation of the British brigade was much deeper than that of the Soudanese; and this was undoubtedly a disadvantage, because they were unable to deploy so quickly after passing the *zeriba*. But this formation was assumed in the belief that the *zeriba* was a much more formidable obstacle than it actually proved, and that the enemy's fire-resistance would be more severe. It is impossible not to sympathise with General Gatacre's obvious determination—that, whatever happened to the other parts of the assault, the British brigade should burst into the enclosure at all costs. The fact, however, remains that MacDonald and Maxwell gauged the resistance of the enemy more accurately, and adopted formations better suited to the attack on this particular occasion.

The fact that the Cameron Highlanders were extended across the front of the whole British brigade has also excited criticism. It is contended that although in the confusion of an action units must become mixed, every effort ought to be made to postpone or minimise that event. Each battalion should have been made to cover its own front. It was a serious error to place one battalion where it was bound to be immediately mixed up with the leading companies of the other three. The former explanation covers this. General Gatacre over-estimated the power of the enemy. He believed that the covering line would be practically destroyed in the advance and while tearing the *zeriba* to pieces. It was better to sacrifice one complete battalion than to weaken all equally.

The Camerons would suffer terribly; but the fresh battalions, coming up in column, would burst through the gaps they had made, and, carrying on the few survivors, would take the place by storm. Gatacre's formation reveals the fact that he believed sincerely that he was sending one of his battalions to destruction. This explains why he selected the centre of that battalion as his own place and that of his Staff. He has been censured for exposing himself to perils which miff lit have robbed his brigade of its commander. But there is to a civilian a certain grim splendour in the spectacle of the General who would not take the responsibility of sacrificing a regiment unless he himself marched with them.

Happily the *zeriba* proved weaker, and the Dervish fire less deadly, than had been expected. The Camerons, who should have acted as the containing line, rolled in as the first wave of the assault, and, with the exception of a few stolid heroes who continued to pull the *zeriba* to pieces, they became mixed with the leading companies of the columns. In fact, there was not enough resistance to develop the mighty strength of the British attack. It is possible to maintain that General Gatacre formed his brigade unnecessarily deep, arranged his regiments inconveniently, and exposed himself unjustifiably. But all these defects arose from the original mistake of over-estimating the power of the enemy—a wise and prudent error into which, it is to be hoped, our Generals will frequently fall.

The shortness of the artillery preparation cannot, however, be explained. The batteries came into action at under 1,000 yards, and with practically no loss to themselves they shelled the *zeriba* for an hour and a half. In this period they inflicted a severe slaughter upon the enemy, which is estimated by several competent officers who saw the corpses in the enclosure to have comprised 20 per cent, of the total Arab casualties. This is very satisfactory to the artillery officers. But one is compelled to ask why the bombardment only lasted an hour and a half. If so great a loss could be inflicted in such a short time without any danger or inconvenience to the gunners, why were they not allowed to continue for three or four hours? This certainly is the course which would be suggested by all tactical experience and by all modern books on war. Indeed, it is impossible to doubt that, had the bombardment been prolonged, the Dervishes might have been driven out of the *zeriba* altogether, or at any rate would have suffered so severely that their fire would not have inflicted such severe loss on the assaulting columns, and valuable lives might have been saved. Again, no use was made of the infantry fire in preparation of the assault. If the brigades had fired, let us say, fifty rounds per man into the *zeriba*, they must have killed some Dervishes, and the subsequent attack would have been easier and cheaper. Civilised troops should take full advantage of their weapons; and the spectacle of the assaulting columns advancing on the entrenchments after an insufficient artillery preparation, and disdaining to open fire till they were within a range when their rifles were on an equality with those of the Dervishes, however magnificent it may be, suggests the hog-hunter who dismounted from his horse, flung away his spear, then dealt the boar a tremendous kick in the throat, and eventually made an end of him with his hands.

I have already discussed the bad boots and the improvised bullets, which were the only dark spots on the clothing and equipment of the British troops. As no occasion arose at the Atbara for magazine action, the disadvantage of the bullets was not felt. There is, however, one very delicate matter to which am compelled to allude. It has been said—in the first instance by several silly correspondents—that the Soudanese were the first at the *zeriba*, and that they 'beat' the British brigade. Continuing this absurd competition, the different British regiments each contend as to which of them was first. I have received three lucid statements from officers in the Lincolns, the Seaforths, and the Camerons. All prove conclusively that their own regiment had that doubtful honour. To anyone who has followed the account of the assault in the last chapter the ridiculous nature of this dispute will be apparent. The three brigades were formed obliquely to the *zeriba*, so that naturally the right of Maxwell's brigade was the earliest to strike it. The British, having the longest distance to cover, were of course the last. Besides this, the Soudanese charged over the final hundred yards of ground, as they were ordered, while the British marched steadily up to the *zeriba* in obedience to their different orders. There is therefore no especial merit in having been the first to reach the enemy. Indeed, the palm of honour may with reason be claimed by those men of the Cameron Highlanders who continued to destroy the *zeriba* and made no attempt to close with the Dervishes. Yet the actual truth is that the leading companies of the Seaforths and the Lincolns entered the enclosure simultaneously, preceded by a fringe of the Cameron Highlanders. The Royal Warwickshire Regiment were engaged in protecting the left flank from the possible attack of the Dervish cavalry, and consequently did not penetrate until a few moments later.

While the army was sweltering from the Atbara to Darmali, the Sirdar shared their hardships. The utter defeat of Mahmud brought him no rest. His whole attention, his whole soul, was concentrated on the great task which was entrusted to him. As soon as he reached Berber after the victory, he held a parade of all the troops. A platform was erected and adorned with flag's; on this, surrounded by his Staff, the General took his stand. The Emir Mahmud, his hands bound behind his back, was then compelled to march past at the head of the army, preceded by an enormous flag, on which was inscribed in Arabic characters, '*This is Mahmud, who said he would take Berber*.' Having thus enjoyed the pleasures of victory, the Sirdar turned again to the conduct of the war.

For the final phase of the campaign three new gunboats had been ordered from England. These were now sent in sections over the desert railway. Special arrangements were made to admit of the clumsy loads passing trains on the ordinary sidings. As usual, the contrivances of the railway subalterns were attended by success. Sir H. Kitchener himself proceeded to Abadia to accelerate by his personal activity and ingenuity the construction of the vessels on which so much depended. Here during the heat of the summer he remained, nursing his gunboats, maturing his plans, and waiting only for the rise of the river to complete the downfall of his foes.

END OF FIRST VOLUME

Index

Symbols

A

B

C

X

Y

Z

Printed in the USA
CPSIA information can be obtained
at www.ICGtesting.com
LVHW081501060923
757383LV00005B/30